FORGING
THE
COPPER
COLLAR

Posse members and their prisoners marching
from Bisbee to Warren (July 12, 1917)

FORGING THE COPPER COLLAR

Arizona's
Labor-Management War
of 1901–1921

James W. Byrkit

The University of Arizona Press
TUCSON, ARIZONA

About the Author ...

JAMES BYRKIT's interest in Arizona labor and politics grew out of his boyhood experiences in an Arizona mining town. Born in Jerome, Arizona, he developed early a feeling for the social, economic and political attitudes that characterized Arizona mining communities and the impact these communities had on Arizona's statewide affairs. Byrkit received his Ph.D. in history from Claremont Graduate School. In 1973 he joined the faculty at Northern Arizona University, where he has taught courses in the American frontier, Arizona and the Southwest, and regional images. He has published articles on Arizona resource use and on radical labor unionism in the West.

THE UNIVERSITY OF ARIZONA PRESS

Copyright © 1982
James W. Byrkit
All Rights Reserved

This book was set in 11/12 V.I.P. Palatino
Manufactured in the U.S.A.

Library of Congress Cataloging in Publication Data

Byrkit, James W.
    Forging the copper collar.

    Bibliography: p.
    Includes index.
        1. Trade-unions—Copper miners—Arizona—
Bisbee—History. 2. Bisbee (Ariz.)—Social condi-
tions. I. Title.
HD6515.M72B563   331.88′122343′0979153   82-2075

ISBN 0-8165-0745-7   AACR2

Little copper collars
Little hints at gain
Makes the little fellow
Awfully, awfully vain

Little deeds of malice
To our fellow men
Put you right with Tally
And his gang again

Edith Whitaker
Jerome Sun

CONTENTS

IV. The Quiet Kingdom

Reference Material

Maps

Photographs

Portraits

Warren District, July 12, 1917

Columbus, New Mexico, in late summer of 1917

PREFACE

Arizona copper mining camps before the 1950s were not unlike the British imperial outposts described by W. Somerset Maugham in his *South Sea Tales*. Such Arizona towns as Morenci, Jerome, Ajo and Bisbee were isolated, mercantilistic colonies. There the laboring men enjoyed good wages and a variety of comforts, while local administrators—congregated in a tight, friendly clique—maintained their identities as wardens if not as nabobs. In this circle, as in a military officers' club, an atmosphere intimate and casual prevailed. Unlike pillars of the community in more traditional, familiar American settings, the mine and smelter operators felt no compulsion toward demagogic propriety; their appointive status enabled them to pursue a self-expressive style of life. Too, from their often cosmopolitan origins and training they had acquired gracious and hedonic tastes. These characteristics, together with the natural spontaneity endemic to mining camps, produced a social vitality among the managers and engineers which complemented the street-filled celebrations of the camps' wage earners.

Remoteness, crudity and the glaring heat of the area were probably the first impressions of a newcomer to the upper social stratum of a mining town. The daytime image was quickly softened by the first evening lawn party, garnished with a lavish cold buffet, tinkling ice and gentle laughter. Here tired and overtold dinner party stories were given new life, while bits of benign if not congenial gossip found their audience. Little knots of men chuckled as they joked about the round heels of legislators elected to oppose the influence of the copper companies.

It was in this atmosphere that I heard originally of the Bisbee Deportation. At the time it made no more impression on me than any of the other numerous sensational anecdotes that constituted the routine repertoire of those evening exchanges. More detailed accounts subsequently fleshed out the story — and tweaked my curiosity. I began to realize that something more substantial lay behind the flippant boasts that "we caught those Wobbly deadbeats with their pants down" or "in those days we took care of things the 'old frontier' way."

Since then, I have come to understand that the amenities of Arizona colonial society were only a small, visible part of the state's colonial experience. Like the proverbial iceberg, the great substance of that experience lay out of view. The aim of this book is to reveal some of that substance, a part of Arizona history that has too long remained obscured.

Acknowledgments

Without rival, Anne Beller Byrkit, in every respect, did the most to help bring this book into being. Four people, Professors John Niven, Harwood Hinton, Melvyn Dubofsky and Clark Spence, provided extensive and detailed critiques of the various stages of the manuscript. I am indebted greatly to them for their comments.

After reading the "underground" version of this book, several other scholars helped me—with their encouragement and constructive suggestions—to persevere with my work. They include C. L. Sonnichsen, Jim Foster, Bob Houston, Jim Kluger, Marjorie Haines Wilson, Earl Bruce White, Joe Park and Beverly Springer.

Other people, many from around the state of Arizona, gave me support, too. In particular, John P. Frank, Platt Cline, John Pintek, Selma Pine, Sam and Judy Goddard, Jacquie McNulty, Tom Miller, David Ward and Bishop William Scarlett deserve my deepest thanks for their interest, enthusiasm and helpfulness. Marie Webner of the University of Arizona Press has been remarkably patient and understanding and a firm believer in my perspective in this book. I am grateful to the University of Arizona Press for effecting publication of this work.

—J. W. B.

PROLOGUE

On September 6, 1901, a half-crazed anarchist fired two bullets into the stomach of President William McKinley. Eight days later McKinley died, and Theodore Roosevelt became the 26th president of the United States. This marked the beginning of a new era in American life. Roosevelt's presidency signaled, if only superficially, a fifteen-year decline in popular support for business and industry coupled with a rising national sympathy for labor, farmers and other working-class people.

In the Arizona Territory, as much or even more than across the nation, the "Progressives" enjoyed a phenomenal popularity during this period. Before 1901 the Arizona mining industry—sponsored, owned, and directed by eastern corporations—effortlessly manipulated Arizona politics and society, making the territory an industrial colony. But such Progressive territorial governors as Alexander O. Brodie, appointed by Roosevelt July 2, 1902, and Joseph H. Kibbey (1905–09), also a Roosevelt appointee, disturbed the easy and absolute control which the corporations had enjoyed for two decades. By 1908 middle-class and working-class Arizonans had become a political force in the territory. These people gained control of the territorial legislature between 1908 and 1912. They dominated all twenty-four committees in the 1910 Arizona Constitutional Convention, producing a document which Arizona mine operators and conservatives found "radical" and deplorable.

Progressive-minded, anti-corporate politics characterized the Arizona State Legislature from 1912 to 1916. During this period liberals enacted laws which provided for the eight-hour day, women's suffrage, workmen's compensation, the right to picket, the recall of judges, better and safer working conditions and other legislation which enraged corporate interests. In particular, the Progressives enacted taxation laws distasteful to the mining companies. By 1916 the copper corporations were so furiously frustrated that the mining companies' managers, previously often at odds with each other, organized themselves in a counteroffensive against the state's liberals, especially the state's unionists.

By early summer of 1917, the mining interests controlled the state's governor and its legislature, and they owned or controlled most of Arizona's newspapers and banks. In July, as the climax of their campaign, the mining companies took advantage of wartime hysteria, which had influenced public opinion throughout the nation away from Progressivism to support industrial and governmental repression of "unpatriotic" liberal dissent and labor agitation.

By 1921 the corporations had reestablished their control of Arizona politics and society. But Arizona old-timers carry with them even into the last quarter of the century the bitterness of this great labor-management war.

This book is about power: about eastern power sponsoring and manipulating economic, political, social and cultural life in the American West; about corporate interests in Arizona gaining power, using it, abusing it, losing it—and regaining it. This corporate power of the late nineteenth and early twentieth centuries, was so great and complete and sure that someone like Senator William Andrews Clark, the Montana and Arizona copper baron, could say, "I don't believe in lynching or violence of that kind unless it is absolutely necessary," and be taken very literally.

The Cockeyed World

We've been from hell to breakfast
But now we're easing back
On any road or rattler
You're sure to hear this crack
When Old Man Hunt is Governor
Wobs needn't give a shit
Red Arizona, boys! The red sun over it.

You peanut politicians
I'll say you birds is through
In a cold, cruel cockeyed world
There's just one thing to do:
Travel on with "Traveling Tom,"
Christ knows he'll never quit.
Red Arizona, boys! The red sun over it.

You Maricopa sod hounds
That smell of ditch and dung
Us eye double double yous
Ain't all been shot or hung.
You'd better watch your haystacks
And maybe so your jit
Red Arizona, boys! The red sun over it.

You bloody Bisbee cousins,
You're going down the trail
A'talking to yourself
A Wobbly on your tail;
Us Wobs is sitting pretty,
I'll say we're fixed to sit —
Red Arizona, boys! The red sun over it.*

---

*"The Cockeyed World" (fugitive doggerel in files, Arizona Historical Society, Tucson).

THE BISBEE DEPORTATION OF 1917

In the summertime, bulging, silvery-bottomed cumulous clouds nose northwestward across southern Arizona. Having gathered their cargo of moisture over the Gulf of Mexico, they sail above the high Sonoran sierras, billowing majestically, their lacy white caps reflecting the sun as they seek the cold air that will condense their burden and release it in torrential downpours. In July and August, usually in the late afternoon, the clouds burst and drench the Arizona desert, often to the accompaniment of violent thunder and lightning.

Early in the morning on Thursday, July 12, 1917, a *posse comitatus*, two thousand strong, swept through the streets of Bisbee, Arizona, and arrested more than two thousand people. Led by Cochise County Sheriff Harry Wheeler, armed vigilantes composed of members of the Bisbee Workman's Loyalty League and the Bisbee Citizens' Protective League picked up anyone they deemed "undesirable." The deputies herded their prisoners into Bisbee's downtown plaza, while two machine guns commanded the scene.

For two weeks a labor strike had crippled Bisbee, a copper mining town. The Industrial Workers of the World, commonly known as the "Wobblies," called the strike on June 27. Only about three or four hundred men in Bisbee belonged to the radical IWW, but approximately 50 percent of Bisbee's 4,700 miners went out on strike. Mining officials wanted production back to normal; every strike-bound day meant a loss of generous wartime profits.

Included among the captives were numerous Bisbee business and professional people who supported or sympathized with the strikers. The vigilantes arrested four or five women, too, but almost immediately released them. Executives of Phelps Dodge and the Calumet & Arizona Mining Company planned and coordinated the roundup. Phelps Dodge's mine, the Copper Queen, was the richest in the state.

Though the affair was handled with extreme foresight and efficiency, Bisbee's vigilantes were not without fresh example for their actions. Only two days earlier, citizens had deported sixty-seven men from Jerome, another Arizona mining town several hundred miles north of Bisbee.

From the plaza the deputies marched the arrested men to the local ball park. There mine managers gave those workers out on strike one last chance to return to work; many men agreed and were released. At gun point, the remaining prisoners, 1,186 of them, climbed into waiting boxcars of the El Paso and Southwestern Railroad, a subsidiary of Phelps Dodge. The train took the men to Columbus, New Mexico, one hundred and seventy-three miles east of Bisbee, where many of the deportees remained for two months. Only a few ever returned to stay in Bisbee.

At first glance, the Bisbee Deportation appears as merely one more sensational incident in the history of the American labor movement. It contained those traits which characterized the bitter conflicts between labor and management in that seventy-year period from the end of the Civil War until the New Deal. The Haymarket Riot, the Homestead Lockout, the Ludlow Massacre stand out as representative events of this part of American economic history.

But just as each of these other sensational and tragic episodes had its own peculiar qualities and explanation, so did the Bisbee Deportation, upon closer examination, have a unique and extended significance.

The deportation provokes at least five questions of a broad nature: (1) Since the Industrial Workers of the World seemed to play an important role in the affair, to what degree was the deportation related to the radicalism that characterized this period of American history? (2) How much or in what way did the deportation reflect the general conflict between labor and capital, particularly as this conflict developed within the national domestic atmosphere of World War I? (3) How did the affair fit into the "Progressive Period," and to what extent did the philosophy, national policies and public attitudes regarding "Progressivism" shape the conditions which surrounded the deportation? (4) Given the place (Arizona) and the time (1917), can the deportation be seen as some kind of late American "frontier experience," or, at least, did vestigial elements of American frontier life contribute in any way to the nature of the event? and (5) What relationship did the Bisbee Deportation have to Arizona life and politics during this formative period of the young state's history?

Several months after the deportation, President Woodrow Wilson sent a commission to Arizona to investigate the labor problems there. Serving as secretary for the commission was young Felix Frankfurter, who was destined later to become an illustrious member of the United States Supreme Court. On November 6, 1917, the investigation into the situation at Bisbee having been concluded, Frankfurter sent a report of the commission's findings to the President. Although the federal investigators found the deportation to be unprovoked and unjustified, they failed to see any significance in the event beyond the immediate and obvious labor-management conflict.

Some of the obstacles to understanding the deportation lie in the complexities that Felix Frankfurter and the commission failed to discern. Like other industrial crises, this incident was woven tightly into the background of national and state politics and economics. But it also was a manifestation of the peculiar pressures of the times, antagonistic pressures that cannot be explained simply in terms of conventional polemics: liberal-conservative, management-labor, middle class-proletariat.

The Bisbee Deportation stemmed from a desire on the part of resident managers of the copper companies in Bisbee to satisfy the demands of mine owners for greater profits. In particular, the Phelps Dodge Corporation and the Calumet & Arizona Copper Company, the two largest, pressured operators for greater earnings. Irritated by the recent assertion of labor strength in Arizona politics, mine managers grew alarmed at the growth of the national union activity that was benefitting somewhat from the permissive mood of Wilsonian liberalism. Wartime conditions and the attendant patriotic hysteria provided an atmosphere in which these managers could reclaim their own threatened economic and political power. The possibility of unprecedented but transitory wartime profits in the copper industry further pressed the operators to assure for themselves absolute rule of the copper business. This rule would dismiss permanently management's power struggle with labor and other anti-corporate interests.

In their attempt to preserve the profits of wartime production, the mine operators made every effort to block intrusions by any labor organization. Heightened by wartime fevers and the general inability of people to differentiate one union from another, the popular fear of radicalism enabled the mine operators to call all union members "radical." Responsible organizations such as the International Union of Mine, Mill and Smelter Workers (the IUMMSW) were easily labeled "seditious." By exploiting patriotic fervor, the company officials in Bisbee convinced the public that more than 4,700 miners in the Warren district were dominated by less than four hundred desultory card-carrying Wobblies and a handful of agitators.

In the October 9, 1967, issue of the New York-based newspaper *The National Observer* there appeared an account of the Bisbee Deportation. Fifty years had elapsed, and the newspaper article commented that the story had become a "hazy memory." *The National Observer*'s account, a lengthy narrative with a photograph and a map, emphasized the IWW radicalism explanation.

But this version, by John V. Young, speaks of what the company records "don't show" and contains no new information. It is a standard account found in the 1917 popular newspapers.

If one looks around, the Bisbee Deportation appears to be even less than a "hazy memory." Contemporary liberal journalists showed a spirit of great outrage, yet the Bisbee story faded fast. Perhaps it was because any historical significance was beclouded by World War I or because anti-radicalism accelerated to new and more sensational heights with the Red Scare and the Sacco-Vanzetti case. But a routine check of ten new and popular general college survey textbooks for American history will reveal no mention whatsoever of the 1917 labor strife in Arizona. The fantastic and intriguing story of the Bisbee Deportation has been treated—and forgotten—as another routine and incidental event lost in the backwash of time.

Forgetting it did take a few years. Gordon S. Watkins, one of the most sensitive industrial economists of his day, wrote in 1919:

> No other incident in recent years, outside of the Mooney case, has proved more irritable to organized and unorganized labor forces than the deportation of workmen from the Warren district, Arizona, to Columbus, New Mexico, on the morning of July 12, 1917.[1]

Two years later labor historian Alexander Bing shared Watkins' opinion when he called the Bisbee Deportation the "most deplorable act of industrial violence which has occurred in the history of our country."[2] During 1919 at least four other dramatic labor events, each sensational in its own right, rose to obscure the Bisbee Deportation. The Seattle general strike, the bituminous coal strike, the great steel strike and the Boston police lockout collectively seemed to mark the Armageddon of the early twentieth century labor movement. By 1921 the Palmer Raids and a short but strongly felt depression had distracted the public and, subsequently, most historians' attention. Also, on December 19, 1921, the United States Supreme Court declared the 1913 Arizona anti-injunction law unconstitutional. Arizona's span of labor glory now appeared as a brief flash-in-the-pan, an ephemeral and sleazy sideshow off the spectacular midway of the country's history. Bisbee's remote location did little to convince anyone that anything could happen there to merit it a place in the mainstream of American life.

American novelist and essayist Mary Austin mentioned this out-of-the-way quality of the region. In 1923 she commented that despite Arizona being far away, "everyone" knew about the Bisbee Deportation. She wrote, "In spite of the effort of organized labor to make of what happened at Bisbee an item of capitalist strategy, it remains in fact a characteristically Arizonian incident." Miss Austin apparently laid aside her usual liberal and insightful compassion to return—with the

decade—to normalcy. Unike the "liberal element," she roman-
tically attributed the deportation to "the spirit of the old days"
when gentlemen were obliged "to throw the drunken cowboy
out of the dance."[3]

Thus was the whole affair dismissed. Easterners and other
image-makers were not going to allow their fantasies about the
wonderful, simple, primeval West to be ruined by some
spoilsport's illusion of industrial warfare and radical politics
where there should be nothing but buckboards and bar-b-ques
and soft guitars.

For people everywhere the West represented a reaffirmation of those earthy, simple, honest values for which America,
in popular historical accounts, was supposed to stand at one
time. The frontiersman and the Wobbly, respectively—high-
minded, pure and courageous—symbolized absolute American
good in conflict with absolute cosmic and human evil. For all
kinds of romantics, the American West years ago became the
appropriate scene for a morality play.

The disenchanted eastern urbanite has long seen "the
West" as a corrective to the past and an alternative to the
present. Caroline Kirkland wrote in 1842, "The future—the
bright, far-ahead, vague Western future—is to make up for
all." As compensation for some uncertain yet deeply felt
failure, the West has represented to eastern romantics the primeval goodness of America's noble "lost dream," a great,
open arena for the acting out, if only in their fantasies, of
that dream.[4] The Bisbee Deportation and its social, economic
and political significance simply did not fit in with the rest
of the country's mythological conception of what Arizona's
place was supposed to be in the scheme of things. The incon-
gruity of wage scales or immigrants in a starry, cactus setting
was not acceptable to those who longed for simpler, nobler,
cleaner times. Arizona should be a refuge from all that; so
the deportation rapidly faded from the nation's consciousness.

At the same time he denounced the intelligentsia for allowing itself to become infected by the hysteria of World War I,
James Oneal, in the April 1927 *American Mercury*, attributed the
deportation to "white terror" reacting to radicalism. Bisbee was
lumped in with hundreds of other witch hunts and red purges
the country over.[5] That year historian and socialist Mary Ritter
Beard attributed the action to "mob spirit."[6] Andre Siegfried,
in *America Comes of Age* (1927), cited the "famous deportation

from Bisbee, Arizona, in 1918," as a good example of the "tradition of direct action" which involves a group of citizens that "usually comes forward spontaneously... to execute the law—often an unwritten law which they declare to have been broken."[7] Siegfried's carelessness cost him chronological credibility in addition to an insightful analysis. Few comments from national figures followed. Labor historian John S. Gambs did remark in 1932 that the Bisbee Deportation was "the most important manifestation of violence" during its period.[8]

In Arizona, memories of its most notorious historical act died a little more slowly. Former Governor Campbell confessed around 1940 that the burden of the responsibility for the deportation should be placed upon the mining companies.[9] Writers assigned by the Works Projects Administration observed that the Arizona miners' union had been "crushingly defeated" in 1917 and did not revive for eighteen years, when the Wagner Act gave it life.[10]

After World War II, when there was a resurgence of labor activity in Arizona, the story of the deportation was used by both sides to condemn the other. But by this time facts as well as issues had been forgotten. One old IWW, writing his memoirs, claimed vigilantes killed three Wobblies during the Bisbee roundup.[11] Acid-tongued columnist and anti-Semite Westbrook Pegler was an Arizona resident by 1948. In his syndicated newspaper column he denounced Felix Frankfurter as a distorter of what had happened at Bisbee. Wrathful, caustic, Pegler cited Frankfurter's compassion for the Arizona strikers in 1917 as proof of Frankfurter's "Commie sympathies." Frankfurter's report to President Wilson was held up by Pegler to prove that Frankfurter "might tolerate murder and anarchy by Communists in the United States."[12] Adding to the ignorance about the deportation at this time was a statement in Robert Glass Cleland's 1952 history of Phelps Dodge to the effect that IWWs used violence in Arizona when, in fact, no evidence has ever been produced that anyone other than company goons, vigilantes, deputies, soldiers and police used violence during the labor strikes of the period.[13]

A Phoenix labor journalist, Paul Peterson, wrote in 1955 that the Bisbee Deportation initiated the impotency Arizona labor had felt since 1917. Out of the flotsam and jetsam of intimidation, misinformation, bitterness, garbled motives, romantic rationalizations and other debris that floated in the wake of the deportation, at least one substantial plank had been seized. Though Peterson's article lacked much of the flesh of the episode, the bones and even some of the muscle were there. Peterson claimed many of the "Reds" were imported into Bisbee, a likelihood that yet awaits final proof. He cited the bitter memories old-timers carried with them, quiet frustrations that continued to exist beneath their parched smiles. Most significantly—and accurately—Peterson stated that Arizona's modern labor troubles had begun with the Bisbee Deportation in 1917.[14]

The following week in the same newspaper that featured Paul Peterson's story of Bisbee, the *Arizona Republic,* a rebuttal appeared. This article was written by Frank Cullen Brophy, son of William "Billy" Brophy, one of those indicted for his part in the deportation. Brophy said the deportation "had nothing to do with a legitimate labor grievance or controversy." The trouble, Brophy claimed, was largely the result "of efforts of enemy agents and native subversives." Brophy insisted, despite all the reports from the United States Attorney General to the contrary, that "some of the money that financed this effort ... came from Germany via secret agents in Mexico and San Antonio, Texas." He then picked up the Pegler theme and said that it was in the reports of Felix Frankfurter "that the myth of the wrong done to labor in Bisbee took root and has subsequently flourished as a result of the solicitous care and culture of 'liberal' practitioners over the years." The men responsible for the Bisbee Deportation, Brophy continued, "were men who did big things in their state, and they were men who did not hesitate to risk their lives and reputations in behalf of what they thought was right." Then Brophy's comments about the deportation put him squarely in the genre of the hysterical anti-communist paranoia identified with U.S. Senator Joseph McCarthy. McCarthyistic thinking which had crested nationwide a year before but, typically, was still at high tide in Arizona:

> But the men who created the situation [the IWWs] which led up to the Bisbee deportation knew what they were doing, and I suspect Mr. Frankfurter knew what he was doing when he wrote his reports .... The pattern from Bisbee, 1917, down to the recent scandals at Fort Monmouth, the Rosenbergs, Oppenheimer [sic], or Alger Hiss is cut out of the same piece of goods; and whatever the material may be, the color is Red—the color of blood.[15]

Brophy's explanation may or may not have been the final word in the popular Arizona mind. A "right to work" law (banning closed-shop and union-shop contracts), passed on a popular referendum in 1946, had made it clear how eager the majority of Arizona's citizenry was to help the cause of labor. Some union literature still referred to the deportation for the benefit of its own membership, but did not make capital of it.[16]

In her 1919 travels around the state, Dr. Alice Hamilton heard one interesting interpretation of the deportation that no other source reveals. A "mining official" in Ajo told her: "But then, the Phelps-Dodge people never meant to deport so many — the thing got away from them." Getting rid of fifteen or twenty agitators, he explained, would have sufficed, but the outsiders Phelps Dodge brought in and deputized were too aggressive. (Twenty-three boxcars for fifteen or twenty agitators?) After they were arrested, the miners were "too mad and too proud and too loyal to each other" to accept the offer to go back to work. But the record of the copper company's policies in Bisbee after the deportation gives little credence to this peculiar piece of back-pedaling.[17] Old-timers who had been adults in Bisbee and other mining towns in Arizona in 1917 all have some dramatic impression of the event branded in their memory. Most of them confused or exaggerated the details, but for all of them, the Bisbee Deportation remained a high point, if not the most sensational experience, of their lives. All reacted strongly to it and all had maintained fierce opinions about which side was "wrong" or who was "to blame." But they all agreed that the deportation had been the climax in the social and political development of the state.

But even old-timers, their memories clouded by time, became vague about the nature of the deportation. One Bisbeeite recalled only that it involved "a bunch of German spies or something like that."[18] Another remembered that the strikers claimed they only wanted higher wages, "But I know it was just to curtail production to help the Germans."[19] A deportee, Si Morris, said of the miners' strike fifty years afterward, "We just wanted higher wages; the price of copper was going up, so why not?"[20]

PART I

THE ENABLING CONTEXT

1

THE SETTING

Bisbee's history is the American mining frontier history of harshness and violence. Whatever astonishing might have happened, it took place within the quite credible dimensions of the American mining West.

Early Copper Mining in Arizona

Although white persons apparently mined copper in what later became the United States as early as the first half of the seventeenth century, it was not until the middle of the nineteenth century that copper mining became a vigorous and substantial American enterprise. The year 1845 saw the first developed commercial production of copper in the United States. The first copper production in the far Southwest came from the old Santa Rita region of New Mexico.[1] About the same time, miners extracted some copper at Ajo. But transportation difficulties limited production to very high grade only.[2]

After the Treaty of Guadalupe Hidalgo in 1848, several northern railroad routes to the Pacific coast were proposed. Since these routes promised continued commercial ascendancy for the North, they were opposed by the southern states. When

Jefferson Davis was appointed Secretary of War in 1853, he ordered a survey for a southern railroad route. This route, intended for use by the Southern Pacific Railroad, included some land still owned by Mexico. On December 30, 1853, James Gadsden, United States Minister to Mexico, signed a treaty with the Mexican government that sold, for ten million dollars, 29,670 square miles below the Gila River from the Rio Grande to the Colorado. This treaty, ratified by Congress on April 25, 1854, and signed by President Franklin Pierce, included the rich copper veins that were to explain Bisbee's existence.[3]

Investors and grubstakers wasted no time exploiting the mineral wealth of the new region. Copper was first mined in Arizona at Ajo in 1854 by the American Mining and Trading Company, which several entrepreneurs formed in San Francisco.[4] The Planet mines, on the banks of the Colorado River, opened up about the same time. This ore together with that from Ajo went by water all the way to England to be processed.[5] In the late 1860s Henry Clifton discovered copper in eastern Arizona; by 1876 the Clifton-Morenci district had two large-scale mining operations. In the meantime, Globe became a booming silver camp. That same year Morris A. Ruffner worked for the first time the rich United Verde copper ore body in Jerome, Arizona. (It had been discovered eleven years earlier.) All of these developments took place before the first mining located at legendary, notorious Tombstone was recorded (1878). But what was to prove the richest find of all occurred in 1877 twenty-five miles south of Tombstone and seven miles north of the Mexican border in Mule Gulch, a branch of Tombstone Canyon, near Mule Pass in the Mule Mountains.[6]

Bisbee's Beginning

Traveling through southeast Arizona in 1864, J. Ross Browne, an adventurous journalist, found the region an "inhospitable place." Despite poor roads, fierce Indians, "burning suns and chilling nights," the area had begun to develop mining as early as 1857. Browne also discovered that the vicissitudes of the Arizona desert had left a "wayside lined with the bleached bones of unfortunate men," a pardonable exaggeration for a harsh and forbidding country.[7]

In 1875 Hugh Jones, a prospector, discovered ore in Tombstone Canyon. But not until 1877 did Jack Dunn stake the first claim. Dunn was not a prospector but a government scout

out of nearby Fort Huachuca. Looking for water with an army officer, Lieutenant Rucker, and some friendly Indians, Dunn detected traces of silver a little east of what later became Bisbee townsite. In a prominent iron cropping (an outcrop of what was significantly called, later, the "Dividend Fault"), he found pockets of gold and silver ore with a small trace of copper stain. The two officers knew of the rich oxidized copper outcrop which later became the Copper Queen mine, but for very practical reasons their interest concentrated on gold and silver — the place was too isolated to make copper ore shipment profitable.[8] Rucker and Dunn filed their silver claim and then grubstaked miner George Warren of Fort Bowie to work their Mule Gulch mine for them. In that same year, 1877, Warren was also sponsored by George Staples of Eureka Springs to locate the copper outcrop of the district. Warren found it and named the mine the Mercury.[9]

Rascality and caprice played a part. In 1878 George Warren got drunk and told about the wealth in Mule Gulch. Warren and several others then went to the area, staked claims on the north side of what was to become known as "Copper Queen Hill" and had them recorded collectively as the "Copper Queen." This enterprise included the jumping of the Dunn-Rucker claim. Shortly after, Warren anteed his share when he bet that he could outrace a horse for a hundred yards around a post. Warren lost the race.[10]

Also in 1878, one of the Copper Queen owners, George Atkinson, together with several partners, made claims adjoining the Copper Queen. The principal locations included the Copper Prince, Copper Jack, Czar, Atlanta, Hendricks and Neptune claims.[11]

But lack of capital, isolation and distance from a railroad precluded work on any of these claims. When the Southern Pacific finally reached Benson in 1880, the possibility for profitable operations soared. In the spring of 1880, Edward Reilly, a lawyer, engineer and mine broker, came to Bisbee from his own mine in Elko, Nevada. After talking to its owners, he and Levi Zeckendorf, a Tucson storekeeper, obtained an option on the Copper Queen claim for $20,000. Reilly went to look for investors. In San Francisco he persuaded two railroad builders, John Ballard and William Martin, to investigate the Copper Queen. Encouraged by their technical mining advisors, the brothers Ben and Lewis Williams, Ballard and Martin sent their attorney, DeWitt Bisbee, to take up the option and purchase the Copper Queen. Reilly and Zeckendorf retained a one-third interest.[12]

The Copper Queen Mining Company was founded with a capitalization of $2,500,000. The group named Martin as manager and Ben Williams as mine superintendent. Lewis Williams was to build and operate a smelter. They christened the camp in honor of their attorney, DeWitt Bisbee.[13]

In June 1880, with the smelter completed, Ballard and Martin began actively operating the Copper Queen. The mine's great wealth manifested itself immediately; while clearing away the brush on the claim's west side, the new owners exposed a circular sixty-foot-wide body of almost clear carbonate copper. Continued excavation revealed a high-grade ore that reached 25 percent copper content. They shipped their black copper for analysis to a chemical works at Phoenixville, Pennsylvania, that was managed by Dr. James Douglas, an expert in chemical geology. Douglas was much impressed by the shipments from the Copper Queen. He obtained a commission from some eastern investors to investigate various copper mines in the Arizona territory. The trip intensified his interest.[13]

A year after his return from Arizona, an old American mercantile and import firm, Phelps, Dodge & Co., asked Douglas for advice about their building a copper smelter on an island in Long Island Sound. Douglas' opinion was negative, but in the course of the conference with the Phelps Dodge officials, they engaged him to inspect several copper properties in a forthcoming second trip to Arizona. Here was born an association which was to make Phelps Dodge one of the largest copper mining companies in the world. It was to make Dr. Douglas a multimillionaire.

In February 1881, Douglas went to Arizona and subsequently advised Phelps Dodge to buy properties in both Morenci and Bisbee. Immediately the Phelps Dodge partners, William E. Dodge, Jr. and D. Willis James, agreed to buy the Detroit Copper Company in Morenci. A year later, Phelps Dodge, accepting Douglas as a one-tenth sharing partner in the venture, obtained the Atlanta claim in Bisbee.[15]

After several years of expense and despair for its owners, the Atlanta began to pay off. With this encouragement, Phelps Dodge, acting through Douglas, bought the Copper Queen mine for $1,250,000 in 1885. Douglas was appointed mine manager, while the Lewis brothers became the mine and mill superintendents. The very next year another large ore body was discovered in the Copper Queen; in time it became the richest mine in Arizona.[16]

Other operations in Bisbee flourished, too. In 1889, an obscure Michigan development company headed by Charles Briggs acquired the Irish Mag, a promising but undeveloped claim adjacent to the Copper Queen. After several months of disappointing exploratory work, Briggs' group discovered a huge deposit of high-grade copper ore. They thereupon organized the Calumet & Arizona Mining Company, a venture that soon became one of the most profitable in the territory. In addition, a small group of Arizona speculators headed by Lemuel Shattuck, discovered ore and in 1906 began producing copper. It is said that the Shattuck-Denn mining company was at one time the "highest-grade, lowest-cost producer in the world."[17]

In October 1904 the *Engineering and Mining Journal* commented on the obvious wealth of Bisbee's resources. It was easy to predict, said the *Journal*, that "the growth of Bisbee during the next two or three years will be more rapid than any other important copper district in the country."[18]

Bisbee's Growth

Bisbee's social and cultural development paralleled that of other frontier communities. Crudity, violence, boredom, filth, barbarism and drunkenness characterized the way of life in southeastern Arizona. Despite mining and associated economic activities, little change took place before 1880.

Restless, ungainly, growing quickly, Bisbee had a youth as rough as the local terrain. By 1881 Bisbee had a school. To avoid the "depradations" of the Apaches, the school held classes in the Miners' Union Hall at Brewery Gulch. Indian drill was held regularly. Sometimes when the Apaches raided, the teacher took her pupils to the nearest mine tunnel.[19] According to Dr. Douglas, one night in 1881, "when the Indians were out, . . . the women were put for safety into the mine, and every man who could handle a gun was on the alert."[20]

The "criminal element" moved in (but never took over) in the eighties. In what became known as the "Bisbee Massacre," robbers killed four people in December of 1883. One of the outlaws, captured within two weeks, was sentenced to life in prison and then promptly hanged from a telegraph pole by a lynch mob.[21]

Eventually Bisbee, at 5400-foot elevation, occupied about two miles of the upper and steepest section of six-mile-long Mule Pass Gulch. The buildings of the town, many clinging to the canyons' sides, were arranged in tiers, and residents of the upper levels could reach their homes only by flights of stone or wooden stairs. Brewery Gulch, with bawdy houses and bars lined along its lower part, intersected Mule Pass Gulch at a right angle.[22] Like other Western mining towns, Bisbee featured a number of gambling houses equipped for poker, faro, craps and roulette.

Older than Tombstone, Bisbee was tougher, lustier, richer, more lawless, less cultured than even the myths suggest about its neighbor twenty-five miles away. J. Ross Browne had observed that in the mining towns of barbarous Arizona one could occasionally find "men of refinement and education connected with the mines." Seeing a lynch victim swinging from a tree, a Reverend Pritchard remarked in 1882, "Something must be done to civilize these savages." Upon his return to New York, he sent Bisbee a collection of personally selected books.[23] The lynch law revolted Dr. James Douglas, too. According to one source:

> The gruesome sight of a body of a Mexican desperado, left dangling by a self-appointed vigilance committee from the limb of a convenient tree, brought home to Douglas, especially, the rough, lawless nature of Bisbee society in 1885 and the immediate need for establishing those cultural and ameliorating agencies which he believed the development of a self-respecting, law-abiding community required.... Whether the story is true or apocryphal, the company's camp at Bisbee ... soon had its church, hospital, company store, and recreation center.[24]

Reverend Pritchard's philanthropic program of moral uplift seems to have been misdirected, and Dr. Douglas' paternal example appears to have failed, for thirty-five years later it was a New Yorker, a progeny of Dr. Douglas', not an uncivilized native, who ordered Bisbee's best-known act of lawlessness.

Bisbee's growth reflected the development of Phelps Dodge. As Bisbee grew, it lost much of its frontier crudeness —on the surface, anyway. By 1900 several fine homes had

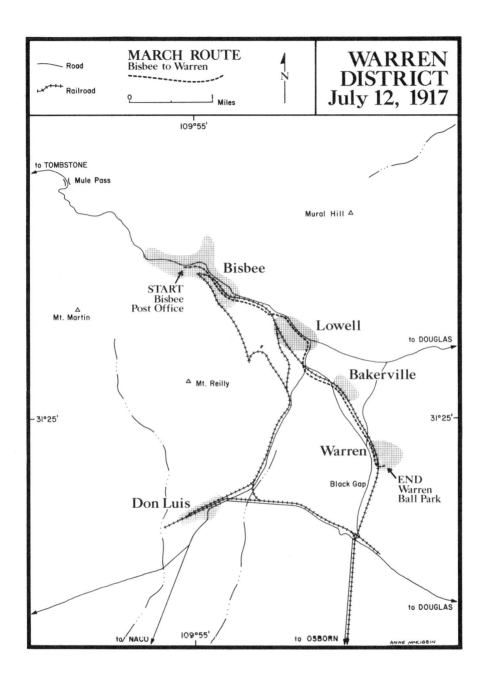

been built by managers and engineers. On January 9, 1902, the town of Bisbee was incorporated.[25] A tremendous flood during the summer of 1908 brought desolation to the town, and a few months later it suffered a half-million dollar fire. But as the town was rebuilt, substantial structures in brick and stone replaced the old, flimsy frame ones. Several suburbs grew up beside Bisbee, and the entire area became known as the "Warren District," in honor of George Warren.[26] By 1917 the Warren District boasted the third largest population of any community in Arizona.[27] In 1905 a reporter for the *Tucson Citizen* visited Bisbee. "Bisbee," he wrote, "the city of foul odors and sickening smells, the busiest burg in the territory." Brewery Gulch, he reported, is a street "covered with a slime several inches deep and about four feet wide." The street was part of the Bisbee sewer system, and women were "caused, while walking, to hold their skirts high....In Bisbee there is lots of business and mere existence."[28]

Sister Cities

The similarities of Butte and Bisbee played a strong part in shaping the labor history of the two camps. For both, the Dantesque image obtained—sulphur, slag, glaring heat, perpetual subterranean fires, roasted landscape. An early twentieth century journalist reported: "The city of Butte seems to fulfill the abomination of desolation of scripture. This great desolate waste embraces the working place of the men, the homes of their families, and the playground of their children."[29] Both towns were widow-makers; falling rock, fires, underground gas, electrocution, explosives, cave-ins, uncovered holes, runaway cages, rotten timbers and silicas exacted high payment in human life.[30]

Unlike Butte, however, where "the War of the Copper Kings" raged sensationally for decades among F. Augustus Heinze, Marcus Daly and William Andrews Clark, Bisbee's three mining companies got along well together. Marked by a guarded friendliness, the three companies cooperated so well that each allowed the other unlimited access to its mine. All three exchanged geological information freely. Perhaps this happy condition prevailed because, despite Shattuck-Denn's high-grade ore and Calumet & Arizona's profits, the Copper Queen reigned supreme. Bisbee was recognized by everyone as a one-company town.[31] Similarly, citizens around the state of

Arizona understood that when someone spoke of "the company," the reference was to Phelps Dodge.

Frontier Melting Pot

One thing made living in either town worthwhile: money. Discussing conditions and wages in Bisbee in 1913, *The Arizona Labor Journal* stated that the "pay roll ... is the envy of many other cities of the state." With almost everyone earning above the county average, even Bisbee's teachers enjoyed high pay. In 1914, *Arizona*, a public relations magazine aimed at potential tourists, gave Bisbee lavish praise. In the tone of *Sunset* and other genteel, promotional magazines of the period, it said, "Today it [Bisbee] is the richest copper camp in the southwest and believes it will soon be termed the richest copper camp in the world."[32]

By 1917, the year of the deportation, there were 4,718 men employed in the Bisbee district.[33] The place was booming. George Wharton James, the celebrated Southern California dreamspinner, visited Bisbee early that year and could report, "The wages paid are the highest of any camp in the United States."[34]

The people who came to Bisbee were varied. In the early days Cornishmen or "Cousin Jacks" comprised the majority of miners. For them mining was a craft, a family tradition. They brought their wives and children to Bisbee and identified fiercely with the profession of mining. Although they were prideful and defiant of arbitrary authority, their loyalty to their employers was unwavering. But the "new immigration" began to affect Bisbee after 1900, particularly as increased technology reduced the need for skilled miners and created a greater demand for the low-paid, unskilled laborer. Brawny southern and eastern Europeans—many imported or enticed into Bisbee—began to rival in numbers the Anglos. Most of the Bohemians, Serbians, Austrians, Montenegrans, Czechs and Italians, known better by such appellations as "Bohunks" or "Bear Dancers," did not bring their families, and they lived together in their respective quarters.[35] Racial and ethnic tensions began to grow. Yet Bisbee remained a "white man's camp"; company policy said Mexicans could not work underground.[36] Orientals were not welcome; one person recalls that "one of the unique traditions of Bisbee is that no member of the celestial kingdom may remain in town overnight."[37]

2

LABOR
AND POLITICS
IN THE WEST
AND ARIZONA

From the middle of the nineteenth century, western mining camps shared a loyalty to each other and a discriminating, passionate sense of community.[1] Despite great, forbidding physical distances, the sister cities of Ely and Coeur d'Alene and Globe were tied together in a close sorority. No two communities·shared circumstances more than Butte and Bisbee. Their common sulphurous setting, occupational dangers and sensitivity to market vagaries bound them tightly. Communications were frequent, and the routes and resting places between them seemed as familiar to the copper miner as neighborhood streets and bars did to the city dweller. Western Union telegrams flew back and forth hourly across the two thousand miles of wire that separated the two towns.

Yet, for all this sodality, an even more conspicuous condition typified nineteenth and early twentieth century western mining camps. As historian Rodman Paul put it, "If any one characteristic stood out in common to the mining West, it was instability."[2]

The history of Arizona shows that power politics and interest groups were not new to the state during the early twentieth century. Arizona became a territory for many of the same reasons that it became a state—so that certain interests might be better able to have political control over the area's affairs. Arizona was a pawn in the expansionist politics of the antebellum period. Acquired in the Treaty of Guadalupe Hidalgo (1848) and the Gadsden Purchase (1853), Arizona played a part in the northern attempt to mollify southern discontent over territorial acquisitions. Arizona was made a territory of the Union during the Civil War, on February 20, 1863, partly as a response to the claim of the Confederacy which had made Arizona a territory of the Confederacy on January 18, 1862.[3]

Arizona's forbidding qualities of aridity and heat, and its fierce Apaches, delayed the development of labor activities as they delayed the development of mining itself. But where mines did open up in the West, labor had special problems. Insular and autocratic industrial managers operated under anachronistic frontier values. Management's belief in local autonomy and rugged individualism made the miner's life a nightmare of overwork, unsafe conditions and job insecurity. The miner, usually unqualified in the skilled trades, found little in the existing national labor structure to support him.

Labor: 1890–1915

To counteract employer absolutism, western mine workers developed their own organizations.[4] In 1863 a metal miners' union had been founded in Nevada. This was followed by organizations in South Dakota (1877) and Butte, Montana (1878). The Western Federation of Miners, founded in Colorado in 1893, affiliated briefly with the AFofL—from 1896 to 1897. Soon after the organization of the WFM, the Mine Owners Association was formed. It was the efforts of the WFM to gain company recognition which led to the great and bitter industrial battles of the turn of the century—Leadville, Coeur d'Alene, Telluride and the well-known Cripple Creek Wars of 1903 and 1904. During these struggles, the operators had the active support of the local governmental authorities and the press. Facing this kind of opposition, the unions met defeat in practically every major strike.

Despite strike failure, growth of membership in the WFM increased and enabled it to exercise limited political action. WFM-supported legislation led to eight-hour-day laws in many

Southeast Arizona and
Southwest New Mexico
(1980)

western states. Rejoining the AFofL in 1911, the WFM, which in 1916 changed its name to the International Union of Mine, Mill and Smelter Workers, supported national labor goals.[5] For more than twenty years, it exerted as much political force as any other group in the western states. With other labor unions, the IUMMSW effected several pro-union laws. Labor historian Philip Taft claims:

> The codes of labor and welfare on the statute books of the state governments are largely, if not wholly, attributable to the persistent efforts of the state federations of labor.[6]

During the 1890s labor reached the peak of its power in many western states. By taking advantage of the Populist mood, labor oftentimes coalesced noncapitalist elements in a state:

> In most mining communities local farmers, businessmen, and professionals allied with labor unionists; and public officials, including judges, elected by union votes, often supported labor's goals. Instead of class being pitted against class, local communities united in coalitions cutting across class lines to combat "foreign" capitalists.[7]

It was this pattern of politics that enabled Arizona labor to gain the upper hand in the years 1908–16.

But legislation, as in so many other situations involving the cause of the common man during this period, did not mean much change in practice by mining companies. Backed by the higher courts, the companies expressed their independence of the law with impunity. In the meantime, mine operators developed their own collective counterattack. Copper tariffs, "worse than impotent" in the 1880s, were strengthened, thus improving profits. Exchange of ideas and decreased secrecy among companies hastened the development of copper metallurgy in the 1890s, enabling even more profits. The western mining companies were growing up.[8] By 1900 they were girding for a full-scale offensive against labor organizations. The sensational events related to the assassination of pro-mine owner Governor Steunenberg of Idaho and the subsequent kidnapping and trial of Bill Haywood and others dramatized the bitterness of the conflict.[9]

The repression continued. In Colorado, ruthless use of the summary discharge, the black list, armed guards and spies culminated in the swing of state, county and town officials to the side of the mining companies.[10] On April 20, 1914, a strike at the Rockefeller-owned coal mines near Ludlow ended with the wholesale massacre of thirty-nine strikers and their families including two women and eleven children. Strikebreakers, national guardsmen and deputies, after soaking the strikers' tent colony with coal oil, set the tents afire. As people ran screaming from the blazing tents—some people on fire—machine guns and rifles cut them down. Many of the traits that identified the Bisbee Deportation—absentee ownership, feudal rules, company-owned towns, brutal managers, immigrants, detectives, strikebreakers, cooperative authorities, company violence, indictments against strikers, twaddly federal intervention —described Ludlow.[11]

Not only did the Ludlow Massacre signal the end of effective unionism in Colorado and the lengths to which big money would go to crush workers' independence, it heralded in the West an innovation of paternalism—the company union. In Ludlow it was called the "Colorado Industrial Representative Plan" or the "Rockefeller Plan." Ludlow miners voted for it as an alternative to nothing by a close majority in October 1915.[12]

The end to union effectiveness came to Montana in the same year as the Ludlow Massacre—1914. Capitalizing on an internecine union struggle in Butte, the copper companies restricted employment by use of a "rustling card" and were able to end job control, which had existed in Butte for thirty-six years.[13] To cap the union defeat, the Butte Miners' Union Hall was blown up by several expertly placed charges of dynamite in June 1914. The books of the union were destroyed, as was the collective will of the miners. The mine owners blamed the agitators and the malcontents, but the radicals said that it was an act of the mine operators perpetrated in order to discredit the union. If possible, the workers claimed, the operators hoped to disrupt union cohesiveness and bring about an open-shop camp. Whoever was to blame, the blast *was* followed by an open-shop, non-union situation.

From the fall of 1914 to June of 1917 no effective miners' organization existed in the Butte district. A new union formed a few months after the dynamiting called itself the Butte Mine Workers' Union. Branded "IWW" by Anaconda, the union was suppressed by martial law and the state militia. Union members vehemently protested the IWW charge, and testimony by union leaders indicated only about seventy-five Wobblies worked in Butte at the time.[14]

A little more than one month before the Bisbee Deportation, on June 8, 1917, a terrible disaster occurred in the Speculator mine in Butte. One hundred sixty-four men were smothered or burned to death when fire broke out. Four days later miners formed an IWW local in Butte. The Speculator disaster had crystallized miner dissatisfaction, but subsequent strikes failed.[15] Montana mine owners—like those in Arizona—had triumphed.

Though the hostile and unattractive environment delayed Arizona's entrance into large-scale mining, the region could not escape forever being exploited. The wealth awaited, and it was only a matter of time before Arizona advanced to the front of the nation's copper-producing regions. Between 1871 and 1875 Arizona produced 1 percent of the nation's copper; by 1885 copper production amounted to 15 percent of the nation's output.[16]

Western mining throughout its history had been distinguished by its hectic, violent frontier nature. In addition, the labor problems of the frontier paralleled—in some cases, anticipated—those of the urban East.[17] But Arizona, arriving on the mining scene the last, became the last to experience the wrenching tensions of labor-management warfare. Arthur L. Walker, General Superintendent of the Old Dominion Copper Company in Globe, Arizona, from 1887 to 1893 and later Professor of Metallurgy at the Columbia University School of Mines, recalled that there was "no questioning or dissatisfaction" about obeying orders or doing work. The workers, as he remembered, had been primarily Anglo-Saxon; the implication by Walker being that Arizona labor-management harmony could be somewhat explained by that fact. [18]

In the late 1800s little unemployment could be found in Arizona's mining camps. These camps, for the most part, were tight, feudalistic societies. Workers often were paid with scrip or performance *boletas* which could be exchanged only at mining company-owned stores. Removed from national trends and issues, the mines and their workers existed as closed, isolated social and economic entities. As Governor Nathan O. Murphy observed in 1891, "The supply and demand are fairly equalized, wages satisfactory and labor contented." [19]

Arizona's labor forces pulled themselves together toward the end of the nineteenth century. The first lodge of the Arizona Railroad Brotherhoods was established in 1883. Always the center of twentieth century labor activity in the state, Globe saw the birth of mining unionism in the Arizona territory in 1884. The first notable strike in Arizona's labor history took place that year; soldiers were sent to the Tombstone district to stop disorders growing out of a reduction in pay and in working hours. However, union membership throughout the territory increased slowly. Despite some discontent with lower wages during the depression of 1893, labor took no action. Most miners in Arizona, owing to the limited size of mine operations, had a close relationship with their employer until 1900. They felt no need for a union until the companies became oppressive. [20]

Oppression soon was felt. Martial law was invoked at Globe in 1896 (the year after Arthur Walker left) as a result of employer influence during a strike protesting wage cuts and the employment of Mexicans. In a manner that seems ironic when compared with Bisbee twenty-one years later, the WFM local told the mine managers to grant their demands or be escorted out of town. Naturally law officers supported the company officials, and the strike was suppressed. But Globe became known, then, as the center of territorial labor agitation in Arizona. [21]

At the same time this labor-management conflict was establishing itself in Arizona, a national atmosphere of tolerance and industrial peace had begun to grow. The climate of public opinion had become more favorable to union activity. Muckraking writers produced some sympathy for the plight of the workingman, and ordinary newspapers expressed such unprecedented sentiments as, "Capital must make up its mind to get along with organized labor." The National Civic Federation, formed in Chicago in 1896, initiated a joint campaign between worker and employer to maintain industrial peace across the country. Composed of such diverse and unlikely leaders as Mark Hanna, Samuel Gompers, Grover Cleveland, Charles Eliot, John D. Rockefeller, Jr., John Mitchell, Archbishop Ireland and Charles N. Schwab, the Federation endorsed unionization and trade agreements. In several situations, it helped bring about management-union settlements. (Its only attempt to settle a major dispute failed when the United States Steel Corporation crushed a bitter strike in 1901.)

This mood, together with President Theodore Roosevelt's mediatory policy toward the anthracite strike of 1902, prompted some people to term the years 1898 to 1904 "the honeymoon of capital and labor." An industrial commission, authorized by Congress in 1901 to investigate "Capital and Labor Employed in Mining Industry," filed a well-documented and compassionate report.[22]

Workers in Arizona during this period enjoyed improved conditions. A schedule of mine wages at Jerome in 1904 showed that shift bosses, blacksmiths and hoist engineers rose to $5 a day while miners earned $3.50.[23] This substantial pay did not have the blessing of all mine owners. Certain labor-sponsored legislation provoked further managerial dissatisfaction. The Arizona Railroad Brotherhoods attempted to secure laws providing for tenure and increased wages as well as laws guaranteeing safety measures. For their efforts, the Brotherhoods succeeded in getting the Arizona territorial legislature to pass a law in 1903 limiting trainmen to sixteen consecutive hours on the job. In this sympathetic spirit, territorial Governor Brodie signed on March 13, 1903, an eight-hour-day bill for underground miners.[24]

Understandably, the mine operators searched for adjustments. In Morenci and Clifton, where no union existed, the copper companies proposed a pay cut to accompany the newly legislated reduction of work hours. The workers walked out. To show their authority, the copper companies persuaded Governor Brodie to order Arizona Rangers to Morenci on June

6, 1903. On June 11, President Roosevelt had military detachments sent to Morenci from Fort Grant and Fort Huachuca.
Shortly afterward the strikers were enjoined by court order to
return to work.[25] Thus, early legislation, like in so many other
states and at the national level, proved largely ineffectual in the
face of corporate-influenced judiciary.

For a long time the organizers of the Western Federation of
Miners found a poor reception in Arizona mining towns.
Grubstakers with a handful of loyal muckers were responsible
for almost all Arizona mining activity during the nineteenth
century. With the growth of large corporations, this close
employer-employee relationship began to break down. By 1905
nine WFM locals and a territorial union, Arizona State Union
#3, had appeared.[26]

In Bisbee, it is true that the Cornish-born "Cousin Jacks"
dominated the skilled laborers. They appeared too "hard-
bitten, clannish, conscientious, too independent to be pushed
around by boss, foreman, or superintendents, too self-reliant
to welcome the activities of labor-union leaders or other outsiders in their affairs."[27] These were "professionally skilled"
miners, and the operators relied upon, consulted with and patronized them. Even as late as 1903, labor-management relations remained good. The *Bisbee Daily Review* reported that:

> the year 'round three shifts of men...go down into the
> Copper Queen, and rarely do the names on the payroll
> change, as long as a good man wishes to remain in the
> company's employ, and a more contented, money saving,
> industrious, sober and thrifty list of employees cannot be
> found anywhere upon the face of the globe.[28]

By using a policy of trust and generosity, Dr. James Douglas
made Bisbee a city with high loyalty and morale. As times
changed, this loyalty deteriorated. More arbitrary policies
under less benevolent authority stirred uncertainty among the
older miners, while mining industry growth and new employment practices brought more independent workers to Bisbee.
But the strong vestiges of old worker loyalty helped to provide
the cohesiveness and spirit which accounted for the way in
which the mining camp responded to the "invasion by the
I.W.W." during World War I.[29]

Copper production in Arizona soared between 1871 and
1905. The territory's yearly average between 1871 and 1875 was
189 short tons, 1 percent of the national total. The years 1876–80

averaged 1,168 tons per year. In 1885, thanks substantially to the bonanza strike at the Atlanta claim on the basis of Dr. Douglas' educated guess, Arizona produced 11,353 tons of copper. Twenty years later, in 1905, the state was up to 113,000 tons.[30]

Times were changing. Dr. James Douglas, in his development of mining and metallurgical techniques, was contributing to the general industrial trend of decreasing dependence upon skilled labor. In the meantime, the United States, upon the influence of the owners of the growing industries in the land, saw thousands of homeless, wretched Europeans pouring through the lamplit golden door to create a huge unskilled labor pool. Thus improved technology, a flooded labor market, a decline in the demand for skilled specialists, poison dreams, empty, hopeless promises and irresolute economics created a new situation, a new loss of security and stability.[31] The gap between mucker and manager grew.

From the beginning, working conditions in Bisbee had been treacherous and miserable. The miners worked in wet stopes and drifts often in water up over their shoe tops. They breathed wet, foul air.[32] Ironically, despite the constant and dangerous presence of water and uncomfortable humidity, drilling was done "dry," thus creating the dust that produced the deadly pneumoconiosis which struck down many Bisbee miners. The temperature in the mines ranged well over 100°. In the wintertime men emerged from the sweltering adits and, without benefit of shower or change of clothes, walked home through the subfreezing cold. Numerous accidents occurred despite Dr. Douglas' unusual safety precautions. By 1905, Bisbee miners began to feel less loyal and more dissatisfied.

At a meeting on February 26, 1906, John B. Clark secretly organzied the first Bisbee labor union, a local of the Western Federation of Miners. Immediately the Bisbee Merchants Association passed a resolution opposing the WFM. Also, Bisbee miners showed little interest in organizing. In an open election held on March 1, 2,888 miners voted against the union, 428 for it.[33] The copper companies promptly fired four hundred men who had voted for the union, this prompted one hundred more workers to quit in indignation at this retaliatory act.

A year later, in February 1907, WFM activity revived in Bisbee. Bisbee Miners Union, local No. 106, organized by

Joseph Cannon and Percy D. Rawlins, prepared for a strike. "The press and the pulpit" lined up against the strikers, and at the same time the Bisbee small businessmen gave all their support to the copper companies. The copper company–controlled newspaper began a campaign of abuse against the miners and their officials.[34] As before, the three big mines laid off hundreds of men—ostensibly to do repairs.

In March the companies announced a wage raise. The *Daily Review* carefully pointed out that the raise was not a result of a "demand or request from the men."[35] Knowing not every miner could be bought off, the companies continued their inquisitional process. Eighteen "spotters" were employed on each shift. Within a month, 600 men were fired; by April 10, the number of discharged men reached 1,600.[36] The union then decided to call a strike for higher wages and to protest the use of Mexicans as well as the heavy layoffs. Three thousand men walked out. But the companies held firmly against recognition of the union.[37] As Joe Cannon, the WFM organizer, remarked, "They have a closed shop in Bisbee—no one but a scab can work."[38]

At the WFM convention held in June and July, Thomas Booker of Butte received a hearty ovation when he reaffirmed the sense of community that existed between Butte and Bisbee. He promised:

> Butte No. 1 will enlist in this Bisbee fight, not for one year but for twenty years if necessary.... We will not only give you our cordial assistance with our hands, but we will swell your fund with the necessary coin of the realm to help down any corporation that is as soulless as the Copper Queen is.[39]

The companies did import strikebreakers, some coming from as far away as England, and within six months most of the strikers had been replaced. In July 1907, the Copper Queen officials obtained an injunction which, in addition to prohibiting picketing arriving trains, even forbade the use of the United States mail to inform anyone outside that a strike was on in Bisbee. Throughout the strike, company police arrested men for vagrancy, illegal assembly and many other trumped-up charges. As if in rehearsal for the 1917 drama, company officials denounced the strikers as un-American and "alien agitators." Having accomplished nothing, the union called off the strike on December 27, 1907. To placate the workers, two years later the Copper Queen Mining Company announced that it was inaugurating a system of sickness and accident insurance for its workmen.[40] The insurance program was the first of several "fringe" benefits the company developed over a period of years to induce company loyalty.

Sometime before February 1907, Walter Douglas, then the general manager of the Copper Queen, had said that the Western Federation of Miners should never organize at Bisbee. Rather than see such a calamity occur, said Douglas, the mines would shut down. In so saying, he laid down a personal vow which became almost an obsession with him. Yet, in the next ten years, Douglas neither closed his mines nor effected lasting legal repression of unionism. When Phelps Dodge pressed charges against the strikers for such things as vagrancy and illegal assembly, no defendant was convicted. It was, as the *Arizona Labor Journal* observed several years later, "all the more remarkable when it is considered what were the type of men that the copper company had selected for trial judges and deputies." Everyone could see that Arizona labor was not totally under the thumb of the copper companies.[41]

In 1909 the Globe-Miami area strengthened its reputation as a hotbed of Arizona labor activity. That year the Globe mine operators closed down the mines until the unions removed their "walking delegates." A dutiful Globe sheriff jailed two members of the Industrial Workers of the World who paraded under a red flag.[42] This kind of intimidation failed to discourage Globe union growth. By January 1915, the WFM was strong enough in Globe to call a wage strike. Immediately, in a portentous move, Globe citizens formed the Arizona Business Improvement League. On January 23, the strike ended with the acceptance by both sides of what was to become a landmark and object of frequent dispute in subsequent Arizona labor relations—the "Miami Scale."[43] Designed by union men eager to share the wartime profits, the Miami Scale was a sliding wage rate based on the market price of copper. Arizona labor considered it a qualified victory.

Aside from another short strike in Ray in July 1915, the Arizona labor war remained free from sensation or violence until a landmark event in Clifton-Morenci in the fall of 1915. The organization of the Arizona State Federation of Labor on

January 20, 1912, had brought no other new developments to the Arizona labor-management picture.[44]

Politics and Labor: 1901–1910

There is no doubt about it, "one central theme unifies the entire twentieth century—the interaction of Arizona with external economic and political forces."[45] But even before the turn of the century, absentee investors in Arizona copper mining recognized the importance of the political control of the territory if they were to enjoy the fullest profits. (Accordingly, since it was less well financed and lacked the manipulative skills which had accrued to employers through years of apprenticeship in the art of fulfilling ulterior motives, labor lagged behind.) Most importantly, local mine managers were expected to make the right connections and sponsor the right candidates to keep down property taxes.

In 1891 William Andrews Clark assigned a Louisianan, Henry J. Allen, as office manager and financial agent to Clark's newly acquired United Verde property in Jerome. Clark had come to know Allen in Butte where Allen had served Marcus Daly of Anaconda, one of Clark's most hated enemies in the notorious "war of the copper kings." Allen had worked for Daly as a director of Daly's political affairs—arranging newspaper advertising and editorials, securing orators, scheduling torchlit parades and manipulating elections. Allen's energies succeeded in bringing about a defeat of Clark in 1888 in one of Clark's early bids for political office. Clark hired Allen away from Daly and sent him to Jerome.[46]

In Jerome, Allen's administrative duties were nominal; his most important function was, as it had been in Butte, political. He was expected to use his charm and persuasive skills to make sure the political climate in Arizona was favorable to the interests of William Andrews Clark. Clark budgeted a generous fund for this purpose. Allen's primary job was to keep down mine taxation and obtain other favorable legislation.

A story about Allen relates that on one occasion a bundle of bank notes that Allen had drawn to use at a legislative session in Phoenix somehow or other had been marked. Someone plotted, apparently, to catch Allen and the United Verde at bribery. The money went out and then began to reappear in payments made by legislators. When Allen contended that he had spent the money for purchasing mules for the United Verde Copper Company, the word got around, and that particular legislative session became known as "the mule legislature."[47]

Allen enjoyed only limited success. He managed to gain the support of Phoenix' *Arizona Republican,* but the *Republican*'s business manager Harvey J. Lee informed Allen on June 16, 1900, that ex-Territorial Governor Myron H. McCord had acquired 51 percent control of the other Phoenix paper, the *Gazette.* Lee told Allen that McCord and the other *Gazette* owners "apparently intend to play to the gallery and give the railroads and mining companies the worst of it. They have little or no money and it will be a case of the big mit. With McCord in they will be able to make some trouble probably for us all." Lee went on to advise Allen that McCord, along with another Arizona political aspirant, Charles H. Akers, intended to use the *Arizona Gazette* "to club all corporate interests into line by advocating a bullion tax and the abolition of tax exemption for railroads." "You know the crowd as well as I do," Lee told Allen, " the way it looks now, the next legislature will probably be democratic. In that event the *Gazette* would shine." Then Lee concluded, "If there is anything in particular that you have up your sleeve against the common enemy do not be backward about mentioning the fact if the *Republican* can be of service to your interests."[48]

But these were good times for "the gallery." Even more in Arizona than across the country, labor received residual agrarian-stockmen Populist support (what there was of it in the arid zone) and incipient middle-class Progressive support (what there was of that in a pre-commercial industrial state) in its bid for power. Labor drew most of its strength, of course, from the thousands of miners who toiled for the copper companies. Whatever Henry Allen might have had up his sleeve would have to wait. His appointment had been ill-timed; in Arizona labor's star was rising.*

---

*"Labor" here means labor unions *and un*organized working men. At no time has "organized labor" alone ever been a potent political force in Arizona. Most wage earners in the state at this time identified with middle class values and ambitions, even though their rhetoric, resolutions and even reality may have had a conventional proletarian ring.

Allen soon fell out of Clark's favor. As his resentment toward Clark grew, Allen began to suffer prolonged periods of mental depression. Having been a trusted employee, privy to if not agent for many of Clark's outrageous and criminal manipulations, Allen decided to write an exposé. On January 6, 1904, Allen mailed the sensational exposure to the muckraking *Gazette*. A few hours later he changed his mind and through a United Verde lawyer tried, unsuccessfully, to recover the manuscript from the postal authorities. Deranged, Allen killed himself on January 8 at his ranch a few miles from Jerome. Charles Clark, outside the ranch house door at the time of Allen's suicide, immediately investigated Allen's affairs. He contacted the United Verde counsel who informed Clark of Allen's efforts to recover the expose. What Allen failed to do through legal process, Clark quickly achieved with ten thousand United Verde dollars.[49]

For several years, Arizona labor enjoyed indeed a phenomenal political potency. Sometime before Arizona's statehood in 1912, anti-corporate influence was felt. On March 12, 1904, the territorial supreme court ruled that the supervisors of Yavapai County, a group controlled by the copper interests, had no authority to lower the taxes of the United Verde Copper Company.[50] Since the Progressive-minded President Roosevelt usually picked open-minded men for territorial appointments, the territorial executive branch often supported labor, while the elected legislators and county officials usually represented management. Although labor strength was growing, the copper concerns prevailed in this dispute since farmers and railroad interests shared the mining companies' antipathy toward labor's political efforts and helped the copper men to dominate Arizona before 1909. What is more, as George W. P. Hunt claimed, despite occasional bits of gubernatorial "Progressivism" and despite impressive periodic flashes of pro-labor potency, every Arizona territorial legislature was under the control of the corporations. Federally appointed governors, though often symbols of hope for Arizona laboring men, had their price, too. George Hunt quoted a territorial governor's veto as going at $2,000.[51]

Across the nation, workers developed more political awareness and muscle. Arizona labor, too, became more politically active. In addition to enjoying the nationwide blessing of the Progressive movement, Arizona labor's interests were solidified by the Bisbee and Globe labor problems of 1907 and 1909. In 1908, angered by the recent adverse Supreme Court decisions related to the injunction, the boycott and federal mediation, Samuel Gompers decided to throw the weight of the AFofL to the Democrats.

Following the example of their national counterparts, Arizona's Democratic leaders pledged to pursue labor's objectives in the territory's 1908 election. Feeling its power rise and the recent sting of defeat in Bisbee and Globe, Arizona labor combined with other non-corporate interests and declared its ambition to be the control of the copper companies.[52] Although the Democrats lost to Taft and the Republicans in the national election, they won in Arizona. For the first time supporters of labor controlled the territorial legislature.

This labor legislature immediately turned on its former benefactor, Governor Joseph Kibbey, and in an attempt to strip the governor of some of his power abolished the Arizona Rangers.[53] The rangers had been created to be vigilant in the interests of the cattle business, but they had been used by Governor Brodie in 1903 in Morenci and by Governor Kibbey in 1907 in Bisbee to aid local officers in maintaining peace during the labor troubles. Ranger Harry Wheeler earned the respect of the strikers when he told them that any thugs and gunmen employed by the copper companies would have to reckon with the Rangers. In fact, Wheeler became friendly with the strikers and even gave them protection. This rankled mine owners who quietly advised the companies' deputies that corporate money was behind any gunman who might get into trouble. One of the deputies later admitted this, and he said he understood the pledge of support to be an invitation to commit murder. To compensate for Wheeler's impartiality, the copper companies requested Governor Kibbey to have federal troops sent into Bisbee. Indignant, Wheeler informed the governor that the Rangers would see to it that no trouble would come to Bisbee unless the "peace officers" started it. Kibbey sent no troops. Much to the ire of Phelps Dodge, Captain Wheeler and the Rangers had steadfastly remained unbiased. In desperation, the companies resorted to an injunction. But apparently the 1909 labor legislature had no room for sentiment. The bill to abolish the Rangers was vetoed by the new territorial governor, Richard Sloan, a conservative. Led by George W. P. Hunt, the legislature overrode Sloan's veto with the necessary two-thirds majority vote. Liberal strength was now substantial.[54]

After the Rangers were eliminated, Harry Wheeler got himself elected sheriff of Cochise County where he remained a favorite of workingmen up until the Bisbee Deportation— when he changed his own sentiments.

More confident by 1910, the Bisbee Miners' Union organized a labor party, though it disbanded within a short time upon the advice of G. W. P. Hunt who warned that a liberal third party would weaken the Democrats. Calmer, more organized, labor plotted its course. Always a persistent advocate of statehood (even though its defenders during territorial days had been federal appointees), labor had by now begun to push for a congressional statehood enabling act.[55]

With all this liberal activity in Arizona it was inevitable that certain political leaders would emerge who bore the Progressive stamp. In February 1918, when President Wilson's Mediation Commission reported to him on the effects of migratory labor, it declared that the migratory laborer "has helped spread ideas of liberalism into our industrial life."[56] If Western mining company officials saw spreading liberalism as a plague, they saw George Wiley Paul Hunt as its infectious carrier. Born in Huntsville, Missouri (a town founded by his grandfather), November 1, 1859, Hunt received about eight years of education in public and private schools. He went to Colorado in 1878, where he initiated himself into the mining community by prospecting for gold and other minerals. This adventure apparently failed. He came to Globe, Arizona, in July 1881, penniless, driving a burro. Hunt waited tables in a restaurant for two years and then worked as a laborer for some time in the Old Dominion mine. He drove a delivery wagon for the Old Dominion Commercial Company store; ten years later he was president of that mercantile organization.[57] Along with his commercial activities he became a banker and for several years ranched on the Salt River. When Globe was incorporated, Hunt became the town's first mayor. But he never forgot his mining experiences and the misery of the mucker's life. Hunt was elected in 1892 to the Arizona Territorial Legislature where he served as a moderate-Populist-progressive-minded spokesman in an assembly invariably dominated by corporation representatives. He served in the territorial lower house from 1892 to 1896 and in the Council, the upper chamber, from 1896 to 1900 and from 1904 to 1910.[58]

Perhaps the greatest evidence of George Hunt's political acumen and capacity for calculation was the fact that, despite

Arizona labor's political surge in 1909 to encourage Progressive legislation, the territorial legislature failed to pass strong anti-corporate laws during its last four years of existence. As he laid the groundwork for both Arizona's statehood and his governorship of that state, Hunt took care not to build his image as a "radical." At the same time this moderate stance perhaps lulled the dozing giant of Arizona mining into further complacency. As the most active and conspicuous member of the territorial legislature, Hunt often even seemed to represent corporate interests. His friendship with Arizona mine managers and their political representatives was an open fact. He spent most of his energy crusading for statehood, an ambition shared by mining men and other Arizonans alike, although for dissimilar motives.[59]

Among the "best people," it was fashionable to deride G. W. P. Hunt. Some said that he ate with his knife; others snickered about his poor English. But he got votes. A careful politician who "took care of his friends," he played the demagogue by campaigning in old clothes. Like his Republican contemporary, William Howard Taft, George Hunt was hugely corpulent, and a thick, droopy mustache gave him a walruslike appearance. His election as President of the Constitutional Convention in 1910 testified to his liberal record and to his popularity with the Arizona workingmen.

Even though Hunt's politics showed definite support for labor during the Constitutional Convention and during his early terms as state governor, one study has shown that Hunt, rather than being a spokesman for "labor" or for "liberalism," actually represented a phenomenon of the times, the "Progressivism" of "middle-of-the-road" small businessmen. Arizona's practical politics of the period included labor as an important segment of the Progressive coalition.[60] After being elected first governor of the state of Arizona, Hunt went on to hold that office, sporadically, for six more terms. He died in 1934.

Arizona Statehood

Under the leadership of Hunt, the legislature made known labor's desire for statehood. Arizona had made earlier bids for statehood—in 1891 and 1901.[61] In 1902 an amendment in Congress to an Arizona statehood bill provided that Arizona and New Mexico be admitted as one state. This "jointure" move failed to pass, as did the Arizona bill. But a controversial question had been raised: Were Arizonans desirous enough of

George W. P. Hunt

statehood to team with non-industrial New Mexico to enable statehood? The railroads and mining companies were horrified at the idea of being joined to the agricultural population of New Mexico and thereby be forced, through high assessment, to subsidize the New Mexicans. Moreover, a popular antipathy was felt by Arizona's prevalent Anglo-American population against New Mexico's predominantly Spanish-speaking Mexican population. Racism had its hand in the formation of the new state.[62]

A greater roadblock than the "jointure" possibility stood between Arizona and statehood. Albert Beveridge, the imperialist-minded and influential Senator from Indiana opposed Arizona statehood on the grounds that Arizona would, once a state, send two Democrats to the United States Senate. This would mean a weakening of the already tenuous Republican control of that body. As time went by, Beveridge's argument in opposition to statehood grew to include a realization of and an opposition to the railroad and mining "interests." Beveridge argued that these interests were attempting to establish state independence in order to escape the conservation-Progressive-oriented authority of the federally appointed territorial administrators. "Arizona," said Beveridge, "is just a mining camp" and should remain under the trusteeship of the United States federal government.[63]

President Taft, motivated by protective thoughts of a somewhat different nature, visited Arizona at this time and expressed a fear of too much liberalism in state constitutions. Taft warned against permitting labor groups to determine the fundamental law of a new state. Following more warnings from Taft, the necessary Congressional enabling act was passed and signed by the President on June 20, 1910.[64]

Labor's interest in obtaining statehood was shared by the mining and railroad corporations who wanted to get away from the strict territorial laws concerning public financing of corporations, taxation privileges and use of natural resources.[65] Too, the "Progressive" territorial gubernatorial appointees disturbed the easy political control mining men had enjoyed before 1901. They reckoned elected governors could be more easily manipulated. The corporations had their own ideas about how the new constitution should be written, but as it turned out, liberalism was not to be denied Arizona's citizens. In the election campaign for convention delegates that ensued the enabling act, the Republicans charged that Democrats were introducing socialism "to destroy the American form of government."[66] Corporation-controlled newspapers cautioned against using the constitution for legislative purposes. Unimpressed by Republican or corporation propaganda, voters drifted from their former position supporting big business. Fuming, the copper companies sat by and watched labor take over Arizona politics.

In 1904, Will L. Clark (no relation to Senator Clark) was appointed Henry Allen's replacement at the United Verde operation in Jerome.[67] In a letter written to Charles Clark which reflected the abject situation of the mine operators, he complained: "Both classes of newspapers are claiming that the other is dominated by the Corporations." Continuing, the new assistant general manager observed the strong anti-capitalist mood in the Arizona political atmosphere:

> I think it is a mistake for them to stand on such red-eyed platforms as the Democrats have throughout the Territory—for it appears they will carry the election and the "isms" will surely go into the Constitution.[68]

The Bisbee miners, representing the largest single bloc of voting power in Arizona, called for a meeting of representatives of all labor unions in the state of Arizona. This group convened in Phoenix on July 11, 1910, to decide which provisions Arizona labor should demand in the new constitution. After some debate, a long list of liberal proposals was drawn up into the labor platform. These demands included measures for popular sovereignty, equal suffrage, the anti-injunction, employer liability, direct election of United States senators, authorization of state seizure of property, public payment of court defense costs, short terms for elected state officials and other Populist-Progressive guarantees. The laborites felt that the two major political parties would find these provisions unacceptable. It was at this time that the Bisbee miners urged the formation of the labor party. G. W. P. Hunt, fearing the crippling of the Democratic party by the loss of the labor constituency, persuaded the Arizona Democrats to endorse labor's constitutional goals if labor would pledge its support to the Democrats. A deal was made and thus labor came to dominate the convention.[69]

By now, labor was only one interest group opposed to the mining corporations. Small property owners and businessmen, jumping on the Progressive bandwagon, became eager to deprive the corporations of the political control they were thought to have had in the territorial legislature. And so the general public, what there was of it in middle-classless Arizona, supported the Democratic candidates, hoping to squeeze more tax money from big business and ease the burden on its own pocketbook. On the day of the election of convention delegates, September 12, 1910, true to Will Clark's prediction, the liberal victory was overwhelming. Of fifty-two delegates elected, forty-one were strong liberals. Forty of these were Democrats. The Cochise County delegation, ten in number, was the largest of the thirteen counties represented. (Greenlee County's organization had not yet become official.) Only Maricopa County, with nine delegates, even approached the Bisbee-Douglas domination of the Constitutional Convention.[70]

An Arizona pioneer with liberal tendencies, Frank C. Lockwood, wrote in retrospect in 1932: "It was a thoroughly representative body of men who met to write the Constitution of Arizona." Straight-faced, almost righteous, he quoted someone describing this "representative" body:

> The delegates from one county [Cochise] were composed of a machinist, a plumber, a locomotive engineer, two miners, three lawyers, a butcher, and a railroad switchman who had defeated in the election one of the greatest mining operators of Arizona.

"Labor," Lockwood observed euphemistically, "was manifestly in the saddle."[71]

Up at the United Verde, Assistant Manager Clark wrote General Manager Clark, who was at his home in San Mateo, "The result of the election was as I had predicted." He then reaffirmed the corporate "lay-low, wait-and-see" attitude:

> I do not find any change in the situation, for even Atty. Ellinwood, who is elected in Cochise County, has publicly stated that every pledge of the Democratic platform would be written into the constitution.
>
> It appears that our attitude, so far, has been clearly the most expedient one....[72]

Even Will Clark could not divine the devious scheming of Democratic candidate for Cochise County convention delegate Everett E. Ellinwood. Although a man of unquestionable copper company loyalty, Ellinwood did indeed endorse the radical measures. He told the Cochise County Democratic Constitutional Delegate Convention on August 20 that he supported a blend of the Oklahoma and Oregon constitutions, and he denounced President Taft for his objections. He repeated this point of view at the Bisbee Opera House on August 27 where he was rousingly cheered for his impassioned support of the popular sovereignty provisions.[63]

Ellinwood's brazen radicalism angered the Republicans — and fooled the Cochise County Democrats; he, like the other Cochise Democrats, received overwhelming support at the delegate election. The frustrated *Tucson Citizen,* strongly middle-class Republican, spoke up warily. It said that Ellinwood knew the radical provisions would be rejected in Washington and that as a phony liberal he stood to serve the copper companies no matter what happened at the convention. If Phelps Dodge cat's-paw Ellinwood got an extra-liberal constitution passed, it would be turned down by Taft; if he wrote a conservative document according to his true interests, he would get what he was paid for. Either way, the corporations would win and the labor-middle-class coalition of Arizona would lose. The *Citizen* (itself often ingratiating toward the railroads) did feel Ellinwood's gambit amounted more to a long-shot gamble: "The people see the corporation collar underneath the cloak of socialism."[74]

Apparently Phelps Dodge had an *agent provocateur* among the delegates at the 1910 Arizona Constitution Convention. It was reported that delegate Ellinwood was the most vigorous and outspoken conservative in the convention. And when he became desperate, he used disruptive methods. Ellinwood showed himself to be "skilled in the game of controversy. ...Whenever he saw that his [conservative] views could not carry, with change of tactics ... [he] would advocate the most extreme radicalism in an attempt to swing his opponents into an untenable position."[75]

The convention assembled on October 10, 1910, at the territorial capital building, where all of President Taft's apprehensions were realized. Despite the intense difference of political goals among the members, the mood of the convention most of the time was one of congeniality, informality and even, at times, fraternal high spirits. Attendance was often poor; the members were distracted by such diversions as the Territorial Fair which was going on at the same time. On one occasion the delegates, by chance in an untypical irritable mood, were serenaded by the Copper Queen band.

G. W. P. Hunt was elected president of the convention.[76] Bisbee's hand in the formulation of the document was clear from the start; E. E. Ellinwood fought the hardest to protect corporate interests while the principal spokesman for labor was Bisbee machinist Thomas Feeney. Hunt proceeded to appoint liberal Democrats to the chairmanships of all twenty-four established committees.[77] Later, one Arizonan commented that the body of the constitutional convention "was distinctively a radical organization." To him its proposals paralleled the "freakish" Oklahoma constitution, and he deplored such "radical" measures as the initiative, referendum and recall.[78]

The delegates also used the Oregon primary law as a model.[79] Confident of public support and eager to guarantee popular sovereignty, they prohibited the governor from vetoing initiative or referendum measures approved by a majority of the voters. In the spirit of reform the delegates adopted fashionable Progressive ideas hoping to mitigate long-smoldering discontent with existing conditions. While they had a chance, they also hoped to stunt the potential power of big business in the new state. By pledging *not* to form a third party and getting the Democrats to pledge, in turn, to support labor's objectives, labor was able, without a majority, to strongly influence the Constitution. Since many middle-class Republicans—secretly or openly—despised the big corporations, these three dissimilar groups—agrarian Populist Democrats, small businessmen and labor—combined in a temporary alliance to give labor its apparent control from 1910 to 1916.[80]

And yet the convention was not "radical" enough to pass such labor-sponsored objectives as an anti-injunction measure or a limitation of the use of Mexican labor. The latter proposal would have allowed the employment of only 20 percent alien workers and would have ensured for labor a favorable ratio of eligible voters in mining camps. Understandably, Maricopa County and other non-mining delegates, despite their pledge to support labor's goals, were not as pro-labor as they were anti-corporate. These two measures would have strengthened labor's hand at the expense of both corporate *and* non-mining commercial class interests.[81] The labor-bourgeois coalition had its limitations.[82]

The copper company operators watched these proceedings with wary sensitivity. Will Clark at United Verde wrote Senator William Andrews Clark in Butte:

> In view of the rapid changes that are occurring in the political situation East, notably the recent speech of Senator Root in favor of direct legislation, the conservative people here, including our Governor [Territorial Governor Richard E. Sloan], are rapidly changing opinion as to the likelihood of the Constitution being rejected on account of containing ... radical features.[83]

In the same letter the United Verde assistant manager bemoaned the resolution that excluded lobbyists from the convention. He went on to denounce Charlie "Acres" [Akers], the proprietor of the *Arizona Gazette,* who had supported the resolution, and the fact that the *"Gazette* bolted the Republican Ticket in Maricopa County this year, although it has always heretofore been a strong partisan Republican paper." Then Will Clark cut through to the heart of 1910 Arizona politics:

> The particular point on which I desire your advice is this. It is manifest that if by this resolution this Phoenix gang could drive every mining man or corporation man away and leave them a clear field, they would be much delighted and this condition would continue throughout the succeeding legislatures.[84]

The *Gazette* had, indeed, supported the anti-corporate forces in the convention. During the election campaign for delegates the *Gazette* wrote: "Direct legislation is opposed only by the shortsighted, the corporation politician and those interests that cannot trust the people, but can buy the legislatures."[85] The *Gazette* lashed out at all Arizona corporations and the "corporation press," saying they actually opposed statehood. It accused the *Arizona Republican* of being a pro-corporation, "railroad interest" newspaper.[86]

The validity of Will Clark's analysis of the situation was matched by the truth of his prognostication concerning "succeeding legislatures." Only after the corporation interests had pulled themselves together were they able to turn the popular tide of liberalism sweeping across the state. As it turned out, that process would take more than five years.

On November 5, Will Clark continued his day-by-day report on the Arizona Constitutional Convention to Senator

Clark. He noted a fear on the part of the "Democratic papers and of merchants and men about town at Phoenix" of too much radicalism in the Constitution. "A rumor has been promulgated," wrote Clark, "that if the Recall is put in, including Judges, the Constitution will undoubtedly be rejected by President Taft." He then quoted "Proposition No. 70," passed by the convention that day:

> That no law shall be enacted by this State limiting the amount of damages to be recovered for causing the death or injury of any person.... Any contract or agreement to waive any right to recover damages for death or injury shall be devoid.[87]

These employer liability measures were particularly upsetting to the copper companies in view of the dangerous nature of mining and the loss of profits involved both in improving conditions of safety and in the payment of settlements. Will Clark's antagonism seemed directed mostly at the Phoenix businessmen who, he said, "will endeavor to make the Constitution as radical as possible, yet cunningly calculated to secure the approval of the President and Congress."[88] Will Clark had, apparently, a practical insight into the convention more astute than that of the *Tucson Citizen*.

What was to become the most controversial—and subsequently publicized—feature of the Constitution, the recall of the elected judiciary, originated in the early twentieth century. Emanating primarily from mine workers who believed corporation-dominated judges discriminated against them, the judicial recall was intended to unseat any judge who opposed their attempt to organize. The recall-of-judges feature had labor's fervid support as a backup to the even more controversial and "radical" anti-injunction proposal. If labor could not stop the courts from issuing strike-prohibiting injunctions, it could oust the judges who issued them.[89]

The liberal momentum was such that the delegates ignored the rumor concerning the acceptability of the recall-of-judges provision. In fact, Taft had made his disapproval clear, but the convention refused to heed the warning.[90] The Reverend Seaborne Crutchfield, the convention chaplain and father of a Maricopa County delegate, invoked divine partiality when he prayed, "'O Lord, we are not willing to believe President

Taft will turn down our constitution on account of such a small matter as the recall, initiative and referendum."[91] Taft, if he heard a call, did not respond.

To add elective power to mining districts, the Constitution provided double representation in the state senate for those five of the total fourteen Arizona counties (Cochise, Gila, Maricopa, Pima and Yavapai) in which mining interests, as well as labor interests, were the strongest.

For this reason, plus partisan loyalty, none of the delegates from the non-mining counties of Coconino and Santa Cruz voted for the new Constitution. Each of the five members of the Pima delegation—all Tucson business and professional men—voted against the ratification, too. Their motive might have been party loyalty but more likely they had been selected to represent the interests of the Southern Pacific Railroad.[92]

On December 9, 1910, the convention adopted the Constitution by a forty-to-twelve vote. One Democrat—Phelps Dodge attorney Ellinwood—and eleven Republicans refused to sign. Territorial Governor Sloan called a special popular election. By an overwhelming majority of four to one, Arizonans, on February 9, 1911, gave their approval.[93]

Will Clark offered to Senator Clark his usual lucid account and incisive assay of what had happened. In Jerome 173 had voted yes, 72 no, for a 70 percent majority. No one in nearby Cottonwood voted against the Constitution. The voters of Pima County, whose five delegates had unanimously voted against the charter, supported ratification two to one. Predictably the yea vote was much stronger in Cochise County. In one precinct where the United Verde "knew the names of those who voted," the fact intimidated few; "the returns show that outside of the office clerks and heads of departments, the rest voted solidly for ratification." The Jerome agent explained the techniques and motives:

> You will understand that in general it was a combination of Democrats and Socialists, but here the Socialists made a canvass during the past two days and secured the signatures on little red cards of all the voters amongst the working men. The main argument they used was that they would get workman's compensation and damages for all injuries.
>
> This is important for you and the other large owners of property in Arizona to know, that is that the working

class are well organized and now well informed and I consider it of the highest importance that immediate consideration should be given to these subjects.[94]

Taft kept his promise. His veto, though, had been interpreted as more than a fulfillment of his promise to nullify any
document which might include the recall of judges; the veto
also was part of the general reaction to what appeared to be
excessive liberalism within the Progressive movement.[95]

Actually Taft and Arizona mining interests had less to be-
wail than they asserted. Considering the potential labor power
in the convention, it is striking that most of the "radical" labor
proposals, including the anti-injunction measure, were not incorporated into the Constitution. Such extreme measures as
state control of minerals were decisively defeated.[96]

In these decisions against certain pro-labor proposals by
the delegates, the mixed loyalties that later enabled public and
labor support of the Bisbee Deportation can be found. The general endorsement of the popular rule proposals reflected the
true temper of the convention as a body.[97] Almost everyone in
the convention favored the direct sovereignty provisions. Since
corporate interests had been extremely successful in dominat-
ing the territorial legislature, the copper companies were
shrewdly aware of the electorate's knowledge of its dependence on copper mining in Arizona. This symbiosis explained
the vacillating trends of the period, since the mining representatives knew that their power in state government, too, lay
ultimately in the hands of the voter.

Ironically the direct sovereignty provisions can be interpreted as a victory for the operators. They knew that the
"thoroughly representative body" of workingmen in the convention felt an ambivalence toward "radical" labor goals, an
ambivalence that reflected an essential loyalty to their
employers. Although part of the Constitution indicated a temporary setback, mine operators knew, if only subconsciously,
that they could eventually count on the average voter. And a
legislature was much easier to manipulate than a governor.

On the labor side, the Constitution did include measures
providing employer liability for industrial accidents and the
outlawing of blacklists. It created an eight-hour day for state
and local government employees and placed controls on child
labor. Moreover, it directed enactment of additional employer

liability and workmen's compensation legislation. The Constitution also reserved the right of workers to sue for damages in the event of an injury with no statutory limitation on amount, prohibited employers from demanding a release of liability from employees as a condition of hiring, created the office of a state mine inspector and established several "limitations and controls" of corporations.[98] All of these the conservative delegates found both radical and deplorable.

Arizonans knew that President Taft, too, would find the proposed Constitution radical and deplorable. So a committee headed by G. W. P. Hunt went to Washington to lobby for its adoption. Along with Hunt went two other Democrats, Phoenix *Gazette* owner Charles Akers and Eugene B. O'Neill. One Republican, Phoenix banker and subsequent Bull Mooser, Dwight B. Heard, was assigned to the committee but elected to travel separately. When the Democrats got to Washington, they found Heard on the scene. He told them that he had already conferred with various Republican leaders who had assured him that if the Arizonans would drop the initiative, the recall and the referendum, Arizona would undoubtedly gain statehood. Heard pleasantly and tactfully related all this while entertaining the Arizona Democrats at a gracious breakfast. When they refused to agree with him, Heard suddenly turned furious, paid the bill and stalked out leaving the others to finish their meal.[99]

After Taft's veto of the statehood bill on August 15, 1911, the recall-of-judges provision was stricken from the proposed Constitution. The Arizona voters ratified this revised document December 12, 1911, and returned it to Washington.[100] As President Taft signed the Statehood Bill on February 14, 1912, making Arizona the forty-eighth of the United States, he said: "Well, it is all over. I am glad to give you life."[101] Therein lay a clue to one of Arizona's mistakes. Chaplain Crutchfield had misdirected his prayer toward heaven instead of toward Arizona's real creator—the White House. To compound this slight, the people of Arizona gave Taft an even harsher slap. On November 5, 1912, an amendment by popular referendum restored the recall-of-judges measure.[102] By a vote of 16,272 to 3,705, Arizonans showed their heretical, ungrateful nature.[103]

G. W. P. Hunt won the first election for governor on December 12, 1911. The Democratic candidate, Hunt led his opponent, E. W. Wells, 11,123 to 9,166.[104] In this same election Democrat Henry Fountain Ashurst, after conducting literally a two-fisted campaign (on June 2, 1911, during a primary election campaign rally in Prescott, he won a brawling fight with his opponent, M. G. Burns), was chosen as one of Arizona's first two United States senators. Democrat Marcus A. Smith was the other. Carl Hayden, another Democrat, won the race for Arizona's lone representative to Congress.

United Verde Copper Company Assistant General Manager Clark, in his series of reports to Charles Clark and Senator William A. Clark on the political currents of Arizona, touched on some more of the nationwide trends and the "rapid changes that are occurring in the political situation East" that had helped create the adverse political climate for Arizona copper companies. He observed that "both classes" of newspapers had adopted the "red eyed platforms" of such Progressive programs as direct legislation and control of corporations. Clark told his employer that "the West has not yet awakened up to the danger of the conservation measures that Roosevelt and Pinchot will attempt to put through Congress." Although he conceded that the "working class are getting so well educated that they will vote as a unit on any matter they believe directly affects them," Clark deplored "that we are in an era of the wildest misrepresentation in regard to the isms, and so far there has been no concerted, active effort of an effective nature put forth to correct them."[105]

In July 1910, agent Clark informed Charles W. Clark that in Jerome "of course radical movements continue in full swing."[106] Apparently the agent had reason to assume that the United Verde general manager was well aware of the May 23, 1910, Jerome city election in which the Socialist Party candidates captured two of eight city offices, losing several of the other offices by narrow margins; the vote for marshal was lost by the Socialists by only fifteen votes out of two hundred twenty-nine cast.[107] In the next few years Socialists and liberal Democrats won many more public offices throughout the state.

The tide of public opinion that enabled "radicals" (or, at least, "liberals") to enjoy victories at the polls grew rapidly after 1910. The developments of protective legislation (with the negatory effect of the courts in mind) between 1907 and 1917 was, as labor historian Henry Pelling said, "remarkable."[108] It was this mood which left the temporarily ostracized Arizona corporations brooding helplessly on the sidelines. Together with the fact that the various copper companies had never seen fit to organize themselves, the public rush to liberalism left Arizona corporations politically impotent. Will Clark urged Senator Clark on October 20, 1910, "I therefore think that it is advisable to take some public part in these matters ... and that a meeting should be called and the attitude of the industry set forth." Four months later Clark repeated, "I consider it of the highest importance that immediate consideration should be given" the subject of the well-organized labor classes in Arizona.[109]

But Clark's manifesto for organized operators would take time to become realized. In the meantime, the mining companies remained helpless as labor dominated the Constitutional Convention and the early state legislatures. Pro-labor attitudes prevailed around the country. The sympathetic national response to such events as the 1912 IWW strike in Lawrence, Massachusetts, showed potential public support for labor, and such brutal tragedies as the Ludlow Massacre in 1914 brought a surge of protest on behalf of the unions.[110] Following the trend, American scholars began to lavish attention on the labor movement.[111] By 1915 labor had reached its peak of popularity in the United States. The Walsh Commission Report gave recommendations revealing the most extreme popular sympathy with the travail of labor while liberal journals chastised business severely. *The New Republic* proclaimed labor's zenith:

> After what labor has endured, something more is required for good-will than an offer to kiss and make-up. The employers will have to make very tangible sacrifices and renunciations before workmen can afford to believe that the new good-will is something more than a desire to avoid inconvenience. Capital will have to meet labor more than half-way before it has any right to expect an easy human friendliness in the fixing of industrial relations.[112]

The Walsh Commission recommended such radical changes as tough inheritance tax laws "so as to leave no large accumulation of wealth to pass into hands which had no share in its production." It also suggested strict government control of natural resources, guarantees of "workers' rights," "comfortable" minimum wages, strict safety and sanitation controls and many other federal controls of ownership regulations to restrain big business.[113]

However, capital, in Arizona and around the land, had shown not an iota of any desire to "expect an easy human friendliness." Whatever sympathy or influence labor achieved was done in spite of capital. In most cases both sympathy and influence were quite transient if not imaginary.

Arizona, for a short while, was an exception. Between 1910 and 1916, labor and its supporters enjoyed what is probably the greatest success of any effort by labor in the history of America in gaining political power. The national labor movement may have realized certain deep ambitions by seeing growing membership, some favorable federal legislation and considerable public support. Many workingmen and their leaders found these gains to be acceptable substitutes for political mastery; any substantial power was fantasy on labor's part. In Arizona, however, for a few short years the mastery was real. While unionism within the state failed to realize an efficacy satisfactory to itself, *un*organized labor voted as an enlightened, self-interest bloc. With a sense of certainty and purpose, wage-earners united with other anti-corporate voters throughout the state. The labor-bourgeois coalition maintained not a secretive but an open, dignified, legitimate command of the substance and direction of Arizona political life.

The first state legislature convened March 18, 1912, and passed minor laws favorable to labor. In addition to the recall of judges referendum, another—for women's suffrage—passed the legislature. Voted on by the general public in November of 1912, the women's suffrage referendum was endorsed 13,452 to 6,202. Many laws regulating mine safety, taxation, workmen's compensation and election campaign donations also passed in this legislature.[114]

But another referendum law ran into trouble. In an effort to offset the liberal Constitution and the thrust of even more radical legislation, the companies began to counterattack in concert. When operators hired Mexicans and other foreigners in the mines because these aliens would work for less and could not vote, labor organizations in 1913 circulated initiative petitions for an eighty percent American citizen hiring law. Enough signatures were obtained to get the measure on the ballot.[115] The proposal read:

> Any company, corporation, partnership, association or individual who is or may hereafter become an employer or more than five workers at any one time, in the State of

Arizona, regardless of kind or class of work, or sex of workers, shall employ not less than eighty percent qualified electors or native born citizens of the United States or some subdivision thereof.[116]

By a popular vote majority of 10,694 on November 3, 1914, the bill passed—overwhelmingly in the mining communities. Apprehensive delegates had turned it down at the Constitutional Convention, but labor foresaw no difficulties for the law once it was enacted.[117]

Immediately the eighty percent law provoked a worldwide controversy. While the British and Italian governments condemned it as abusively discriminatory, Italian, Japanese and Chinese residents of Arizona sought to bring action against the state.[118]

Logically enough, the test case originated in Bisbee. Mike Raich, a cook at William Truax's English Kitchen restaurant, was an Austrian alien; his presence on the English Kitchen payroll put Truax in violation of the new law.* Within a few days after the law went into effect, county authorities arrested Truax.[119] Immigrant cook Mike Raich petitioned the federal court through high-powered Arizona corporation attorneys to issue a restraining order on the enforcement of the state law until it could be reviewed. Federal Judge William H. Sawtelle agreed. On January 7, 1915, after proceedings involving John S. Williams of Bisbee and former Judge John H. Campbell of Tucson as attorneys representing Raich and Arizona Attorney General Wiley R. Jones assisted by William B. Cleary of Bisbee representing the State of Arizona, a federal tribunal reached a ruling. The United States District Court in San Francisco found the Arizona law in conflict with the Fourteenth Amendment to the United States Constitution and therefore void. On November 1, 1915, the United States Supreme Court upheld the ruling of the district court.[120] Although it disapproved of the Arizona anti-alien law and affirmed the Supreme Court decision, *The New Republic* expressed strong reservations:

> We should not overlook the fact that states like Arizona have a very serious problem in the mining or industrial camps financed by absentee capital, manned by

---

*Truax and the English Kitchen figured in another case, *Traux v. Corrigan*, a landmark Supreme Court decision in 1921 which found anti-labor injunction legislation unconstitutional. See pages 313–15.

alien labor, and governed despotically by a little group of higher employees. In such camps nothing like an American form of local government is possible. The anti-alien law attempted to substitute, for an exploited body of aliens, citizen laborers, by education and temperament fitted to check the arbitrary tendencies of mining camp capitalism.[121]

With this judicial support the mine owners, who recognized the truth in Will Clark's message concerning the intelligence and unity of the working class, won their initial major battle in their counteroffensive against the political power of labor. Another proposal that failed in the Constitutional Convention, the anti-injunction, passed also in the 1913 legislature. This, too, met defeat in the courts. The copper men could depend upon the federal judiciary to protect their interests from the colonial upstarts.[122]

One episode, in particular, illustrates this judicial preferential treatment. In October 1913, two Phelps Dodge officials were indicted on charges of illegal traffic in arms. William H. Brophy, general manager of the Phelps Dodge Mercantile Company, and F. E. Cole, manager of the mercantile company's hardware department, faced charges in the Arizona District Federal Court at Phoenix of conspiring to privately export munitions of war to the Carranza government during Mexico's civil war of that period. Witnesses stated that Brophy and Cole sold 90,000 rounds of ammunition which were paid for in United States bills and Mexican gold coin. The bullets were to be used for Carranza's soldiers against Huerta's revolutionaries. Ramon P. DeNegri, a financial agent of Carranza's constitutional government, testified that, although he purchased the munitions from Phelps Dodge, he had not told the copper company officials exactly how the arms would be used.

Brophy and Cole filed demurrers while two Mexican co-conspirators pleaded guilty. The story circulated that Phelps Dodge paid the Mexicans to confess in order to avoid having their testimony and the evidence against them produced in court. Since the United States prosecuting attorneys could not prove Brophy and Cole knew the destination of the ammunition, Judge Sawtelle advised the jury to render a "not guilty" verdict on the two Phelps Dodge administrators. The judge fined the two Mexicans but $200 each and told them he proba-

bly would have done what they did. Openly and without compunction, Judge Sawtelle endorsed Phelps Dodge's behavior.

The court proceedings were handled with dispatch and
extreme discretion. The initial hearing was tacked on to the
court schedule "after the usual business of the court" had concluded and almost everyone had gone home. As a result, the
matter got little publicity. In time, it became known as the
"Phelps Dodge case."[123]

Even with this judicial advantage, Arizona corporations
were being inundated by a tide of popular liberalism. As yet
their confidence that they would eventually receive the support
of the Arizona citizenry was not being realized.

In 1914 the voters sent more liberals than ever to the legislature; fifty-three Democrats were elected to state office while
only one Republican, Thomas Campbell (the same man who
occupied the governor's chair during the Bisbee Deportation),
had success. A native-born Arizonan and a man popular
throughout the state, Campbell was elected State Tax Commissioner. There is little doubt his campaign had the strong
support of the copper interests. George Hunt was re-elected
governor. The governor's campaign had displayed the basic
humanitarian stand of the Progressive movement. By now
described as a real "radical," he referred to the teaching of
patriotism as "anomalistic" and supported such reforms
at the state prison as the abolition of the ball and chain, the
silence system, the tight-cropped head and the striped uniform.[124] Hunt's drastic steps stunned much of the electorate.
Many Arizona citizens declared that they were shocked
and offended. His real test of strength and popularity was
approaching rapidly. Copper company strategy had put the
mine owners on a collision course with the governor.

Clifton-Morenci

One historian of the Clifton-Morenci strike in the fall of
1915–16 has pointed out that it was one of the rare "successes"
labor experienced during this period. Mainly, he said, this first
major labor difficulty after Arizona's statehood was "successful" because no one got killed or badly hurt and the strikers
enjoyed the protection of the governor and the local sheriff.
That the settlement included no more for labor than management had originally offered did not seem to detract measurably

from this "success" assessment. A contemporary journalist, John A. Fitch, found similar satisfaction. He compared this Clifton-Morenci strike of 1915 with the Colorado coal strike of 1913–14 which resulted in the Ludlow Massacre. He saw the labor-controlled Arizona strike, in which the operators charged the governor and local law officers with taking orders from the miners, as "an exact reverse" of the employer-dominated Colorado strike. In Morenci, for example, deputized strikers guarded the mine properties and drew company pay for doing it. Moreover, the militia received orders to keep strikebreakers out.[125] The copper companies financed strikers who served as watchmen "under the direction of the sheriff" of Greenlee County.[126]

Other qualities, too, mark the Clifton-Morenci strike and settlement as a high-water event. Besides the unique peacefulness of the affair, the strike provided an opportunity for the growing collective strength of Arizona mine management to be tested against the established power of labor. In this showdown at least three important political developments took place: (1) Governor Hunt and labor proved their strength to maintain the status quo for a while; (2) manifest labor strength helped to forge the amalgam of previously apathetic or mutually antagonistic copper companies; (3) out of this conflict emerged the Phelps Dodge Corporation and Walter Douglas as the central force and leadership of the anti-union campaign in Arizona that climaxed in July 1917, with the Bisbee Deportation and the crushing of politically effective organized labor in Arizona.

The Phelps Dodge Corporation at no time ever neglected its interest in its Morenci property. Before it had acquired any holdings in Bisbee, Phelps Dodge, on the advice of Dr. James Douglas, had helped finance Morenci's Detroit Copper Company. In 1881 the company had invested $30,000 in the Morenci property, and even though the mine never paid off to the extent of the Copper Queen, it was a reliable operation. As in Bisbee, Phelps Dodge dominated Morenci; the Edinburgh-administered Arizona Copper Company had more influence in nearby Clifton. The Arizona Copper Company was acquired by a group of Scottish investors in 1883, and a smaller mining concern, the Shannon Copper Company, had been organized in 1901 by Boston investors.[127]

Morenci, like most other Arizona mining towns, was geographically isolated. Over the years it had, like Bisbee and

Jerome, developed into an industrial barony. Most miners in this district were illiterate peons imported from Mexico. The three copper companies, with Phelps Dodge as their leader, "controlled almost every aspect of the workers' lives." The men accused bosses of "selling jobs" to employees and compelling workers to buy chances for the raffling of "worthless articles." No one said conditions were unbearable, but numerous complaints of minor irritations could be heard, and the workers felt they were not getting their share of the profits. This last dissatisfaction became more meaningful as the wartime price of copper soared in 1915.

When the WFM attempted to organize the workers in 1915, it became obvious that the companies were very active in trying to obstruct unionization. All three fired many men who joined the union or failed to sign a petition of "loyalty and satisfaction" (a form of "yellow-dog" contract, which had been upheld that year by the Supreme Court). On September 11, 1915, after the mine managers denied the union organizers a request for a hearing, the union committee decided to strike. For several weeks the mine managers refused to meet with WFM representatives, and the strike remained at an impasse. The mine officials established a "refugee camp" where those who "found it uncomfortable in the strike district" could enjoy free food and tent lodging. Then, it was suspected, the operators tried to discredit the strikers by throwing the main switch in the power plant and putting the mining camp in darkness. Although it seems absurd, they also appeared guilty of harmlessly detonating a large amount of dynamite in another frame-up attempt.[128]

This operator stubbornness was reinforced by the fact that for several months the Phelps Dodge Corporation had been able to gain control of several newspapers around the state and had begun a barrage of propaganda against Hunt. In particular, the newspapers condemned Hunt for his failure to repress the Clifton-Morenci strike. The publications accused the governor of siding with unpatriotic radicals. One of the most obvious of the corporate mouthpieces was the Phoenix *Gazette,* which only a few months earlier had been a strong critic of the copper companies. The *Gazette* emphasized Hunt's collaboration with the WFM.[129]

On September 3, the Bowie, Arizona, *Enterprise* defended Hunt against attacks by the *Gazette*.[130] The strike had become a political issue. One week later the *Tucson Citizen* announced that the Copper Queen had obtained a "string of newspapers" in Arizona.[131]

September 23, Phelps Dodge executive Walter Douglas arrived in the district on the same train with WFM President Charles Moyer. Each met to talk with his respective associates.[132]

The strikers in Morenci then decided to negotiate without asking for union recognition. But the managers still rejected the miners' proposals. Requested to come to Clifton to help break the stalemate, Governor Hunt left Phoenix by train and arrived in Clifton on September 28. Declining to accept the hospitality of the copper men, Hunt interviewed the workers to discover their complaints and discussed the strike with WFM leaders Moyer and George Powell.[133] On Thursday, September 30, Hunt appeared in the Clifton plaza to make an address. He said that in view of the workers' complaints he believed the existing condition "does need adjustment." As to the mine managers' refusal to meet with labor representatives, Hunt told the crowd that he would put everyone in the "bull pen" if that was what it took to talk it over.[134]

Then the liberal Democrat got down to basic reality. "I was told when I came over here that I would cut my throat politically....Time as it rolled on has said that those people who had the temerity to stand up for their rights are heroes, and not traitors."[135] On the same day the *Gazette* reported a statement made by Walter Douglas in Bisbee concerning the Clifton trouble. In counterpoint to Hunt's reference to the political nature of the Clifton-Morenci deadlock, Douglas said, "It was apparent to all disinterested parties in the district that the sole aim of the leaders of the Western Federation of Miners was to secure political domination of this state." Not only did Douglas have politics on his mind, he knew something about worker manipulation, too. The Federation knows, Douglas was quoted as saying, "'how easily the Mexican workmen are led and how easily they are intimidated.'"[136]

Hunt returned to Phoenix right after his Clifton speech and for the next few days the state's newspapers bandied about the story of his presence in Clifton and his speech there. Several sources which had previously supported the governor either wavered or they criticized and denounced him. Tension continued to build in Morenci. In the late afternoon of October 2, ostensibly on the strength of several demonstrations, the mine managers of Morenci attempted to create the effect that their safety was imperiled and they commandeered a locomotive to stage a melodramatic flight from the mining district. Progressive journalist, John A. Fitch, obviously delighted by this piece of histrionics, reported in *The Survey* the ordering of the mine managers' arrest by Sheriff Cash of Greenlee County. To intercept the train engine, Cash had wired ahead to Lordsburg, New Mexico, and had the mine managers arrested and charged with "inciting to riot." After a hearing, the local justice of the peace released them and allowed them to continue to El Paso where they remained for four months. Their obvious effort to give the false impression that they had escaped from harm prompted a bemused Governor Hunt to term the entire affair "theatrical and true to the techniques of the movies."[137]

The Morenci mine managers may have been flying a histrionic flag, but the state's newspapers found their humbug adventure to be good copy. An extra of the *Gazette* headlined: "MINE MANAGERS FLEE FOR THEIR LIVES."[138] Governor Hunt wrote the refugee operators saying that no conditions in Clifton-Morenci warranted their hasty departure. He told them their flight must have been prompted by their desire to get sympathetic support from uninformed outsiders.[139] *Dunbar's Weekly,* a pro-labor paper, found more specific political motivation behind the mine managers' caper. The action, it said, was "part of a well-laid plan to frighten foreign investors and keep their money out of the state, in order that times might be hard and the administration held responsible."[140] A letter from El Paso signed by the mine managers and addressed to "The Committees Representing the Former Employees" of their companies was made public. In addition to blaming Governor Hunt and Sheriff Cash for the Morenci-Clifton labor troubles, the letter said the mines "will remain idle indefinitely." The statement added that the managers "may take a different view of the situation" when the influence of the WFM was "dissipated."[141]

National Guardsman arrived in the Clifton-Morenci district on October 4, where they remained on duty for a little more than a month. The exiled managers did agree to talk to miners' representatives; a conference was held in El Paso from Saturday, October 16 to Saturday, October 23, where nothing was accomplished.[142] Charles W. Harris, adjutant general of the state militia, traveled with the labor delegates to El Paso but was denied entrance into the conference room. He reported that the mine managers were very uncooperative and said the managers "at no time indicated any desire to meet the employees 'half-way.'"[143] On the other hand, the Phelps Dodge-owned Tucson *Arizona Daily Star* printed an extensive account of how the WFM had destroyed the El Paso conference.[144] So the strike wore on. Since Governor Hunt and others had requested federal mediation, Secretary of Labor Wilson detailed Joseph Myers of El Paso and Hywel Davies of Lexington, Kentucky, to effect a settlement in the dispute. But their presence did little to break the deadlock.[145]

Meantime, the press had a field day. The usually discreet *Mining and Scientific Press*, T. A. Rickard's venerable San Francisco-based operators' journal, suggested that some of the Clifton-Morenci strikers' claims were justified. In a prompt defensive, indignant reply, Walter Douglas informed Rickard of the latter's ignorance about the issues at stake. Douglas also reiterated his resolve not to negotiate with unions. Rickard, who usually avoided controversy, was not intimidated. In an editorial reply, he said, "We doubt whether the principle of collective bargaining ... can be ignored successfully."[146] How wrong his opinion proved to be.*

After almost five months, the strike ended. In the sense that peace characterized the strike, strikebreakers were kept out, management was kept on the defensive and union representatives were recognized, the Clifton-Morenci affair emerged as a huge victory for Arizona labor. The workers returned to their jobs on January 26 having relinquished almost all of their original demands. The WFM had been disavowed.[147] In its first big test of industrial might after having shown political power, labor was satisfied to break even. It even called a draw a victory.

The flight of the Morenci mine managers may have been symbolic of labor's "Golden Age" in Arizona affairs, but it was also symptomatic of management's intractable attitude. In addition, it gave substance to corporate allegations that Governor Hunt encouraged labor tyranny. Voters' doubts began to grow rapidly.

---

*Rickard also learned to be a little more humble toward Arizona copper magnates. See p. 298.

About the only thing that could be called a "victory" about the strike settlement was the absence of violence. Workers got a pay increase, but it amounted to much less than they had asked for. Compared to the soaring price of copper, the raise was humiliatingly infinitesimal. The workers had "won" the right to "organize" but had to disavow their own union, the WFM. Also, the men, in reaching a settlement, "conformed almost completely to the terms laid down by the managers."[148]

Yet everyone saw positive qualities in the settlement. The mine managers asserted vigorously, "Governor Hunt had absolutely nothing to do in any way with an amicable adjustment of the strike."[149] Hunt offered his own analysis. He said the handling of the affair had "no parallel in the industrial history of the United States." He asserted this had been accomplished despite the fact that the newspapers around the state, controlled by corporate interests, had published grossly exaggerated and untrue stories of terror and violence perpetrated by the strikers. Hunt said there was no evidence of any truth to these reports.[150]

While Governor Hunt suggested that the breach in Arizona political life was in danger of widening, and both Hunt and Douglas had recognized the political nature of the Clifton-Morenci event, some official sources responded blindly to the strike settlement. Secretary of Labor Wilson wrote Hunt praising the "enlightened spirit" which characterized the handling of the strike and said that an "auspicious outlook in the industrial field is thereby assured."[151] A few days earlier, on February 10, Federal Commissioners of Conciliation Davies and Myers wrote Hunt to summarize their findings regarding the strike and to say that the "settlement" of the Clifton-Morenci strike should "bring about an era of good will that means peace and prosperity to the state at large."[152]

The commissioners had not been paying much attention to activities around the state during their trip to Arizona. Their optimism lacked any sensitivity to the continued latent anger and frustration not only of the laboring men of Arizona but, particularly, of the mine managers. The mining interests had not only stiffened their defense at Clifton-Morenci—they had begun a vigorous political counter-offensive against Hunt in Maricopa County. A recall petition circulated, the legislature did a dramatic turn. As early as June of 1915, the liberal funding and budgetary practices of the Hunt administration came under attack. Provisions were written into the appropriations bill for the following fiscal year lowering the budget and limiting the power of both the governor and the state auditor to authorize—or limit—expenditures. National Guardsmen on duty at Clifton-Morenci learned that they would have to accept non-negotiable scrip until the Supreme Court could provide a ruling. Suddenly everything seemed to be turning against the governor. At Clifton-Morenci embattled management decided to hold ground in the Arizona labor-capital war of the nineteen-teens.[153]

3

ARIZONA TURN-AROUND

The real issue and significance of the Clifton-Morenci affair were yet to erupt. On January 22, 1916, *The New Republic* carried a routine Progressive eulogy of the peaceful nature of the strike and cited this Arizona procedure as a model for labor-management relations elsewhere. The New York periodical pointed out the necessity Phelps Dodge felt in discrediting the Clifton employees' tactics "lest they be adopted at other mines." The article expressed the belief that "the opportunity is present in Arizona for organized labor to prove that it can win its struggles for industrial democracy if only the government protects the strikers in their rights." Skipping from one basic point to another, *The New Republic* observed, "This situation illustrates the dependence of labor on enlightened opinion." Then the article came down to one key issue:

> There remains our responsibility for institutions that leave the state powerless to interfere with a process by which a handful of owners in New York, Boston or Edinburgh can impose upon ten or fifteen thousand men and women the choice between surrendering their liberties or starving.[1]

A Mine Manager's Leader Takes Charge

Management's time for a declaration of war had come. *The New Republic* article, without mentioning any one person's name, had a specific target: Walter Douglas, newly appointed vice-president and member of the board of directors of the Phelps Dodge Corporation. Governor G. W. P. Hunt called Douglas "the consort of the queen of Arizona copper mines," but Douglas had managed, remarkably, to keep himself anonymous. Although he was the single most influential person affecting the affairs of the Phelps Dodge Corporation and although he held directorships in the state's most powerful newspapers and banks, his name rarely appeared in print. In fact, when referring to him, even his enemies rarely mentioned his name. Yet he was the link between the executive suite of Phelps Dodge's New York office at John and Cliff streets and its Arizona copper mines.

Walter Douglas' ability to maintain anonymity in Arizona is all the more remarkable considering his background, connections and seeming omnipresence. He was, along with James S. "Rawhide Jimmy" Douglas, a son of the illustrious developer of the Copper Queen, Dr. James Douglas. Walter was born in Quebec on December 18, 1870, to Naomi Douglas, and he went to Canadian schools. Before coming to Prescott, Arizona, as an engineer in 1890, he took a course at Columbia University School of Mines in New York. After a brief association with a smelting and refining company in Kansas City as a metallurgist, Walter returned to Arizona in 1894 to join his father's company. At age thirty-one he was appointed general manager of the Copper Queen.[2]

Walter early showed executive ability, and Phelps Dodge groomed him for an administrative rather than a technical career. In this respect he reflected the rapidly developing nature of America's industrial-corporate society. Walter seemed to have a feeling for organization and the political-economic realities of the new, complex system. By 1916 he had risen to vice-president of Phelps Dodge; the following year he replaced his ailing father when the board elected him to the company's presidency.[3] Walter maintained a residence in Warren and was naturalized as a United States citizen in Tombstone in 1913.[4] He entered into New York society as a lesser figure.[5]

In an effort to avoid the high rates and other unreasonable demands placed upon it by the Santa Fe and Southern Pacific Railroads, Phelps Dodge decided early in the 1900s to build its own railroad from Bisbee to El Paso. The company gave the responsibility for this task to Walter Douglas. After being forced to use some unorthodox and crudely direct methods to overcome the resistence of the Southern Pacific, Douglas got his railroad—the El Paso and Southwestern—through. (Phelps Dodge paid cash for this capital asset.) Later Douglas became prominent in the operation of seven railroads. When the Southern Pacific eventually bought the El Paso and Southwestern (at a fantastic profit for Phelps Dodge), Douglas served as a director on the larger line's board. From this position he later became chairman of the Board of Southern Pacific Railroad and president—prior to its nationalization—of the Southern Pacific of Mexico. Illness forced Douglas into early retirement in April 1930. He died on October 3, 1946, at seventy-six.[6]

Whereas Dr. James Douglas' talents lay in innovation and refining techniques of processing copper ores profitably, Walter Douglas' skills in organizational management stamped him. In particular, during the early twentieth century political and economic crises of Arizona did Douglas manifest effective leadership. No only did he pull together the loose ends of Arizona mine management to enable the concert of interest that eventually crushed the state's liberal political influence of that period, Douglas made himself a figure of national prominence as well. He was a forceful member (being careful not to become a colorful personality) of the American Institute of Mining Engineers. In 1916 he was elected national president of the American Mining Congress and in that capacity focused the Congress' attention on new matters. By using the Congress' journal, Douglas dramatically redirected the emphasis of the organization from the technical problems of mining and metallurgy to social and economic issues. At the same time, the popular patriotic swing back to the support of the wartime mobilization of business and industry aided Douglas in his effort to help rebuild the tarnished image of industry and to strengthen the power of mining corporations. Douglas appeared to have a shrewd sense of public relations. During the years 1915–18 Arizona mining from the operators' point of view received an overwhelmingly disproportionate share of attention in national periodicals. Douglas was voted to lead the American Mining Congress two more times.[7]

Dr. James Douglas had been interested in obtaining more profits through more efficient production; Walter Douglas discovered that such sources as wages, taxes and workmen's compensation could be substantial profit drains. Dr. Douglas argued that the entire industry could benefit if each company would let down its barriers of secrecy and open up its methods to everyone; his son found openness to be a distinct handicap.

Maintaining a strict secrecy in all its matters had long been a Phelps Dodge rule despite Dr. Douglas' wishes to the contrary.[8] "Perhaps it is because Phelps Dodge is deriving more than an equal proportion of benefits from its relationship with Bisbee that the company conducts its business in a secretive manner," one person has written.[9] Whatever the reason, Walter Douglas managed to maintain, considering his masterful influence, incredible corporate secrecy and personal anonymity during the years of Arizona's labor-management warfare. *The Bisbee Daily Review* almost never mentioned the name of its number one citizen in *any* context. Douglas' arrivals to and departures from the community rarely got any notice of any kind. Other publications around the state either did not know about him, did not understand his importance or were afraid to mention his name. Such an educated and involved labor leader as Henry S. McCluskey did not realize the basic fact of Douglas' power. McCluskey stated that his only knowledge of Douglas' role in the Bisbee Deportation was "hearsay."[10]

There appears to be no question of Douglas' responsibility in the Bisbee affair. Even the official Phelps Dodge historian, Robert Glass Cleland, acknowledged that "the orders for the actual deportation by the railroad were issued by Walter Douglas, president of Phelps Dodge."[11] Too, Douglas was a primary defendant named in the federal charges brought against the deporters in 1918. How did so many people fail to see Douglas' role as the kingpin in Arizona during this period? Even more significantly, why did so many people, once they had perceived his role, refuse to mention his name? Governor George W. P. Hunt referred to Douglas only as the "consort of the queen of Arizona's mines" and as the "largest employer in the state." *The New Republic* wrote of Douglas' "autocracy and exploitation" and then identified Douglas simply by calling him "the owner of one of the Arizona copper mines."[12] When commenting on the perpetrators of the strike, Robert Bruere, reporting boldly otherwise, said, "At the forefront of the 'patriots' who had engineered the deportation were the executives of the greatest metalmining corporation in America."[13] The *New York Sun*, seemingly removed enough from any wrath of the Arizona copper baron, referred to Douglas only as "the Vice-President of the El Paso and Southwestern" and as someone "who is also interested in the Bisbee mines."[14]

Despite Douglas' relative invisibility, he kept busy slipping around behind the scenery of Arizona's political puppet show. When he surfaced, he almost invariably could be found only in print. Douglas' writings appeared in San Francisco or New York publications. His *New Republic* statement and articles and letters in *The Mining and Scientific Press* indicate that Walter Douglas was the only Arizona mine owner or manager involved with the broader industrial picture who appeared in national print.[15]

Douglas used *The New Republic* article on the Clifton-Morenci strike as the antithesis of his position. With indignation not quite under control, Douglas wrote to the liberal journal and categorically refuted *The New Republic*'s point of view and provided many clues to his motives and strategy that led to his Bisbee Deportation sixteen months later. After he dismissed the "verity of the statements" in *The New Republic*'s article on the Clifton-Morenci strike, Douglas mentioned "the fact of my official connection with some of the mining companies involved in the strike, to anyone adept in modern civic or quasi-political discussion." Douglas apparently expected, or at least hoped, that literate metropolites (as opposed to unschooled Arizona folks) knew of his place in the scheme of things. He also emphasized his "quasi-political" role as opposed to his industrial role. After a lengthy defense of the copper companies' position and a praise for their restraint, Douglas denounced the motives and methods of Governor Hunt in handling the strike. Then Douglas lost his composure and referred to *The New Republic*'s editorial as "inflammatory invective" and said that "half-baked philosophy from the high-brows merely tends to increase the difficulties." Douglas concluded by calling the horrors of the Ludlow Massacre "fabled" and alluded to the near-sightedness of people seated in "an editorial chair three thousand miles away."

More important than all this was Douglas' account of the conduct of certain Clifton-Morenci citizens during the strike:

Conditions in the strike district finally became such that a large number of wholly disinterested citizens organized a species of vigilance committee, which undertook to protect law-abiding citizens from oppression by the strikers. Thereafter, when the strikers' committee ordered a man to leave the district, this vigilance committee made an issue of it and of course prevailed. The man remained. An Arizona vigilance committee commands instant attention and respect.[16]

It was in this group of "wholly disinterested citizens" that Douglas knew his political support and vigilante membership lay. It was from this example, too, that Douglas could have drawn his model of technique and his confidence of support for bringing off the Bisbee Deportation. The Bisbee vigilance committee simply reversed the procedure of the Clifton-Morenci vigilantes.

The fact of Douglas' strong reaction to an intellectual-Progressive journal like *The New Republic* raises several questions: (1) Did Douglas fear the journal had belittled him in the eyes of genteel New Yorkers whose acceptance he craved? (2) Was he trying to make respectable his actions by carrying the Arizona mine managers' counteroffensive into the New York literary and social circles? (3) Was he building a broad base of justification for a long-planned assault on a currently respectable segment of America—labor?

The New Republic remained unimpressed. It had "the highest authority for stating the facts," it said and disagreed with Douglas on his opinion of the strike situation at Clifton-Morenci.[17] Four weeks later Governor Hunt joined *The New Republic* forum and, reinforcing the journal's account, refuted Douglas' side of the story. He, in closing, again got to the heart of the affair:

Regarding ... intimidating measures employed against me during the strike, there is much that could be said, but as these developments were in a sense political, and in view of my disinclination to foster in any unnecessary way a controversy with Arizona's greatest employer of labor, thereby widening that breach between classes which must inevitably be regarded as deplorable by every thoughtful public-spirited citizen, further comment is needless ....[18]

The battle was getting more intense.

Wartime Wealth

Why were Arizona miners, even a small number of them, willing to embrace any radical labor movement? The answer to that question lies primarily in the economics of mobilizing for World War I. Copper is an essential part of warfare weaponry. No substitute has been found for copper shell jackets. Communications' wire and cable, too, are vital. By 1916, thanks primarily to the demands of the munitions suppliers for the respective belligerents of World War I, American copper production climbed to fantastic heights. In October 1916, Walter V. Woehlke wrote in *The American Review of Reviews* that the current American mining boom had been obscured by the "epochal events of these super-extraordinary times." This boom, Woehlke proclaimed, in "quantity and volume surpasses all similar episodes in the history of American metalmining." The value of copper produced in America, he pointed out, had increased in ten years from $137,000,000 in 1905 to $242,000,000 in 1915.[19]

In 1917 $210,000,000 in copper, gold, silver, lead and zinc were mined in Arizona — an all-time record to that year. As early as 1909 Arizona led in the world production of copper.[20] The value of copper mined in Arizona climbed from $40,000,000 in 1910 to $95,000,000 in 1915 to $200,000,000 in 1917.[21]

In 1916 the Bisbee District produced 190,303,591 pounds of copper, a figure that remained an all-time high for twenty years. The total value of profitable minerals produced in the Bisbee District more than doubled from $15,837,974 for 1905 to $32,177,576 in 1915. In 1916 this jumped to $51,367,739. The Copper Queen's share was $10,377,818 in 1905, $16,492,070 in 1915, and $25,81,630 in 1916.[22]

While the production of copper leaped upward (apparently unimpeded by the labor unrest), the price of copper almost doubled from 13.4¢ a pound in July of 1914 to 26.5¢ a pound in July 1916.[23] In 1916 Phelps Dodge produced copper at 9½¢ a pound. This fact allowed Phelps Dodge in 1916 to enjoy a 218 percent increase in net profits over the previous year — from $10,981,512 in 1915 to $24,030,905 in 1916. By May 1916, copper producers made 400 percent greater profit than they made a few years earlier when copper sold at 12 cents a pound. Since it was paying dividends as high as 325 percent a year on the investment, Phelps Dodge decided to recapitalize. On March

14, 1917, officials authorized the Copper Queen Mining Company to increase the value of its capital stock from $2,000,000 to $50,000,000. The newly organized corporation announced its first dividend three months later—$2.50 per share *plus* an extra dividend of $5.50 per share on the *newly devalued* shares.[24]

Other copper companies enjoyed profits as great as those of Phelps Dodge. Profits in the copper industry nationwide for 1917 ranged from 33 to 800 percent on the capital investment. During the time the price of copper hovered in the twenty and thirty cents per pound bracket, the expense of producing copper ranged only from eight to nineteen cents per pound, depending on the recovery cost.[25] Low grade, high cost copper mines, at other times unprofitable, opened up throughout the state each week.[26]

Early in 1916 Phelps Dodge had announced a voluntary wage increase.[27] Pay to workers in 1917 prompted popular California essayist George Wharton James to remark that year, with some fairness, "The wages paid [in Bisbee] are the highest of any camp in the United States, the men and their employees working together for the best interests of each."[28] At least the men were working for the best interests of their employers. Statistics indicate that for the workingman wartime profits were hard to realize. According to some studies, purchasing power of the American worker actually fell.[29] The *Monthly Labor Review* for June 1920 shows that cost of living increases, based on a 1913 index, rose to 104 in December 1915, and to 142 in December 1917.[30] From 1913 to 1917, consumer prices rose almost 40 percent while union hourly wage rates rose only, on a national average, 14 percent.[31] Meanwhile union wages, per week, only rose to 102 in 1915 and to 112 in 1917. This resulted in a decrease in purchasing power to 93 percent in 1916 and 77 percent in 1917. A report of the Railroad Wage Commission shows that increases in family expenditures "due to increases in cost of living" from January 1, 1916, to January 1, 1918, amounted to 52 percent for food, 10 percent for rent, 44 percent for clothing and 31 percent for fuel and light.[32] These statistics meant as much in Bisbee, Arizona, as they did anyplace else in America.[33] Robert Bruere, writing in *The Nation* in 1918, observed that the high market price of copper during this period had given the mine operators "a sense of urgency."[34] Urgency surged, too, in miners who ogled corporate profits and squinted at their own slightly increased take-home pay.

Offered their greatest opportunity to claim a more reward-
ing role in American life, workingmen found themseves in a
stalemate not altogether unlike that which engulfed Europe.
Corporation managers, single-minded in their effort to increase
profits without a hindrance, became more intransigent every
day. Employment increased, but so did labor turnover. Arbitrary managers hired and fired capriciously. Hundreds of men
drifted in and out of Bisbee each month.*

The Arizona *Messenger* picked up the tensions of the day
and on May 26 declared "that there will be serious labor troubles is not improbable."[35] Arizona miners had come to feel
desperate enough to consider something radical.

The Gist of It All

The battle of Clifton-Morenci may have been where Walter
Douglas and the copper companies decided to make their stand
in the labor-management political war of early twentieth century Arizona. But the demands of labor for higher wages and
more fringe benefits did not constitute the biggest drain of
corporate profits. The "radical" Constitution and the liberal
First and Second State Legislatures had struck at the soul of the
copper companies by creating a taxation program that pared
earnings and contradicted corporate attitudes toward laissez-
faire economics. In addition, the expensive new workmen's
compensation laws rankled the mining men.

Had it not been for these thrusts of the state's hand into
the copper industries' pocketbook, little effort probably would
have been made by mine owners to interfere in the lives of the
people of Arizona. Had the Arizona legislature not passed laws
to restrict maximum profits, Walter Douglas and Phelps Dodge
would not have bothered so much to regulate the affairs of the
colonial outpost. There is no evidence that either man or company wanted power in Arizona for its own sake; New York and
the world were their ambition as a court. Douglas must have
seen his duties in respect to combatting an industrial workers'

---

*Answering letters of inquiry in 1916 about work in Arizona, one state period-
ical wrote: "Arizona is the best place in the world for a working man, because it is a new and developing country and where there is no job today,
there may be half a dozen tomorrow." ("Labor in Arizona," *Arizona*, Vol.
VIII, No. 1 [November–December, 1916], p. 16.) The article failed to mention
the more likely converse of that condition: "Where there are a half-dozen
jobs today, there may be none tomorrow."

uprising in a frontier setting as an awkward nuisance at best. Tax laws, corporation laws, labor laws, skimpy depletion allowances and employer liability laws all cut into the money-making success of the absentee owners. These men knew that in America just as money gets political power, so does political power get (or at least save) money. It was management's unpleasant chore to secure the political atmosphere favorable to these money-making ambitions.

As it turned out, the counteroffensive by management grew to include the control of every aspect of Arizona life — economic, political, social and even religious. The mining men intimidated editors, threatened ministers, bought sheriffs, seduced lawmakers and bullied union leaders. They rigged elections and manipulated the legislature. Phelps Dodge even forced its propaganda into the public school curriculum. When all this was not enough, the mining companies continued to enjoy especial preference in the courts. Between 1915 and 1918 the companies, led by Walter Douglas, completely reversed the direction of Arizona politics and destroyed the liberal influence in the state. By 1921 they had secured a closed society.

The money matter was uppermost — even solitary — in the minds of the mine officials, but the corporate offensive depended on masking corporate greed in order to gain public support. The operators had to get the Arizona voters to prescribe their own distasteful medicine of assuming the tax burden so that the corporations could make more profits. For the mining companies this meant ridding the state of George W. P. Hunt's Progressive program and replacing it with political policies more in keeping with the avaricious appetites of the copper men. This also meant using tactics that would inflame the middle-class Arizona voters and antagonize them toward the Hunt regime. Toward that end the companies, over-shadowed by Phelps Dodge, emphasized the radical nature of Hunt's penal reform and his desire to abolish capital punishment. The governor's stand in the Clifton-Morenci strike was widely publicized as proof of his support of union radicals. His fiscal practices were described as "wasteful," "irresponsible" and "corrupt." This corporate tactic — aided by wartime hysteria — finally worked.

The copper companies' biggest concern in Arizona had always been the politics of taxation. Non-corporate citizens shared this concern. Apart from the popular sentimental desire

for the sovereignty of statehood, the strongest drive that motivated most Arizonans in their movement for statehood was the
desire to be able to tax the mines, railroads and even the few
big stockmen. Arizona citizens resented the profits from their
mineral wealth and from exorbitant railroad rates going back
East. Throughout territorial days, notwithstanding unsympathetic appointees to territorial administrative positions, the
mining and railroad companies had seen to it that the burden
of taxation fell on the more numerous but less prosperous
citizens.[36]

Prior to 1900 copper companies had easily controlled
Arizona politics. Charles Poston, Sylvester Mowry and Sam
Heintzelman had urged Congress to give Arizona territorial
status so that they could more easily protect their mining interests. The nineteenth century Territorial Assembly always, and
governors usually, treated mine tax laws in a way favorable to
the corporations. A territorial governor's veto, as George Hunt
commented, could be bought for $2,000.[37]

As early as 1881—the year Phelps Dodge acquired its first
property in Bisbee—the Territorial Legislature, under the influence of Arizona's mining companies, passed a bill repealing an
earlier bullion tax law. The *Phoenix Expositor* on April 8, 1881,
observed:

> It is not a good financial policy to exempt the product
> of these mines from taxation. The mine owners have
> carried their point. They are mostly non-residents who
> don't care a button for the prosperity of Arizona beyond
> the mines in which they are interested.

With what proved to be an astute prophecy, the commentary
continued:

> When Arizona becomes a state and the whole cost of the
> Government falls on the property of that territory, it is not
> at all likely that the product of mines will escape taxation.
> ... Mines ought not to be taxed because they have no
> certain value, but the product of the mines, the title to
> which has been acquired without cost, ought to contribute
> to the cost of maintaining the local government, and the
> equity is still stronger where mines are returning large
> dividends to the owners.[38]

A "bullion" tax was a type of excise tax derived from the market value of the metal actually produced. Since states varied in

their assessment of this tax, it was difficult for metal producers to pass the tax on to the consumer. Another tax, the "ore reserves" tax, a kind of property assessment, became more widely used in the twentieth century. A levy based on an arbitrary—and usually very conservative—estimate of the value of remaining ore deposits, the ore reserves tax was subject to a "depletion allowance." The depletion allowance allowed the ore reserve evaluation to be reduced by yearly amortization. Theoretically (depending in practice on the provision of the law) the property could be reduced to zero valuation while still producing generous quantities of metal with no accurately predictable end in sight.

Whereas nineteenth century mining operators created a political issue by their absolute resistance to the unsophisticated "bullion tax," modern mining companies have promoted legislation that has allowed them to refine their tax dodges. The advantages of arbitrary "depletion allowances" and "estimated reserves" as well as "risk write-offs" related to capitalization, adverse operating conditions and market price fluctuations have found acceptance with the unknowledgeable general public. Today's extractive industries have, like other American businesses, rationalized, complicated and thus made palatable the fact that they pay minuscule fees in order to rape the land for profits.

Owing to the repeal of the bullion tax, property tax rates for individual property-owning citizens leaped up. At the same time, property assessment of mines for tax purposes was very low. The mining companies paid taxes only on their "improvement," that is, on their surface structures at the mine sites. The surface land value rather than the mineral value of the mining property was also included. This rocky, isolated, dreary ground had almost zero valuation.

Territorial Governor Nathan O. Murphy, a Benjamin Harrison appointee in 1892, did support a mine profit tax. Taxes, clearly, were the copper companies' chief political concern, and the Territorial Legislature protected their interests faithfully. Murphy, appointed a second time as Territorial Governor by McKinley in 1898, urged that the mine operators be forced to pay a fair amount of taxes, stating that it was wrong that Arizona's great riches in gold, copper and silver should be plundered to be distributed in the East and in Europe with scarcely any tax paid in the territory. In 1894 the total assessed value of property in Arizona amounted to $27,000,000, a quarter of the state's true taxable value. By 1899 the Arizona mine value alone was estimated at $100,000,000, but the mines were appraised for tax purposes at $2,000,000. That year another bullion tax bill met defeat in the Territorial Legislature.[39]

Many bills were introduced in the legislature to effect Murphy's request; all were defeated. Legislative efforts to create the office of mine inspector and to regulate the hours of underground work were defeated, too. In 1901, Murphy again asked for a tax on mining; again the tax failed.[40]

But in 1902, Arizona power politics began to take a new direction. This turn would last about twenty years. Alexander O. Brodie, a member of Theodore Roosevelt's famous Rough Riders, was appointed Territorial Governor by his former commander. Well liked in Arizona, Brodie was to reflect many of Roosevelt's liberal attitudes which characterized the nation's "Progressive Period" from 1901 to 1917. He refused a "special appropriation" from the legislature and amplified the pleas of the previous governor for a tax on the mines.[41] In his January 19, 1903 address to the Territorial Legislature, Brodie said:

> Great wealth has for many years been taken from the mines in this Territory and distributed as dividends in other sections of the world. Assessments have been made of, and taxes levied on, the surface structures and reduction plants at these mines; this has been done, apparently without taking into consideration the value of the individual property as a revenue producer.
> I believe in justness and fairness, that owners of producing mines in this Territory would willingly pay a tax on the output of their mines.

Still, in 1903 the tax situation did not change significantly. Spokesmen for the average Arizona citizen continued to demand a bullion tax to "allay the feeling of those engaged in other pursuits than mining that they are bearing more than their share of the expense of maintaining the Government."[42]

But the tax bill remained a bill.

This legislature may have defeated the tax proposal, but it did act to limit underground miners to an eight-hour day and it stopped the mining companies from forcing workers to accept coupons, scrip, punchouts and store orders instead of legal tender. A substantial new hope now rose in the breast of Arizona's laborers.[43]

After the supervisors of Yavapai County lowered the taxes of the United Verde Copper Company in 1904 (Will Clark having apparently been more forceful than Henry J. Allen), the Territorial Supreme Court enjoined the supervisors to reinstate the old tax schedule. The supervisors refused and, allied with the supervisors of mining counties Mohave, Graham and Cochise, entered the lists against the territorial administration. By 1905 a full-scale battle was in effect. But to the copper companies' advantage, the struggle bogged down in litigation. The Copper Queen mine, producing more than twelve million dollars' worth of copper a year, was assessed in 1905 at fifty-six thousand dollars.[44]

In 1905, Brodie again complained about the permissive mine tax program in Arizona:

> It is evident to all fair minded men that the Territory has extended leniency and fostered this industry beyond the years of expediency. Having grown to immense proportions under the care of the Territory, it now becomes obviously a question as to what portion of its product shall be exacted in support of Territorial institutions. A very small tax on the gross output of mines would yield to the Territory an aggregate sum commensurate with that industry's importance among those other varied industries which have always borne their share of taxation.[45]

In 1907, the mines found the greatest legislative effort ever to tax them. A new governor, another Roosevelt appointee, Joseph F. Kibbey, aroused public sentiment enough to stage a battle. Actually, in August 1905, the Territorial Board of Equalization had raised the total assessed valuation of mines from 2.5 million dollars to 11.5 million dollars. But the mining counties' Boards of Supervisors failed to comply.

The following year the Territorial Board of Equalization found on the assessment rolls returned from the counties that Cochise, demesne of the Copper Queen, was the most derelict in its assessment procedures. In March 1906, the United Verde Copper Mine was assessed at only $835,504 when it was actually worth $150,000,000.[46]

The board ordered a fourfold increase in the Cochise County assessments, double in Yuma County and an increase of but one-third in Senator Clark's Yavapai County. In Graham County, locale of the Clifton-Morenci operations, the procedure was found acceptable.* The absentee Boston and Edinburgh owners were providing a sharp discordant note in the Arizona mining corporation concert by complying with the law. Although the "corrected" assessed valuation ordered by the board was still ridiculously low, mining companies contested the order.[47]

An Arizona Supreme Court decision forced a 400 percent increase of the Copper Queen assessment; Phelps Dodge appealed to the U.S. Supreme Court ... and lost.

Kibbey laid it on the line to his 1907 legislature:

> It is easily conceivable ... that a county assessor, or a county supervisor, who owes his election to assistance received from a mining company or to any other influential single interest may find it easy to believe that suggestions from that mining company or that other interest relative to its assessment should have too favorable consideration.[48]

Partly as a result of Progressive Territorial Governor Kibbey's aggressiveness and partly as a result of increasing popular support for anti-mining legislation, the first session of the Twenty-fourth Territorial Legislature passed a bullion tax law which raised Arizona's total mining assessments to $20,000,000. But this "special mine tax bill," approved by Kibbey on March 11, 1907, was written so as to exempt "productive" mines (those which produced $3750 or more of mineral wealth per year) from regular property taxes. Instead, it provided for the valuation of a producing mine for taxation purposes of an amount equal to 25 percent of its gross annual output. Actually, the new law increased mine taxes only slightly, but it brought a great cry from the copper companies.[49]

For the most part the Twenty-fourth Territorial Legislature still supported the mining interests, while Governor Kibbey, intent on gaining greater tax equalization, continued to insist on a heavy taxation of the mines. The companies denounced Kibbey as an "agitator" and aligned him with the "radical" element of the territory. After two years of this pressure from the mining bosses, Kibbey retired in 1909 and was replaced by

---

*In 1909 the territorial legislature gave Clifton-Morenci its own county, Greenlee, by cutting off a piece of Graham County.

Judge Richard E. Sloan, a Taft appointee and a friend of the corporations. At once the old order of things was revived. The average Arizona citizen felt a sharp jolt; the picture became much clearer. But this condition, despite a now-growing liberal movement in Arizona, prevailed until after the First State Legislature convened in 1912.[50]

Even though the pro-labor representatives captured the 1908 election for the territorial legislature, no drastic new tax laws were passed before statehood.[51] At the Constitutional Convention thirteen delegates were appointed to the committee on "Public Debt, Revenue and Taxation"; no other committee had more members. But the items finally included in the basic document regarding taxation merely authorized future legislation. Probably the mine owners found the workmen's compensation section to be the most irritating feature of the primary law. This section included a "fellow-servant" provision compelling corporations to contribute collectively to a fund that would reimburse industrial accident victims when another worker rather than the employer was found responsible for injury or death.[52]

After a meeting on October 28, 1912, attended by a special committee of the Arizona mine owners, the State Tax Commission proposed a "Mine Tax Law" based on only one-eighth of the gross and 100 percent of the net production. In addition, the mine managers submitted as the evaluation of their mines a figure more than $1½ million *less* than the value they had been assessed in 1912. Sensing the impending anti-corporate direction of the 1913 Arizona political breeze, the commission revoked its endorsement of the mine operators' tax proposal.

The First Arizona State Legislature had wasted no time in exercising its constituted power to enact taxation laws. On March 18, 1912, it passed legislation repealing the special mine tax law that had been passed in 1907 by the Territorial Legislature. Classifying mines and mineral claims with all other taxable property in the state, the new law provided that a mine's assessment be determined on an *ad valorem* basis "at its full cash value." This legislation together with another law passed on May 17, 1913, tripled the assessment of Arizona mines since, in addition to the *ad valorem* levy, it taxed the copper companies on an amount equal to four times the net plus one-eighth the gross of the previous year's output. All machinery, smelters and improvements were assessed *beyond* these valuations.

More onerous to Arizona's mining interests than any legislation ever, the 1913 law was self-repealing as of June 30, 1915. The State Tax Commission, by recommending legislation drastically contrary to corporate desire, had openly defied copper mining power and had reflected the current Arizona mood which insisted on a greater tax burden for the mines. Indeed, the commission expressly stated it would not endorse any proposal "or any other measure calculated to cause the great producing mines of this state to bear any smaller percentage of the burden of taxation than has been borne by them in the past." While the mine operations declared the taxable valuation for 1913 should be $31,320,077.95, the commission reported that assessable mining property valuation for 1913 should be in excess of $108,000,000.[53]

During the years 1913 and 1914, in accordance with the new law, Arizona taxed its producing mines in a way that amounted to a triple levy: an excise or "bullion" tax, an income tax and a surface property tax. As yet the lawmakers had wisely avoided the treacherous "deposit reserves" assessment form. The mine operators were frantic.

In the same two years the entire matter of implementing the tax procedure was left in the hands of the Arizona State Tax Commission which arbitrarily designated the amount due for all taxpayers. The tax commission did observe certain "reconciliations" between the commission and the mining companies; still mines and machinery paid 35.7 percent of all taxes in the state for 1914. The following year that percentage rose to 38.3.[54]

Despite their previous differences, their natural competitive condition and their profound mutual suspicion of and, in some cases, mutual contempt for each other, the operators now collectively provoked by these new tax laws were bonded in league. No other attack could have created a greater degree of positive mutuality than this slash at their ledgers. Their common enemy had at last made itself dramatically, convincingly manifest.

By June of 1915 the mine operators had united enough to influence the legislative proposals related to budgetary appropriations. Employing an expensive lobby campaign, the operators initiated another "Special Mine Tax" bill to shift approximately $900,000 of annual taxes from the copper mines to the farmers, stockmen, wage-earners and small property owners. The State Senate, by now rapidly succumbing to mining company influence, voted to cut the biennial public school appropriation from $500,000 to $100,000, but Governor Hunt vetoed this bill. Later Hunt pointed out the new tax measures would have "not only materially reduced the taxation responsibilities of the large mining companies, but [would have] virtually provided that each company be its own assessor."[56] One appropriations bill, passed by a special legislative session in June 1915, provided a condition restricting the renewal of previous statutory appropriations if the governor should fail to approve the new bill. Hunt vetoed this confusing piece of legislation, but it created such a legal squabble that it was referred to the Arizona Supreme Court for review. The court would not meet for six months. In this way the mine interests obtained a delay on certain expenditures. Without re-enacting the 1913 mine tax law or any other law providing for the taxation of the mines, the 1915 legislature adjourned. Although he had lost liberal legislative support by the summer of 1915, Hunt was able to exercise his anti-corporate will for one more fiscal year through his constituted administrative agencies and executive powers.

The failure of the most recent "Special Mine Tax" bill and the other copper company–sponsored tax law changes angered still further the copper people. They now began, through their controlled newspapers, an extensive public denunciation of Hunt's fiscal practices and policies.[57] Though clearly not in command of broad popular support, Hunt did not back down. His support was strong enough to reverse the pressure for the "Special Mine Tax" bill and effect a fourteen-cent general reduction in the tax rate for the following fiscal year. This reduction was made possible by the Arizona State Tax Commission which used its constituted authority and raised the valuation of producing mines in Arizona from $118,026,003 for 1915 to $172,731,913 for 1916.[58] First among the individual mines was the Copper Queen, evaluated at $36,159,000; second was the United Verde with an evaluation of $20,687,011. All other non-mining property valuation in the state of Arizona in 1916 amounted to $39,569,706.66.[59]

The commission cited wartime profits and expanded operations as the reasons behind their action. To ascertain mine taxation, the commission adopted a formula based on net income from an average of the preceding three years. Net earnings of all copper mines were taxed 15 percent with no deductions for depletion, bond interest or any other loss. Included in the valuation was all property—machinery, improvements and the mine itself.[60]

This was not a decision calculated to please the mining companies; it drew them closer together and further stiffened their pledge to take over the control of Arizona politics. Within a short time their pooled ingenuity and resolve enabled them to evade increased taxation. While the tax commission may have demanded—and got—higher valuation from mining county assessors, the copper company–elected county boards of supervisors lowered, quite legally, the county tax rates. Some valuation was appealed to the Superior Court and eventually to the Supreme Court. In other situations, the copper companies simply refused to pay, the delinquent taxes merely accumulating until the tax commission sought payment through court order. During the drawn-out time involved, both in waiting to go to court and in carrying out litigation, production and profit-making continued uninterrupted. Since most Arizona jurists appeared to wear the "copper collar," eventual judgments usually favored the corporations.

Whatever tax payments the mining companies eventually did make between 1914 and 1919 were quite negligible alongside the huge World War I profits. Overall, the corporations gave up little control of their tax situation; they were allowed to estimate their own valuation, they elected their own county assessors and supervisors' board (and thus determined valuations and tax rates), and their legislative influence, even during this time, resulted in a tax formula so complicated that its interpretation could easily be manipulated, particularly by the best and most expensive corporate tax attorneys in the state—most of whom worked for the mining companies. Still, the companies resented whatever little taxation they had to pay.[61]

The mining men claimed they could make no money. On September 28, 1915, Walter Douglas announced (in his own newspaper, the *Arizona Daily Star*) that owing to extreme expenses, "It is obvious that the companies are barely able to earn the interest on their investments." In his statement Douglas claimed Phelps Dodge was selling its copper at 14¢ a pound. In June and July, the price had been over 19¢, while it climbed to above 20¢ by December 1915. The average market price paid for domestic copper in 1915 was 17½¢ per pound, almost a 50 percent increase over the previous year.[62] Throughout 1915 and

1916 the mining men of Arizona bewailed their plight. As the price of copper rose higher, profits leaped upward almost geometrically.

Comforting the mine owners as they lamented the handicaps to profit-making in Arizona was the knowledge that the federal government was more cooperative. It had relaxed its corporate income tax law by adding an amendment making mine depletion allowances more favorable to the hard-pressed companies. Mine operators acknowledged this relief on November 16, 1916, by a resolution of appreciation passed at the nineteenth annual meeting of the American Mining Congress.[63]

Signs pointed to a similar favorable shift in state policies. With national wartime sentiment moving quickly to support American industry, it was only a matter of time before Arizona's electorate, too, would swing away from its Progressive posture. The state's legislature had already shown the way.

Hunt Loses Ground

The revolt of the "liberal" legislature was only the beginning. For several months many newspapers which had earlier endorsed Hunt had commenced to snipe at his fiscal policies. But editors began to condemn his use of troops at Clifton-Morenci as poor economy while Hunt's protection of the strikers was depicted as support for the WFM. By the end of summer 1915, not only the publications controlled by Phelps Dodge—the Tucson *Arizona Daily Star,* the Phoenix *Arizona Gazette,* the *Bisbee Daily Review,* the Douglas *International Gazette* and the Clifton *Copper Era*—but other statewide newspapers, too, denounced the governor.[64]

A movement to recall Hunt which had begun early in 1915 was announced on October 22. By this time Hunt's outspoken liberalism plus his penal reforms and his generous budgetary proposals had caused some doubt among more conservative Democrats who feared for the party's chances in the 1916 election.[65] Hunt's support of the strikers and Phelps Dodge's power of the press caused Arizona's growing middle class to solidify their doubt into a concrete recall campaign. C. H. Akers of the Phoenix *Gazette,* and O. S. Stapley, a state senator from Mesa, led the campaign. (In the gubernatorial election only a year before, Akers had strongly supported Hunt.) The recall spokesmen claimed they opposed Hunt not for his labor position but for "wasting money," vetoing good legislation, over-taxation, catering to radical elements, general incompetency and "wanton disregard for state laws."[66]

The recall movement appeared to be centered in the Mesa area, a Mormon agricultural community in Maricopa County about fifteen miles southeast of Phoenix. Besides Mesa resident Stapley, the recall leaders included R. F. Johnson, a Mesa rancher. Although it had been organized in Phoenix, the campaign moved to Mesa to avoid being identified with either the politicians at the state capitol or the mining operators of the other larger Arizona communities. The relocation was an attempt to give the recall movement a broad, popular "plain folks" or "grass-roots" image. But when Hunt supporters managed to nullify a pro-recall resolution on October 26 at the Mesa Commercial Club, it was apparent that not all voters had swung over to the corporation position.

During the last week of November, State Senator Stapley led a reorganization of the recall committee. Fifteen of the first twenty-one people who signed the new recall petition were farmers. But nothing more came of it.[67]

Hunt's strength, somewhat diminished, was reflected in several newspapers that remained true to the anti-corporate politics of the 1908–14 period. The *Arizona Labor Journal* wrote that while Maricopa County farmers led the recall movement, it was actually a far-sighted political move on the part of the corporations. "The opponents of the governor and of organized labor in Arizona figure that a little recall talk will do the people good and put them in the humor to vote against George W. P. Hunt at the general election next fall."[68] Typical of the newspapers from the smaller non-mining towns of Arizona was the *Winslow Mail*:

It will be a sad day for Arizona if it ever permits ... the mine owners ... to control the state government to the exclusion of the rights of the other people.... The mine owner seems to think his rights never cease so long as there is anything in sight that he wants. With a string of hired satellites — shyster lawyers and political mountebanks — their whole policy seems to be to threaten and intimidate the strong, and cajole or bribe the weak into doing their bidding, and they profess surprise that anyone should say them nay. It is these same shyster lawyers and political mountebanks who are engineering the recall movement against Gov. Hunt, and they bear the same relation to the mine owners that the unscrupulous non-resident agitators bear to the labor element.[69]

After the Mesa Commercial Club override, the recall attempt sputtered. One Eastern syndicated columnist, Gilson Gardner, attributed the ouster movement exclusively to "mine owners seeking his [Hunt's] recall." Gardner said, "The chief owners are Cleveland H. Dodge, William Church Osborne and some other New York millionaires." Hunt himself denounced the men of the recall movement as puppets of the "Cateses, Carmichaels and Ellinwoods."[70] (He, like so many others, could still not bring himself to name the ringleader, Walter Douglas.)[71] Hunt condemned the campaign by *The Arizona Gazette* to malign him. After referring to the *Gazette*'s "numerous malicious falsehoods," the governor spoke of a

> great conspiracy which has been set on foot with a view of ultimately ... establishing ... a hierarchy of special interests, who, by placing their puppets in power, might straight away set about the revision of the Arizona Constitution, the transference of the main burden of taxation from the large corporations to the individual freeholder.[72]

Hunt then went on to claim that the members of the 1915 legislature trying to recall him were the same individuals who supported the "Special Mine Tax" bill.[73] The mining companies had concocted a tax bill that would lighten their load and still have the support of the alternate taxpayers of the state. It now appeared that State Tax Commissioner Tom Campbell, the only Republican elected to state office in 1914, was not the only friend the copper interests had in political Arizona. But Hunt held on.*

By the spring of 1916 it was clear that the real political issue in Arizona involved labor and non-mining people versus the mine owners. A pro-labor paper, the (Miami) *Arizona Silver Belt*, condemned as "corporate piracy" the "corporate depredation ... which refuses to aid in building Arizona roads, which

---

*The *Port Orford* (Oregon) *Tribune* spotlighted an irony: "'The very people who had made the air vocal with dire predictions of the disaster impending over Arizona if the Constitution carrying the recall feature should be adopted were the first to invoke it.'" (Kluger, p. 92.)

opposes the development of free schools, which even goes to the length of controlling a coroner so that when a man is accidentally killed in its employ it can secure a verdict favorable to a lenient settlement." This control of Arizona economic and political life by "absentee capitalists" had "caused a deep distrust of all capital ... in Arizona." "Governor Hunt," commented the *Silver Belt*, "may have taken political advantage of this deep distrust of the absentee capitalist in Arizona, but Governor Hunt did not create this distrust."[74]

But even the *Silver Belt* vacillated. It admitted that "the people seem to have tired of so much radicalism and they seem to want to get down to something sound and substantial." For that reason they were allowing big business "to flirt with" them. But, the *Silver Belt* explained, "That doesn't mean that the people are trying to turn our government over to the big corporations by any means." Arizona businessmen and farmers formed the balance of power between labor (the radicals) and big business (the conservatives). The "big representatives of the absentee capitalists" should not mistake the shopping around this balance factor seemed to have been doing lately, warned the *Silver Belt*. The present anti-radical movement should not be construed as support at all for big business. The message was clear; it was the beginning of "back to normalcy" for the Arizona swing vote. Arizona middle-class enchantment with liberalism had outlasted the national phenomenon by about a year.[75]

Probably no Arizona newspaper spoke better for the wavering "middle Arizona" vote than the *Silver Belt*; even miners had strong bourgeois aspirations and fears. The paper's general tone in 1916 was one of tolerant independence.[76] It reported in early June: "Phoenix Getting Nearer and Nearer to Copper Camps." Phoenix city businessmen were allying with the copper interests "through investment." *Petit bourgeois* shopkeepers, enjoying the war boom, were becoming *nouveau riche*; mining prosperity had produced an influx of commercial class people while the Salt River Project together with a wartime economy had stimulated Arizona agriculture and stock-raising; the *Republican* estimated the voting strength of Arizona labor had dropped to 12 percent.[77] Arizona politics, in turn, was showing more secrecy, more organization, more sophistication and less atomization.[78] On June 24, Secretary Charles A. Tanner of the Globe Miners' Union wrote in the

Silver Belt about the "Labor Forward" movement. "The golden hour of opportunity is here," claimed Tanner.[79] But he was whistling in the dark; the nemeses of organized labor were out, about and all around.

Throughout the late summer and fall of 1916 the *Arizona Silver Belt* became more restrained in its political viewpoint. It showed much less individualism; at times it seemed fearful. The paper even apologized for allowing itself to be too controversial in the past.[80] Uncertainty and a reactionary mood were rapidly developing.

The Election of 1916

Apparently Arizona voters did not appreciate Hunt's conservation of their tax dollar enough to offset the worry they felt concerning his seemingly drastic reform steps and tolerance of radicalism. Many Arizona citizens who had been offended by Hunt's penal reform now viewed his support of the Morenci strikers as open sedition. Hunt, it is true, had not gone much beyond the period's conventional and nationwide Progressive politics. He had not tried to appeal so much to organized labor as he had to the Arizona workingman and other non-corporate voters. His image, however, like that of Arizona unionism, had been stained. Meanwhile the relative population of such middle-class counties as Maricopa had begun to rapidly climb. Contrary to labor official Tanner, labor's golden hour of opportunity had passed. It was the copper corporations' turn.

Intent upon regaining legislative control and stimluated by their success in effecting Hunt's popularity decline, the mining companies continued to push. For several months after the Clifton-Morenci confrontation the mine owners cast about for someone they could enter in the Democratic primary race against Governor Hunt. In February 1916, their newly found man, banker George A. Olney, announced his candidacy. Olney's general record was untainted, but the identity of his specific backers made clear his manipulated role.[81]

Shortly after Olney's announcement of candidacy, the Democratic state committee held a meeting at the Adams Hotel ("the 'real capitol' of Arizona") in Phoenix. It was here, at the Adams, that the mining companies maintained their legislative headquarters. Several unlikely figures from around the state comprised the committee. One man—purporting to represent "the people" of Arizona—was George Purdy Bullard, an attorney retained by the Arizona Eastern Railroad and also by the Phoenix Pacific Gas and Electric Company. Bullard, along with Neil Bailey, superintendent of the United Verde Railway, Colonel Breathitt, right-of-way agent for the Arizona Eastern and Southern Pacific railroad companies, and John H. Robinson, secretary and political manager of the Arizona chapter of the American Mining Congress, had been the "big four" in the original public advocacy of the Olney candidacy. The alliance of these men and their support of Olney indicated that the mining companies, in addition to organizing themselves, had teamed with the two other largest corporate industries in Arizona—the railroads and utilities —to gain political strength. Still, many people suspected that the mining bosses alone were directing the Olney campaign.[82] Olney campaigned under such slogans as "He Made the Copper Men Pay Taxes," a piece of fraudulence used to "refute the argument advanced against him that he is a corporation man."[83] Actually, Olney had been a publicized supporter of the pro-corporate "Special Mine Tax" bill the year before.[84]

Olney enjoyed tremendous financial contributions. *Dunbar's Weekly* reported on April 29 that "a prominent Douglas mine owner" contributed $7,000 to the Olney campaign.[85] Not many "prominent Douglas mine owners" availed themselves to pick from so that the mine owner in mind must have been Walter Douglas. The *Weekly's* refusal to use his name was another example of the reluctance of all Arizonans to identify the kingmaker of Arizona.

At the same time, Walter Douglas' *Arizona Daily Star* kept up its condemnation of Governor Hunt and the labor movement in Arizona. When Hunt announced his candidacy on March 30, the governor addressed his statement to the "farmers, proprietors of small businesses and home-owning workers." Hunt told them the issue was

> whether Arizona, loyal to her Constitution, shall continue steadfast on her course of adherence to Progressive ideals, of constructive, representative government, and of absolute freedom from corporate tyranny, or whether, following the painful precedence of many another state, she shall come under the yoke of dollar despotism, [and] bend the knee to special privilege.

At issue, Hunt continued, was whether "the people of Arizona shall continue to govern themselves or shall they supinely surrender their natural heritage to those same powerful corporations." The *Star* reacted with daily attacks on Hunt.[86] It claimed Hunt's third term campaign showed he was interested solely in labor objectives, and the paper asserted Hunt was trying to "herald to the world that he is bigger than the [Democratic] party."[87]

The growing surreptitiousness about political activity began to bother some people. In late May, *The Arizona Silver Belt*, with the smoke-filled rooms of the Adams Hotel in mind no doubt, deplored the secret meetings that appeared to be directing the coming primary elections. "The people feel there is something going on behind closed doors," the *Silver Belt* stated. "And the people are right in feeling this way, for it is the truth."[88] Arizona's corporate machine, well-lubricated and free of internal friction, was moving smoothly, effectively, behind the facade of legitimate politics. Arizona's closed society was tightening.

The primary was scheduled for September 12. On September 1 *The State Herald* included a large cartoon showing two boxers in a ring. One clean-cut fighter was tagged "People's Interests" while the other boxer, his right glove containing a horseshoe labeled "Special Mine Tax Bill," represented George Olney. In one corner sat a water bucket marked "Fake News." Two groups of spectators, one on each side of the ring, had identifying banners above them. On the left, supporting the "People's Interests," sat "Arizona Farmers, Stockmen and Wage Earners." On the other side (appropriately the right) were the "Absentee Copper Barons." No specific names identified the group on the left, but the capitalists had tags; W. Douglas, L. Cates, "Arizona Mining Chapter" and J. Birdno were included. Charles Akers was shown holding a string attached to a little dog labeled "Arizona Gazette"; the dog sat on a box marked "Mortgage." The whole cartoon was called "The Horseshoe in the Glove." Polemical lines had been drawn and at least a few Arizonans were quite aware of where their political interests lay.[89]

Covering all bets on the primary, the copper companies supported State Tax Commissioner Tom Campbell as the uncontested Republican candidate. Final Democratic primary returns showed 18,122 votes for Hunt, while Olney had only

12,261.[90] The Arizona voting Democrat had not as yet been bought off or stampeded away from liberalism. Hunt issued a statement as soon as the count was in which said that the election showed "that the people of Arizona will not readily submit to the yoke of organized greed." Hunt said he hoped that now all Democrats would support Arizona's liberal Democrats in November.[91] He knew he would need all the loyalty he could get to defeat popular Tom Campbell.

Tom Campbell's popular appeal lay in his background. He was a rarity in Arizona in 1916—a native son. He stood out among the carpetbaggers. Born in Prescott, January 18, 1878, Campbell was a member of Prescott High School's first graduating class.[92] He went to California to attend college for three years as a geology major, apparently preparing for a mining career. Without completing his degree, he returned home and obtained a job in the post office. At age twenty-one Campbell moved to Jerome, where within a short time, thanks to his technical education and an adventurous spirit, he became a successful development promoter. In Jerome he met and married Gayle Allen, the daughter of United Verde Copper Company branch agent Henry J. Allen. In 1901 President McKinley appointed him Jerome postmaster.

Restless and ambitious, Campbell entered politics and was elected to the territorial house of representatives. While there, he introduced the eight-hour-bill which was passed. This deed gave him a reputation of being friendly to labor. From 1907 to 1914 Campbell served as Yavapai County tax assessor; in this position he proved his basic loyalty to the copper companies. Apparently this fact did not diminish his wide popularity, and in 1914 he won the election for Arizona State Tax Commissioner, the only Republican to survive the Democratic avalanche of that year.[93]

Campbell's broad general popularity and his service to the copper companies made him the logical Republican candidate for the gubernatorial race. In mining town Miami on October 19, Campbell received a standing ovation after a campaign speech. While soliciting votes in Bisbee, Campbell crossed a strikers' picket line to have a meal at the Truax' English Kitchen restaurant. Labor lawyer Bill Cleary spread the news of Campbell's patronage of the cafe. That night when questioned about it, Campbell told a predominantly labor crowd that he would not have patronized the place if he had known the cafe's

Thomas E. Campbell

labor troubles had not been settled. Back in anti-labor Phoenix, Campbell bragged about his contempt for the pickets.[94] Hunt, on the other hand, exploited the English Kitchen strike in his own way. During his Bisbee campaign, he ceremoniously boycotted the cafe, giving a little sidewalk speech nearby on labor's rights, and then walking into another restaurant.

Openly and unanimously endorsed by the state's mine operators, Campbell nonetheless maintained an image of incorruptibility. Six feet three inches, a pleasant drawl, an easy and engaging smile and a ten-gallon Stetson hat reassured the voters that Campbell was everything the noble, chivalric, courageous western cowboy and he-man should be. His appeal needed little editorial embellishment. To many Arizona voters, middle-class and workingmen alike, he represented the tall, strong hero come home to clean up the corruption. Campbell won the general election for governor on November 7, 1916, by 30 votes out of 58,000 ballots cast.* Immediately Hunt demanded a recount.[95]

In this same election the voters rejected the creation of a state department of labor by a 3–2 majority. Little doubt existed by now as to the mellowing nature of their political sentiment.

Arizona's judicial wheels turned slowly for Hunt. On December 16, 1916, the Superior Court denied his initial complaint to contest the election. Two weeks later, on December 30, both Hunt and Campbell took the oath of office. Since Hunt refused to give up the gubernatorial chambers in the Arizona capitol, Campbell set up an office in his Phoenix home. On January 25, 1917, the Superior Court of Maricopa County agreed to hear Hunt's appeal. Two days later the Arizona Supreme Court declared Campbell *de facto* governor. He entered office on January 29.[96]

As it turned out, only crude skulduggery beat George W. P. Hunt and the liberal Democrats. The recount efforts revealed gross tampering at the polls by the corporate interests. Inconsistencies in vote-counting procedures were reported in Maricopa, Gila and Greenlee counties. Although the minority party, the Republicans had been able to dominate the polling

---

*Hunt's defeat failed to end Walter Douglas' attacks on him. An editorial in the November 23 issue of Douglas' Tucson-based *Arizona Daily Star* accused Hunt of being a Socialist. (Editorial, *Arizona Daily Star*, November 23, 1916, p. 4.)

and vote-counting committees in several key Democratic precincts. When a ballot was marked for a straight Democratic ticket but also included an "X" for Campbell, officials counted the vote for Campbell. But when other improper markings appeared that could not contribute to Campbell's victory, the ballots were thrown out. In Snowflake, a Mormon community, a complaint accused the Bishop of the Church of the Latter-Day Saints of fraudulent ballot marking in favor of Campbell.[97]

Other irregularities showed up in Douglas and Bisbee. Testimony brought before the court indicated that in Douglas the jugglery got very involved.[98] Bruce Stevenson, assistant Cochise County attorney and Campbell supporter, testified on the witness stand that Art Pearson, an inspector in Douglas Precinct No. 1, had been drunk on election day and that, in fact, the whole election board was composed of people who ran things "in a very loose and crooked fashion." Pearson, who had claimed he favored Hunt over Campbell, was alleged to have erased and re-marked forty ballots of the one hundred twenty-three vote majority that the precinct cast in Hunt's favor. The Campbell people told the court that Pearson could not be found in the state, and thus they could not produce him as a witness.[99]

Then the plot thickened. Hunt's attorneys located Pearson, and he went on the stand. Pearson swore that Thiel detectives who said they were employed by Campbell's people (the mining companies) offered him a bribe to change the votes and then get out of the state. The anti-Hunt faction had conspired to invalidate the vote count in the entire precinct and have *all* the votes thrown out. Pearson told of extravagant debaucheries at the expense of the detectives. Numerous other witnesses, man after man, substantiated most of what Pearson said. Instead of rigging the election to favor their candidate, the forces behind Campbell presented false testimony about the irregularities in Hunt strongholds in order to have *all* the ballots of those precincts thrown out.[100] By creating a case for fraud in the princincts where Hunt was expected to win and by framing the Hunt supporters as the guilty ones, the copper companies hoped to negate the Hunt strength in enough key precincts so as to eke out a victory in what they knew would be a close election.[101]

The Bisbee election was equally invidious. In Bisbee Precinct No. 1 Hunt had received a two-hundred-vote majority. This margin would have been much greater if voters had been able to get to the polling booths. Although forty booths had been erected in the city jail, they were empty most of election day. Hundreds of voters stood in line for hours while John Curreto, an Italian immigrant and Republican poll judge, struggled to locate the names and numbers of voters on the register. Semi-literate and unfamiliar with the English language as well as with the voting process, Curetto fumbled helplessly as he tried to process the voters. It took each registered voter twenty-two minutes to process and cast his ballot. Of 1,300 registered voters in Bisbee Precinct No. 1, only 852 voted. Several hundred remained waiting in line when the doors were closed on them at six o'clock. Many more became restless during their wait, fell out of the line and went home. Another poll judge, L. R. Roscoe, was equally slow about his work. Since the state law prescribed that a maximum of ten minutes be allowed for each elector to cast his ballot, the *Campbell* people asked that the Bisbee Precinct No. 1 procedure be called an irregularity and that all the ballots be judged invalid.[102] Not denying that their own Republican judges caused this irregularity, the Campbellites insisted that since there was no evidence of fraud or crookedness, overt or furtive, they could not be held criminally liable. Yet they insisted that all of the votes of Bisbee Precinct No. 1 should be disqualified.

This line of logic apparently made sense to Maricopa County Superior Court Judge R. E. Stanford. (Judge Stanford did not disqualify any precinct *in toto*. But he did show preference for Campbell in judging which ballots were invalid.) On Wednesday, May 2, 1917, after several months of litigation, Judge Stanford awarded the governorship to Campbell. Hunt then appealed to the Arizona Supreme Court. In the meantime Campbell was sworn in as *de jure* governor, a fact that contributed to the favorable atmosphere for the Bisbee Deportation which must have, by then, been well past the formative stage in Phelps Dodge's plan.[103]

PART II

THE TRIUMPH OF CONSERVATISM

ENTER ORGANIZED RESISTANCE

The broad view reveals the Bisbee Deportation as an important part of an intricate plan of management's general assault against American labor between 1900 and 1920. While drawing little attention to their national scheme, employers worked within a grand design to hobble the unruly workingman. The Bisbee event happened to be one of the more glaring examples of their handiwork. If industrial battles are to be judged by their success and decisiveness, however, Bisbee was a *coup de maître.* Bisbee's deporters expressed their pride for years afterward.

Arizona Mine Managers' Disunity

Preparations did take time. Back in 1910 United Verde's Will Clark advised that the various operators of the Arizona copper industry unite and "take some part in these matters." Clark had gone on to say, in early 1911, that he considered it of the "highest importance that immediate consideration should be given to the subject of the well-organized labor classes in Arizona."[1] But the copper companies of Arizona found cooperation difficult if not contrary to their best interests. The three Bisbee corporations seemed harmonious enough, but that was not a typical situation. Despite the feeling of community shared by most of the people involved in the western copper mining business, the mining companies themselves could not get along with each other. One writer explained:

> In the nineteenth century the big concerns could and did fight each other because they had the resources, were producing at costs well below even low market prices, and wanted still further to reduce costs through larger operations, and to keep their places in the sun.[2]

In America there was but one way for people and corporations "to keep their places in the sun": make more money. Since the primary concern of the absentee owners was to expand and increase profits, local managers thought about little else. Labor difficulties were secondary considerations before 1910. Mining administrators saw no need for cooperating with each other.[3]

The *Arizona Mining Journal* reported on September 22, 1909, that "the present situation of the copper market is one of extreme dullness, due possibly to commercial inactivity, increased production and over speculation."[4] But "extreme dullness" of the market had not kept the Phelps Dodge Corporation from enjoying sales that resulted in record-making profits. For the first half of 1909 dividends of $2,224,730 for Phelps Dodge reflected the fact that Arizona was leading that year in the world production of copper. There was little time for mine managers to think about an impending constitutional convention.[5]

The failure of the copper companies to work together in Arizona paled beside the great copper wars of Montana. A titanic struggle for power there between three aspiring "copper kings"—Marcus Daly, Augustus Heinze and William A. Clark—had left the Montana copper mining industry chaotic and diffuse. As one person noted in 1916, "One may hazard a guess that there never will be a United States Steel Corporation in the copper industry."[6] As so often was the case, however, this weakness was only relative and apparent. Though the warring copper companies were permissive toward the Butte WFM, internal struggles kept the union from achieving any substantial authority in miners' affairs. For a while labor, however, enjoyed limited state and local political strength and until

1914 had considerable voice in the hiring and firing process of mine employees. Because of this, the Butte WFM gained demands that made it the "Gibraltar of unionism."[7]

This industry-wide rivalry was felt on a lesser scale in Arizona. That the absentee owners had different backgrounds and headquartered themselves in different cities provided the greatest handicap—in addition to the competition for profits —to intercorporate concord. One reason, perhaps, that the Morenci strike saw no greater collective action on the part of the mine owners could be attributed to the fact that, while Phelps Dodge's executives centered their activities in New York City, the home office of the Arizona Copper Company was in Edinburgh, Scotland. Morenci's third copper company, Shannon Consolidated, operated out of Boston.[8]

Bigotry played a part, too. Three copper companies operating in Arizona were owned by Jewish interests: Kennecott and Ray Consolidated by the Guggenheims and Miami Copper Company by the Lewisohns. Both of these groups had a more permissive, even compassionate, attitude toward workingmen. The Miami Copper Company initiated the "Miami Scale," and in 1914 S. R. Guggenheim testified before the Federal Commission on Industrial Relations that "employees are fully justified in organizing ... outside the plant." Guggenheim, in a very uncapitalistic way, told the commission that the "high cost of living is partly responsible" for industrial discontent. To someone like Walter Douglas this sob-sister attitude must have appeared tantamount to treason. Guggenheim then went on to commit the heresy of heresies among industrialists. He said the men were entitled to more of the luxuries of life; the government should tax the rich, and corporations should allow workers to share more of the profits.[9]

Sam Lewisohn showed similar lenity. Before Felix Frankfurter made his trip to the strife-torn Arizona copper camps, he talked to Lewisohn, a good personal friend. The Lewisohn investments included the Inspiration mine at Miami where several thousand miners were employed. Lewisohn had been assured by the Inspiration mine manager that the men were loyal and that "'they may strike at Phelps Dodge,[10] but they won't touch us.' When they struck," Frankfurter commented, "every mother's son in the Lewisohn mine went out." The mine manager broke down with a mental collapse. According to Frankfurter, Lewisohn said,

> There must be something so wrong when that can happen. When a man who thought he knew his men can be one hundred per cent wrong, probably something drastic needs to be done....I can tell you now that whatever recommendations you give on the spot after your investigation we will support.[11]

Lewisohn pursued his commitment. When he arrived in Arizona, Frankfurter received a telegram (October 15, 1917) from Lewisohn saying that he had instructed the manager, B. B. Gottsberger, "to put no obstacles in way of a common settlement."[12] When they heard of this kind of cooperation, less permissive mine owners must have been hotter than fresh blister copper.

Even Walter Douglas' father, Dr. James Douglas, like Guggenheim and Lewisohn but at an earlier time, had been thinking of the labor-profits problem. The elder Douglas read Herbert Spencer's works on Social Darwinism, and he firmly believed in man's social evolution. To him, the rise of corporations had an adverse affect on employer-employee relations. Showing a sense of stewardship, Dr. Douglas wrote:

> In the case of any of our great corporations the effect of personal intercourse between labour and the actual heads would be vastly more influential than conferences between the men and their managers, between whom there is too generally a high and wide barrier of distrust and dislike.

Dr. Douglas revealed other equivocal attitudes in this respect:

> I have just been reading Wallace's *Social Environment and Moral Progress* and I am troubled by the thought that I must be very wicked because I have become moderately rich. There is too much truth in his arraignment of businessmen and methods and of society and its recklessness, but Christianity has been applying much the same measures of relief as many modern critics.[13]

Unlike his son, Walter, Dr. Douglas saw his glass as half-full rather than half-empty. His expressed doubts reveal the feelings that help explain the lack of passionate corporate single-mindedness before 1910 in denying the Arizona workingman a share in the territory's natural abundance.

Walter Douglas experienced other frustrations in achieving intercorporate unity. Like so many Americans, many of his managerial colleagues failed to discern where their true political interests lay. One excellent case in point was the matter of John Greenway, the Calumet and Arizona manager at Bisbee, and Greenway's support of Teddy Roosevelt's Progressive Party. Unlike Will Clark, Greenway lacked the ability to make astute political perceptions. Many corporate officials probably had not recognized interest politics by 1912; for someone like Greenway, personal sentiment more than anything appears to have been the major factor in shaping his political loyalties. Greenway and Roosevelt had maintained their friendship after serving together with the Rough Riders.[14] No matter what prompted Greenway to support the Progressives, the fact reveals the absence of unanimity among Arizona mining officials.[15] When Douglas' circumstantial colleagues—the Greenways, the Guggenheims, the Lewisohns—failed to guide their actions toward the "best interests" of the copper companies, Douglas had to assert a more direct and influential leadership. Thus did he and Phelps Dodge become the prime force behind the corporate counteroffensive that began in earnest in 1915.

National Employer Offensive

Douglas did not have to operate in a vacuum. Many things, including the recent rise of Progressivism, the growth of Democratic power, and the anti-corporate attitude of many Americans, put employers on the defensive.[16] The hearings, findings and bitter denunciation of corporations by the United States Commission on Industrial Relations counterpointed by its favorable review of labor helped to further upset employers.

The honeymoon period of labor-management between 1896 and 1902 was over quickly. Although little organized opposition to organized labor appeared before 1902 (the courts had sufficed quite nicely), the national offensive against labor could be detected as early as 1903.[17]

In the earlier stage of the fight, management did not rely exclusively on vigilante action and patriotic deportations to crush labor upstarts. As they gradually became aware of the necessity for unified action, employers became more dependent upon the services of managerial associations. Anxiously responding to labor's considerable gains, American industrial leaders formed employer organizations in an open and, at times, masterful effort to check the tide of union expansion.

The intrusions made by unions into the area of "managerial function," particularly, caused employer distress. To combat these intrusions, employers began a united drive to guarantee open-shop conditions and restore management's authority.[18]

Among other things, the employer groups hired salaried business agents, retained lawyers and imposed assessments on their membership in order to maintain financial reserves. To carry out their collective assault on labor, they arranged and, if necessary, subsidized banking agreements and contractual obligations during drawn-out sales, slow-downs or production stoppages. To companies involved in strikes, employer associations could offer special benefits. These organizations not only maintained employment offices, they helped strikebound firms fill orders and encouraged special orders from strikebound shops.

In an attempt to plug all gaps in their defense, the organizations provided such "employment services" as "certificates of recommendation" (rustling cards) for employees and an elaborate system of employee "records" (black lists), and they pressured businesses to keep an open shop. They lured away effective union leaders and encouraged yellow-dog contracts; they helped organize company unions, and they furnished detective services and strikebreakers to members. Since employer organizations were financially able to provide sophisticated professional services, they of course kept all types of extensive records and published a plethora of anti-union propaganda. The employer groups used their political influence and a generous supply of money to put public authorities on their side. Civil police as well as the military came to the aid of business. By the beginning of the twenties, more than two thousand associations in the United States had aligned themselves with the crusade against labor.[19]

Actually, by 1916 the public sympathy for labor was fast dissolving and the federal courts kept up the cooperation management had been enjoying for some time.[20] In 1917 the United States Supreme Court supported the employer offensive when, in the Hitchman Case, it upheld the right of employers to make yellow-dog contracts. By forcing a hungry job applicant to sign a promise not to join a union as a condition of his employment, management severely handicapped labor union recruitment.[21] The members of the National Association of Manufacturers, meeting in New York that March, enthusiastically applauded an appeal to support a "great spring drive" against unions and to "stiffen their lines for a nation-wide offensive against the American Federation of Labor."[22]

Walter Douglas Strengthens His Command

The determination of employer organizations tended to be exceeded by that of individual companies. Corporations had less generous attitudes than employer organizations while many individual executives hated unions still more. These executives had equal contempt for both the IWW and the AFofL. The copper companies, in particular, discriminated against members of unions. In Butte, William Andrew Clark said he would rather flood his mines than concede to union demands. One American labor-management historian cites the Phelps Dodge Corporation as the most representative of the uncooperative, troublesome corporations of this period.[23] The great spring drive initiated in April of 1917 to rid Arizona of unionists was part of a national offensive, but it reached its most dedicated, ruthless form in the copper mining communities of Jerome and, most of all, Bisbee.

With Tom Campbell in the chair as *de facto* governor and the Morenci-Clifton fiasco fresh in their minds, operators organized behind the leadership of Phelps Dodge and wholesale discharges of union members from the mines began.[24] But the mine managers had in mind, as George W. P. Hunt had earlier speculated, something other than merely crushing the IUMMSW. (Hunt called a claim to this effect by Douglas and the other mine managers "a handful of dust in the eyes of the public."[25]) They were determined to undercut public political support of labor by maligning the image of *all* independent-thinking Arizona workingmen.

At least one incident must have provided anonymity-seeking Douglas with a painfully ambivalent reaction. A state newspaper called him a "petty official" and identified Phelps Dodge Counsel E. E. Ellinwood as the *real* power behind the throne. Referring to Ellinwood as the "Kaiser of Cochise," the article claimed it was Ellinwood, not Douglas, who manipulated the recall movement for Hunt, the financing of Olney's campaign and the financing of Campbell. Ellinwood also was credited as the one who conceived of the use of "rule by force" through liberal employment of gunmen. But Ellinwood was merely the front man for much of the Phelps Dodge highbinding, nothing more.[26]

As part of the national employer offensive, the Arizona mine managers formed a unique operators' organization—a state "Chapter" of the American Mining Congress. The mining men by the spring of 1915 had realized that their attention should not be focused exclusively on the technical aspects of mineral extraction. They admitted, as one of their spokesmen put it in the summer of 1915, that

> business men, generally, are waking up to the importance and necessity of giving a larger part of the time they have heretofore given to working out economics in their business, and forming combinations, to trying to find out what the trouble is that stands in the way of general prosperity throughout these United States, and are taking steps necessary to remove the difficulties, giving business a chance.

To facilitate the "taking steps necessary to remove the difficulties," the Arizona Chapter claimed as its members "the most influential and substantial citizens of our State—men whose judgment is accepted by those who do not have the time ... to follow-up as closely as is necessary, the most important features of our industrial and political life."

These "influential and substantial citizens" of the state began to "obtain and record for analysis, complete data upon which to determine the best line of procedure to be followed in the conduct of the affairs of the State." The Board of Directors of the Arizona Chapter, in acquiring this knowledge and calculating "the full deserts of each and every citizen," was bent upon formulating "a line of procedure from which the best possible results can be obtained, eliminating the political schemer" in order to establish fair play and eradicate "personal advantage." The existing conditions forced the businessmen and the taxpayers, "including the day laborer," to pay extravagant bills. Political opportunists, alleged the Chapter, had denied the workingman good pay while limiting businessmen with "embarrassing and harrassing conditions as to make prosperous conditions impossible." This statement, which might be considered a manifesto of the Arizona mining men, concluded by stating:

The business men can and must come to the front,
and lead the way, as they have undertaken to do through
the Arizona Chapter of the American Mining Congress.
Thanks to The American Mining Congress for helping
Arizona get started on the right track.[27]

Walter Douglas was not satisfied to limit to the state of
Arizona his activities in organizing mining men. He had a more
comprehensive—and thus more thorough—plan. His articles
relating to the Clifton-Morenci strike appeared in national
magazines in the winter and spring of 1916. Some time during
the summer of that year, Douglas managed to convince another
professional organization—the American Institute of Mining
Engineers—that it should deviate from its tradition of holding
the Institute's annual convention in a large, cosmopolitan city.
Douglas proposed that the fall meeting be held in Bisbee,
Arizona. Persuaded, the AIME directors chartered a train
which would originate in New York and as it moved westward
would lengthen as new sections were added in Washington,
Chicago, St. Louis, and points in between.[28]

The train left New York City on September 14, and, for the
first time in its forty-five year history, the American Institute of
Mining Engineers headed toward a convention site outside a
major American city. After tours of mines in the Hurley, New
Mexico, area and the new smelter at Douglas, the AIME members went to Bisbee where the chairmanship of the annual
meeting was turned over to Walter Douglas by Dr. Louis D.
Ricketts, chief consulting engineer for Phelps Dodge and 1916
President of the AIME. For the next few days the mining men
enjoyed meticulously planned, graciously executed and
thoroughly entertaining hospitality. Their host and his corporation left no detail unattended, no comfort neglected, no want
unfulfilled. Everyone agreed that the October 1916 meeting of
the American Institute of Mining Engineers was an unqualified
success.[29]

The following month, at the national convention of the
American Mining Congress in Chicago, the mine operators of
America repaid Walter Douglas' cordiality; they elected him
president of the Congress for 1917. (Most mining men held dual
memberships in the two professional organizations; accordingly, the Institute and the Congress operated in tandem.)[30] A
portrait of Walter Douglas was featured on the cover of the

Walter Douglas of Phelps Dodge Corporation
(photo by Marvin Erwin, 1930)

December issue of *The Mining Congress Journal*. Unbearded, youthful, self-assured, Douglas appeared to be the personification of the modern, aware corporate leader.[31] At the smoker on November 14, the final night of the convention, while their wives were being entertained at a theater party elsewhere, the members of the Congress reveled in their solidarity. More than six hundred of them occupied places in the great ballroom of the Hotel LaSalle. After some refreshments and entertainment, they sang some "old-time songs." Aided by a musical director and an orchestra, they "made the place ring" with songs like "The Star-Spangled Banner," "Hello, Hawaii, How Are You?," "Hail, Hail the Gang's All Here" and "Don't Bite the Hand That's Feeding You."[32]

Under the presidency of Walter Douglas, the American Mining Congress' major interests shifted from geological and metallurgical concerns to labor, politics, employer organization and taxation. The excitement of World War I obscured to the general public Douglas' dynamic role. But so satisfied was the membership of the American Mining Congress with Douglas' direction of the organization, it did not bother to convene again until 1919; unchallenged, Douglas held his influential post for three consecutive terms.[33]

Walter Douglas wasted no time in making use of his new office. *The Mining Congress Journal* showed immediately his editorial influence; the first issue under his direction dramatized the organization's switch in emphasis to matters economic and political. Affairs in Arizona mining circles received hugely increased attention. In May 1917 the *Journal* carried the longest article ever on non-technical matters. Entitled "Arizona Chapter of Mining Congress Shows Long List of Achievements," the article listed the influence of the Arizona Chapter in promoting or defeating certain state legislation. It called this political activity "an example to the other mining states" and said the article would enable mining men throughout the entire country to "have a more definite idea of what may be accomplished by a state chapter of the American Mining Congress."* The article acknowledged that "the present executives of this Chapter entered upon their duties about the time of the assembling of the State Legislature in regular

---

*There is no evidence that mining men in other states chose to emulate the Arizona model and form a state "chapter."

session." These representatives of the operators addressed
themselves to the task of "assisting the curtailment of new and
superfluous legislation." The *Journal* reported that the mining
men had been

> endeavoring to convincingly disseminate the Chapter's
> views among legislators as to proposed measures which
> were considered to contain elements that would retard the
> general prosperity.

That the copper interests' primary target was taxation relief was
openly discussed:

> The very large measure of the tax burden being carried by
> the mining industry in Arizona, and the great bulk of the
> employment in the state being provided directly and indi-
> rectly by the mining companies, it will readily be seen that
> such efforts as were directed had the largest benefit to the
> mining districts.

In a generous, conciliatory style, the report claimed that the
mining operators had cooperated with local union organizations and the State Federation of Labor in an attempt "calculated with the utmost possible endeavor at fairness." (This
claim of intercombatant harmony was based on fugitive example.) The article discussed the mine operators' efforts in bringing about the defeat of a new alien labor bill (the Kinney bill)
and the defeat of a bill proposing that two-men teams be required on the "single-man" drill. Perhaps anticipating the need
for vigilantes, the copper people snuffed out proposed legislation that would curtail the deputizing powers of local sheriffs.
Their defeat of a school tax measure, the mining men explained, "was supplanted with legislation of fair character"
since the proposed legislation (a continuation of the policy of
the previous two years) provided conditions under which "the
sparsely settled agricultural districts would have benefited at
immense cost to the thickly populated mining districts." What
was more, the article boasted,

> A number of other measures indirectly placing hardship
> upon the mining districts to the unfair advantage of other
> centers were likewise displayed in their real colors, with
> the result that the majority of the legislators stood for
> fairness and either disapproved the bills in toto or so
> amended them as to remove their unfairness.

The Arizona Chapter report credited the Chapter's executives with being so effective in their persuasive and didactic efforts that

> It may be said that more was achieved in putting down a firm foundation for rational legislation and the ending of haphazard lawmaking than brought about by the performance of any previous legislative body since Arizona entered statehood.
>
> The exceedingly few new laws placed upon the statutes by the legislature, it may be added, recommended the body very highly to the Arizona public. The legislators set, through the display of conservatism and thoughtful consideration of business that came up, an example that future Arizona legislatures will doubtless make endeavor to follow.[34]

But the lawmakers had really only been driven to a do-nothing impasse. This was the same legislature which failed to pass the "Special Mine Tax" bill. Arizona mining men had yet some distance to go before they would enjoy the power they had imputed to themselves in the May 1917 *Mining Congress Journal*.

Phelps Dodge Widens Its Assault

In the same *Mining Congress Journal* article which publicized the legislative prowess of the Arizona mine operators and admonished mining men in other states to do likewise, mention was made that "the Chapter has not been idle in matters of larger publicity for the mining districts of Arizona." This euphemistic assertion informed the reader that the "larger publicity" had served "to the end of advancement of the interests of all legitimate, conservative enterprises" as well as informing people "in every part of the state of the very great importance to the public welfare that successful mining operations represent."[35] In its polite, restrained tone, the article continued to discuss "the cooperation of the Press" throughout the state. But the substance of its remarks was far too modest.

Stung by the Clifton-Morenci debacle and now supported by other copper companies as well as by the railroads and utilities, Phelps Dodge recognized that the best way to gain more political strength was to influence voter thinking. So it went into the newspaper business.

Arizona small town newspapers (outside mining camps) revealed strong state and regional loyalties. Their editorials and news emphasis expressed the fact that many Arizonans were suspicious of outsiders. The support labor received in Arizona from 1908 to 1916 from non-mining communities can be attributed somewhat to this suspicion of copper companies and their managers. The population of the larger cities was more sophisticated and tolerant. Tucson and Phoenix businessmen appeared to be envious of and awed by the big New York–based copper executives. Newspapers in the two cities reflected this hankering for a more cosmopolitan tone.

The circumstances of their relationship with the copper people often forced the deference of Arizona newspapermen. Before 1900 Charlie Akers, manager of the *Gazette*, had been a loyal Republican. That year he went over to support the liberal Democrats. As late as the election of 1914, Akers remained a booster of George W. P. Hunt. But shortly after Hunt's 1914 re-election, the paper switched to a fervid pro-corporate position. The *Gazette*'s change of loyalty came about after Rawhide Jimmy Douglas reportedly picked up $5,000 worth of the *Gazette*'s outstanding bonds early in 1915. *Dunbar's Weekly* claimed that Dr. Louis D. Ricketts, president of the Valley National Bank (Arizona's biggest) and Phelps Dodge's chief consulting engineer, also had invested in the *Gazette*.[36]

The major Phoenix (and Arizona) newspaper, the *Arizona Republican*, was owned and managed by banker-realtor Dwight B. Heard. A leader in the Arizona Republican party, Heard had never been strongly supportive of anti-corporate politics. His siding with the copper companies at this time meant only a small shift starboard.[37]

A statement of management of the Tucson *Arizona Daily Star* on April 1, 1916, showed that the publication was owned by James Douglas, Walter Douglas and Phelps Dodge General Manager Stuart French.[38] George W. P. Hunt claimed in October 1915 that the same interests controlled the *El Paso Herald*, the *Douglas International*, the *Arizona Gazette* and the *Copper Era*. Of the *Bisbee Daily Review* there was no question.[39]

As the war situation drew closer to them, small town Arizona residents strengthened their national identity and patriotism, and many began to take pride in Arizona's copper production. Their political support began to shift; most of the small town newspapers espoused this new view.

While every newspaper in Arizona with a large circulation satisfied copper interest will, a few small papers did—courageously—keep their independence. In spite of threats and the temptation of bribery at least four publications, the *Santa Cruz Patagonian*, the *Winslow Mail*, the *Yuma Morning Sun* and *Dunbar's Weekly*, continued to criticize absentee ownership and corporate power. To them, bending to the yoke of the mining barons was to wear "the copper collar." Much of the apparent copper company support from the state's smaller newspapers did not come from the heart; the mining companies had ways of slipping on the copper collar.[40]

In addition to those newspapers it directly controlled, Phelps Dodge retained the "Arizona News Service" managed by Ned Creighton. Hunt claimed Creighton was no more than a hired puppet of the copper interests. One source stated that Phelps Dodge had acquired eight weeklies and one daily in Arizona which were run by Creighton.[41]

Creighton did more than merely provide "news service." In its January 22, 1916, praise of the handling of the Clifton-Morenci strike, *The New Republic* mentioned that Governor Hunt had been "able to expose the payment of money to newspapers for printing plate matter favorable to the companies" concerning the attempt to recall Hunt.[42]

This revelation must have made Walter Douglas wince when he thought of the refined, cosmopolitan members of his New York Club reading about his foiled attempts to rig news in the far-off barony. He waxed defensive in his angry letter which appeared in the periodical a month later. He stated: "The matter referred to consisted almost wholly of ... affidavits, ... the truth of which has not been questioned."[43]

But libel was not the crime Governor Hunt had exposed. On October 15, 1915, one week before the announcement of the campaign to recall Hunt, Ned Creighton sent a letter to more than forty newspapers throughout Arizona. The letter, which asked for page rates and total circulation figures, said: "Copy for page will contain cuts of strike scenes, affidavits of refugees driven out of Clifton and Morenci." Creighton, using a style and syntax which suggest that he spent much of his journalistic life writing headlines, then explained:

If used must not be labled [sic] advertisement or marked in any way to indicate same as paid matter, as

written copy will clearly state part taken by Western
Federation of Miners in trouble and object of publishing
is to make clear why companies in district refused to deal
with the Western Federation.

Creighton reminded the local newspapers that the entire
matter would be sent in plate form. He also asked them
if they would be interested in running a supplement with
the same content athough he did say he had not as yet approached his "client" with that proposal.[44]

This request of Creighton's involved a violation of United
States Federal Law. An act of Congress on August 24, 1912,
made it a criminal offense to solicit or secure the publication
of advertisements without having them marked as such. On
October 22, 1915, Creighton sent to the *Santa Cruz Patagonian*
cuts by parcel post showing scenes of a WFM demonstration in Clifton-Morenci. A note was attached:

If you use two or more of these cuts in your next
issue, sending me 10 copies of your paper, together with
your bid in duplicate for $10.50 the same will be promptly
paid.

Yours truly,
Ned Creighton[45]

Forty papers ran the unmarked ad, but the *Patagonian* turned
the letters and plates over to the federal authorities. On April
14, 1916, Ned Creighton pleaded guilty in United States Federal
Court to the charges of securing publication of unmarked
advertising and was fined the maximum penalty: $500.[46]

But the propaganda machine of the copper companies
moved on unhindered by Creighton's conviction. More newspaper people switched over to the corporate side. Ernest
Douglas, who had written a story for the November 1 edition
of the *Arizona Republican* that showed sympathy for the Clifton-
Morenci strikers, was hired by the United Verde Copper
Company to edit the *Jerome News*. His attitude about striking
miners changed 180°.[47] The interjournal warfare got hotter;
the pro-Hunt paper *Dunbar's Weekly* called the *Phoenix Gazette*
a "liar." In an editorial condemning accusations by the
Phoenix Gazette that Hunt had juggled his report on automobile costs, the *Weekly* asked: "How about it, Mr. Yellow Dog
Gazette? You have been peddling your filthy truck around here
about the Governor." Defying anyone to prove the *Gazette's*

charges, the *Weekly* demanded, "Now, how does it feel to have your bluff called?"[48]

This kind of invective on the part of *Dunbar's Weekly* may or may not have hurt the copper interests. But a few weeks later the *Weekly*'s editor, John O. Dunbar, received a thick envelope by Wells Fargo Express. The letter had been sent by John H. Robinson, Secretary of the Arizona Chapter of the American Mining Congress. It contained one $100 bill and twenty $20 bills. Prior to receiving the money, Dunbar had met with Robinson and John J. Birdno, receiver of the United States Land Office, in a room at the Adams Hotel in Phoenix. The two men asked Dunbar to print articles in support of George A. Olney and against G. W. P. Hunt. Either the amount was not great enough or Dunbar's loyalties to Hunt, for whatever reason, were too great. He photographed the bribe money and ran the picture along with the story under "Editorial Comment" in his paper.[49] A few of the other Phoenix newspapermen withstood the temptation of the copper money; most, like Ned Creighton and Ernest Douglas, joined the crowd.

By May 1917, the "Arizona Chapter" of the American Mining Congress could report,

> The press has been very liberal in its extension of cooperation and aid in all ways ... , as a whole recognizing the benefits which will be carried to all the people and interests of the state by ... gladly joining hands with the Chapter in the movement.
> A more delicate matter in association with the publicity work in the state has been the gaining of an understanding on the part of newspapermen that the mine manager ... really desires the cooperation of the press in keeping the public aware of the fairness he wishes to maintain, and that he is readily accessible to the newspaperman who comes legitimately in the interests of accuracy and understanding of the aims and work of the company.[50]

The Chapter's report neglected to mention that every large newspaper in the state and most of the small ones had already decided to cooperate with the mining interests of the state.

Phelps Dodge did not limit its incursion into the field of journalism to provincial Arizona. The mine operators discussed a bigger ambition in the *Mining Congress Journal*:

It has been felt in connection with publicity matters that the home field should first be considered, and that with legitimate, well-considered cooperation established here the time would have arrived to extend the publicity work to the broader field represented in various mining publications of good standing in the country at large.[51]

This ambition had been realized considerably through Walter Douglas' election to the presidency of the American Mining Congress; his weight in shifting the focus of that organization's journal was soon made obvious. For the three years under his direction the publication strongly emphasized financial, political, organizational and administrative problems of American mining operators. Politely but directly it poured forth a stream of one-sided corporate propaganda designed to rouse the up-until-then technically-oriented operators. The very first edition under Douglas' tenure as Congress president displayed a stunning change in emphasis. After Douglas' three years in office (having secured his corporation's rule of Arizona during that time), the *Journal* returned to the more technical aspects of mining that had characterized its pre-Douglas era.[52]

In addition to *The Mining Congress Journal*, another professional mining periodical, *The Engineering and Mining Journal*, was said to have fallen into Phelps Dodge hands. Early in 1915 the Phelps Dodge Corporation as well as other Arizona mining companies had decided to use the copper market quotations in *The Engineering and Mining Journal* to determine the weekly wage rates of miners that were based on the Miami Scale formula.[53] Also, on those same copper price quotations, Phelps Dodge based the price paid to small independent mine operators for copper ore delivered to Phelps Dodge smelters.[54]

The advantage to Phelps Dodge in being able to influence these quotations was obvious. As one Arizona newspaper pointed out, the editor of *The Engineering and Mining Journal* could have saved the copper companies thousands of dollars by misquoting copper prices one-fourth or even one-hundredth of one cent. Phelps Dodge was reported to have paid "upwards of a million dollars" for the magazine, the most prestigious in the field.[55] Allegations to this effect appeared in several independent papers. Labor groups then accused Walter Douglas of fraudulently reporting the market price of copper so as to lower the wage rates that were determined by the Miami Sliding Scale.[56]

Resentful at being accused of manipulating the copper price quotes, Douglas wrote a lengthy rebuttal to the charge which appeared in several Arizona newspapers.[57] He insisted there was no fraud or distortion involved regarding the copper price quotations. Discrepancies that had been cited as proof of the charge Douglas explained in a statement as confusing as it was indignant. His basic defense was that any day-to-day "estimate" of market-wide copper price was done with "extreme difficulty." He flatly and emphatically denied any ownership of *The Engineering and Mining Journal* by the "copper interest."[58]

T. A. Rickard, editor of the *Mining and Scientific Press* and a former editor of the *Engineering and Mining Journal*, found Douglas' explanation unsatisfactory. In two articles which appeared in the *Press* following Douglas' letter in the Arizona newspapers, Rickard pointed out that the *Journal's* quotations were, indeed, almost two cents a pound lower during the month of July 1916 than were those of the *Press*. Directly quoting Douglas' claim of innocence in the rigging of quotations, Rickard (who rarely stepped into controversy) stated, "We have every reason to believe that our quotation reflected conditions accurately."[59] Two weeks later the *Press*, as Rickard put it, "reverted to this interesting subject." While Rickard found the "sinister suggestion . . . [that] the large copper-producing interests have financial control of the *Engineering and Mining Journal* . . . to be as baseless," as Walter Douglas claimed, the editor still could not dismiss the puzzling nature of the market quote disparities. "We are at a loss," wrote Rickard,

> to understand why a labor-union or a [small, independent] mining company should agree to base its scale of wages or its settlements for ore upon the guess of a single trade paper, when the suggestion of this arbitrament comes from the buyer of the labor and of the ore.[60]

Arizona's small mine operators and labor union leaders failed to respond further to this controversy.[61] The matter, like so much other knavery of the time, either failed to catch their eye or survive their test of credulity. They had not yet come to reckon with the extreme nature of copper company intrigue.

Along with their ventures into the state and national world of journalism, Phelps Dodge and its officers extended their non-mining interests further and became involved in the

Arizona banking business. Perhaps using New York bank executive, diverse capitalist and Phelps Dodge vice-president Cleveland H. Dodge as a model, several Phelps Dodge officers had been instrumental in developing Arizona financial institutions. Both Dr. Louis Ricketts and Walter Douglas helped to develop the state's largest bank, the Valley National. The Brophys, A. J. Cunningham and others—along with the Douglases—founded and built up the Bank of Douglas, the Southern Arizona Bank & Trust Company and several smaller savings and loan institutions. The statewide political and social advantages of this kind of economic leverage need no explanation.[62]

An industrial health inspector from Chicago, Dr. Alice Hamilton, heard in Globe that all the doctors there "'were copper.' Only one labor doctor could I find in all that region; the rest were deeply dyed copper. Some of them more royalist than a king." What is more, she heard from someone, "'The lawyers are copper too, all but the one the union hires.'"[63] Long-time Cochise County attorney W. K. Meade stated in 1917 that the rule in Arizona had been for the bar to "hide and cover-up" rather than expose corporate lawlessness. "Corporations as a rule," said Meade, "quietly support dishonesty in legislatures, courts, attorneys at law, and officials.... Since statehood, honesty has largely prevailed along executive lines, but the courts and legislators are strongly tainted with corporate poison."[64]

The "achievements" listed by the "Arizona Chapter" of the American Mining Congress in its May 1917 report included a program in the Arizona public schools sponsored by the "Chapter." The mining men had developed "an extension of the study of political economy under competent direction" and had provided "an increase in the number of reference books upon the subject in the school libraries." The report said that no other effort could "be extended more laudably in any direction." It continued:

> Experience in the Bisbee [school] district is that with the study confined to but half of the last period of the high school, a great many errors are corrected in the minds of the young people as to the relations of capital to labor. These corrections do not stop with the students in their benefits, but are carried into the homes, with results of the best, and that might be attained in no other way.

The report expressed the hope that "means will be found" to enable "cooperation with the superintendents of the schools" throughout the state "and in the several mining districts in particular to introduce this study in the last year of grammar school, at least, and to carry it through all of the periods in the high schools." In addition, the Chapter hoped for the cooperation of the State University in this endeavor to the extent that some qualified person would serve as an advisor on copper company "political economy" to the teachers "in the schools of the state."[65] Forcing its propaganda on the school curriculum was but one more way in which the copper industry extended its influence.

Even more audacious was the mining bosses' attempt to dictate the ecclesiastical affairs of the state of Arizona. Along with the press, the pulpit had become a traditional support upon which the copper men could rely. In most situations the Phelps Dodge Corporation appeared to have had the thorough blessing of the most authoritarian and conservative church in the state: the Church of the Latter-Day Saints.[66] Such people as Reverend A. D. Raley, a strong copper company sympathizer, spoke for the majority of the Protestant sects.[67] When Dr. Hamilton went to Arizona in 1919, she discovered that "most of the ministers are copper."* Only Dean William Scarlett of the Phoenix Episcopal Cathedral was mentioned to Dr. Hamilton as "being labor."[68] But he was too much for the mine operators to tolerate in their campaign for a totally closed society. Years later Dean Scarlett (who, after leaving Arizona, became Bishop of the Diocese of Missouri) wrote to Henry S. McCluskey:

> Do you recall that ... I went to lunch at Bishop Atwood's only to find him in a dither because James ["Rawhide Jimmy"] Douglas had just been there demanding that if he did not put me out of the Church ... they would sue me?
> Do you also recall anything to the effect that one or more of the copper crowd were, as Governor Hunt put it in a letter to me, 'doing everything in their power to prevent my being elected Bishop of Arizona?'[69]

---

*At one time during the July 12 roundup, Bisbee authorities contemplated the deportation of Father Brewster, Bisbee's liberal Episcopal vicar. Only the fact that he was out of town on business saved him. (Bishop Scarlett, interview, March 13, 1972.)

Wage scales and the morning news, voting booths and Sunday school, home mortgages and doctors' calls, all the day-to-day affairs of the people of the state of Arizona had come under the surveillance and say-so of the copper kings. More importantly, by 1917 such large corporations as Phelps Dodge and the United Verde Copper Company had developed several techniques which enabled them to avoid payment of the taxes they had found so abhorrent in 1913, '14 and '15. Tax evaluation remained high in the mining counties, it was true. But thanks to a growing corporate awareness of popular ignorance and a lessening of corporate heavy-handedness in political manipulation, the copper companies had come to regulate or at least influence their tax expenses. From the start, and the fact never changed, mining property and production—no matter how zealous the tax commission may have been to increase valuation—remained far below actual valuation. When requested to submit a valuation estimate, a mining company presented one that was absurdly low. If the tax commission rejected this, the eventual adjustments or "reevaluations" constituted only a slight compromise for the mines.

Invariably, the copper companies owned the assessors and supervisorial boards of Cochise and Yavapai counties. Tax rates in these two counties were 30 to 40 percent below that of the state average. Frequently appealed valuations were often stalemated in superior and supreme court litigation for months or even years. Taxation formulas, already complex, became labyrinths for tax evasion. While fantastically high World War I profits made any Arizona copper company taxes seem negligible, stubborn, parsimonious mine managers could avoid even these by simply refusing to pay. If their delinquency in this respect eventually brought them to court, they could count on a sympathetic, ex-corporation lawyer judiciary to get them off in a relatively inexpensive way.[70]

Devious Weaponry

As the management offensive widened and hardened, public support for corporations grew. With public backing, western mine operators met only limited resistance in their organized effort to repress union activity. To aid them in their confrontation with militant unionism, operators hired the services of private detective agencies. For the Ludlow Massacre, the Baldwin-Felts Agency had supplied several hundred gunmen, most of whom had been temporarily mustered into the state militia or deputized. The Byoff Brothers Agency kept a card file of more than ten thousand able mechanics who could be dispatched within a few hours to a strike scene. Supplying "guards" to employers with labor trouble any place in the country made Robert A. Pinkerton a wealthy man.[71] William J. Burns, former head of the W. J. Burns International Detective Agency and Chief of the Bureau of Investigations of the Department of Justice, used his official position to aid his private agency in a campaign of "copper interests of the Southwest against the I.W.W."[72]

Some Burns detectives found work with the United Verde Copper Company, but most of the detectives hired in Jerome, Globe and Bisbee were provided by the Thiel Detective Agency, a Los Angeles–based operation.[73] Thiel detectives joined Arizona labor unions to spy on union activities and make reports to management. Spying seemed to be pervasive at all levels and was part of what Robert Bruere called the "stool-pigeon psychology" of the industry. Bruere said:

> I know mining camps where the local managers keep secret agents on watch over the foremen; where the foremen bribe men to spy upon their fellow-workmen down in the mines; and where the absentee owners in the East employ detectives to report on the managers.[74]

A long-time accountant of the United Globe Mines told how his company hired an "expert detective" from the Thiel Detective Agency in Los Angeles. The "operative" was an ex-Pinkerton man who had served in the United States Secret Service. He was, therefore, able to command a "fancy salary." The agent went to work as an underground miner, joined the union, served on committees, worked his way up to secretary and treasurer and finally became president of the local. All this time he was "reporting union business and activities by letter to the mining companies [sic] manager, signing the letter with a number." The only person who knew the detective by sight was the accountant, who paid him the difference between his wages as a miner and his contractual salary. The detective "faithfully reported all radicals on the payroll and many of them were discharged."[75]

It was well known that the IWW in Arizona was infested with detectives. As one person observed, "The I.W.W. thrives where the tactics of the employers are so autocratic as to breed intense resentment and distrust among the men."[76] Certainly this was true in Arizona; IWW activity was the greatest in Jerome and Bisbee. Comparatively few IWWs could be found in Clifton, Morenci, Globe or Miami. On July 1, 1917, The *Bisbee Daily Review* commented that Wobbly leaders "are paid for their work. They are professionals."[77] The *Review* suggested German money financed Wobbly leadership. The evidence shows that more likely the copper companies themselves paid IWW organizers and agitators. At least one active Wobbly, William Holther, was proved to be an employee of the Thiel Detective Agency.[78] Some people believed another Bisbee IWW organizer, James Chapman, also was a detective. After Chapman went to Globe the first week of July 1917, he and two other suspected *agents*, Roger S. Culver and H. F. Kane, were described as "the most energetic and vociferous" Wobbly organizers in Globe.[79] Several Wobbly leaders deported from Jerome and incarcerated for several days in the Prescott jail turned out to be professional "operatives " These detectives' dedication to keeping their true identity secret was probably matched by their fear of being found out by bona fide IWWs.[80]

One of the slickest roles of the inside detectives was to act as an *agent provocateur*. John McBride, the federal mediator sent to Arizona in 1917, wrote eight years earlier that Pinkerton detectives

> are employed to terrorize the workingmen and to create in the minds of the public the idea that the miners are a dangerous class of citizens that have to be kept down by armed force. These men had an interest in keeping up and creating troubles which gave employers an opportunity to demand protection from the state militia at the expense of the state, and which the state has too readily granted.[81]

Usually the most common *provocateur* was simply a professional police agent who coldly engineered a single provocative act designed to "set up" leaders for roundup and arrest. Burn's detectives were expelled from the IWW for advocating force and violence, while other *agents* planned to give radical workers IWW cards so that they might be arrested. Furthermore, administrators of the Sherman Detective Company directed its representatives "to stir up as much bad feeing as you possibly can" between nationality groups.[82]

To carry out their instructions, Sherman spies filed reports on union membership, wormed their way into IWW leadership, gained the confidence of the workers and got elected to union office in order to be able to spread dissension among the membership and cause the union leaders to be run out of town. According to the Sherman service, all this was done in the interest of "'constructive thought, Americanism and truth.'"[83]

Evidently *agents provocateurs* found employment in Arizona in 1917. In addition to Holther and Chapman in Bisbee and some "operatives" at Jerome, many other IWW leaders were suspected of being copper company plants. Testimony in the President's Mediation Commission hearings included charges that company-hired detectives had infiltrated Arizona miners' unions and had provoked the strike of 1917 as well as other labor unrest.[84] Robert Bruere's findings convinced him there was "no doubt that the so-called *agent provocateur* had a hand in fomenting the strikes . . . from Butte . . . to Bisbee."[85]

Some "homemade" *agents* were used in Arizona. During the short strike at the Consolidated Copper Company in Ray, Arizona, in July 1915, General Manager Louis Cates hired a Phoenix man, Carlos Aldai, to start a fight with a rooming house proprietor known to be friendly with unionists. Aldai waited until the man came along the street and then knocked him down. Immediately both men were arrested, but Aldai was quickly released. The rooming house owner received a one hundred dollar fine and a ninety-day sentence subject to suspension on condition that he leave the camp. This he did.

Cates also paid Aldai to steal a trunk containing the local union's records and documents. According to Aldai, "The Miners' Union was holding meetings in Ray until we got away with their books and that seemed to have broken them up." Ray miners never participated significantly in subsequent labor agitation.[86]

So suspect were all IWW activists in 1917 that even Frank Little, the IWW organizer lynched in Butte, had his doubters. It seems unnecessarily reckless to impugn the trustworthiness of Frank Little, but the fact that there was doubt held by someone adds to the argument that the possibility of conspiracy was rife at all IWW levels and knew no limitations. One story has it that R. S. Culver, Arizona IWW district secretary and a local IWW grievance committee chairman, was arrested in the big fall 1917 IWW roundup and made it all the way to the Chicago trial before Judge Landis discovered Culver had been planted by the Federal Secret Service.[87]

Agents and other detectives had a way of working themselves out of jobs. After the Arizona deportations of July 1917 had broken the back of unionism in Arizona, operatives continued to report to the companies that "the I.W.W. movement is growing." No evidence exists to show that the copper companies allowed themselves to be taken in by claims from detective agencies that IWWism was stronger, better organized and more threatening than ever.[88]

The *agent provocateur* was, perhaps, the big gun in the huge arsenal of the employers in their offensive against organized labor prior to the Wagner Act. But the hiring of *agents* only partially reflected the determination of mine officials. The cooperation and unity of mine managers also indicated the degree of the mine operators' belligerence. In interviewing "the ablest mining employers in the State" of Arizona in 1917, Robert Bruere found that they proposed to remedy the problem of "agitators" by "taking them out in the country and shooting them."[89] Insistent on dealing with individual employees, employers refused to recognize unions or their representatives. Not only did the copper companies refuse to bargain, they discriminated especially against members of trades unions.[90] When W. A. Clark spoke of lynching and flooding his mines, he only was expressing in more explicit language the other mine owners' determination to withstand unionism.

The Butte Miners' Hall, blown up in June 1914, symbolized the militancy and desperation of Clark and the other copper mine operators. Twenty-six expertly placed dynamite charges ripped the hall to rubble. The editor of the WFM magazine reported that agents from a private detective agency working for the mine owners set the charges. It may have been an assassination attempt; WFM President Charles Moyer was in Butte at the time.[91]

The dynamiting of the union hall represented other aspects of the employer offensive. It showed the efficacy of the radical "bogey" tactic since the general public (who believed the mine owners' contention that union members themselves had done the job) tended, after 1914, to see the Butte IUMMSW as "radical." This label, in turn, created internal conflicts within the IUMMSW that weakened it and brought about an open shop.[92] The Butte blast was followed by a three-year quiescence in Butte labor activity. Regardless of reponsibility, Butte mine operators found that a violent act could dampen union energy effectively. Similarly, management in Arizona found a way in Jerome, in 1909, to keep labor under control. By manipulating local union affairs, operators subdued labor. Mine officials were learning that if they could manipulate and intimidate union members, perhaps they could stifle labor movements completely.

5

THE ILLUSION
OF CHANGE

Ordinarily corporations have secured their closed societies with relative ease. An objection here could, as a token of tolerance, be indulged. A criticism there could be expunged overnight with a flood of indignation from the controlled press. A real threat could be quietly and completely and quickly suppressed. (Promote that charismatic union steward to foreman.) The mythology of alternate power should be encouraged as long as the claim of that power remained mythological. Management could allow labor unions to *say* and *believe* that they shared in the shape and direction of things as long as they stayed in their place. Usually this worked. The illusion of democracy satisfied most people. Indeed, the *real* responsibilities of decision-making would have overwhelmed most of them. Studies confirm this. Labor's ups and downs usually have been more related to political and social changes than to any collective action on the part of labor itself. Yet, for a while during the early twentieth century, labor enjoyed a brief period of relative popular blessing along with some small improvements in its condition. Most of the advances for labor were granted politically and not through labor exerting any pressure in its own behalf. Similarly, most of labor's claims to "growth" or "power" were measured more by counting names on membership rolls than by citing actual political and social changes effected by the energy and will of the labor movement.

The Progressive Myth

The somewhat benevolent attitude toward labor during the years 1900 to 1918 was derived from a popular discontent Americans were feeling toward business administration and the entrepreneurial ethos. Labor benefited from the "backlash" that had developed toward the monopolistic abuses of the late nineteenth century. As Henry D. Lloyd had stated in 1884, "We have given competition its own way, and have found that we are not good enough or wise enough to be trusted with this power of ruining ourselves in the attempt to ruin others."[1] Popular "progressivism" (as opposed to "political progressivism") was a surfacing of latent innocence and indignation. In the press and on the streets, in city councils, in state legislatures and in Congress, the Progressives went after the city bosses, the Robber Barons, the sweatshop owners and the food and drug adulterers.[2]

Most impressive during the period was labor legislation at the state level. By 1912 thirty-eight states had child labor restrictions. Within another year, nine states had minimum wage laws. Reflecting the influence of Progressive pressure, an eight-hour day and workmen's compensation laws prevailed in twenty-five states by 1915.[3] Actually, however, the real wages of many industrial workers declined. Many of labor's gains in the period must be interpreted as a conciliatory gift intended to absorb protests of war profiteering or exceptional business growth[4] "Labor" as a movement failed to coalesce into any substantial or enduring political effort. Labor's failure to pull itself together to support either an independent labor party or a socialist platform may be explained by the basic vitality of American capitalism (despite its temporary dip in popularity during the period), the middle-class psychology of American workers, the American's faith in "individual rights," the conservative features of the American political system, the anti-socialistic views of the Roman Catholic Church, and the anti-socialistic leadership of Samuel Gompers.[5]

But these circumstances were unacceptable to many unskilled, disillusioned industrial workers. They searched for some vehicle with which to redress their complaints. Politics seemed pointless. And so, in the late nineteenth and early twentieth centuries, radical organizations in America usually found themselves part of the labor movement.

As the influence of Marx, Sorel, Bakunin and other European radical thinkers began to find its way to the United States (usually as part of the mental and physical baggage of immigrants), it crept into the platforms and literature of various labor groups.[6] Labor radicalism found its largest nineteenth century audience in the unskilled membership of the Knights of Labor. After the allegedly anarchist-inspired Haymarket bombing, public anger turned upon the Knights and the radical aspect of the labor movement. The demise of the Knights brought the flowering of the American Federation of Labor, a non-politically-oriented, basically conservative amalgamation of traditional craft unions. By 1905 the AFofL had a reputation of being cooperative, benign and respectable. Unskilled workers, impatient and disillusioned, looked for more viable, more promising ways to challenge the American social order.

The IWW

Most studies of the growth of trade unionism in the United States recognize that the aims of labor movements were practical and conventional and that "most American wage earners do not start with any general theory of industrial society."[7] However, if any one industrial union in America did base its rationale for organization on ideological concepts, it was the Industrial Workers of the World, the "IWW" or the "Wobblies."[8] Actually, three categories or levels characterized IWW thinking. First there were the salon intellectuals based in Chicago and New York and other large cities. This tiny segment included people such as Mabel Dodge Luhan and Daniel DeLeon. The more dangerous and earthy business of labor organizing and leadership belonged to the second category of Wobbly.[9] Rough, dedicated men like Bill Haywood, Vincent St. John and Frank Little composed this group. They boiled their ideological beliefs down to bread and butter issues that the third level, the membership—the ten-day bindle stiffs* in the mining and lumber camps—could understand and respond to.

---

*A "ten-day bindle stiff" was an itinerant ("ten-day") hobo-laborer or "stiff" who carried his worldly goods including his bedding in a bundle or "bindle."

A dash of romance flavored the radical vision of the eastern intellectuals. They saw the western IWW in much the same way as others saw the western cowboy—an innocent, courageous primitive, the affirmation or rebirth of a lost American dream.[10] And so the dirty, hungry bindle stiff was endowed with a saintliness, a mystique of frontier proletarian nobility. Although Mabel Dodge Luhan invited Big Bill Haywood to her New York "salon," most trans-Mississippi muckers and lumberjacks and field hands took little interest in the pamphlets and books produced by the radical intelligentsia; Joe Hill's Wobbly songbook was enough for them. Conversely, the eastern intellectuals shaped and altered the IWW image to satisfy their causes and dreams, paying little concern to the day-to-day plight of the western workingman.[11]

The American general public hardly knew of the existence of the IWW before 1915. Organized in Chicago in June 1905 by several prominent men in the socialist and labor movement, such as Bill Haywood, Eugene Debs, "Father" T. J. Hagerty, Daniel DeLeon and William E. Trautmann, the IWW was founded on the belief that trade unions and existing industrial unions alike were powerless. Its most important forerunner was the short-lived Knights of Labor; from the start the IWW saw in the AFofL and its craft union policy a hateful enemy.[12] Its legacy from the Knights—"An injury to one is a concern of all"—was translated into the IWW mottoes of "We shall be all," "Solidarity" and "One big union." However, the IWW differed from the Knights of Labor in that it placed absolutely no confidence in conventional political methods.

Bravado rather than action distinguished the Wobblies. As one contemporary source said: "The Wobblies preach violence without practicing it, while the Knights practiced it without preaching."[13] One analyst contends that this "all blow and no show" reputation hastened the decline of the Wobblies:

> The I.W.W. was too revolutionary to attract the support of the basically conservative forces of American labor, and in spite of the violence of its propaganda, too cautious to be successful as a revolution. The only thing in which it fully succeeded was in arousing popular fears of violence . . . .[14]

Despite numerous criminal charges and many arrogant claims by the Wobblies themselves, no IWW other than Joe Hill was ever convicted of destructive or injurious acts. IWWs went to prison on "conspiracy" convictions.

Direct motivation for organizing the IWW arose out of the profound indignation and frustration that western miners experienced in the bloody Cripple Creek, Colorado, labor wars of 1903–04, which lasted for thirteen months. Eventually crushed by vigilantes, hastily deputized sheriffs, police and the militia, the Cripple Creek strike was the first major radical outbreak of the western miners.[15]

Although the wretched western miners, lumberjacks and other vagrant workers of the period understood little of economic and social theory, the philosophy of the IWW leadership was derived from the teachings of George Sorel, the French syndicalist. The visionary promise if not the arguments of his ideas found acceptance among those workers and organizers whose attitude had become radicalized by what they felt to be the failure of the American system and the harmless, empty nature of the WFM and the AFofL.[16]

The WFM represented radical industrial unionism more completely than any other union in the West. But its failure in Colorado and other mining areas drove WFM members to look for more effective methods and hardened their resolution. It was from the militant miners of the WFM that the IWW gained "most of its...bone and sinew...for setting in motion machinery of the new union....It is safe to say that had it not been for the Federation, with its practical strength and the stimulating example of its history, there would have been no I.W.W."[17] The seeds of rivalry were sown in fertile ground.[18*]

Radical industrial unionism also grew out of the failure of the AFofL, covetous, snobbish and traditionally conservative, to recognize the need for industrial organization and out of the AFofL's direct opposition to radical movements. Most organized American labor has always been more craft conscious than class conscious.[19] One labor historian has noted: "The American Federation of Labor, as the alleged embodiment of

---

*The IWW remained a thorn in the side of the WFM. At the twenty-first convention of the Federation in 1914, it was noted that "...there seems to be a concerted movement on the part of the I.W.W. to get in where the W.F.M. are doing good work and disrupt the union." (Brissenden, *The I.W.W.* ... , p. 320.)

everything 'crafty,' has always been the arch enemy of the I.W.W."[20] This rivalry and antagonism proved useful to industrial management, particularly in Bisbee, Arizona, in the summer of 1917.

To the IWW, existing labor organizations were merely convenient adjuncts to capitalistic employers, *de facto* company unions. The opening statement of the IWW constitution reads: "The working class and the employing class have nothing in common."[21] Early organizers and the membership of the IWW were drawn from divergent interest groups who shared a hatred of the capitalistic scheme of things. They felt that the craft organization created three types obnoxious to the labor movement: the "aristocrats" of labor (craft union members), the "union" scabs (union members too "respectable" to strike) and the "labor lieutenants" (union members with loyalties stronger to employers than to the workingmen's cause). Industrial unionists were convinced that collusion existed between labor leaders and certain capitalists. For instance, many times between 1905 and 1910 the AFofL provided strikebreakers to undermine and frustrate the efforts of the IWW.[22] Devout Wobblies never dreamed how much more their own organization would serve American employers as a profitable tool.

A general rise in socialist strength occurred in the United States during the first fifteen years of the twentieth century. By 1910 the Socialists had captured the political control of more than thirty American cities including Milwaukee, Wisconsin; Berkeley, California; and Butte, Montana. Bisbee, Arizona, had a strong Socialist constituency. Eugene Debs, running for President on the Socialist ticket, got 900,000 votes in 1912. Perhaps a third of the delegates at the AFofL conventions at that time were Socialists.[23] By 1911, though, there was a growing hostility toward the IWW by the Socialist Party. The Socialists opposed the professed methods and tactics of IWWism rather than its point of view, organization or its proposal for a society of the future. Having adopted the "boring from within" tactic to change and control existing unions, the IWW avowed (but rarely practiced) a concept of "direct action," i.e., the use of violence and sabotage.[24] Resentful of the IWW militant reputation, the Socialists voted in 1912 to expel from their ranks anyone who advocated violence. The last tie between the IWW and the Socialist Party was broken in February 1913, when Bill Haywood was recalled from the National Executive Committee of the Socialist Party.[25]

After 1913, two distinct branches or characteristics of the IWW began to develop: (1) the doctrinaire eastern wing, more syndicalist, disciplined and dogmatic; and (2) the more libertarian western wing, decentralized, more anarchistic and less Marxist. The antagonism felt toward the WFM and the monolithic AFofL by the westerners was much more intense. Authoritarian IWW leadership was more suited to the masses of immigrant workers in the East than was collective authority. These people appeared to have a greater need for more centralized, affirmative unity and leadership for the long-lasting industrial action which their situation and temperaments demanded. Institutionally oriented, these "new immigration" easterners craved dogmatic platitudes, not skeptical radical thought or western anarchism.[26]

So the IWW looked westward to its birthplace.[27] As it organized toward the Pacific, it met qualified success in the South and Midwest.[28] But the mining and lumber regions of the frontier held the greatest promise for Wobblyism. One writer explained it this way:

> The form which this new kind of unionism [the IWW] took in the next few years owed everything to American conditions. Frontier society in the mines and logging regions of the West was unsophisticated. There were employers on one side and workers on the other. Law enforcement was poor . . . .[29]

The scene demanded a more spontaneous, flexible and comprehensive labor organization (or "disorganization," as some called the IWW) than that needed in settled eastern regions.[30] The IWW appealed to rootless, voteless, womanless, alienated men.

In 1917 the *Seattle Post-Intelligencer* reported that 75 percent of the IWW membership in the Pacific Northwest was 15–21 years of age.[31]

The IWW promise embodied and made dramatically tangible the beliefs, dreams, hopes and visions that promised to the victims of industrial capitalism an escape from the futility of their lives.[32]

There is a "restless temper" among Americans, a compulsion to be mobile. This wandering "theme" or "tradition" has become a well-known American character trait.[33] But not always has it been voluntary. The western IWW oftentimes was a helpless victim of industrialization and he tended to be a drifter who moved westward as a last hope. "The American I.W.W. is a neglected and lonely hobo worker, usually undernourished and in need of medical care," wrote sociologist Carleton H. Parker in 1915," ... a byproduct of the neglected childhood of industrial America."[34] Lured by advertisements promising available work, high wages and permanent employment, job-hunters trekked westward to mining and lumber camps only to be laid off in a short time owing to the caprice of the foremen, company policy and the market. One-half were native Americans. For the immigrant, in spite of the melting-pot slogans and the visible abundance of the nation, America, for them, had become a "kidnapper, a gospeler of false promises, an indifferent and cruel step-mother."[35] Ninety percent of the men were unmarried; the annual labor turnover rate was estimated at 600 percent.[36] By 1916 the discontent of the western ten-day bindle stiff reached a desperate level.[37] His reputation as a cunning, malevolent bomb-thrower, caped and smirking, grew to legendary proportions. With windy braggadocio, the Wobblies delighted in reinforcing their identity as villains *sans rival* in the catalog of American folk myth.

As America grew, more advanced mining technology created a greater need in the mines for the unskilled laborer and, at the same time, decreased the significance of the skilled "miners." Thus the gap between workingman and operator grew greater, the alienation stronger, the ethnic tensions tighter. Militant unionism's time had arrived. At the IWW tenth convention at Chicago in 1916, Dan Buckley asked in the afternoon session of November 23 for an appropriation of $2,000 to organize miners in the West. The Committee on Organization and Constitution carried the proposal 4–1. When Buckley's resolution came before the general committee on November 25, where it also passed, the secretary recorded the remark that the "time is ripe for organization in the mining districts of the West."[38]

While the complaisant mood of Progressive America prevailed, the IWW met little widespread criticism. Though public sympathy during the IWW strike at Lawrence may have been directed mainly toward the brutalized children of the strikers, the Wobblies still were not objects of broad, national contempt.

Taken as a movement, the IWW in 1912 was seen as peaceful. One observer remarked that the IWW should be "more an object of pathetic interest than of fear."[39] But the press and other sources were beginning to discover substantial influence and even treachery in the Wobbly movement. Even certain scholarly sources found power in the feeble feints of the Wobblies.[40] Hostility toward the radical union began to show itself; the IWW became an object of hatred. As contemporary journalist John Fitch observed, an attitude "grew up which permitted 'good' citizens to break the law with impunity when dealing with 'bad' citizens." Fitch wrote in 1915:

> Baiting the I.W.W. has become a pastime in nearly every place in the United States where that organization has made its appearance. Members and leaders have had their constitutional rights atrociously invaded by officials and by "good" citizens.[41]

The IWW bogey idea quickly spread and intensified. Reactionary business interests, eager to discredit any union, wanted the public to see an image of the Wobbly as a lazy hobo whose philosophy was "sabotage" and the overthrow of capitalism. Whatever constructive qualities the IWW possessed, the press suppressed. Tales of IWW outrages gave newspaper readers a thrill.[42] Sensational stories like that of the Everett Massacre in November, 1916, reinforced the iniquitous reputation of the Wobblies, even though the IWW was cleared of blame.[43] American publications carried innumerable stories of IWW sabotage and tyranny. Ole Hanson, the pious mayor of Seattle, later summarized the invective used during this period to describe IWWs:

> The I.W.W. is a sneak and a coward.... Morally dabauching every member by the teachings of cowardice and hate.... The American bolshevists (I.W.W.) fired wheat fields when our army needed wheat, put dead rats and mice in canned food, spiked logs in order to destroy machinery... and did every damned and cowardly thing....[44]

With the coming of the war, logic was discarded and the national excitement colored all issues. Little sympathy could be found for the IWW at the popular level.[45] The *Bisbee Daily Review* carried these verses by Ned White, a Bisbee miner, in its July 10, 1917, issue:

When Kaiser Bill slapped Uncle Sam
and punched him in the face
And Uncle started out to make the
world a decent place
The wobbly saw a chance to knife our
country in the back,
To flag the train of Liberty and blow
it off the track.
They threw right in with Kaiser Bill,
the Turk and all the rest
And did their very best to wreck the
nation they infest.
But Uncle may get tired some day
and clean the rotten mess,
And when he does there's bound to
be a little fun, I guess.

The Wobblies failed to disclaim this invective, almost seeming to wallow in their notoriety. Impotent, illusory, the tiny IWW struggled toward a piteous affirmation of an image that assured its complete defeat. Proud and romantic, the Wobblies refused to admit, or even see, that they were being manipulated to effect the permanence of all the conditions they so desperately sought to change.

Less emotional and more judicious writers perceived the self-destructive weakness of the IWW. These more even-tempered contemporary sources failed to see IWWism as either a menace or a viable social and economic movement. Even in 1912 *The Outlook* commented, "The Industrial Workers are weak as yet," and went on to describe IWW disorganization, innocence, crudity and rawness.[46] A year later, R. F. Hoxie declared that

the American public has been frightened by the impressionistic school of reporters and magazine writers into a vital misconception and tremendous over-estimate of the power and significance of the Industrial Workers of the World.

The union had a "pathetically weak membership" at that time (14,000), and it had never reached 10,000 before 1913.[48] Hoxie pointed out that the IWW as "a body capable of local and spasmodic effort only.... The fact is that the I.W.W. is not an organization but a loosely bound group of uncontrolled fighters." He claimed that the IWW would not be able to make a successful assault on the present social and industrial organization. "The bulk of American workmen," Hoxie contended, "...cares little for the remote future of the revolutionary ideal."[49] A stout Wobbly defender, also writing in 1913, admitted the IWW had "embarrassingly little constructive to offer."[50]

Other weakness debilitated the Wobblies. Leadership inadequacies seemed to plague the organization throughout its existence. Without effective leadership, the IWW constantly found itself in a state of chaos. As one historian noted later, the restless, unstabilized nature of the Wobbly floaters and immigrants left them "an unruly band...unwilling to follow any leadership."[51] The IWW, despite such dynamic organizers as Bill Haywood, was shot through with distrust and stubborness. The lack of constituted authority enabled outsiders to work themselves into positions of power quickly and without attracting suspicion. From its origin, the IWW movement had known opportunists, detectives and other frauds. An "I.W.W. strike" may or may not have been managed by the I.W.W. "Also it may [have been] managed by the I.W.W. leaders but include[d] no appreciable proportion of 'Wobblies' among the strikers."[52] With their representatives in positions of IWW leadership as *agents provocateurs*, employers could discredit the IWW and use the resultant charges of disloyalty and anti-patriotism to obscure the basic economic issues.

So far as the general public was concerned, thanks in part to the *agent provocateur*, all Wobblies were evil and virtually all union members were Wobblies. Since the employer and public officials could typify IWWs (and all other union members) as arch-friends and the dregs of society, they could easily adopt a "hang them all at sunrise attitude." One western small town sheriff was quoted as saying they were "having no trouble at all with the Wobs. When a 'Wobbly' comes to town, I just knock him over the head with a night stick and throw him in the river. When he comes to he beats it out of town." Any poor man without visible means of support "is assumed to be, *ipso facto*, an I.W.W."[53] Paul Brissenden summed up this business:

> By means of an insidious extension of the I.W.W. bogey idea, either that organization itself or some other labor body or both of them are made the "goat" in dis-

putes in which the I.W.W., as an organization, has no part. If a lumber company, for example, gets into a controversy with the shingle weavers union of the American Federation of Labor, it has only to raise a *barrage* and shout through its controlled news columns that "they are 'Wobblies!'" and public opinion is against them. Nor does the misrepresentation stop there. All who openly sympathize with the alleged Wobblies are, forsooth, themselves Wobblies![54]

At one point during the "Big Drive" in the Warren ball park on July 12, 1917, the *Bisbee Daily Review* noted that the distinguishing mark of a "Wobbly" was the refusal to promise to go back to work.[55] One IWW source claims that in the 1913 Wheatland, California, hop riot, *one* IWW was among the 2,300 strikers. Yet the IWW was charged with four deaths in the riot. As capital intended, the frame-up hurt the AFofL in the long run.[56]

Regarding the purported violence, the comments of a Los Angeles policeman seem apropos concerning Arizona. The policeman claimed the Wobblies in his area had committed no overt acts and that the police, raiding IWW halls, were the only ones who were destructive. "In fact, we policemen have been made the tools of big business interests who want to run things," he said. "I'm ashamed of myself for consenting to do their dirty work."[57]

Slackers and Saboteurs

In the effort to further discredit and eventually outlaw the IWW, the baiters of the IWW seized upon the anti-war statements of the Wobblies to capture the attention and outrage of the public. After April of 1917, in particular, the Wobbly refusal to support the war became an expanded and effective propaganda technique.

Single-minded, self-advancing labor groups have been traditionally anti-militaristic. Fearing a domestic use of the army and conscription of workers for capitalistic purposes, labor leaders of the past often sided with pacifists.[58] The IWW vigorously opposed war and conscription, and Bill Haywood articulated the IWW's pacifistic stand.[59] Spiteful union members, reacting to the choice of "slaving to enrich capitalists or dying to protect them," remained passive toward patriotic duties.

When United States Senator Charles S. Thomas of Colorado on June 28, 1917, told his colleagues that the IWW was "sending out the vilest kind of literature showing...that they are against conscription and the war in general," he was not exaggerating.[60] Just a few days earlier, on June 23, the secretary had recorded in the minutes of an IWW meeting in Bisbee that the local had affirmed a communication from the central executive committee in Seattle recommending a general strike throughout the United States as "protest against persecution of I.W.W. members on account of alleged anti-conscription activities."[61] The previous October, at the IWW Tenth Convention, the delegates had resolved to make a "desperate effort to get the working classes to ignore" the United States conscription proclamation of October 3, 1916.[62]

After the conscription proclamation, Jack London stickers "Why Be a Soldier?" had been distributed by Wobblies.[63] One IWW leaflet read, "General Sherman said, 'War is Hell.' Don't go to hell in order to give a bunch of piratical, plutocratic parasites a bigger slice of heaven." From Jerome on April 10, four days after the United States' declaration of war, Frank Little telegrammed Bill Haywood suggesting that a conference of all radical organizations be called to fight compulsory enlistment and to advocate a general industrial strike.[64] *Solidarity*, the organization's weekly, proclaimed in April of 1917:

> A slacker is not a slave who refuses to slit throats or get his hide perforated for the master class. A "slacker" is one who is too cowardly or stupid to join with his fellow workers against the exploiters of labor—one who neglects the interests of himself, his wife and family and of his class in order to make efficient profit or cannon fodder out of his worthless carcass.[65]

While some Wobblies simply refused to register for the draft, many members went to Mexico or into hiding; they often were helped by other people who looked upon draft evasion as a proper and honest thing.[66]

The general pacifistic attitude of labor and the intense anti-war expressions of the Wobblies helped feed the propaganda machine of the anti-IWW forces. National popular sentiments against IWWism rose to an hysterical level. The Wobblies were called the "industrial Ku Klux Klan," as well as Bolsheviks and pro-German traitors.[67] Although the Wobblies boastfully confessed to the charges made that they had wreaked havoc through sabotage across the land, "no members were ever found guilty of planting dynamite or endangering life or property by acts of sabotage" in a court of law.[68] Yet popular will decreed that something had to be done to curb them. On April 11, 1917, a bill (H.R. 2763) was introduced in Congress by Representative Warren Gard of Ohio "to punish acts of interference with the foreign relations, the neutrality, and the foreign commerce of the United States, to punish espionage, and better to enforce the criminal laws of the United States." After a brief stay in the House Committee on the Judiciary, the bill emerged and became the "Espionage Act" on June 15, 1917.[69]

Momentum built up. In the spring and summer of 1917, United States troops, authorized by President Wilson to repress "disloyalty," harassed IWWs. The United States' Department of Justice moved through several policy stages in the summer of 1917, each stage more intensely repressive than the last. Beginning with a concern that was purely local or statewide in scope, the dimensions of repression became a broad federal matter as demands for government action poured in. On July 11, the day before the Bisbee Deportation, all agents and district attorneys were put on the IWW alert. The Bureau of Investigation authorized its agents to infiltrate high IWW positions.[70]

The IWW threat was taken less seriously in the East than in the West. On the other hand, Westerners showed less concern than the Easterners about the war. To Westerners, Socialism and German plots were men-of-straw issues or part of the western rhetoric to get eastern support for the federal repression of Wobblies. Western senators and congressmen condemned the IWW while condoning the mob action they felt was necessary in the absence of federal statutes or the failure to prosecute under existing law.[71] Referring to this behavior on the part of western lawmaker and citizen alike, *The New Republic* observed that "a flame of terror has spread from Bisbee throughout the West." The best thing to do, the journal cooly advised, was to allow the Wobblies to preach their ideas since it was impossible to attribute, specifically, a single lawless act to the IWW.[72] Such attempts to publicize the reality of IWW harmlessness only drew such comments as this one from Montana's Governor Stewart:

It is fatal to attempt to conciliate this element [the IWW].
Get them before they have a chance to start anything, and
put every mother's son away where they can tell their
troubles to the wardens and prison guards.[73]

The general clamor for Wobbly blood resulted in two bills
introduced in the United States Senate in August to suppress
the IWW. As one moderate source noted:

None of these measures attempts to deal with any of
the economic causes of the unrest in the industries
affected—copper mining, lumbering and agriculture, but
all propose to make certain acts on the part of workingmen
punishable as crimes.[74]

A crackdown was underway, and President Wilson gave it his
blessing. IWW philosophy, strikes, and pacifism combined
with molded public opinion, western patriotic zeal (allied with
eastern wartime hysteria) and frontier justice had prompted the
"manhandling" and eventual destruction of the IWW.[75]
One of the most amazing aspects to this story of repression
is the rapidity with which people in America became so hateful
toward Wobblies. The war, the fear of sabotage and treason
and the propaganda from repressive, reactionary and "patriotic" sources had quickly heated public feelings. Writing in
Sunset, Walter V. Woehlke made clear as late as February 1917
that he felt no compulsion to condemn the IWW: "The I.W.W.
is not an immediate menace. Despite the numerous outbreaks
on the Pacific Coast, its far-western ramifications are almost
negligible."[76] The following September Woehlke wrote in *Sunset*: "During the last seven or eight years the Industrial Workers
of the World...have become a major problem in the United
States." True to America's wartime spirit, Woehlke added that
IWWism had "taken up the cudgels for the 'wops' and
'bohunks.'"[77] Thus Americans were primed for the massive
IWW raids of that month, September 1917.[78] Easterners' failure
to take the IWW threat seriously was emphasized by the fact
that in all the IWW roundups everyone arraigned was arrested
—except for those in Chicago—west of the Mississippi River.

"New Blood" and Old Bogies

Soon after the Arizona Constitutional Convention, Will
Clark of the United Verde wrote to Walter Douglas. At that time
(1911) Douglas was general manager of Phelps Dodge's western

operations. Clark ostensibly wrote the letter to agree with the Copper Queen's plan to raise wages; for many years collusion had existed among the mining operators concerning the regulation of wage scales around the state. The letter also made clear the continuation of Clark's interest in getting the mining companies together for an offensive against labor. Somewhat casually he mentioned to Douglas that although Jerome was "not experiencing any labor troubles at present," the WFM had "promised the local agitators that they may start very active trouble in the various Arizona mining camps."[79] This probably was not fresh news to Douglas.

In Walter Douglas, Clark had an ally who could more than match his own zeal for countering labor's political power in the state. Douglas had made little attempt to hide his ambition to rid Arizona of all organized labor.

Labor historian Alexander Bing, looking back over the events of 1916–18, found that where the employers were the most reactionary in Arizona, the union leadership management was the most aggressive and radical. It appeared axiomatic— excessive management conservatism equaled fiery, extreme labor leadership. Bing's studies led him to conclude that ruthless and illegal reprisals by both employers and government officials, although purportedly directed against the IWW, really were attempts to suppress the AFofL and other conservative unions.[80] In his examination of the problem, Vernon Jensen discovered much the same thing. Radical elements of the WFM-IUMMSW (i.e., the IWW) were always much stronger in Arizona than in other states. This characteristic strengthened the charges that Phelps Dodge and other Arizona mining companies hired expert *provocateurs* and imported militant IWWs. But whether the situation was manipulated or natural, it played into the hands of the copper companies. Legitimate IWW leaders had pledged to destroy the IUMMSW.[81]

The IUMMSW (WFM) started downhill in the fall of 1916.[82] By February 1917, for several reasons, the IUMMSW was declining rapidly. When the IUMMSW refused to issue a charter to its Arizona branch owing to the radical and independent nature of the district's constitution, the IWW had a good chance to carry out its November 1916 resolution to organize the state.[83] In Jerome, where Robert Tally and the other operators were so insistent on maintaining an open shop, the conflict between the operators, the Jerome Miners' Union (IUMMSW) and the IWW grew. In addition to importing

Wobblies and hiring detectives, the company took advantage of the growing bitterness between the two unions. More and more men were becoming dissatisfied with the IUMMSW because it was not aggressive enough to challenge the recalcitrant operators.[84]

A new feature developed out of the Arizona labor troubles in 1916–17—the "New Blood" movement. In early 1916 the "New Blood" movement represented part of the national IWW phenomenon. It involved more aggressive, "direct action" techniques than did the older "soapbox" Wobblyism. Since it started with the Agricultural Workers Organization in the wheat fields of the Midwest, the movement reflected the temperament of the western wing of the IWW.[85] The "New Blood" found popularity in Arizona, particularly with the copper mine operators. Galvanized by the Clifton-Morenci affair, resident administrators began to promote the "New Blood" movement in Arizona. They preferred odious radicalism to respectable unionism.

Originally the Arizona "New Blood" movement included a few WFM members in the several districts who began to talk of joining the IWW. One reason these men gave for an allegiance shift was dissatisfaction with the conservative WFM president, Charles Moyer. Moyer, who by now fearfully opposed the IWW, supported continued WFM affiliation with the AFofL. But the greatest cry for "New Blood" came from the mine operators themselves. Phelps Dodge, the United Verde, even the Guggenheim interests wanted Moyer's WFM removed and replaced by the IWW. The Pinkerton Detective Agency echoed this preference. W. A. Burns, a bona fide unionist from Virginia City, Nevada, claimed that whoever supported the "New Blood" slate was consciously undermining legitimate unionism. He stated:

> I am not in accord with the policy pursued by the New Blood advocates....I saw the work...in 1914 by some men who are now advocating the New Blood slate — detectives and others who do not want any union. ...They may be able to accomplish the destruction of the Western Federation of Miners.[86]

Copper Era, a trade paper financed by the copper corporations, vigorously endorsed two "New Blood" union leaders in Arizona, J. L. Donnelly and George Powell. Some people questioned their loyalty to labor interests; both men were described by old-time unionists as "self-seeking."[87]

Late in January 1917, IWW organizer Grover H. Perry left Chicago to found an Arizona state IWW chapter in Phoenix. Arriving on February 1, Perry by chance met state IUMMSW leader J. L. Donnelly who asked Perry "what so many Wobblies were doing in Arizona." Donnelly, showing considerable frustration, complained about the unwillingness of the IUMMSW local at Bisbee to endorse a national charter. In a gesture of conciliation, Donnelly then asked that Perry's IWW support Donnelly and Powell "in bucking Moyer." In that case, prognosticated Donnelly, "everything will turn out lovely." To a smiling, unresponsible Perry, the Arizona labor leader concluded that the Wobbly organization should consider his offer since the IWW "had no future in Arizona." Called "Metal Mine Workers Industrial Union #800," the IWW chapter intended to organize active IWW locals in all of the state's mining camps. Frank Little and Pedro Coria were the most successful recruiters.[88]

Throughout Arizona in February and March the IWW accelerated its organization drives. Then in April, men who carried IUMMSW union cards were discharged in the Globe-Miami area with the simultaneous hiring of those who did not. Arizona IUMMSW organizer H. L. McCluskey claimed later that copper companies imported IWWs at company expense to take the jobs of discharged IUMMSW members.[89]

Company officials allegedly imported "New Blood" supporters to work in the mines so that managers could claim that radicals existed among their workers. The operators then had an excuse to discharge older employees who belonged to the IUMMSW. The "New Blood" movement served as a single identity for all unionists. In the fall of 1916, after the Western Federation of Miners changed its name to "International Union of Mine, Mill and Smelter Workers," a newcomer to Bisbee, James Chapman, took little time getting himself elected to secretary of the Bisbee local of the IUMMSW. Chapman bragged of having broken the Butte IUMMSW union. In the spring of 1917, he became an aggressive IWW organizer. Many people felt sure James Chapman worked for the copper companies.[90]

AFofL officials and other union leaders began to protest that the cry of "I.W.W." had been raised by employers in order to stamp out all unionism.[91] In Jerome the *Sun* later charged:

> It was only last spring that the United Verde Copper Company assisted in bringing organizers of the I.W.W. into the state for the purpose of fostering it as a rival of the regular miners' union and to use them to bump their heads against each other and eventually demolish organized labor in Arizona.

The *Sun* claimed that this condition finally reached a state in which "every person not agreeing with Mr. Tally in everything was an I.W.W."[92]

One IWW source claims that before the Jerome strike of June 1917, IWW leaders realized the copper companies were playing the unions against each other. The Wobbly leaders thereupon dropped some of their demands in an attempt to ally themselves with the IUMMSW.[93]

The patterns in Jerome and Bisbee were similar. In each place the IWW tried to take over the IUMMSW. In each place the regular union was weak, and in Bisbee radicalism had never been a real political threat. The loyalty and independence of the Cornish Cousin Jacks had always complemented the dedicated anti-union attitude of Phelps Dodge.[94] As elsewhere, men were discharged or refused work in Bisbee because of their political affiliations.[95] Bisbee miners had been politically active for years, but company officials did not fear bringing Wobblyism to Bisbee. Glisio Chukovich, a deportee, claimed, "The company put their own 'stoolies' in the unions. The company then sponsored a drive to get rid of the unions. They feared a non-company union."[96] The situation provoked suspicion, and the principal organizer of the IWW in Bisbee, James Chapman, did appear, indeed, to be an *agent provocateur*.[97]

John H. Walker, a member of President Wilson's Mediation Commission sent to Bisbee to investigage labor problems in November 1917, declared Chapman was "a gunman and stool pigeon and private detective for the copper companies."

At least two events aided the corporation's defamation of the IUMMSW in the spring of 1917 in Arizona. First, the recent inauguration of Tom Campbell as governor gave the companies more confidence to deal forthrightly with labor; responsible IUMMSW members who opposed the IWW made charges that mass dismissals started when Tom Campbell became governor. Second, the declaration of war on April 6 intensified public hostility toward radicals. It inspired the mayor of Globe to designate April 8 as "Loyalty Day" at which time the IWW received a vitriolic denunciation as being un-American. For the majority of people outside of labor who made no distinction between the IWW and the AFofL, *all* union members *were* Wobblies and traitors.[98]

Arizona mine operators welcomed Wobbly activity. Without effective leadership, without a sizeable membership, the Arizona IWWs served as a useful counterforce against more independent and conservative unionism. Shrewdly the operators gained control of Arizona labor activity and directed it according to their will.

6

MOVING TOWARD A SHOWDOWN

For a number of reasons, labor unrest increased in 1917. Workers were dissatisfied as a consequence of extraordinary wartime corporate profits, high prices, overwork and labor's being asked to surrender its few privileges. Also, some of the general conditions that came to characterize later twentieth century labor dissatisfaction already were in evidence: inefficiency, lack of security against unemployment, the feeling of anonymity and impotence of working in a huge organization and in disagreeable, unclean, unhealthy, unsafe and tedious working conditions.[1] Wages were not keeping pace with rising costs and workers wanted security against unemployment to do their best. One writer at the time could have been speaking about the Arizona problem when he said that "the rapid growth of large scale business has widened the gulf between master and man. Shop managers and foremen have been appointed because of their technical knowledge rather than their knowledge of men."[2] Gordon S. Watkins, an American labor economics scholar, later added: "The fact that mining...industries of the West are owned and controlled by persons who reside in the East has a significant bearing upon the growth of industrial unrest." He went on to say that owners, managers and directors were indifferent to the importance of labor problems. The primary concern of administrators in industry, Watkins pointed out, was profits. Managers lived in constant fear of owners.[3]

Mining, smelting and refining copper ore required enormous capital investment. Therefore only large corporations could make production profitable. In an effort to keep down costs, copper companies, like other businesses, invested in professional efficiency experts and other engineering talent. As F. Harcourt Kitchins wrote in October 1917,

> Our big industries of the present-day are run by professional managers who...are put in charge of their industries because they have proved their capacity to conduct them successfully. Capital buys the brains and experience of those men and pays them handsomely, but values them absolutely by results—by the profits which they are able to earn.

Concerned with making money, management, Kitchins explained, knew little and cared less about the struggles of labor.[4]

Miners' Revolt and Public Reaction

Gordon Watkins, searching for particulars, observed that employers insisted on dealing with individual employees. More specifically, he claimed that the copper companies discriminated against the members of trades unions. Obviously the enmity managers felt for the IUMMSW resulted from the pressure they received from the head office to capitalize on the wartime opportunity. Workers responded accordingly. "Industrial unrest is in itself a symptom and not a disease," Watkins claimed. The laboring population was not disloyal but wanted its wages adjusted to the high prices of the war if it could not share in the added profits. "The failure to establish collective regulation of the conditions of employment," he said, "may be characterized as the central cause of our labor difficulties."[5] Arizona miners, having had a taste of real power in Arizona from 1908 to 1916, could not be passive or benign. Like their fellow workers around the country, they felt compelled to do something.

National union membership, which was 2,582,600 in 1915, rose 7.4 percent to 2,772,700 in 1916 and then climbed 10.4

percent to 3,061,400 in 1917.[6] Mobilization for war caused employment dislocation and a shifting of the labor population. This produced, in many places, a great wage disparity among workers. A general labor shortage plus employee awareness of the huge corporate profits gave labor the greatest leverage and motivation in its history.[7] A cessation of immigration in 1914 contributed to the labor shortage and strengthened union confidence.

As union membership soared, so union ferment increased. The year 1916 saw three times as many strikes as did 1914, while a greater percentage of the strikes was provoked by demands for an increase in wages (two-thirds in 1916 as opposed to one-half in 1914). The high employment turnover and faulty distribution of labor resulted in large numbers of migratory workers who were restless, insecure and dissatisfied.[8]

American labor unions called four thousand two hundred and thirty-three strikes in the war year of 1917. A record national high up until that time, it remained a record for some years to come. Three thousand of the strikes occurred between April 6, 1917, and October 6, 1917. The mining industry accounted for four hundred and seven of the strikes. In metaliferrous mining, strikes totaled forty-three in 1916, ninety-four in 1917. Arizona strikes totaled seven and twenty for the two respective years.[9] Provocative conditions and new strength made labor more active than ever before. And the mining companies were stiffening further their intransigence.

In Arizona, the first significant strike to follow the Clifton-Morenci deadlock in 1915–16 began in Ajo in November 1916. It lasted only sixty days before the miners capitulated. So thoroughly broken was this Ajo walkout, that Ajo did not even become part of the massive strike program in the spring and summer of 1917. The first strike in Arizona in 1917—an IWW affair—did not, interestingly enough, hit the copper mines. Wobblies first struck the Goodyear Rubber Company at Litchfield, west of Phoenix, where Goodyear was attempting to grow Pima long-staple cotton to make cording for tires. The German U-boats had cut off the supply of Egyptian long-staple cotton.[10]

The first strike in the copper mines for the year 1917 was not IWW led. It was called at Jerome on May 25 by the International Union of Mine, Mill, and Smelter Workers, the newly adopted name of the old Western Federation of Miners. Aimed at securing higher wages and union recognition, the strike ended quickly, on May 31. Interference by the IWW with the IUMMSW prompted the bulk of the miners to return to work.[11] Jerome workers were not yet ready for radicalism.

In Globe and Miami, the IUMMSW voted on June 30 to strike at 7:00 A.M. But on July 1, the IWW called a strike for that afternoon. The mines shut down and seven thousand men went out. The new governor, Thomas Campbell, went to Globe on July 4. A federal conciliator, John McBride, was brought in, and ex-Governor G. W. P. Hunt was appointed President Wilson's special investigator to study the labor problems in Arizona.

After the Globe walkout, strikes sprang up around the state—one in Morenci, another in Jerome, and one in Bisbee, where the workers went out on June 27.[12]

Demands seemed legitimate. In brief, the Arizona strikers wanted safer working conditions, the abolition of any kind of discriminatory hiring practice, more job security, a small wage increase and some form of union recognition.[13]

Taking advantage of the general mining prosperity of the times, a new publication, the *Arizona Mining Journal*, appeared in June 1917. In its maiden edition the *Journal* dared to say, "We feel deeply that there is much more in the employment of a man than an exchange of chattel value."[14]

This was a minority attitude. Most newspapers and other periodicals condemned the workers for their greed, lack of patriotism and outright sedition. The IWW, already branded "un-American," had now become a symbol for treason, sabotage and conspiracy. Even the cosmopolitan *New York Times* carried many editorials questioning the loyalty of the foreign-born (including the "disloyalty" of the Lutheran Church). It indicted, tried, convicted and sentenced the IWW. The program of the IWW, claimed the *Times*, "calls for the destruction of industries until capital surrenders."[15]

On July 1 the *Bisbee Daily Review* headlined that the citizens in Helena, Montana, had asked for protection from the "IWW mobs." That same day, the *Review* carried an editorial warning that the "I.W.W. and their tools and agents and dupes are striking against the success and safety of our government's soldiers when they strike in the great copper mines that must be depended upon to furnish guns and shells for our armies...." Calling the strike "vicious, wicked, senseless, unpatriotic," the *Review* praised those miners not on strike, "those soldiers in the trenches at Bisbee."[16] The *Los Angeles Times*, the same day, claimed the strike demands were an "excuse for anarchistic aims." "Their aim," the *Times* said of the strikers, "is socialistic assimilation of all property."[17]

Showing no less propensity for peddling hysteria, *The New York Times*, also on July 1, quoted a letter from Butte: "The I.W.W. . . . are known in this community for their radical views of the most violent socialistic type . . . [and] the . . . strike is being engineered from German sources and financed by German money."[18] Two days later, the *Review* editorialized that for Arizona, "the youngest state in the sisterhood, is reserved a cross heavier than the bloodthirsty Iroquois" which cursed New York in the old days or the Ohio floods or the Dakota blizzards or the Kansas grasshoppers. "The agents of the I.W.W. travel across the state like a pestilence."[19]

An ugly mood was building for a showdown. Public hostility, spurred by the exhortations of the press, increased daily. The intensity of war hysteria in Arizona may have lagged behind that felt along the East Coast, but public animosity toward "seditious elements" gradually increased.

With labor divided and reeling, the strategy of the employer offensive shifted. By protesting the war in general and demanding more of industry's earnings, labor had played into the hands of management. Labor's apparent greed shocked the American people. Following through, employers worked the sedition explanation of labor unrest to conceal from the public eye the basic reasons for the workingman's dissatisfaction.[20] By reminding the public of the Mooney-Billings case of the year before, management's propaganda advertised the treasonous nature of the IWW and the presence of "enemy aliens" in the labor movement.[21] The strategy worked. In the spring of 1916, at the Third Session of the Arizona State Legislature, Mrs. Pauline O'Neill introduced a resolution "denouncing the I.W.W. and all its works." Thirty-one representatives voted for it, none against.[22]

This shift in popular opinion resulted not only from the newly discovered opportunity on the part of management to stamp radical labor groups as "treasonous." For some time management had maintained a general campaign to promote a fanatical antagonism toward all organized labor. In 1917 employers labeled all strikers in Arizona as "Wobblies," "aliens" or "pro-Germans." The companies pictured as anarchists and saboteurs anyone who criticized them.[23] On the other hand, accounts of war-profiteering intensified workers' frustrations causing them to react in a way that made it easy for employers to accuse them of "treasonous activities." Labor's unenthusiastic position on conscription and its inherent pacifism seemed indeed to support the allegations of the employers.[24]

But after the declaration of war in early April of 1917, the true conservative nature of many Arizona union members began to show itself. In particular, those from the craft groups, indignant at what they felt was a lack of patriotism, broke away from miners' unions. And so the never very strong Arizona labor movement, despite the general unhappiness over labor's failure to share in wartime profits, broke further apart. Thus divided, its conquest was inevitable.[25]

With labor itself split into two passionate sides, the IWW sensed an opportunity to strengthen its membership at the expense of the IUMMSW. It continued its aggressive campaign to organize the mining camps of Arizona in the late spring of 1917.[26] Where employer resistance and propaganda were strongest, the IWW found its most frustrated and promising candidates. Operators appreciated this IWW response to employer adamancy since conservative union members offered too unconvincing a target to arouse the kind of public antipathy and hostility management desired. After his trip to the West, New York newspaperman Robert Bruere quoted large lumber operators as saying that "we have taken advantage of the general prejudice against them [the IWW] as an unpatriotic organization to beat their strike."[27] The copper companies used the same technique. Through their newspapers and public relations spokesman, they tried to inflame the public against the "Wobblies," which meant practically any member of any union. In Montana the situation reached a condition similar to that in Arizona. One historian has commented:

> Anaconda seemed intent on a showdown. Its detective informers were high in the ranks of the Butte I.W.W. In violently incendiary speeches these company provocateurs encouraged their cohorts to adopt a position

that the government would define as seditious and disloyal. In other words, the copper company was having its
paid agents help organize a wartime strike against itself
as a ruse for the indictment and elimination of the local
"radical menace."[28]

Arizona managers also knew the public had learned to
label all union activity as "seditious." Operators were educated
and sophisticated enough to know that no real danger was
involved.[29] Apart from the rhetoric, studies have shown that
employers tended to be indifferent to social ideologies. In fact,
employers preferred and encouraged militant, radically dominated unions to tractable, conservative ones. By using the IWW
radicalism as a smoke screen, they could easily bring ruinous
action against all unions. From their own experience, mine
employers knew they risked nothing by such tactics and in fact
would gain much.[30]

One can see that mining operators might welcome the
IWW to their mining camps and even pay for their importation.
To carry out the rest of their plan, however, they needed the
support of law officers and some citizens of the community.
This proved to be quite easy.

Through the years, an attitude had blossomed in the
United States which implied that "good" or "respectable" citizens may with impunity break the law when dealing with "bad"
or "disreputable" citizens.[31] The IWW had declared in 1910,
"What the mine owners fail to do by force [themselves] they
have accomplished through civic federation methods."[32] Without the military, warned the "Council of Defense" in Butte,
citizens would be forced to take the law into their own hands.
"I can get a mob up here in twenty-four hours and hang half-
a-dozen men," boasted W. A. Clark.[33] Vigilantes served
employers gladly.

Despite the public railing against the Wobblies, IWW
members received peculiar favors from the copper companies.
In Butte, as in Bisbee, a large number of Wobblies were working in the mines, although several thousand non-IWWs had
been dismissed or refused work. There were more IWWs working where the rustling card was used than where it was not.
Understandably, the employers in Arizona who were charged
with importing IWWs into the state were denying employment
to staunch IUMMSW men. But most of even the informed public overlooked these facts. In his Sixth Annual Report (1918), the

United States Secretary of Labor noted that unusual IWW strength existed in areas where management had taken the strongest stand against union growth. But he drew no conclusions. When responsible public officials such as Secretary Wilson could not see any but the most obvious connection between IWW strength and anti-war sentiment, it is not surprising that public opinion should have been so obtuse. The stage had been set in Bisbee for the Workman's Loyalty League and the Citizen's Protective League.[34]

Apart from its political triumphs, organized labor did make a few gains in Arizona between 1900 and 1917. But the history of the struggle between labor and management in the state during this period must be seen as only a flash of hope for the workers. Some advances were indeed realized, but they were extremely limited. No peaceful forms of collective bargaining had been established; the adamant stand of the managers in resisting the closed shop had paid off handsomely. Major legislation that favored labor was never enforced. Much of it was later repealed or declared unconstitutional by the courts. Many of the liberal Arizona constitutional provisions were eventually ignored. Rather than being a reflection of any substantial influence gained by labor, the legislation which remained appeared as a sop to reformist middle-class sentiment. Most of the concessions involving working conditions were minor ones.

After the controversial defeat of G. W. P. Hunt in the disputed election of 1916, mass discharges began of men who had been prominent in union or political activities. Not only did the war afford a favorable situation for the copper companies, it intensified their desire to rid Arizona, once and for all, of any irritation from organized labor.

Since investigations indicated that no acts of violence or sabotage could be attributed to IWW or other union activity in Bisbee prior to the deportation, the reputation of sedition that labor unions managed to acquire seems all the more remarkable. In its dispatch from Bisbee on November 6, 1917, the President's Mediation Commission reported that up until the day of the vigilante roundup, "Conditions in Bisbee were, in fact, peaceful and free from any manifestations of disorder or violence."[35]

But in the statewide offensive against labor, operators had effectively roused public antagonism toward striking miners.

Bisbee was but one example. In Jerome, Bisbee's Arizona sister mining camp more than three hundred miles to the north, a similar (but less dramatic) pattern of circumstances had developed earlier among its managers, miners and townspeople.

The Precedent of Jerome

Many of the conditions that preceded and characterized the Bisbee Deportation could be found in Jerome. Indeed, Jerome was a close member of the copper mining family which included Butte and Bisbee. All three mining camps were located in remote and barren sites. All three were dominated by autocratic copper barons.[36]

In 1865, Al Sieber, a noted guide and army scout, spotted mineral promise near the deposit which later accounted for Jerome's existence. But he never filed his claim or worked it. The first recorded claim in Jerome (which conflicts with some of the local stories) was made on February 19, 1876, by Josiah Riley, John O. Dougherty and John P. Kelly. Later in 1876, a rich outcropping of copper was discovered there by Morris A. Ruffner. Two claims, the "Eureka" and the "Wade Hampton," caused a small boom. Shortly before becoming territorial governor in 1882, Frederick A. Tritle, representing a New York syndicate, purchased the claims made by Ruffner, Dougherty, Kelly and others. That same year, 1882, a group led by Tritle formed the United Verde Copper Company. The organizers named the camp for Eugene Jerome, a New York lawyer and manager of the enterprise.[37]

In his first trip to Arizona in 1880, Dr. James Douglas visited the Verde Valley to inspect the Ruffner holdings. Although at that time Douglas considered the location too isolated to be profitable, he recommended the property to two Philadelphia investors, and they purchased it. In 1887 Douglas returned to the site, by now in new hands and named "Jerome." Deciding the property was very promising, he recommended its purchase to Phelps Dodge. Negotiations proceeded smoothly up until the last hour when the Tritle group raised the price to a level unacceptable to Phelps Dodge.

Two years earlier, in 1885, the notorious copper king of Montana, William Andrews Clark, had developed a strong interest in the United Verde. When the Phelps Dodge people dropped their negotiations for the property in 1888, Clark stepped in and acquired it.[38] He built a narrow-gauge railroad into Jerome and, from 1912 to 1915, constructed a huge, modern smelter on the valley floor, two thousand feet lower than the mine and four miles down the mountainside from Jerome at "Clarkdale." Clark was the sole operator of the United Verde until his death in 1925.[39]

In May 1917 the IUMMSW, which had made its first strong organizational move in Jerome six months earlier, failed to enlist a sizeable membership. Although the Jerome miners felt as dissatisfied as those in Butte or Globe or Bisbee over the rising cost of living and the failure to share in copper production profits, few dared to be unionists. The United Verde assistant general manager, Robert E. Tally, denied it, but the men felt that their jobs were at stake if they organized local labor unions. Their fears had substance; many who joined a union found themselves immediately dismissed.

Like Bisbee, Jerome had its labor problems. For the first few years of the twentieth century, unions in Jerome did not thrive. Organizers of the WFM and IWW got only a scattered, passive response. Company agents usually handled union officials with ease. But in 1909, the IWW officers in Jerome suddenly became so difficult that the United Verde Copper Company put up its own candidate, John Opman, for office of union secretary-treasurer. The men were paid to get out and vote. Opman was elected 108–58—in a camp with several thousand miners. The Jerome IWW executive board then became company appointees. Such was the extent of pre-war Wobblyism in Jerome.[40] In addition to the war boom, 1917 saw a new bonanza strike in Jerome. After several years of property acquisition and development, James S. "Rawhide Jimmy" Douglas, Walter Douglas' brother, hit a large, rich mass of high-grade copper ore. In 1917, this United Verde Extension mine produced 64,000,000 pounds of copper.[41]

When the IWW campaign to organize the western mining camps hit Jerome in 1917, the mine managers maintained their easy control. The managers easily broke the first strike at Jerome; after a strike vote was taken on May 21, 1917, practically every man who voted "yea" was discharged.[42]

Any IWW threat in Jerome in 1917 was illusory. Participants in the May strike, for example, included only 100 Wobblies among 4,000 miners. Yet the IUMMSW members and even non-union miners found it difficult escaping the IWW label. To be a miner, it seemed, was to be an enemy agent.

In February, the state IUMMSW representative, H. S. McCluskey, hoping for cooperation, had gone to Jerome and advised against a walkout. (Men seen talking to McCluskey were fired, although most were later reinstated.) However, miners' discontent accelerated and by May 22, McCluskey, chafed by the intractable managers, endorsed the strike. That night McCluskey was awakened and taken from his room by armed and masked men. They drove him out of town about thirty miles and dumped him there. He walked to Dewey, the nearest stage stop, and by way of Prescott was back in Jerome a day later.[43]

On the evening of May 23, UVCC Assistant General Manager Tally gave a demonstration of the kind of uncompromising determination the Arizona mine managers had finally resolved to adopt. Tally met with Arizona American Federation of Labor President J. L. Donnelly and a committee from the Jerome local IUMMSW. The committee had, again, asked for the Miami Scale, the closed shop, the check-off and a grievance committee. Tally informed them that the Miami Scale had gone into effect on May 16 (after being set up in the company's favor), but he refused to consider their other demands.[44]

The next day Tally met again with the miners' representatives together with McCluskey and W. A. Burns, executive board member of the IUMMSW. Burns, who had been Tally's boyhood friend in Virginia City, Nevada, even tried to appeal to the mine manager's side.[45] But the mine operator was unyielding. Tally said the United Verde Copper Company had "a contract to supply the United States Government with copper during the period of the war." Then he claimed the union strike was "irregular and crooked." With restrained indignation, Tally went on to praise the "fair and just manner" of the union representatives, but he called the union "selfish and unpatriotic." His implication was clear enough; he wanted to recognize the men in his office only as people apart from the union they were supposed to represent.[46] This stubborn unwillingness to recognize the unions characterized the two Arizona copper kingdoms.

Tally and the IUMMSW representatives discussed the situation further. McCluskey denied charges that the IWW had infiltrated the Jerome local, that the union had used any intimidation in getting a strike vote or that the vote was in any way "irregular and crooked." "We deny it, absolutely," McCluskey asserted. The two sides talked for about forty-five minutes; the union men rephrased their earlier complaints and attempted to cajole Tally into some kind of compromise. But the mine managers remained steadfast, even unperturbed. Finally Tally, his patience wearing, announced: "Now to be frank, we are going to do what we can to operate...we realize, and you realize, that something is likely to happen, and things then go from bad to worse. But my instructions to our men are that we are on the defensive." McCluskey then notified Tally that the union men understood if an agreement was not reached in this meeting, the four o'clock shift would not report. Burns made one last personal plea to Tally, but Tally replied, "We are going to fight it out."[47]

On May 24, at 7:00 P.M., about 1,500 employees of the United Verde walked out. It was the first strike in Jerome's history, the first wartime copper strike in Arizona and, some said, the first strike ever against property owned by William Andrews Clark. At the last minute the pay rate of miners was boosted from $5.00 to $5.25 a day, but this raise did not apply to muckers and trammers. United Verde was playing upon the elitist values of the workingmen to divide them. But the miners failed to be satisfied. They wanted still higher wages, a closed shop, the check-off system and, most of all, union recognition with bargaining power. Two hundred Mexicans, affiliated with the Liga Protectora Latina, remained at work and were daily escorted through the picket lines by armed guards.[48]

As soon as the strike started, Secretary of Labor William B. Wilson appointed John McBride, a prominent union labor man, as federal mediator. McBride went to Jerome, as did Governor Thomas Campbell and Lt. Col. J. J. Hornbrook, Seventeenth Cavalry (sent to find out if troops were needed as claimed by the sheriff), on May 28. Since the copper company officials refused to recognize the union, separate daily meetings were held between the managers and McBride and between the union leaders and McBride.[49]

The IWW seized the opportunity to intrude. Some clashes erupted between the IUMMSW members and IWWs. At an IWW mass meeting in the Opera House, well attended by mine managers and town businessmen, IWW organizers Frank Little and Grover Perry received liberal applause from the non-union segment of the audience. It became clear that the IWW and the managers had a common rival. Afterward, the Jerome miners charged the IWW members with being union smashers and with having company detectives as their leaders.

According to the *Jerome Sun*, the United Verde Copper Company owned the Opera House. When he heard the lessee of the Opera House had granted its use to the Jerome Miners Union, Tally told the lessee that he would cancel the lease if the meeting was held. Yet two days later the IWW not only was permitted to use the Opera House for its mass meeting, but the company paper, the *Jerome News*, extravagantly publicized the affair and encouraged everyone to attend.[50]

On May 26, the Jerome Miners Union accused the mine officials of staging the Opera House meeting and of giving jobs to IWW members while denying employment to members of other labor organizations. The next day the IWW representatives, realizing the benefit to management of their divisive role, said they would be willing to cooperate with the IUMMSW.[51]

Tension rose in Jerome, and the officials on the scene did little to mitigate it. On Monday, May 28, without any apparent provocation, Jerome Mayor J. J. Cain sent out a "dodger" with "WARNING" emblazoned across it, declaring that all women and children were prohibited from being in the business section of Main Street until further notice. This same warning was carried in the local newspapers for several days.[52] Jerome citizens paid little attention, however, and life went on as usual.

Mine owners felt the miners would accept a crumb; on May 31, 1917, Tally wrote to Conciliator McBride saying the company would not grant the check-off or the closed shop but that the Miami Scale was acceptable. (Tally had set that up two weeks earlier, to the company's advantage.*) He also promised not to discriminate against members of any union and to rehire all former employees. But the United Verde did not intend to recognize any union; Tally's letter specified that he would only recognize grievance committees "representing the employees," and he said that the committees were "to be selected from men actually in our employ."[53]

By a close vote on June 2, the miners accepted Tally's "concessions" 467 to 431, and the union formally declared the strike off on Sunday, June 3.[54] The men went back to work; but the settlement was to be very short-lived. A brief interlude would

---

*In both Bisbee and Jerome, one of the IWW demands later in the month was to *eliminate* the Miami Scale and provide a guaranteed daily wage. The Miami Scale had proven to be full of loopholes (among them the alleged fixing of copper price quotations) that were to corporate advantage. (Callender, "True Facts...," p. 10.)

enable both sides to rally for the decisive battle in the war for control of Arizona.

Bisbee: January–July, 1917

The Jerome strikers acted in concert with disgruntled miners all over the state; their actions anticipated by only a few weeks a broader program of strike activity. The same unrest existed in Globe-Miami, Clifton-Morenci and, of course, Bisbee. Ajo, the only other large mining area in the state and even more isolated than these other communities, had seen its weak, tentative challenge of corporate power smashed beyond recovery in January. The IUMMSW appeared strongest at Globe, but Globe miners, heeding advice from their organizers, did not strike. They felt they were strong enough to get recognition. They were wrong. P. G. Beckett, general manager of the Old Dominion, the largest and best-known mine in Globe, was just as stubborn as other Arizona resident administrators.* The miners' protest remained a stand-off. But the IWW in the Globe-Miami area failed to get the strength it had found in Jerome; the IUMMSW had too much support. So the Wobblies looked for someplace more vulnerable.[55]

More so even than the Jerome local, the Bisbee Miners Union was weak. Although the Bisbee local was one of the oldest and most politically active in the state, it had never really dared to challenge Phelps Dodge and the other mining companies directly. This fact itself added to the ignominy of the workers, particularly those newer, less skilled men who felt faint loyalty to the copper companies. So overpowering was the copper companies' campaign to inhibit successful unionism in Bisbee, that those men who dared to continue their WFM (IUMMSW) membership had to do so almost surreptitiously. Some carried their membership cards in their shoes for years.[55]

Popular belief has it that the IWW did not organize in Bisbee until the spring of 1917. But a book published in 1914 which discussed only the "potential power" of Arizona labor activity, listed three IWW locals in the state in 1914: Phoenix (Local 272), Bisbee (Local 65) and Lowell (Local 65, branch 2).[56] Apparently the local, dormant through 1916, was activated

---

*The capital stock of the Old Dominion Copper Mining and Smelting Company was held by the individual officials of Phelps Dodge rather than by Phelps Dodge itself. (Cleland, p. 134.)

on January 27, 1917, as part of the broad IWW organization drive pledged at the November 1916 Chicago convention. The IWW easily captured the IUMMSW local by the middle of May 1917.[57]

On June 1, Grover Perry sent out a bulletin to the several Arizona branches of the "Metal Mine Workers Industrial Union No. 800" announcing that the Arizona chapter's first annual convention would be held in Bisbee on June 15 at 9:00 A.M. in the Miners' Union Hall on O.K. Street. "All paid up members eligible to attend," stated the bulletin. Describing the Jerome strike as a victory for the miners, Perry's announcement said the union "now must go after the six-hour-day."[58]

At the conference in Bisbee the subject of a strike came up, but organizers Frank Little and Grover Perry advised against it. But the strike fever was too strong and the membership drew up some standard demands. The items were voted on and approved, but the miners decided to claim their demands were coming from the IUMMSW instead of the IWW. When he got back to his Phoenix office, Grover Perry sent a wire to the Chicago IWW office advising Haywood that the miners were on the verge of a statewide strike. Perry asked the Wobbly chief if he could come to Arizona to help restrain the emotion-driven workers, but Haywood—his hands full with IWW activity in all parts of the country—remained in Chicago.[59]

On June 26 spokesmen for the Bisbee IWW announced their goals. A committee headed by Chairman Ben. H. Webb and composed of local labor leaders M. C. Sullivan, W. H. Davis, J. G. Payne, A. S. Embree and Charles Tannehill presented the strikers' demands to the Bisbee mine managers. (Noticeably absent from these names was that of suspected *provocateur* James Chapman, the most rabid of the Bisbee Wobbly organizers.) Nothing extreme lay within the prosaic list[60]:

1. Abolition of the physical examination.
2. Two men to work on machines.
3. Two men to work in raises.
4. Discontinuance of all blasting during shifts.
5. Abolition of all bonus and contract work.
6. Abolition of the sliding scale of wages. All men working underground to be paid a minimum flat scale of $6.00 per shift, and top men $5.55.
7. No discrimination against members of any organization.

The union had aimed the demands in two very practical directions: increased safety for men in the mines and protection from company exploitation. Job and wage security were paramount; the Miami Sliding Scale had proven to be a perfidious pitfall. Also, the demands did not reflect in any way on IWW ideological commitment to George Sorel's industrial syndicalism.

These particular demands got little publicity. Instead, the wire services reported a more drastic list issued by Arizona IWW Secretary-Treasurer Grover H. Perry as representing the Bisbee miners' request. Most of the items on Perry's list were either similar to or as routine as the Bisbee demands. But this publicized requisition did include such extreme demands as the closed shop, the six-hour "collar to collar" day and the six-day work week. From Salt Lake City on July 10 Grover Perry sent a letter to the Bisbee IWW Executive Comittee saying the demand for the six-hour day was imperative. Somewhat irritated by the Bisbee local's independence, Perry took the opportunity to admonish the local for going out too soon. The Bisbee convention in June had decided, Perry reminded the Committee, to wait for a universal or statewide strike announcement. The Bisbee local had acted too independently, and Perry insisted that now the six-hour day "must be included" in their demands. These instructions reached the committee only after its members had been removed to Columbus, New Mexico.[61]

As might be expected in Bisbee, the mine managers—the most implacable in Arizona—ignored the demands. In a gesture of contempt, Copper Queen Mine Superintendent Gerald Sherman tore up the list presented him. This act, more than any other one thing, infuriated, solidified and made more resolute those miners who were dissatisfied. The local union leaders immediately called a strike without the benefit of a general vote. All the leaders then identified openly with the IWW.[62] The assonance of the names "International Union of Mine, Mill, and Smelter Workers" and "Metal Mine Workers' Industrial Union" (the new IWW name perhaps having been adopted with that thought in mind) confused the already emotionally charged citizens of Bisbee. Quite ignorant of union designations and the details of union organizations and activity, they found it easy to think of any union member as a "Wobbly." Wartime hysteria, provoked by national publicity and fast-circulating rumors, deepened the fear and antagonism of the Bisbeeites.

On June 27 the Bisbee miners walked out. The strike immediately became a focus of national attention. The June 29 editon of the *New York Times* headlined: "Big Copper Strike Blamed on Germans."[63] Company officials claimed IWW leaders in Arizona were working with German agents to stir up German and Austrian miners. Newspapers and other publications over the country, as they had been doing for several months, labeled all strikers as "aliens," "Wobblies" or "traitors." Ethnic insults, in particular, were used, and company officials lined up the loyal Allies vs. the Central Powers as the respective sides in the labor war. A report from Bisbee's sister city, Butte, where a strike was also in progress, cited a German and an Irishman as troublemakers, while "the Cornish, Welsh, and Serbian miners together with the loyal Americans...have consistently refused to have anything to do with what they regard as an effort engineered by German sympathizers to stop the mining of copper and zinc."[64]

The Butte release claimed that the "Allies" represented over 50 percent of the work force, thus suggesting that the troublemaking Central Power agents, i.e., the strikers, constituted a minority. In Bisbee, Phelps Dodge estimated 50 percent of the miners were off at the Copper Queen, but A. D. Kimball, the IWW union secretary, claimed support of 90 percent of the miners.[65] Certainly the "Cousin Jacks" stayed loyal to their employers. By July 1 the copper companies of the West had announced a resolution in which they said they were "determined that under no consideration will they recognize this band [the IWW]."[66]

Phelps Dodge Digs In

One day during the last week of June 1917, officials of the three copper mining companies in Cochise County's Warren District approached Sheriff Harry Wheeler. More intense than usual, the officials expressed concern to Sheriff Wheeler about the great number of unemployed strangers that had been drifting into Bisbee during the preceding few weeks. Their concerns were heightened by the fact that the IWW had called a strike on June 27.

In times of trouble, the Bisbee copper companies always had the quick, unquestioning cooperation of law officers. Now they wanted Sheriff Wheeler to deputize men whom they had

Sheriff Harry Wheeler of Cochise County

selected to guard company property. The sheriff was experienced in helping mine operators control minor problems with workers, but the scope of this request evoked uncertainty on Wheeler's part. There followed a hasty education for the sheriff on the dangers of radicalism. Within a few days he had changed his mind, and a deputized vigilante group, the "Bisbee Citizens' Protective League," was formed.[67]

The managers considered several ways to get the miners back to work. On June 30 the Bisbee mining companies issued their declaration that under no conditions would they recognize the IWW. The Phelps Dodge Corporation used its newspaper, the *Bisbee Daily Review*, to intimidate and coerce the men. But mainly the *Review* tried to touch the miners' sense of guilt regarding their lack of patriotism in striking against a company producing vital war supplies.

On July 1, 1917, a Sunday, the *Review* amounted to a counter-strike special. In a prominent box on the front page, Grant H. Dowell, the manager of the Copper Queen, issued a "Fourth of July Notice" saying that the Phelps Dodge mines and surface operations would shut down for the holiday. "It is well that every liberty loving man, woman and child join in the celebration this day; that our enemies at home and abroad may know that we are dedicated to maintaining the principles of liberty and good government at any cost."[68] Inside, on the editorial page, the *Review* dramatized Phelps Dodge's position. Referring to the Bisbee miners who ignored the strike call as "those men in the trenches at Bisbee," the newspaper emphasized the wartime need for copper. It said the "loyal" miners "know in their hearts they are doing the right thing."[69]

In most of its editions in these weeks, the *Review*, by constantly emphasizing Phelps Dodge patriotism, was saying, "The bosses sacrifice, so should the workingman." Apparently everyone in Bisbee, including the strikers, accepted the notion that Big Business and America were synonymous; no comment, other than that found in the IWW propaganda, included the possibility that Big Business could be unpatriotic or un-American. One arrested Bisbee miner later stated: "I am not going to scab for any corporation....I don't consider a man owes that much to his country."[70]

From a recent speech by President Wilson aimed at profiteering industrialists, the *Review* quoted out of context.

The paper shaded Wilson's comments to suggest that the President was saying that wage increases were not "economical" or "efficient" and therefore not patriotic to ask for. One item noted that the Phelps Dodge Corporation was buying seven million dollars worth of Liberty Loans. This edition included several scare stories which suggested that copper producers' patience was almost exhausted and that closing the mines was a very real possibility. In addition, at least one article proclaimed that more miners every day were becoming impatient with the strikers.[71] The July 1 *Review* included a message from Sheriff Wheeler[72]:

> TO ALL DEPUTIES—I want to impress upon each deputy sheriff the absolute necessity for extreme self-control, cool, calm judgment and patience. Avoid all display of weapons. Remember, you are deputized for protection of self and property and the maintenance of peace. You are subject to my call, a call which will be made when necessary.

Apart from the premonitive implication in the last sentence and the general threatening tone of the entire messsage, the purpose of the announcement seems unclear—unless one examines the nature of the conduct of the striking miners in the district. The strike was remarkably void of violence on the part of the strikers. Whatever mood of fear and danger that might have existed in Bisbee resulted, primarily, from sensational journalism.

All of this new color and vitality in the *Review* may have been explained in a small article on page three of the second section. This article reported that the *Bisbee Daily Review* had just acquired a new general manager, Cullen H. Cain. A newcomer to Bisbee, Mr. Cain, in addition to writing editorials, "... will also write special feature stories for the Phelps Dodge people."[73] Phelps Dodge brought Cain from St. Louis, where he had been a public relations director for the Southwest Bell Telephone Company.[74] Cain's appointment was only one change in a heavy shifting of personnel throughout the community during the period. The place was booming in an atmosphere of wide-eyed, breathless hysteria.

In Bisbee, pro-copper people continued to look for productive wrath. There was even an argument among the Wobbly denouncers; one group denied the IWW was German and said it was socialist—a growing menace in view of the internal uncertainty of Russia.[75] To strengthen the support of the copper companies and underscore their own loyalty, more than a thousand miners formed the Workman's Loyalty League on July 2. Other signs, too, pointed to a diminished support of the strike; three hundred miners left the district, the strike leaders left for Globe and Clifton-Morenci. There were fewer pickets, more men at work.[76]

In response to a request from Governor Campbell, the War Department sent an officer to investigate conditions in Bisbee. The officer, Lt. Col. James J. Hornbrook, arrived Friday evening, June 29. Saturday morning he accompanied Sheriff Wheeler on the local lawman's rounds. The colonel advised the sheriff that, if needed, a squadron of cavalry was available only a few miles from Bisbee. The *Review* said Lt. Col. Hornbrook "would not talk for publication and refused to even state his mission in the Warren District." The paper appeared to have two contradictory intentions in reporting Lt. Col. Hornbrook's arrival in this mystifying way. On the one hand it hoped to assuage the impression on the part of Lt. Col. Hornbrook that Bisbee needed military help. On the other hand it did not want to dilute the program of hysteria-inducing propaganda for its readers.[77]

After looking the situation over, Hornbrook telephoned Governor Campbell saying that "everything was peaceable, with few gatherings of men and no riots." On July 1, Hornbrook called Campbell again. This time he reported "Conditions slightly improved." That day, July 1, Calumet and Arizona Manager Jack Greenway also telephoned Campbell: "Few pickets out . . . no violence or damage to property."[78]

Later on, when asked to square his knowledge that no violence took place in Bisbee with his permissive attitude toward the deportation, Campbell stated: "The strikers [in Bisbee] were not rioting or engaging in violence of any sort, but were threatening to do so."[79] Lt. Col. Hornbrook sent several telegrams to the adjutant general reporting on the conditions in Bisbee. Representative accounts were: June 30, "no violence or disorder"; July 1, "no disturbance of any kind"; July 3, "conditions quiet today" and July 5, "conditions continue quiet."[80] Later Phelps Dodge obtained affidavits from men who claimed they had been threatened by strikers.

The threats had a similar nature; in most cases a picket had yelled at a man going to work, "We'll get you, you scab son-of-a-bitch."[81]

Despite the absence of violence on the part of the strikers, the *Review* stepped up its program of patriotic intimidation with virulent attacks on the IWW.[82] Vigilante machinery continued to move—the Workmen's Loyalty League claimed 1,600 members. On July 3, Mayor Jacob Erickson published a proclamation requesting that the public refrain from gathering in the streets and "endangering the life and limb, as well as impeding and annoying the normal conduct of traffic and passage of pedestrians." The city ordinance which prohibited crowds from creating a disturbance, assured Erickson, would be rigidly enforced. The *Review* said that "Upwards of 500 men," had left Bisbee in the preceding four days. Also, it reported that except for two mass meetings on July 2, "the day was very quiet in every respect."[83]

The reports of no striker violence conflict with the fact of the heightened restrictions after the strike had commenced. Even more, the reports raise certain questions concerning later claims by Sheriff Wheeler and others that "men were assaulted and beaten" or that IWWs inflicted "many, many severe beatings" before the deportation.[84] Not one incident of IWW violence was recorded in the Bisbee newspaper from the strike's beginning on June 27 to the deportation on July 12.[85]

"July 3," noted the *Review* on July 4, "passed quietly and orderly." Only forty IWW pickets stood duty.[86] The *Los Angeles Times* was moved to assert, "It now can be stated with confidence that the strike is broken.... Today more than half the underground men reported for duty."[87]

The Bisbee strikers themselves pledged determination. Even if the copper companies granted their demands they would not be satisfied. On July 2, the Bisbee Metal Mine Workers Union sent a message of sympathy to their brothers, the striking Butte miners. Displaying the community feeling of the western mining industry (the mine operators had their own telegrams going back and forth at the same time, no doubt), the Bisbee strikers promised not to return to work until the Butte operators had satisfied the miners in that city.[88]

The most ominous declaration of all appeared in the Phelps Dodge newspaper on July 5. The *Review* announced that in anticipation of some kind of "violent" and "overt" acts,

Bisbee "authorities" were prepared to exercise exceptional vigil from now on and

> to take stringent measures upon any sign of disobedience to the regulations which have been fixed by them in association with the protective association and the Workman's Loyalty League. These combined forces represent the greatest organized strength that has ever been brought about in an Arizona district for the maintenance of law and order.

The message must have been confusing in view of the lack of any violence. Perhaps it was in response to a Fourth of July incident on Bisbee's Main Street during the parade. One bystander who refusing to remove his hat as the flag passed by wound up with a sock on the jaw for his stubbornness. This was the only "violence" reported by the *Review* during the whole time leading up to the deportation.[89]

Phelps Dodge, no doubt, was setting the emotional stage for the deportation. But there is another possible explanation for the preparedness. One mine manager later frankly declared that the mine operators had feared government intervention in Bisbee. The copper companies, by emphasizing the peacefulness of the situation, were able to avoid military interference and handle the matter the way they wanted.[90]

Everyone in Bisbee was urged to participate in the Fourth of July parade. Heavy thundershowers on the evening of the third had flooded the lower streets, but the water drained leaving the town rinsed and cool for Independence Day morn. Bisbee observed the holiday in a way described as "the most patriotic anniversary of the declaration of American Independence ever celebrated in this state." The IWWs defiantly declined participation, and many spent their time, unfruitfully, watching the incoming trains for strikebreakers.[91] Yet the community did not lose its labor strife-produced tensions. The Bisbee miners continued to press for their goals.

Far from gaining endorsement by the national Mine, Mill office, the strikers' demands and their sponsors were disavowed. Charles Moyer, president of the IUMMSW, overwrought by the strike in Bisbee, wired Arizona's Governor Campbell on July 3 from Chicago. He insisted that the Bisbee union was a maverick. The strike, he declared, was unauthorized. Three days later Moyer revoked the charter of the IUMMSW local.[92] He charged the IWW was exploiting the situation and trying to put the IUMMSW "in a bad light."[93]

On July 6, the *Review* announced that the "death knell of I.W.W. activity in the Warren District" had been sounded by the vigorous support of the League. Otherwise, there was little mention of the strike. Around the state, things were quieter. The same day, despite their feelings that the Bisbee miners had struck prematurely, Frank Little and Bill Haywood telegrammed Bisbee strike leader, A. D. Kimball: "Entire organization back of you. Must win. No compromise." Since the die was cast, Little and Haywood urged Kimball to make the most of the situation. "Send all news to the papers. Tell the diggers and muckers [not out] to double up on the machines." Their exhortations, however, revealed their own awareness of the strike's flagging nature. On the eighth, despite scare stories of "plots" around the country that had no substance, the *Review* recorded that "peaceable conditions prevail throughout" and that the "backbone" of the IWW "was broken."[94]

Between July 8 and July 11 the situation in Bisbee appeared to be stabilizing. On July 11 the three copper mining companies notified all employees that they would not be considered employed if they had not returned to their jobs by the night of July 13. The *Review* announced, "I.W.W. Menace in Warren District Steadily Dying," and it claimed that more men every day were returning to work.[95] There seemed to be no more hysteria, no violence and an apparent faith that everything would soon return to normal. The passion and the superlatives apparently had spent themselves. The climax had been reached and the relaxing, downhill glide to peace offered no provocation for desperate action. The mining companies had triumphed without physical conflict and had asserted their supremacy in the industrial affairs of Bisbee, if not the whole state of Arizona.

Apparently supremacy was not power enough for the copper companies—they wanted unchallenged, exclusive, absolute control of the state. This meant eliminating all union influence in every Arizona mining camp. But Arizona labor's central bastion of union strength—Globe-Miami—appeared too formidable to be overcome; Bisbee was manifestly more vulnerable. Moreover, although Globe-Miami had shown itself to be the hub of organized labor activity in the state, Cochise County's workingmen had held the greatest sway in early twentieth century Arizona politics. Management's most devastating assault would ultimately have to be on that southern flank.

But the strategy of the collective copper companies included first an attack in the north, at Jerome, where organized labor had never been much stronger than in Bisbee. District action here would also serve as a test of the feasibility of such an extreme technique as physical deportation of "undesirables." The Jerome deportation on July 10 was part of the integrated mine operator campaign against Arizona labor in the summer of 1917 and a prelude to a similar but much grander event in Bisbee two days later.

The Jerome Deportation

Although the deportation at Jerome was carried out on a smaller scale and in a more casual manner than the one at Bisbee, the act merits considerable attention since its development and details so closely resemble those in Bisbee. This similarity, in turn, suggests that the mine operators' offensive against labor in 1917 was broadly and carefully coordinated.

After the workers returned to their jobs in Jerome on July 4, 1917, the IWW continued to agitate. Wobblies made the same demands in Jerome they had made in Bisbee, which the copper companies labeled "extortionate" and most people, including miners, saw as revolutionary.[96] Robert Tally later analyzed the labor difficulties in Jerome and the motives of discontent among the Jerome workers. In doing so, he conceded some of their less treasonable complaints. On August 3 he wrote that the strike in Jerome was caused by "conscription; lack of immigration due to the war; high cost of living; the taking advantage of the above conditions by professional outside agitators, who come into our district and peddle lies and misstatements. Also, to pro-German and anti-government agitation."[97]

At the most, the Jerome Wobblies numbered about one hundred twenty-five. But after the Jerome Miners' Union accepted the terms of Tally's May 31 offer, the Jerome IWW, vehement, aggressive and comparatively disciplined, made itself conspicuous. The organization openly asserted itself in its own name and on July 6 called a strike.[98] After putting up picket lines, the Wobblies harangued the miners coming on and going off shifts and used the colorful insults and invective peculiar to the vernacular of the western miners. In most cases, workers called the IWW bluff, so Wobbly efforts produced little result. Only a small number of the IUMMSW members refused to cross the picket lines. In an attempt to affirm worker solidarity and loyalty to the early June agreement with Tally, a Jerome Miners Union meeting was held on July 7 where the union secured a vote of confidence. A substantial majority (470–194) opposed the IWW action.[99]

Several fist fights and rock-throwing incidents between members of the rival unions prompted two arrests, but no real threat to the security of the community was apparent. Some tension could be sensed, and at least one small mine, the Green Monster, closed. However, the United Verde continued to operate at full force. Despite signs of tranquillity, various Jerome citizens decided drastic action was needed to restore peace and full employment.

In the afternoon of July 9, several hundred men, many of them members of the Jerome Miners Union, signed their names to a roster of "emergency volunteers."[100] That evening a secret meeting was held at the Jerome High School where the men made plans to run the Wobblies out of the camp. It was to be a citizen's vigilante affair—no one was deputized as in Bisbee. The vigilante leaders notified the Jerome police of their plan and the lawmen supported it (though not in a conspicuous manner).[101] The United Verde Copper Company provided two cattle cars for the deportees and two flat cars for the armed guards. The vigilantes agreed to identify themselves with white handkerchiefs tied around their arms, as they would in Bisbee two days later.[102]

By 4:00 A.M. on Tuesday, July 10, over two hundred men had armed themselves with rifles, pick handles and "billies." Sifting through more than 2,500 Jerome miners, they found one hundred four Wobblies and marched them "in ones, twos and threes" to the city jail.[103] Fears that the Wobblies might be armed and would offer desperate resistance to the deportation proved to be unfounded.[104] By nine o'clock the crowded jail resembled "pandemonium, Hades and a smelter combined and rolled into one." Spectators were packed outside. A frivolous air prevailed; impish and cavalier remarks came forth from those incarcerated. "Put Dan Jones in; he's a Wobbly," yelled one; a newcomer called the experience "the happiest moment of my life." The issues in the Jerome situation were as grave as those in Bisbee, but the deportation had a humane, even festive tone.

The jail air got bad and, mercifully, the Wobblies were allowed outside. Surrounded by vigilantes, they were marched up Jerome Avenue, by the Miller Store and the Catholic Church toward the railway track. Near the Episcopal Church, the crowd stopped momentarily, but then continued to the United Verde office building. There, on the steps of William A. Clark's Arizona headquarters, each "Wobbly" had a "trial." By "ones and twos," again, each prisoner had a chance to prove he was not a member of the IWW. A three-man review committee— which included state IUMMSW organizer H. S. McCluskey and a man who checked the Jerome Miners Union register—judged the union affiliation of each man.[105]

By this process thirty-seven of those arrested were released but were "told to keep their mouths shut." The dual memberships of the "two-card men" cost them a pardon. But several Wobblies were allowed to go free because they were family men or had been long-time Jerome residents. "Dutch" Hausman implored the committee to let him stay since he had been thrown out of the IWW only the day before. This fact and his genial reputation won him a narrow reprieve, and "he lost no time waiting for the grass to grow before beating it back to town."

One man, "a large fellow, big enough to work a double jack single," well-enough dressed to "have passed for a gambler, minister of the gospel or most any other sort of a professional man," was ordered out of town. A stranger—in fact he had arrived only the night before—he was James P. "Red" Thompson, a national lecturer for the IWW, who had been programmed for a series of soapbox orations during the strike.[106]

Finally the vigilantes escorted the remaining sixty-seven men to the waiting cattle cars. Two of the prisoners had lived in Jerome for fifteen years or more, "but that cut no ice." As the gates were lifted and the men climbed in, there was considerable horseplay. One man had waited until this late minute to state that he was leaving behind four children, one of whom was only four days old. But Mayor Cain announced he had had his chance. "It's too late now," said Cain, and the cattle car playfulness subsided. One bitter Wobbly, pointing at the vigilantes, said he "would be ashamed to be in that bunch."[107]

Although none of the prisoners, it was presumed, had eaten breakfast, they were given only water which was placed in the cars. While the deportees waved their hats and jeered at the good-natured crowd, fifty armed men climbed on the flat cars placed before and behind the two cattle cars. As the train pulled out, several deportees shouted that they would be back, but probably only a handful ever saw Jerome again.[108]

The train went to Jerome Junction, twenty-seven miles away, where a mounted posse under Deputy Sheriff John H. Robinson met them. Prescott citizens had organized the posse fearing the deporteees would descend upon them. It was made up of fifty armed deputies and a number of volunteer "home guards." A mounted group, they had raced cowboy-movie style across twenty long, hot Arizona miles to intercept the "Wobbly special" after hearing of the roundup in Jerome by telephone.

Deputy Sheriff Robinson requested the Jerome guards to identify the IWW leaders. He then arrested nine men and took them to the county jail in Prescott. In the meantime Yavapai County officials chartered a special Santa Fe coach which arrived with the regular northbound train at 2:50 P.M. The unarrested IWWs were herded into the coach, and the train went to Ash Fork, on the Santa Fe main line. At some time, the deportees were transferred back to a cattle car, their proletarian presence apparently deemed unfit for the elegance of a day coach. In Ash Fork their car was linked to a westbound freight train which the guards planned to take to Needles, California, where they intended to deposit the deportees. However by the time the train reached Kingman, the guards had tired of their duty; they desired to free their prisoners. Mohave County Sheriff J. N. Cohenour had other ideas. He told both Wobblies and guards to get out of town.[109]

Out of Kingman, across the Colorado River into California to Needles rolled the train and its shipment of *personae non gratae*. By then it was almost morning of July 11, and there, by the dawn's early light, the guards and their charges could see another armed posse.

Some of these armed people had been deputized and were acting under orders from the district attorney of San Bernardino County, who said, "California won't be made the dumping ground for Arizona's undesirables."[110]

The Needles posse ordered the whole troupe to return to Arizona; the wary Californians had received a load of deported Wobblies from several Mohave county mines only the day before. Guards and prisoners were back in Kingman by 7:00 A.M. where the deportees were turned over to the sheriff. Then the guards returned to their homes in Prescott and Jerome. Upon their promise to be good, the Wobblies were released.[111]

Actually, pressure from Arizona Governor Campbell had effected the release of the IWWs.

Campbell had been notified of the deportation by United Verde Assistant General Manager Tally on July 10. Tally had wired: "About ninety-five percent. Jerome Wobblies left on special train ten o'clock this morning. Most of them wished on Needles...." Telegrams from San Bernardino County Attorney T. W. Duckworth to California Governor William D. Stephens protesting Arizona's exportation of undesirable citizens prompted Stephens to appeal to Campbell to "put a stop to such practice immediately."[112] In the meantime Arizona's Mohave County Sheriff Cohenour, uncertain as to how to handle the deportees, had wired Governor Campbell for instructions. Responding to Governor Stephens' appeal and the sheriff's request, Campbell called Mohave County Superior Court Judge John Ellis. Campbell told Judge Ellis to release the men if no charges were pending against them. By that time only forty-one remained in custody. The rest had drifted off. Within a few hours, all were let go.[113]

Several Wobblies remained in the Kingman area to work in the local mine; the rest dispersed. Deputies held the nine men in the Prescott jail for several weeks pending arraignment. Federal authorities contemplated treason charges against the prisoners, but none of them was ever indicted. Two of the men, Gillette and Brennen, called Robert Tally in Jerome for help. They were United Verde spies who had played their roles quite well. Tally had Sheriff Young turn them out and buy tickets for them to Butte, Montana.[114]

The Jerome deportation did not escape the attention of other union members around the state of Arizona. While it was going on, the Executive Committee of the IWW at Globe telegraphed Governor Campbell protesting the Jerome deportation and demanding protection for the deportees from the governor. "If protection refused," said the wire, "you must assume consequences ...." Campbell replied that afternoon informing the Globe Wobblies of the deportees' release and expressing his dislike for "the threatening tone of your telegram." He warned that any further such communication would be "sufficient cause for immediate action against responsible party or parties."[115]

The Globe IWW committee sent a similar but more respectful telegram to President Wilson on the same day. Wilson did not respond.[116]

These protests of the Globe miners failed to inspire either Governor Campbell or President Wilson to condemn deportations or to warn the mine operators against other forms of extralegal action. Neither did public disapproval materialize. (The middle-of-the-road *Outlook* described it as a "picturesque occurrence."[117]) Thus encouraged, the copper companies felt free to expand their offensive. The July 10 Jerome deportation was a successful trial run. Besides being a test of the organization and methods for rounding up people and deporting them, it strengthened the confidence of the copper men that they could continue their direct assault on labor with impunity if not approbation.

The Decision to Deport

This narrative of the Jerome deportation provides insights that add new dimensions to the Bisbee Deportation. It is difficult to believe that the two deportations were not consciously related, "master-minded," so to speak. The *Bisbee Daily Review* carefully chronicled the Jerome affair, as if to give precedent and, therefore, authorization to Bisbee's own more spectacular drive on July 12. The *Review* quoted Jerome Mayor J. J. Cain as though he were an authority to be emulated: "'Jerome citizens have demonstrated that they knew how to deal effectively with an undesirable element.'"[118] The *Review* intended the quote to be, obviously, didactic. For several days the *Review* provided a catechism for dealing with undesirables.

The idea that the deportations were individually spontaneous is diluted by the mass of evidence that indicates this technique had long been standard American operating procedure. There was considerable truth in an editorial which appeared in the *El Paso Times* several years after the Bisbee event: "Only in its magnitude was the proceeding [the Bisbee Deportation] very different from the practice common enough all over the country of running undesirables out of town."[119] Deportations and other forms of violent repression had been authorized, carried out and defended by the public for some time.

In 1904 the Western Federation of Miners was weakened by the complete defeat of its strike at Cripple Creek, Colorado, when "by a combination of forces led by the Mine Owners' Association and the local Citizens Alliance... [its] members in the area were simply driven away and replaced by foreign immigrants and country boys."[120] That same year more than a hundred men were deported from Telluride, Colorado. On June 25, 1913, vigilantes deported two IWWs from Marshfield, Oregon.[121]* The president of the IUMMSW, Charles Moyer, was deported from Hancock, Michigan, on December 26, 1913.[122]

This tradition of deporting unwanted people from American towns provided both a model and a precedent for the Arizona mine managers. Deportation, however outrageous it might have appeared to some people, was a relatively conventional and well-practiced method of getting rid of undesirables. Miners knew this, elected officials knew it—and mine operators knew it. Forced expulsions on a grand scale, however, demanded very careful planning and coordination. The unity of the Arizona mine managers, tenuous at best before the prominence of Walter Douglas, had finally developed to a refined state. At least one incident prior to the July deportations demonstrated that the mining companies were finally in close league in their campaign to destroy Arizona unionism. This incident involved the "Arizona Council of Defense," a wartime auxiliary government agency.

Before the United States entered the war, Newton D. Baker suggested to President Wilson the idea of a civilian agency to study the nation's economic and human resources in order to facilitate wartime mobilization. Wilson approved the idea enthusiastically, and a bill was introduced in the House of Representatives as "the President's own." The bill created the "Council of National Defense," which was charged with the coordination of resources and industry but had no decision-making power. When it functioned, it served as a forum for the mediation of domestic wartime problems.[123]

---

*In court action which followed this Oregon deportation, Oregon Supreme Court Chief Justice McBride ruled: "While the conduct of these men was probably insulting to the feelings of the community, and their denunciation of the government and the flag calculated to provoke decent citizens to wrath, and to invite breaches of the peace, this furnishes no legal justification for the course pursued toward them." Oregon legal precedent, quite plainly, meant nothing in Arizona.

On April 18, 1917, a special session of the state legislature formed an Arizona branch of the National Council of Defense.[124] Governor Campbell created various committees and appointed their members. Campbell named Phoenix banker, editor and real estate man Dwight B. Heard president of the Council. Seven representatives of labor and seven mine managers composed the labor committee. The governor named John L. Donnelly, president of the Arizona State Federation of Labor, chairman of the Labor Committee. Dean of the Episcopal Cathedral in Phoenix, William Scarlett, was appointed to the labor committee as a "representative of the people." Scarlett, a Harvard graduate and an outspoken liberal, had been actively denouncing corporate practices from the pulpit.[125]

The legislation creating the State Council of Defense provided for branch councils in each county of the state.[126] Each county complied except Cochise, home of the Copper Queen. Feeling that the authority of the State Council might intrude on the sovereignty of the Warren mining district, both capital and labor in Cochise County failed to respond and organize a county council.[127] Bisbee people did serve on the State Council of Defense. John Greenway, Harry Wheeler, Stuart French, Grant Dowell and eleven other men from Bisbee represented the copper interests on the state level. Shortly after the miners struck at Bisbee in June, these men wired Arizona State Council of Defense Chairman Heard and requested authorization to "round up" the IWWs in Bisbee.[128]

On May 5 Chairman Donnelly announced a resolution calling for "harmonious cooperation" among the people of Arizona's industries for the duration of the war. The executive committee of the State Council had drawn up the resolution. According to later testimony, Donnelly and Thomas French, another labor representative on the committee, had prepared a resolution advantageous to labor.[129]

Donnelly called for a meeting of the committee of the seven representatives of labor and the seven representatives of management. The chairman set Tucson as the place and May 10 as the date. After the mine managers asked for a postponement in order that they might have time to agree upon a common policy, Donnelly advanced the date to May 17. He changed the place to the state capitol in Phoenix. At the appointed hour, 10:00 A.M., Donnelly, Dean Scarlett and four labor committee members were waiting, but not a single mining man arrived.

Those present, however, knew that the mine managers were together in the suite of the Arizona Chapter of the American Mining Congress headquarters at the Adams Hotel.[130]

Governor Campbell went to the Adams and prevailed upon the operators to come to the meeting. After a lengthy delay, one of them, Louis Cates, appeared at the capitol, glanced in the committee room and scurried away. Heard and Dean Scarlett hastened to accost him and asked that he induce his associates to attend. Several of the mining men finally came to the capitol. When the meeting was called to order, Grant Dowell, manager of the Copper Queen, moved to table the "cooperation" resolution. Robert Tally of the United Verde immediately seconded Dowell's motion. When Donnelly and Dean Scarlett urged the operators—on patriotic grounds—to reconsider, the mine managers bluntly refused. The managers then took charge of the meeting, disavowed the purpose of the labor committee and never again recognized its existence.[131]

This example of stubborn unwillingness to cooperate with labor even according to national wartime provisions indicated Arizona mine management's attitude about compromise. Yet the mining men experienced no criticism of their independence. In the meantime, unions were being denounced as "treacherous" for proposing strikes which would "handicap preparations for defense."[132]

Other developments in America at this time appeared to excuse or even sanction industrial management's extralegal behavior. During the first week of June, United States Attorney General Hubbard dismissed all the indictments against management and political officeholders involved in the notorious Ludlow Massacre of 1914, thus giving federal sanction, even license, to determined and uncompromising mine operators.[133] The arrest of numerous people by federal officers on May 1, 1917, under the newly passed Espionage Act, plainly advertised the government's approval of dealing severely with "anarchistic aliens."[134]

In Arizona deportation seemed to be epidemic. On Thursday, July 7, the sheriff in Kingman had obtained warrants for the arrest of fifteen Wobblies for calling a strike that the general body of miners had voted against eight to one.[135] In Chloride, Golconda and Mineral, Arizona (all, like Kingman, in Mohave County), authorities, on July 10, gave IWWs twelve hours to get out of town. This rash of similar symptoms suggested a widely coordinated cleanup.[136]

Globe-Miami

There were several reasons why the mine managers could have selected Jerome and Bisbee for the major deportations. Each town had weak labor organizations, each was already dominated by unusually authoritarian mine owners and each was located in a remote and isolated part of Arizona. A look at what was happening in Globe-Miami helps one to appreciate these facts.

Circumstances in Globe-Miami were different. Globe miners, working under less isolated and less authoritarian conditions, maintained a strong IUMMSW local. They allowed neither the IWW nor the mining companies to control the situation. The Globe-Miami strike vote was taken on the evening of June 30. The combined results were 1,437 "yes" votes to 416 "no." The miners walked out the next day.[137]

The *Bisbee Daily Review* headlines on July 7 played up a Globe citizens' meeting of about "500 people" who pledged their support to the companies. In a camp of 7,000 men, most of whom were out on strike in support of the union, this opposition to the union amounted to an insignificant number.[138] The striking miners practically controlled the district. Governor Campbell arrived in Globe on July 4. The tensions there were much greater than in Bisbee or Jerome since the Globe miners' organization appeared more invulnerable. The "citizen's posse" felt less than confident. There was much feinting and bluster together with some small incidents of violence. Most of the activity involved threats and counter-threats and devious attempts to cross picket lines. The greatest concern of the copper companies was for the pumps which needed to be kept in operation continually to prevent the mines from flooding. Salaried engineers remained in the mines to man the pumps. The engineers were hungry, and the pickets forbade anyone taking supplies to them.[139] A heavily armed truck finally got through with supplies for the men underground. The strikers' unsuccessful attempt to keep the truck from the mine constituted the only threat to an otherwise peaceful strike scene.

Meanwhile former Arizona Governor George W. P. Hunt had received a letter from President Wilson requesting that he do what he could "to act as mediator and conciliator." Wilson said that he was "very much concerned to hear of the serious misunderstanding between the miners and operators in the copper mines."[140] Acting as the President's special representative, Hunt, together with United States Conciliator John McBride, went to Globe. This added to the vexation of the mine managers, since Hunt's background clearly revealed his positive sympathies toward the Arizona workingman.[141]

Management's feelings toward Special Investigator Hunt were soon reinforced. Hunt got to Globe on July 12, the day of the Bisbee Deportation and the day after Walter Douglas left. When he arrived, Hunt was contacted by some suspicious wives who showed him a number of boxcars lined up in Globe, ready for a deportation. He told the army officer in charge, Colonel White, that any such plan must be stopped. A protest against the appointment of Hunt was issued jointly by the Douglas Chamber of Commerce and the Douglas Citizens' Protective League and was forwarded to Senator Marcus A. Smith in Washington. On July 17, after the Bisbee Deportation, Smith answered the protest saying that nothing could be gained by withdrawing the appointment.[142]

The presence in Globe-Miami of duly constituted authorities who at the same time were known to be sympathetic with the workingman intimidated those managers in Globe who were ready to take drastic steps. To the copper men, Globe represented the troublesome independence Arizona labor had shown for the preceding ten years. Globe-Miami had replaced Clifton-Morenci as the symbol of worker freedom and mine manager frustration in the early twentieth century Arizona industrial war.

In a camp such as Globe, whose absentee owners demonstrated less autocratic rule and where bona fide unions flourished, the workingmen exerted unusual power. Also, Globe was closer to Phoenix, the state hub of politics and journalism. Such visibility and accessibility made Globe more subject to investigation by newsmen and various government officials. Globe did not lend itself to effective corporate control through "Loyalty Leagues"—Globe miners felt a weaker community and corporate identity and a stronger class and labor organization identity.

To compensate for their impotency in Globe, the copper men vigorously requested federal military help. Their effort to bring federal troops to strike-bound Arizona mining camps began with a telegram from Cochise County Sheriff Wheeler to Governor Tom Campbell. Wheeler sent a request for troops on June 28, the day after the Bisbee strike was called. On the same day, John C. Greenway, general manager of the Calumet and Arizona Mining Company, wired United States Secretary of War Newton D. Baker to inform Baker of Sheriff Wheeler's request. Greenway emphatically supported Wheeler's efforts. [143]

Governor Campbell sent two telegrams to Secretary of War Baker on July 2 advising military intervention in Arizona. The first message requested that investigating officers be sent to observe the situations in Clifton and Globe; a few hours later, after being pressured by Gila County Sheriff Armer at Globe, Campbell urged Baker to authorize the sending of federal troops to Globe. [144] Campbell later explained that in July 1917 he had no power to call in troops; the Arizona militia (the 150th United States Infantry) was in the process of being federalized and "the governor could petition for help needed but the General had the final say. . . . Upon receipt of said petition, [General] Greene would promptly send an officer of rank and experience from his staff as his official representative and be guided in his future actions by this officer's recommendations."

Campbell's request to Baker accompanied telegrams from several other public and private officials. Gila County Attorney Hugh W. Foster asked Baker to send troops as did Phelps Dodge President Walter Douglas. Douglas volunteered the services of a "special train to handle the troops." Bernard Baruch apprised Baker, too, of the "alarming conditions in the copper mines in Arizona." [145]

Governor Campbell wired Secretary Baker again on July 3 repeating the urgent need for federal help. "Answer my telegram of yesterday advising me what I may expect," Campbell's message implored. [146] A few hours later Campbell had a reply. Baker had referred the matter to Adjutant General McCain; McCain informed Campbell: "Commanding general, Southern Department, Fort Sam Houston, Texas, was directed by telegraph to take necessary action." [147]

The commanding officer of the Southern Department, Brigadier General James Parker, notified Adjutant General McCain on July 4 that Brigadier General Henry A. Greene of the Arizona District had sent Major Charles M. Bundel of the Tenth Field Artillery from Douglas to Globe to investigate the situation and to discuss the matter with Governor Campbell and the local authorities. Major Bundel was to notify General Greene if troops were needed.[148] After investigating, Major Bundel reported that conditions were very bad at Globe with the strikers "in complete control."[149] The following day, July 5, four cavalry troops and one machine gun company (two hundred and forty-two soldiers) under the command of Lieutenant Colonel White bivouacked in Globe.[150]

Some observers felt that the mining officials, the governor and the army representatives exaggerated the nature of the trouble at Globe. United States Attorney Thomas A. Flynn went to Globe before July 12. On the fourteenth he sent a report to the Attorney General stating that the mine owners and the press had magnified the violence and the threats to inflame the general public. He said he had made every effort to verify rumors of German influence or German financing among the strikers; he found nothing. The truck scene at the Old Dominion had been the only real confrontation between management and labor. When the truck broke down, strikers had hooted and cursed the truck drivers and deputies. This was the extent of the "violence."[151]

Colonel White, the army officer in charge of the troops at Globe, reported to his commanding officer that although everything was quiet, the IWWs were "making threats." These "threats" had prompted White to dispatch troops to Miami. Having succeeded in bringing troops to Globe, Governor Campbell broadened his request. The day of the Bisbee Deportation, July 12, Campbell asked that four companies be sent to Bisbee and one each to Kingman, Jerome, Humboldt, Clifton, Morenci, Ajo and Ray. General Parker replied that a state of insurrection would have to be proven to warrant sending more soldiers to Arizona.

The U.S. adjutant general advised Governor Campbell on July 14 that copper mines were not included in an order authorizing military protection for "wartime major utilities." Several days later Campbell asked President Wilson to amend the ruling "for a restoration of order."

A change was made. In addition to those troops already stationed near Bisbee and Douglas, small detachments— usually less than a company—were sent to and remained on duty in Globe, Miami, Ray, Jerome and Ajo between July 1917 and July 1920. These troops were relieved periodically and rarely saw any action. Their presence, most certainly, helped to discourage even minor union activity. Governor George W. P. Hunt made emphatic requests for the removal of the troops during 1918. The army responded by reducing the number to a token few.

The only restraining action by the military involved the dispersal of three hundred IWWs (less than 10 percent of the total number of strikers) attempting to hold a rally on July 8 in a Globe park. A troop of soldiers led by Captain H. G. Fisher drove the Wobblies out of the park and to a nearby hillside. The strikers then went ahead with their meeting. This incident amounted to the only real use of force during the time the troops were in Globe. Colonel White's official report from Globe stated that he prohibited the IWW from holding street meetings but that he *permitted* the Wobblies to use the ball park.[152]

But the frustrated Globe operators had been desperate to get the upper hand. A moot question arose out of the request for troops: did a mining executive like Walter Douglas really want federal troops in the strike-ridden mining towns of Arizona? In Globe, instead of the peaceful demonstrations being broken up, a "most friendly attitude existed between the strikers and the soldiers."[153] Since they had been sent to maintain order, not to take sides, the troops proved of negative value to the mine operators. Certainly this neutral nature of federal interference helped to enrage Walter Douglas. Commanders had been only authorized to arrest or disperse "persons unlawfully assembled" or who threatened to intimidate or harm workers on the job.[154]

On the other hand, an IWW union leader, Roger S. Culver, told United States Attorney Flynn, army Captain Fisher and Department of Justice Agent Claude McCaleb, that the *Wobblies* would *welcome* government intervention in the Arizona industrial war. Culver believed the huge wartime profits earned by the copper companies justified federal expropriation of the mines.[155]

Whatever complaints the copper-producing interests had about the presence of the army, records do seem to indicate that troops in mining camps definitely served the interests of capital. But Arizona mine managers wanted more. The soldiers did not break strikes or smash unions. Only deportations and kangaroo courts accomplished that. With union obliteration as management's goal, the army was an obstacle. Thus some mining company officials developed an antagonism toward the military.[156]

The defiance of the Globe strikers, the helplessness of the Globe managers and the "citizens posse," the presence of "impartial" soldiers and quite partial mediators and the irresolute efforts of Governor Campbell all served to illustrate to Arizona workers, to the American public and particularly to the frustrated mine owners that organized labor could assert itself (however ineffectively) within the limits of the law. To the mine owners this must have been humiliating and intolerable.

The Globe situation, no doubt, strengthened management's resolve to take the situation into their own hands. The Arizona labor-management conflict was about to crest; to delay any longer might mean unwanted government intervention. In Bisbee, for the time being, the army had convinced itself that troops were unnecessary as, no doubt, was the case. As yet, no civilian federal mediators had been sent there.

Phelps Dodge published its opinion of federal conciliators. "Mediation," said the *Bisbee Daily Review*, "judging by the Jerome sample, is a will-o'-the-wisp." The newspaper also headlined that "Mediators at Globe-Miami Abandon Hope," in its attempt to prove that mediation was fruitless.[157]

The hour had come for Walter Douglas and the other Bisbee mine operators to act on their own. Now was the best time to put their carefully designed roundup and deportation plans into effect.

There were several matters with which the perpetrators of the Bisbee Deportation knew they had to reckon: (1) the federal and state government officials had to look the other way; (2) no chance for "mediation" should be allowed; (3) the army could not be allowed to interfere; (4) their act had to be clean, complete and final and (5) the general public, including the citizens of Bisbee, had to be tolerant if not supportive of extreme action.

From the Jerome deportation, the Bisbee Deportation planners learned that neither Governor Campbell nor President Wilson felt a strong inclination to censure community vigilantism. Thus far neither executive had seen fit to send mediators to Bisbee, while Lt. Col. Hornbrook failed to find any need for troops. Corporation ingenuity promised a smooth and efficient execution of the act, while popular approval seemed certain.

The *Review* had been preparing the mood of the citizens of Bisbee for weeks while the same propaganda on an almost equally intense level had been at work across the nation. Public sympathy for labor and immigrants during the Progressive Period had now shifted back to a pro-capitalistic, nativistic, chauvinistic attitude. Their newly discovered sense of patriotism caused Americans to resent news such as strikers bringing about a 25 percent decrease in copper mine and smelter output.[158] Propaganda played upon vague fears related to raids by Pancho Villa on United States border towns and the intrigue suggested by the Zimmerman note.[159] Joseph Erving, a Bisbee resident at the time of the deportation, became convinced that "many beatings" by IWWs occurred before the deportation and by July 12 he decided that running undesirables out of town "was not a brutal thing to do."[160] He was thoroughly persuaded of the great power and menace and evil of the IWW.

The *Congressional Record* tells something about the federal government's mood. On July 13, Senator Henry L. Meyers of Montana told his colleagues that "our country seems to be filled with spies" and that "there should be drastic action to prevent a continuation of that dangerous state of affairs." Meyers explained:

> The labor conditions of our country in the West is [sic] very deplorable.... The mines and smelters of two great mining States of the West are threatened with being closed down in the near future unless a change takes place in the labor situation.... I do believe that much of the trouble was incited by lawless elements, controlled by people who are hostile to the welfare of this country in the prosecution of the war in which we are engaged, with a view to crippling our productivity and our facilities for successfully waging the war.[161]

Despite the favorable mood and all the precautions to assure the success of a massive roundup and deportation, the most obvious evidence implies the possibility that Phelps Dodge General Manager Stuart French did not desire vigilante action. Bisbee, for all the turmoil at Globe, was quiet and rapidly returning to normal. Use of waiting guns and boxcars looked unnecessary. Not until Walter Douglas (just recently appointed as president of Phelps Dodge) appeared on the scene was the deportation suddenly called.

The Clifton-Morenci fiasco had infuriated Douglas a year and a half earlier. On Wednesday morning, July 11, when he arrived at Globe in the "Cloudcroft" he was just as angry with the state of affairs as he had been when he visited Clifton-Morenci. He admitted conditions were improving rapidly at Bisbee.[162] But he had already resolved to do something meaningful and final. Douglas was reportedly "closeted the better part of the day" with Campbell on the eleventh in Globe, and it was believed Douglas told Campbell what behavior he expected of him in the coming days.[163] *Dunbar's Weekly* speculated, "The Bisbee kidnaping scheme was hatched in New York; Walter Douglas, through his boss Cleveland Dodge, was to take care of the Washington end and Copper Tom was to look out for the Arizona end of the tow line."[164] (Actually, Campbell wrote later that one mine manager testified before the President's Mediation Commission "that the Governor was not consulted because if the plans of the operation had been known in advance, the Governor with the aid of the Federal Gov't would have undoubtedly blocked them."[165])

Before leaving Globe for Bisbee, Douglas made his resolve public and he made it clear:

> There will be no compromise because you cannot compromise with a rattlesnake. That goes for both the International Union and the I.W.W.'s. . . . I believe the government will be able to show that there is German influence behind this movement. . . . It is up to the individual communities to drive these agitators out as has been done in other communities in the past.[166]

As soon as Douglas' private railroad car pulled out of Globe, Governor Campbell hurriedly left with his secretary for Phoenix "on what was said to be important business."[167] This was the afternoon of July 11, 1917.

The *Bisbee Daily Review* got Phelps Dodge president Walter Douglas' message at once. In the edition of July 12, the day of the deportation, a *Review* editorial, switching from a reptilian to a medical metaphor, stated it directly:

> 'Those who are not for us are against us. There can be no half-way ground. . . . The strike leaders, the strikers and the aiders and abettors and sympathizers of these

men are getting further and further, every day, outside the pale of the great mass of the citizens of this country who place love of home and pride of city and devotion to flag above every other consideration.... An infected sore may well become a cancer IF IT IS NOT CUT OUT!'

Walter Douglas had apprised the Bisbee citizenry that what on Wednesday morning the *Review* had called a "dying menace" was now a seditious plot which needed immediate and drastic — even lawless — attention.

"We were not asleep," confessed the *Review* the next morning, "but we were surely nodding."[168]

Two days before Walter Douglas' "rattlesnake" comment a "Complimentary Report" based on information supplied by "Operative #5" had been drawn up and sent to Robert Tally by the Thiel Detective Agency in Los Angeles. The report gave substance and reason to Douglas' desire. It stated that

> while the labor troubles in Arizona might be due to a certain extent to German influence, ... they are largely due to the traitors who reside within the State of Arizona, under the leadership of such as Geo. W. P. Hunt and his henchmen.... Operative states that the Unionists of the State can be beaten if the concerted efforts of the different Companies are developed in full force at once....
>
> This operative further states that there will be no better time in the future than there is at the present to fight the matter out....and suggests that the operators of the different mines, decide to fight out to a finish the existing trouble which will end matters once and for all.[169]

Walter Douglas needed no detective agency to inform him that the time had arrived for the supreme assault on labor. No one in Arizona was more sensitive to the rhythms of the labor-management confict than was Douglas. He had taken the initiative at Clifton-Morenci in October 1915, and he had broadened the campaign against labor during the following twenty-one months. Carefully, masterfully, over those months, he had unified the previously uncoordinated Arizona mining operators. By July of 1917, the Phelps Dodge Corporation, together with the other Arizona copper companies, controlled all three branches of the state's government. (The federal district court had been cooperative since 1913.) Yavapai, Gila and Cochise county sheriffs served the mining interests exclusively. Phelps Dodge, by itself, owned, controlled or influenced most of the state's newspapers as well as Arizona's banking institutions. Corporate influence dominated lawyers, ministers and school administrators. Although noisy with protests, conventional unionism in Arizona was ineffectual, while in Bisbee it had virtually vanished. Company-hired *agents provocateurs* had successfully infiltrated and managed to dominate the "radical" IWW locals. In Jerome and other Arizona communities, frontier vigilantism proved still workable and acceptable. Throughout the nation and around the state of Arizona, public opinion, aroused by wartime fears and excitement, now supported industrial policy unquestioningly. Progressivism had sputtered and died; the conservatives had reestablished themselves.

Taking all these developments into consideration, one is puzzled that Douglas and his colleagues were not satisfied. What more did the operators want? Did the debilitated power of labor in the state still arouse dread or animosity among the mining men? What purpose could mass deportation now serve?

Shortly after Douglas' train arrived in Bisbee the afternoon of July 11, Copper Queen general manager Grant Dowell and Calumet & Arizona general manager John Greenway called the meeting for that night at the Copper Queen dispensary. The circumstances suggest they were going to put into operation not a plan to provide protection for their interests but Walter Douglas' vengeful plan to rid Arizona of every trace of "both the International Union and the I.W.W.s."

With clockwork precision, the vigilante leaders executed the plan. By 4:30 A.M. Bisbee's Bell Telephone manager George Kellogg had completed his calls to action; precisely at 6:30 A.M. the vigilantes moved out. Less than two hours later most of Bisbee's "undesirables" were marching to the Warren ball park—and the twenty-three boxcars. So expertly was the roundup carried out, it was hard to believe it had not been frequently rehearsed.

7

BIG DAY IN ARIZONA

It had all been announced the night of the eleventh following the instructions of Phelps Dodge Corporation president Walter Douglas when he arrived from Globe that day on his private railroad car, the "Cloudcroft." The *Bisbee Daily Review* made no mention of Walter Douglas, not even that he was in town. Instead, on July 12, the *Review* reported that " ... the man who was responsible for and led the drive" was Sheriff Harry Wheeler. "He decided that the drive should be made last night," stated the *Review*, and then went on, cryptically, "It required more than courage to make this decision."[1] It also required more than a spontaneous decision to have an arsenal in the infirmary and twenty-three boxcars in readiness.

Preparations in Bisbee

Bisbee officials had, though, considered alternate plans during the preceding weeks of the strike. Several people later proudly claimed authorship of the various considerations. One vigilante, William J. Beeman, boasted that he suggested to Calumet & Arizona assistant superintendent Gene Whitely on about the second or third day of the strike that the Wobbly leaders be taken to Mexico. Whitely agreed and the two went directly to John Greenway's house in Warren. Greenway, the general manager of the Calumet & Arizona, Bisbee's second largest mining operation, liked the idea but said he had to think about it.[2]

On his own, Beeman then went to Bill Truax who, with his father, ran the English Kitchen cafe and was the same Truax involved in the 1921 landmark Supreme Court decision declaring anti-injunction legislation unconstitutional (*Truax v. Corrigan*). Truax and Beeman discussed the proposal with Bisbee assistant postmaster Reuben A. Clampitt, secretary of the Warren District Rifle Club, who also liked the idea. Clampitt remarked that seventy-five or eighty members of the rifle club were all armed and were "all loyal and patriotic Americans." (Within a year Clampitt was in the McNeil Island, Washington, federal penitentiary for post office embezzlement.)[3] But, when Beeman saw Greenway again, the mine manager said he did not believe it could be done. Beeman learned later that Ellinwood and Ross, legal counsel for both Phelps Dodge and Calumet & Arizona, had advised Greenway against the plan.[4]

Sheriff Harry Wheeler, too, was dubious since he had, at times, been a friend of labor. But a minor copper company official, George B. Wilcox, together with John Greenway, succeeded in convincing Wheeler of the nefarious nature of the IWW and the purpose of the strike. The strike fund, they claimed, came from Germany. Wheeler, Wilcox and Greenway were all Spanish-American War veterans. Greenway and Wilcox had both served as captains in Roosevelt's Rough Riders. Up until this time Wheeler's chief fear had been that the local Mexicans would start an uprising, a fear whose credibility is not enhanced by the fact that these same Mexicans had been brought in by the employers. A rumor to this effect found only brief currency in Bisbee. A Mexican had reported that there were many ex-Villista Mexicans among the IWW strikers and that "some of them had cached away large stocks of guns and ammunition."[5] Once they had dispelled the Mexican uprising rumor, the mine managers had but to redirect Sheriff Wheeler's sense of protective responsibility.[6] When Wheeler inquired as to who would bear the expense of such an extravagant undertaking, Wilcox assured the sheriff that the copper companies, not the county, would pay for everything.

Regarding the bonding for "deputy" liability, Wilcox told Wheeler: "You know Jack Greenway well enough to know that he would never leave a friend in the hole." The two men went to Greenway who then confirmed Wilcox's statement.[7]

Miles Merrill, a Phelps Dodge foreman and organizer of the Bisbee Workman's Loyalty League, claimed authorship of the deportation plan. Merrill said he perfected the plan after he had talked it over with Ellinwood and Ross and "an executive officer" of the Copper Queen Mine, presumably Walter Douglas.[8] On the afternoon of July 4, following the big Independence Day parade, seventy or eighty men were asked to meet in the Phelps Dodge medical dispensary. In a brief talk, Harry Wheeler informed the group that seditious outside agitators had come to Bisbee solely to stop the production of copper. After apprising them of the danger, Wheeler asked the men for a show of their support. Each one immediately rose to his feet without looking around "to see what the other fellow was going to do."

After the meeting Wheeler and ten picked men met to organize the "loyal" men of Bisbee in readiness for any "emergency." This group divided the mining camp into ten districts; each man was assigned to a district while Wheeler was to command the entire organization. As a consequence of "suggestions" by Captain Greenway, at least one district was organized along military lines. It was divided into "companies," each with an eventual membership of seventy-five men or more. By July 9 the organization of the preparedness committee was complete.[9]

The Loyalty League learned of the roundup plan more than a week before the deportation. Several more meetings of the League had been held in the dispensary strictly for Copper Queen employees, where Miles Merrill outlined the details for a roundup to be used "in the event of a riot." George F. Kellogg, manager of the local Bell Telephone office, attended the meetings, and he agreed to give the alarm when notified by Copper Queen officials, Miles Merrill or Sheriff Wheeler. Merrill gave Kellogg a list of Loyalty Leaguers containing about two hundred and fifty or three hundred names. Kellogg was instructed to call each person on the list and say merely, "This is the Loyalty League call." League members already knew what to do; the call was their signal to act.[10]

But the deportation part of the plan remained a well-kept secret. Possibly not even Stuart French, the Phelps Dodge general manager, knew anything about the decision to ship the men out of the state. He seems to have gone a long way in handling the situation peacefully. William Beeman asserted, "I know as a positive fact that no one who attended the meeting that night knew beforehand there would be a deportation the next day, until after the discussion which took place at the meeting and a vote was taken."[11] Phelps Dodge had taken great care to create the appearance that the decision to deport was spontaneous.[12]

In late afternoon, July 11, Sheriff Wheeler called his ten district chiefs and informed them of the 8:00 P.M. meeting at the Phelps Dodge dispensary. Even though he had arrived in Bisbee that day, Walter Douglas chose not to attend the July 11 meeting. No one records his presence there, and Dr. Nelson Bledsoe, who did attend the meeting, remembered that Douglas stayed away.[13] Grant Dowell, manager of the Copper Queen operations, called the meeting, and Sheriff Wheeler conducted it. Although John Greenway attended, Lemuel Shattuck did not represent Bisbee's third copper mining company, Shattuck-Denn. There is much to suggest that Shattuck, an old miner and great favorite of the workingmen, found the whole affair obnoxious.[14]

Although Sheriff Wheeler later claimed responsibility for ordering the roundup and deportation, witnesses stated that Wheeler made *no* proposals of any action in the July 11 meeting.[15] It was Greenway, however, who addressed about one hundred "representative citizens" who had gathered in the dispensary, a building which was to remain Loyalty League headquarters for several months.[16] Greenway implied to the men that the planned deportation had the knowledge and consent of the United States government. At least one businessman said later that he had the distinct impression that the United States Army had agreed earlier, through a prearrangement, to receive the undesirables.[17]

Two weeks before the deportation, at the request of Sheriff Wheeler and Arizona Governor Thomas E. Campbell, the army had sent Lieutenant Colonel James J. Hornbrook to investigate conditions in Bisbee and ascertain if federal help were needed to maintain peace. Hornbrook observed that the situation was free of violence and decided against military assistance. But he showed no sympathy for the strikers. Greenway implied in the meeting, however, that the officer had given his direct approval of the roundup and deportation.[18] Greenway merely had told Lt. Col. Hornbrook, "We ought to get rid of this bunch," and Hornbrook had agreed.[19] Later in the day of July 12, after the deportation train had left Bisbee, Lt. Col. Hornbrook reportedly said, "It was the greatest piece of civilian work I have ever seen. I could have not done with my regiment what Sheriff Wheeler did with his deputies today."[20]

The deception by Greenway makes little difference since few men in Arizona at that time would have been disturbed upon learning that no mention of the deportation had been made ahead of time to any outside authority.

For almost three weeks, the *Bisbee Daily Review* had been describing the treasonous, despicable nature of the IWW. All the strikers in town fell into the category of "Wobbly." Now the good citizens of Bisbee had a chance to show their patriotism and save their community. All the evidence clearly pointed to the contrary, but the men at the meeting accepted John Greenway's charges that Bisbee public places were alive with "terror" which included boisterous behavior, jostling, threats and defiance. Moreover, the group heard that a dynamite charge with caps attached "had been found" under the Copper Queen hospital only the day before. These conditions, claimed the speakers, constituted an "extreme situation."[21] The *Review* propaganda had worked; everyone in the meeting accepted the IWW odium. Grant Dowell told the group that a "cancerous growth" had developed in Bisbee and he recommended an "operation." When asked for a vote of confidence, the audience responded unanimously—"everybody jumped to their feet."[22]

Then followed a spirited discussion, and, in what seemed to those present an original, spontaneous suggestion, someone proposed "that we start a drive...in the morning with the Mexican border as our destination." This line of thought led ultimately, with many helpful suggestions, to the decision to deport, "but only after a motion to that effect had been put, voted on and carried without a dissenting vote." Even though John Greenway was the one who proposed Columbus, New Mexico, as the accepted destination, most of those in attendance failed to see the deportation plan as anything other than a creation of that night's assembly. Dowell and Sheriff Wheeler warned the others not to discuss the matter with anyone, including Lt. Col. Hornbrook. After the meeting was adjourned, many men were issued guns from the Phelps Dodge dispensary.[23] At no time during this process or later were any official complaints filed with the sheriff's office or were any warrants drawn up or ever issued.

Bisbee: July 12, 1917

The men then left, having been instructed to rendezvous at their various assigned posts at 4:00 A.M. The plan included directions for arresting " ... on charges of vagrancy, of treason, and of being disturbers of the peace of Cochise County, all men who have congregated here from other parts and sections for the purposes of harassing and intimidating all men who desire to pursue their daily toil." Every "suspicious looking individual" was to be picked up and placed under arrest.[24] Company officials ordered the arrest of a number of other Bisbee residents who had been listed as undesirable because of their outspokenness or admitted sympathy with the strikers. These sympathizers included many storekeepers, contractors and professional people; some were prominent Bisbee citizens. Sheriff Wheeler instructed that upon his cue the deputies were to sweep down the canons of Bisbee, collecting everyone designated as an undesirable.[25]

Shortly after the July 11 meeting, Sheriff Wheeler got word that ex-Governor Hunt, a bitter foe of Walter Douglas, was on his way to Bisbee. Said Wheeler,

"Should the old Governor be in Bisbee after all of his friends had been taken out he would be lonesome, and it will be only an act of kindness to send him along with his friends, so that is what we will do." So it was decided that if Hunt showed up the next morning, he would be placed in the ball park and shipped out to Columbus.[26]

At 2:00 A.M. George Kellogg, aided by several extra switchboard operators, began making his calls. In addition to the Loyalty League members, Kellogg notified numerous members of the Bisbee businessmen's Citizens' Protective League. He made his last call by 4:30 A.M., but deputies continued to keep the switchboard busy with calls to friends and company sympathizers.[27]

The mood was part festive, part evangelical, part theatrical. One source, however, made it clear that "no ribald jests were passed" by the vigilantes during the roundup.[28] Gathered in alleyways, behind fences and in other dark places, the vigilantes waited in small knots, anxious and excited. To identify themselves, they tied white rags and kerchiefs around their arms. The instruction for secrecy was not followed; preparations attracted new recruits while a telephone call brought two hundred reinforcements from Douglas. Within a short time the number of vigilantes swelled to two thousand.[29] At 6:30 A.M. they moved out.[30] A reporter for the *Review* described the scene:

> The captives in the plaza were increased to five hundred men inside of five minutes. They began to mill around. The leaders were haranguing them. The moment was critical. Several deputies raised their rifles threateningly and it surely looked as though blood would run on the streets. But what was this! The steady tramp of men resounded on the streets leading up the canyon. They were coming down, the reserves two hundred strong with their rifles on their shoulders. The front of the line came up to the plaza and someone called halt. The crash of the musket butts on the pavement stilled the mutterings and murmurs of the trapped "wobblies" for the rest of the day. The heart went out of the boldest of the leaders right then and never came back even when the doors of the boxcars yawned a few hours later.
>
> What sights on these peaceful streets. Here came a businessman in overalls and auto cap with two cartridge belts buckled around him and carrying a Winchester forty-four. He was a big man, and in the bright morning light he looked like a giant. In the line of the reserves were old men with thin white mustaches and eyes that burned under their frosty brows like carbuncles. Old Arizona and Texas plainsmen, these, with Colts in their belts. One man in this line was carrying his boy's 22 target rifle. He was certainly a brave man.
>
> At the mouth of Brewery Gulch stood a little man, but he had a big heart and a Krag-Jorgensen and a heavy pistol. He and his men had been through that Gulch and stood with ready rifles while Sheriff Wheeler had gone right up into Union Hall. Every window framed a hostile face and a desperate man. But not a shot was fired.[31]

At 6:30 A.M., newsboys ranging from 10 to 13 years old, and, according to the *Review*, "straining on the leash to get on the dangerous streets with their wares," scurried through the streets of Bisbee delivering the *Review*.[32] Within an hour or so, most of Bisbee's citizens had read Sheriff Wheeler's proclamation: "ALL WOMEN AND CHILDREN KEEP OFF THE STREET TODAY." Wheeler's statement told of the posse's objective and stated the charges of vagrancy, treason and disturbance of the peace. He made clear his opposition to the strikers, and he also proclaimed that threats were "being daily made." He asked for aid and cooperation and requested that no shot be fired, except in self-defense. He assumed full responsibility for the roundup. Wheeler's message concluded: "All arrested persons will be treated humanely and their cases examined with justice and care. I hope no resistance will be made, for I desire no bloodshed. However, I am determined if resistance is made, it shall be quickly and effectively overcome."[33]

In at least one instance, resistance was made. It was, for sure, "quickly and effectively overcome." A former employee and an IWW cardholder, James Brew, awoke when vigilantes started to force their way into his rooming house. Brew had not participated in picket activity or other union demonstrations but had been brooding alone for several days.[34] When ordered out of his home, Brew answered with several shots. He killed Orson P. McRae, shift boss, Loyalty Leaguer and posse member.[35] McRae, unarmed, had been assigned to a deputized detail of five men assigned to pick up IWWs from rooming houses. The deputies assisting McRae immediately killed Brew.[36]

Both men and women claimed vigilantes beat them. One arrested man later stated that he saw Loyalty Leaguers knock down two women and drag them on the ground.[37] Although not deported, Marco Benderack claimed a gunman's beating permanently injured him. A consequent "paralytic attack" left him incapable of manual labor. William Gurovich later said that he and his family were robbed of a watch and chain and $172.50 by the same gunman who took Gurovich away. Nestor Sjofeld was preparing to go for a doctor for his sick baby at 7:30 o'clock that morning when he was met on the front porch by the gunmen. They were deaf to Sjofeld's pleas and answered his wife by throwing her to the floor. One report states that another Sjofeld child, a little girl, remained hysterical for weeks

MARKETS.

WEATHER.

The Bisbee Daily Review

Associated Press Special Leased Wire Service

VOL. 20. NO. 29. THE BISBEE DAILY REVIEW, THURSDAY MORNING, JULY 12, 1917. PRICE FIVE CENTS

ALL WOMEN AND CHILDREN KEEP OFF STREETS TODAY

SLAVS DASHING AFTER FLEEING TEUTON FORCE

Russian Armies Continue Brilliant Advance on Lemberg—Banks of Yser Again Scene of Fierce Struggle.

HAVING broken the strong Austro-German line in the vicinity of Halicz, the Russians are pushing forward from Halicz toward Lemberg. To the south of Galicia, and from Scandian south of Halicz, onward toward the line of the Dniester.

After the capture of Halicz, on the front from Halicz to the river, about 30 miles to the south, General Kornniloff forced the Austro Germans to continue their retreat. In their advance from Halicz the Russians forced the fleeing enemy across the Lomnica and occupied two towns on the western bank of the river. The next natural barrier is the river Stoke, about six miles west of the Lomnica.

Speculation In Grains Dealt Fatal Wallop

STRIKING AUSTRIANS AND GERMANS DENOUNCED BY SON OF FATHERLAND

Bisbee, July 12, 1917

I have formed a Sheriff's Posse of 1,200 men in Bisbee and 1,000 in D ug'as, all loyal Americans, for the purpose of arresting, on charges of vagrancy, treason, and of being disturbers of the peace of Cochise County, all those strange men who have congregated here from other parts and sections for the purpose of harassing and intimidating all men who desire to pursue their daily toil. I am continually told of threats and insults heaped upon the working men of this district by so-called strikers, who are strange to these parts, yet who presume to dictate the manner of life of the people of this district.

Appeals to patriotism do not move them, nor do appeals to reason. At a time when our country needs her every resource, these strangers persist in keeping from her the precious metal production of this entire district.

Today I heard threats to the effect that homes would be destroyed because the heads of families insisted upon their rights as Americans to work for themselves, their families and their country.

Other threats have and are being daily made. Men have been assaulted and brutally beaten, and only today I heard the Mayor of Bisbee threatened and his requests ignored.

We cannot longer stand or tolerate such conditions! This is no labor trouble—we are sure of that—but a direct attempt to embarrass and injure the government of the United States.

I therefore call upon all loyal Americans to aid me in peaceably arresting these disturbers of our national and local peace. Let no shot be fired throughout th s day unless in necessary self defense, and I hereby give warning that each and every leader of the so-called strikers will be held personally responsible for any injury inflicted upon any of my deputies while in the performance of their duties as deputies of my posse, for whose acts I, in turn, assume full responsibility as Sheriff of this County.

All arrested persons will be treated humanely and their cases examined with justice and care. I hope no resistance will be made, for I desire no bloodshed. However, I am determined if resistance is made, it shall be quickly and effectively overcome.

HARRY C. WHEELER,
Sheriff Cochise County, Ariz.

"I Expect Every Man Who Is Not A Slacker to Be at My Side," Is Wilson's Message to Business Men

Serbians Urged To Repudiate Strike of I. W. W.

MEDIATORS AT GLOBE-MIAMI ABANDON HOPE

Governor Campbell Is Threatened by I. W. W.—Hunt Admits Attempt to Settle Strike Complete Failure.

AMBULANCE UNIT ENLISTS 82 MEN

Arizona Red Cross Organization Fast Nearing Completment—Drilling Is Rushed to Hasten Mustering In.

MINERS MUST REPORT TOMORROW OR BE DROPPED FROM COMPANIES' LISTS

after the incident. Vigilante M. C. Denny who took Vuko Delya from his wife and three children at his home in Lowell reportedly beat Delya's children, inflicted a serious scalp wound on his wife and took her jewelry. Denny together with Billy Woods and Bert Grover forced Delya to hand over $425, the last money the family had in the world, and then forced the family from its home. Screaming, bleeding and still in nightgowns, they stumbled into the street.[38]

Since he had been sick for a month and a half, John Ercek was not out on strike. He was sleeping when vigilante Oscar Gilman and another gunman broke into his room. Without bothering to wake him, Gilman grabbed Ercek's foot and started to pull him from the bed. At the same time, Gilman's assistant struck Ercek two sharp blows on the head with a large stick. Seeing one ten-dollar bill and two twenties on a table beside the bed, Gilman took the money and stuffed it into his pocket. After threatening Ercek, the vigilantes forced him out in the street without giving him time to put on his shoes or shirt. Ercek, whose wife was dead, was supporting four children.[39]

Nancy Thomas later testified that gunmen Carl Fuller, Clarence Miller and Billy Woods robbed her home. Charging into John Connor's home, Tom Maddern struck Connor's wife a sharp blow with his elbow. In the street, one vigilante got on his knees and trained his gun on a man who had refused to be a deputy. Sixty-five-year-old Don Walsh, who had lived in Bisbee twenty years, was roughed up. George Rice was eating breakfast when two men shoved their guns through the door and asked if he sympathized with the strikers. He said yes, and they took him away.[40]

While gunmen marched William Eddy from his home, Eddy saw vigilante Mike Denny grab Tony Pereza's wife and give her a violent jerk.[41] Other witnesses saw women with children begging for their husbands and fathers.[42]

Twenty-eight-year-old Fred Watson, born in Cumberland County, England, came to America in 1908. He joined the Bingham, Utah, WFM local on May 24, 1909, and went to Bisbee in 1914 to work for Calumet & Arizona in the Cole Shaft. Later he got a job with Shattuck-Denn as a "tool nipper" (sharpener). His union membership was transferred to Bisbee, but Watson soon discovered the effete nature of the Bisbee WFM local. He joined the Bisbee branch of Mine Metal Workers' Union No. 800

on June 7, 1917, at about the same time other miners had opted for the apparently more vigorous IWW. When union leaders called the strike on June 26, he went out with the others. After spending the evening of June 11 with his lady friend, Dorothy Muat, Watson returned to his lodgings on Brophy Avenue. About 6:00 A.M. Jerry McNartney, Watson's roommate, asked Watson if he wanted to go on the picket line, but he declined in favor of some more sleep. Minutes later he was looking inside the barrels of a shotgun and a rifle, both wielded by well-known acquaintances of his. One was Joe Hope, who had been a school chum of Watson's in England; the other was Tom Maddern, a brother of Jimmy Maddern, the man who owned Watson's boarding house. Nervous and anxious, the two deputies did not even allow Watson time enough to put on his socks.[43]

When one man failed to be aroused by the deputies' knocks, three or four of the impatient gunmen broke down the front door, walked in and pulled the man out of bed. When his wife interceded and begged the intruders to allow her husband to dress, she was pushed aside and the man was dragged out of the house in his nightwear. The wife threw his trousers to him through the window; stumbling and hobbling along, he dressed in the street.[44]

Eight-year-old Matt Hanhila saw his striker father spared similar indignity. Sleeping in the living room, Matt was roused by a loud knock on the front door and looked up to see several men, armed with rifles, silhouetted against the sky. For a second Matt's father, Felix, contemplated a .32 automatic above the door frame; but discretion prevailed, and Matt saw his father whisked away.[45]

Katie Pintek came to Arizona in 1913 from Michigan via San Antonio, Texas, with her husband Mike, a tubercular. Both the Pinteks had originally immigrated to America from Croatia. At the time of the Bisbee Deportation, Katie was twenty-six years old and had two children. The Pinteks lived in a little house in Bakerville, between Lowell and Warren. Pintek's illness made it impossible for him to work in the mines, so he drove a taxi. Most of his customers were miners, and Pintek was known to be friendly with them.

As the Pinteks watched the roundup, they saw many men half-clothed and bleeding. Then, without any explanation, Pintek was ordered into the group of arrested men. He resisted and was pulled out of the house by Claude Clutz. Pintek, who had spent the night coughing up blood, was too weak to walk. Clutz grabbed him by the arms and dragged him one hundred and fifty feet to an ore truck owned by the Franklin Construction and Transfer Company of Lowell. After being loaded into the truck, Pintek was taken to the Warren ball park. Though not a miner or even an employee of a mining company, not a striker or a member of any union, Pintek became a prisoner in the early morning drive on the IWW.[46]

Pintek's arrest was neither unique nor an accident. Not all Bisbee miners owed their soul to the company store. The town's prosperity had attracted numerous independent merchants, contractors, professional people and other small businessmen who provided goods and services for the miners.[47] To build goodwill, they naturally extended credit and, in many cases, shared the ambitions and uncertainties of the workers. During the strike they carried the men's accounts and gave them encouragement. *The Bisbee Daily Review* described these sympathizers:

> Now there is a class of citizens here, fortunately in the small minority, but still a few, we are sorry to say, who are actually ready to encourage — yes, who have already encouraged — such a propaganda as we are now facing and slowly but surely stamping out. Such citizens are little, if any, better than the "wobblies" themselves.... The citizen of your country who extends aid, comfort and abetment to his country's enemies is a traitor.[48]

Thus said the *Review*. Pintek, who recognized the practical need to solicit the favor of his customers, had refused, during the strike, to hire his car to men "with buckets" (scabs). This plus the fact that an AFofL sticker was affixed to his car's windshield branded him "Wobbly" and lost him vigilante blessing. Two men who owned a grocery store next door to the Pinteks were arrested and deported; they had given credit to the miners. As Phelps Dodge and the vigilantes looked the other way, scabs took over the store, sold many goods and fought with each other over the sharing of the remaining inventory.[49] A restaurant owner, Ilija Luke Gobowich, who had purchased $1,500 worth of Liberty Bonds with his savings and had given $25 to the Red Cross, found himself among those arrested. Though not an IWW, he was taken from his business at the point of a gun. Bitterly, he later stated, "I was forced to leave $150 in the cash register and 200 pounds of meat hanging in the meat house yet to be cooked. Meat in my ovens burned up, I guess, because the posse would not permit me to drag it from the stove."[50]

Father Brewster, vicar of the local Episcopal church, had helped the miners build a city park. The only church figure in town whom the miners could trust, he had gained the wrath of the corporations. Vigilantes sought him, and had he not been out of town on business, the vicar, too, would have been deported.[51]

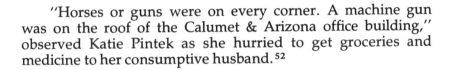

"Horses or guns were on every corner. A machine gun was on the roof of the Calumet & Arizona office building," observed Katie Pintek as she hurried to get groceries and medicine to her consumptive husband.[52]

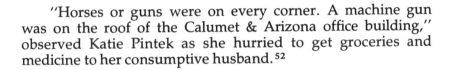

The Eagle Theatre in Bisbee ("The House of Comfort") that day featured "The Super-Deluxe Special Production" of *American Methods* with William Farnum, "The Story of a Red-Blooded American Who Overcomes Prejudice Despite all Obstacles." At the Orpheum Theatre, Enid Bennett was starring in *The Princess of the Dark*.[53]

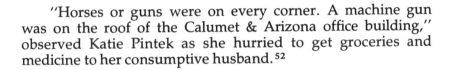

By 7:30 A.M. a huge group had been assembled under guard in the plaza in front of the Bisbee post office. Then, ten abreast, posse members and their prisoners began the two mile march to the Warren ball park. Most were unfed, some were half-clothed; many deputies had been impatient. Armed guards surrounded the procession, while spectators thronged at the rear.* Miners loyal to their employers, observing the "Big Drive," instead of reporting for work hurried home to pick up a rifle and tie a white handkerchief on their arms.[54] Deputy Bruce

---

*The *Review* (July 13, 1917, p. 1) claimed the next day that 3,000 men had joined the vigilante group, while the original delegation of two hundred deputies from Douglas rose to 1,000.

Perley gave one arrested man, Fred Brown, a chance to get out of the roundup line and become a vigilante. Brown refused, stating he "was better off not doing it."[55]

Vigilantes responded in a variety of ways to their situation. One arrested man, William Curnow, said the gunman guarding him in the march had apparently needed some bottled supplemental courage. "He was drunk as a dog," testified Curnow, who later was released in the ball park by Calumet & Arizona foreman Fennotte. Curnow, it so happened, owned the mortgage on Fennotte's house.[56]

One of the most colorful, dedicated and zealous deporters was Dr. Nelson Bledsoe, a surgeon on the Calumet & Arizona hospital staff. Armed with a Krag-Jorgensen rifle, a six-shooter in his belt, a cartridge belt full of revolver shells around his waist, and two *bandilleros* loaded with rifle bullets criss-crossed over his shoulders, Dr. Bledsoe appeared to one Mexican observer to look "just like [Pancho] Villa." Several people later testified Bledsoe "looked like a wild man" and had a strange "light in his eyes." Mike Pintek, who had been a patient of Bledsoe's, said the doctor "was so excited over the work he was doing" that he paid no attention to Pintek's pleas in the Warren ball park. Still others told how Bledsoe would not let deportees accept water offered to them during the hot march from Bisbee. Perhaps the most barbarous deed of the entire roundup and deportation was attributed to Dr. Bledsoe. Three or four people claimed they saw him in downtown Bisbee that morning walk up to a man who was holding a baby and talking to a lady. Without warning or apparent provocation, Bledsoe struck the man with his rifle so that the baby fell to the sidewalk. Bledsoe then forced the man to join the others already arrested. He continued to hit men in the line with his gun stock even after a "Captain Black" and some other gunmen criticized him for being "too strenuous."[57]

While he supervised the roundup and drive, Sheriff Wheeler rode in an open Ford touring car owned and chauffeured by Father Mandin, a local Catholic priest, who had only recently acquired the impressive machine as a gift from his congregation. Mounted on the vehicle, alongside Wheeler, was a new 7.62 mm. Marlin machine gun with a loaded feed belt in position. As the car raced back and forth along the streets of Bisbee, Lowell, Bakerville and Warren, Wheeler shouted instructions, exhortations and praise.[58]

Deputy arresting a striker in Bisbee (July 12, 1917)

Arrested strikers marching through Lowell on their way
from Bisbee to Warren ball park (July 12, 1917)

The parade exceeded in numbers, exuberance and spectacle the "monster" rally of July 4th. As the roundup proceeded
to the Warren ball park, the number of those arrested rose.
Once there, the crowd poured through the northwest gate and
filled the grandstand, while the overflow occupied the baseball
diamond. Vigilantes ringed the entire playing field, making
way for the frequent additions to the collection of prisoners
inside. Several of those arrested showed signs of being badly
beaten; some had long, deep cuts. Throughout the morning
men were added to the collection. Many arrived from Bisbee,
under guard, via streetcar. On the roof of the nearby Calumet
& Arizona office building was the machine gun observed by
Katie Pintek, this one trained on the ball park.[59]

During the hours in the ball-park stockade, most of the
prisoners were given a chance to recant their positions and go
back to work. No one tried to escape. In the meantime, the
IWW leaders exhorted the men not to weaken. Desperately,
John Greenway pleaded with them to go back to work. So did
some of the men's families, friends and others. Women sympathizers outside the park, using strong, explicit language,
exhorted the men not to weaken. They denounced the friends
and family members who offered to intercede and get the men
out.[60] At least one incident reflected a Bisbee, 1917, version of
the age-old conflict between generations. Someone reported
seeing an elderly lady, Mrs. Payne, whose husband was a
gunman, cry out to her two sons to "be men with the men"
and to stay with those arrested. Some men showed contrition
and were released; the rest answered the pleas of Greenway
and the others with catcalls, profane shouts and songs.[61] During this period one of the arrested men, William Cleary,
a well-known Bisbee attorney and long-time successful
defender of the working man against the corporations,
became spokesman for the prisoners.[62]

When Mrs. Pintek arrived at the ball park with the
groceries and medicine for her husband, she could not find
him in the crowd of prisoners, deputies and onlookers. After a
frantic search, she gave the supplies to an unknown man in a
boxcar who promised to get them to Pintek. But luck had
already interceded on Pintek's behalf. While in the line inside
the ball park, Pintek continued to cough up blood. In desperation he stepped up on a little wooden box for a look over the
six-foot-high fence toward the streetcar tracks. By chance he

Vigilantes and arrested strikers marching from Lowell on their way to Warren ball park (July 12, 1917)

Members of Workmen's Loyalty League and Businessman's Protective League guarding arrested strikers at Warren ball park (July 12, 1917)

spied nearby a friend, Constable Percy Bowden, and called to him. Bowden, who knew of Pintek's condition, vouched for him, and he was released.

Actually, almost anyone who either promised to go back to work or who could "get a respectable citizen to vouch for him" was released. At its peak, the number of arrested men had reached around two thousand. This included three women, but they were among the first released. According to one report, lawyer Cleary talked many men into not going back to work. Cleary supposedly promised them he could make the copper companies, particularly Phelps Dodge, pay each one $10,000 in damages if they allowed themselves to be deported. Many other men refused to go back to work out of a sense of worker loyalty, indignation and pride. Taken from the group three times and asked to go back to work, John R. Chase, an old-time Bisbee resident, elected to go out on the train. On the other hand, some gunmen admitted their choice of sides was based more on expedience than on conviction. They knew, as one woman later testified, "Their jobs depended on what they did." By 11:00 A.M., when the train arrived, the group had been pared down to about 1,200 men. Deputies freed Dominic Catero just as he was to step in a boxcar, while at least one man was left behind because there was simply not enough room for him on the train.[63] At no time, it appears, did the men become disorderly.

Just before 11:00 A.M., twenty-three cattle and boxcars of the Phelps Dodge-owned El Paso and Southwestern Railroad rolled into the Warren station; the *Review* reported, "Immediately the Wobblies gave the train a rousing cheer." Twenty-three cars for 1,186 men, however, was nothing to cheer about. Averaging more than fifty men per car meant that few could sit down at one time.[64] Some cars were reported to have had as much as three inches of manure on the floor.[65]

With the arrival of the train, the men seemed eager to start moving. John Greenway made one last desperate plea begging them to go back to work. They responded with hoots and jeers. Dirty, bloodied, hungry, half-clothed, they still seemed high-spirited. The armed guards, in two tight lines that faced each other, formed a winding gauntlet or corridor from the ball-park gate to the train. Greenway, now mounted with a rifle across his saddle, helped guard the right-hand side of the exit gate. Given to shiny leather puttees and a stiff-brimmed campaign

Bisbee and other Warren District citizens watching
arrested strikers at Warren ball park (July 12, 1917)

Corridor of vigilantes formed to load deportees from
Warren ball park to train (July 12, 1917)

Close-up of vigilantes and deportees boarding
cattle car, Warren, Arizona (July 12, 1917)

Boxcars and cattle cars loaded with deportees getting
ready to leave Warren station (July 12, 1917)

hat, former Rough Rider Greenway presented a jut-jawed image familiar to those who read Richard Harding Davis adventure stories. The prisoners were released from the park in groups of forty and fifty and were led—as it were—through a cattle chute to the waiting cars. Within an hour the train had been loaded with men; among them, voluntarily, was the brother of Rosa McKay, a labor representative to the state legislature. Vigilantes loaded some food including bread and oranges in the caboose for the one hundred eighty-six armed guards stationed on top of the cars.[66]

Alice Campbell Juliff, sister of Governor Thomas Campbell and wife of a shift boss at Calumet & Arizona, reported her impressions of the roundup in a poem entitled "Things I Can Never Forget":

The procession of men
Coming down the road from Lowell
To the Warren Ball Park
Across from the railroad track.

The silence awes me,
Sinister, broken only
By the sound of marching feet.
Not a voice was raised,
Company guards, all armed,
Walking on either side of the strikers.

Fear did not cause this stunned silence.
I believe it was surprise.

Bill Cleary, the aristocrat,
Turned bitter because of real and fancied wrongs
At the C. Q. Hands
Made one think of his peers
Of the French Revolution
On the way to the guillotine.
Head high, an occasional glance
Toward his erstwhile friends and neighbors
Among the guards.

The march ended in the ball park,
Where the mutterings and protestings began,
Doubtless at the sight of the train of box cars,
Ready for the deportation.
John Greenway stood in the grandstand
Begging their attention,
Saying anyone who wanted to leave the ranks
And return to work,
Might do so.
He was booed, hissed, cursed into silence.

I watched the march
Up into the box cars like cattle,
Each car had several armed guards on top.
Old friends, neighbors, relatives,
Divided their hate and misunderstanding
Those with guns, others without.

Every lawyer in the district
From the unscrupulous shyster
To the dignified corporation staff
Advised and warned against this
Monstrous thing.
Yes, our side believed we were right,
Blinded by war hysteria, pseudo patriotism
Or was it only self-preservation?

I believed a lot of things
Used to inflame us
Especially that the IWWs
Were saboteurs.
Until a friend and sympathizer
Of the strikers
Was approached by some of the
Smooth, slick agents from the outside,
Offered a fat salary
To go to the wheat fields
Of the north west
And start dissension.
He was so outraged —
He quit his job.

The executors of the roundup and deportation felt that the matter was their own affair and that no one in the outside world should interfere. Accordingly, Harry H. Stout, superintendent of the Copper Queen Smelter, used the fictitious title of "Captain" as he attempted to impose certain conditions of martial law on Bisbee. Calling it "military censorship," he ordered the Douglas manager of the Western Union Telegraph Company to cut off communications between Bisbee and the outside world.[67] When she tried to telegraph President Wilson and United States Senator from Arizona Henry Fountain Ashurst to inform them of the outrage, Rosa McKay, the labor legislatress from Cochise County elected the previous November on the Socialist Party ticket, was knocked down in the Western Union office by gunmen. (A few minutes before, Mrs. McKay was "eyewitness to a man wearing a star, strike a woman in the chest.")[68] By 8:45 A.M., however, Mrs. McKay successfully sent her telegrams. The first, although sent "care Henry Ashurst," was addressed (as was her other message) to President Wilson. In it Mrs. McKay said:

> As representative of state from Cochise County I am asking protection for the women and children before we have another Ludlow, Colorado. They walked men out of town this morning that had not done one thing. Wire answer immediately.[69]

When Harry Stout attempted a similar censorship at the Bell Telephone Company office, Manager George Kellogg refused to obey.[70] But few phone calls were made. W. P. French, a Bisbee auto mechanic, attempted to call both Governor Campbell and ex-Governor Hunt on the morning of July 12. Within four minutes, an automobile filled with armed men stopped in front of French's garage demanding the identity of the person attempting to call out. They had been notified by the operator. French saved himself from deportation by pleading ignorance.[71]

To get the word to authorities outside Bisbee, alert Attorney Cleary, before he returned to Warren to be arrested along with the others, had slipped down to Naco where he telegrammed federal labor investigator George W. P. Hunt in Globe: "Two thousand miners being deported this morning by corporation gunmen.... Stop that train."[72] Cleary obviously chose to be deported. After returning to Warren, he joined the men at the ball park and then elected to board car number five with sixty-four other deportees. This selfless conduct failed to evoke a scintilla of admiration from the *Review*. The Western Union manager allowed Lt. Col. Hornbrook to notify the adjutant general.[73] And so, in the early stages of the affair, the news had leaked out. Later the mine operators gave "humane" reasons for the censorship; they insisted it was necessary to avoid causing a reaction in other counties which might have brought bloodshed.[74]

Little time elapsed before the word reached the ears of elected authorities. Governor Thomas Campbell claims he heard about the deportation on July 12 when R. Allyn Lewis, a Phoenix stockbroker, called to give him the news. Governor Campbell found he could reach Bisbee by neither telegraph nor telephone.[75] Helpless without a militia, he telegraphed Fort Sam Houston asking for troops saying he needed aid because he could not enforce martial law.[76] Responding to William Cleary's message from Mexico, Federal Commissioner Hunt together with federal mediator John McBride immediately appealed to President Wilson to stop further deportations of strikers from Arizona towns "to prevent sympathetic strikes and industrial paralysis." Wilson notified United States Attorney General Whitney who telegraphed Sheriff Wheeler demanding "by what authority of law you are acting. State fully what violations, if any, took place prior to decision to deport strikers."[77] President Wilson contacted Governor Campbell immediately:

> 'May I not respectfully urge the great danger of citizens taking the law into their own hands.... I look upon such actions with grave apprehensions. A very serious responsibility is assumed when such precedents are set.'[78]

Also from Globe, United States Attorney Thomas A. Flynn of the Arizona Federal Judicial District sent a coded telegram to the office of the United States Attorney telling of the deportation in progress in Bisbee.[79]

Train Ride

As the deportation train slowly pulled out of Warren at noon, it blew a warning whistle to several of the deportees' wives who, as they stumbled alongside, cursed Bisbee and its people. Overjoyed with the sight, John Greenway "took off his hat, hollered and clapped his hands."[80]

The train then headed for Columbus, New Mexico, one hundred seventy-three miles east of Bisbee and close to the border of Mexico. A little more than a year before, on March 9, 1916, the Mexican revolutionary bandit Francisco "Pancho" Villa, in one of his thrusts across the United States border, had raided Columbus and killed sixteen people.

While the guards allowed the railroad car doors to remain open, the men, forced to stand for many hours in crowded, airless cars, some in cow manure over their shoe tops, experienced extreme discomfort. The July heat (Columbus recorded one of the hottest days of the year) caused the men in those cars with water to exhaust the supply several hours before reaching Columbus that night. Some became nauseated. From inside the cars, they were unable to see where they were and rumors flew — and grew.

Ten miles northeast of Douglas the deportation train made its first stop, at Lee, an El Paso and Southwestern Railroad station, where train crews were exchanged and water barrels were placed on the cars. There is considerable controversy as to how well the prisoners had been provided food and drink. Some cars had various sizes of water barrels in them, three even with ice. Deportee Fred Brown said later: "There was plenty of water in the car I was in, a big barrel that had held sixty gallons."[81]

Deportee Fred Watson said his car had no water, nor was he allowed to drink when the train stopped for water.[82] Bill Cleary claimed that the water ran out "about 3 or 4 P.M." A few deportees later testified that several cartons of crackers were put on a car at the front of the train. One deputy maintained that much food that had been provided "was thrown away by the passengers in anger or in reckless horseplay." Vigilante William Beeman stated: "All stories about deportees being without food or water are so much bunk.... One full car of provisions and two tank cars of water...[were] on the same train with the men." Photographs of the train fail to support this contention.[83]

None of the deportees was allowed off the train during the twenty minutes it took the engine to get water at Lee Station. Two hundred gunmen, who had left Bisbee in automobiles ahead of the train; lined both sides of the track, while "machine guns on two knolls dominated the situation," one weapon "in a place that looked as though it had taken hours of work to

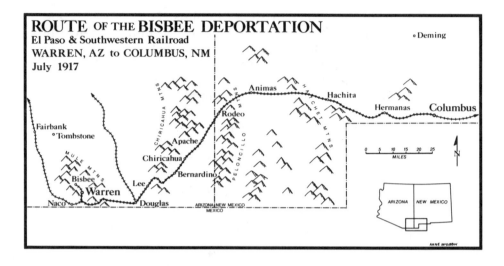

ROUTE OF THE BISBEE DEPORTATION
El Paso & Southwestern Railroad
WARREN, AZ to COLUMBUS, NM
July 1917

level.''[84] These machine guns and those Katie Pintek had observed on the roof of the Calumet and Arizona office building
were, no doubt, the ones sold to Phelps Dodge general manager
Stuart French on April 10 by the Marlin Arms Corporation of
New Haven, Connecticut.[85] Phelps Dodge, indeed, had made
thorough and efficient plans. No one could argue with the
Review editorial of July 14 which said: ''For swiftness of action,
precision of detail and general all 'round success that 'wobbly'
drive will stand as a masterpiece in western annals for many a
long year to come.''[86]

The train then went on to Rodeo, New Mexico, just over
the state line about fifty miles northeast of Lee Station, where
the engine took on more water. Here, at about 3:00 P.M., the
guards allowed the passengers to get out and stretch their legs
a little. Heading east toward El Paso, the train stopped again,
this time at Hachita, fifty-five miles on down the line from
Rodeo. While changing engines here, the deporters again allowed their prisoners to get out and stretch. This time crewmen
tossed bread and crackers to their captives. Deportee Fred
Brown said later:

> I got out and asked the head brakeman whether he
> belonged to the Brotherhood or not, and he told me that
> he did, and I told him who I was, and I asked him if he
> wasn't a little ashamed of the extent he was playing and he

said, "No, we are doing this for Uncle Sam," and I turned to the fellow who had followed me up there and I says, "Do you know what you are doing," and he said, "Yes, I guess I do." And I says, "Under whose authority are you in the State of New Mexico carrying a gun?" And he said, "Sheriff Wheeler's authority," and I said, "Has Sheriff Wheeler any authority to send you into New Mexico with a gun?" And he said, "I don't know that it is an offense, and we are going to take you to Columbus," and that is the first I found out that we were going to Columbus and that the Government was behind it.[87]

But the government of New Mexico, anyway, was *not* behind it. When he learned that the deportees had arrived in New Mexico, Governor W. E. Lindsey ordered the arrest of those in charge. The train arrived at Columbus at 9:30 P.M. Local officials, after arresting F. B. King, district superintendent of the El Paso and Southwestern Railroad, who had been placed in charge of the deportation train, ordered that it turn back. Unlike their Arizona counterparts, New Mexican officials felt no necessity to bow before the Phelps Dodge Corporation. King was released, but the train started westward. At 3:00 A.M. on Friday, July 13, it stopped in Hermanas, New Mexico, twenty miles west of Columbus, where the deporters parked the train on a siding.[88] Many of the captives, despite being without water for more than fifteen hours, were now asleep, even though they could not lie down. Those awake could hear gunmen running back and forth on the top of the train, but the number of footsteps declined until everything was quiet. Fred Brown was so tired he was ready to drop:

> I hollered out and asked the fellow if I could come out and get on top and lay down. I hollered the third time and I got no answer, and finally I saw a black form coming around the side of the car and I waited until he came close, and then I said, "Are you a gunman?" And he said, "No, I believe they are all gone." I slipped out of the car and crawled on my stomach off into the sage brush until I got up with him and then we crawled back to the end of the car and looked across again and we didn't see anyone, so finally the other fellow came over to where I was on top of this—we were afraid to make any noise—and I said, "I believe they are gone," and he said he believed they were too, so we tiptoed up to the head car. About that time the

Drummers' Special pulled in, and I heard more or less noise down at the depot. We were about half a mile from the depot, and we stood there and listened and watched for about ten minutes, and finally we heard a bunch yelling down there at the train and the train pulled out, so we decided then that the men had gone back on this Drummers' Special.[89]

The stiff and weary men climbed out of the cars and built fires. Fred Brown went down to the depot and sent a telegram to Samuel Gompers. Bill Cleary sent messages to Arizona Governor Campbell and President Wilson. Cleary, a steadfast leader, climbed on top of the cars and explained the situation to the men. They all spent the day in Hermanas sending telegrams, writing letters and keeping out of the hot sun. About two o'clock in the afternoon several of the men went around and collected some money. Then two of the deportees caught a freight train to Columbus, where they bought food and tobacco, and they were back in Hermanas by six that evening. About three hours later a freight car attached to a passenger train came in with coffee, bread, crackers, canned goods and tin cups, and these goods were distributed to the men. That night they slept on the ground, in or on railroad cars and on piled railroad ties.[90]

Now more knowledgeable about the situation, New Mexico Governor Lindsey declared that the deportees at Hermanas should be treated humanely. He directed Luna County's Sheriff Simpson to "conduct the fugitives peaceably to Columbus...and feed them at State expense until the Federal authorities take charge." Perhaps Governor Lindsey did not bow before Phelps Dodge, but he was not going to try to challenge the corporation's power by ordering the train back to Arizona. So he wired President Wilson requesting that "the Federal Government take charge and dispose of the matter according to federal law and order."[91] Quickly responding to the request, Wilson alerted his Secretary of War. The War Department, on July 13, gave orders to General Bell—who relayed them to Colonel Sickel at Columbus—to bring the deported men from Hermanas to Columbus and "provide them with rations...if necessary to prevent great suffering." Colonel Sickel was instructed not to hold the men as prisoners. But neither President Wilson nor his executive departments chose to send the men back into Phelps Dodge territory.[92]

While at Hermanas, Cleary, the proud champion of the Bisbee workingman, made a statement for the press describing the purposes of the strike. At the same time, Cleary praised the attitude of the men and condemned the tyrannical way in which the deportation had taken place. A "machine gun was trained on the miners," he complained, even though at no time did any miner offer resistance. Cleary declared:

> While many of the men, it is true, are members of what is known as the I.W.W., nevertheless they are law-abiding and peaceful.... Many who have lived in Bisbee for years — some for as long as fifteen years and have their wives and families there now — are very anxious to return.[93]

There was little evidence the men could return. Not one legally constituted authority suggested that possibility. The copper companies had made clear their intention to maintain exclusive sovereign rights in Bisbee — and Arizona. The Phelps Dodge Corporation spoke through its mouthpiece on July 14:

> Any talk of their coming back is nonsense. They will not be allowed to come back. We have been slow to act, but once started, it is a finish fight. The serious business of this district is the mining of copper ore, not the building of nightly schools of anarchism or idling on the streets or picketing public places and private works.[94]

Four days later, however, when a Bisbee woman on the telephone asked anxiously, "Are the Wobblies coming back?" the *Review* equivocated: "No, madame, they are not coming back; anyway, not soon."[95]

PART III

THE
AFTERMATH

8

SECURING
CONTROL

When roll was called in the Senate of the United States on the morning of July 13, 1917, Senator Henry L. Myers of Montana rose to inform the clerk: "The Senator from Arizona (Mr. Ashurst) is necessarily detained from the Senate this morning by reason of an accident, a misfortune beyond his control."[1] While Senator Ashurst's sudden absence had resulted from a freak accident (an awning collapsed and fell on him, and he was hospitalized briefly), it symbolized the beginning of a series of strong reactions to the "misfortune" at Bisbee. The deportation had unloosed a controversy that would last for years.

Officials and the Press

That same day, "Big Bill" Haywood, president of the IWW, declared the Bisbee event an "outrage."[2] As soon as he got word of the deportation, on July 13, Haywood telegraphed President Wilson in Washington demanding that the miners be returned to Bisbee. Wilson failed to reply. Two days later, upon hearing the men had been moved to Columbus, Haywood telegraphed Wilson again. Still Wilson refused to answer. More

conservative union officials, too, expressed their anger. But
Henry Fountain Ashurst returned from his "accident" to the
Senate. On July 16, after having a telegram from the Bisbee
Loyalty League and the Citizens' Protective League read by the
secretary, he denounced Haywood's Wobblies by quoting a
letter from "a former attorney general of Arizona."

> I myself have heard expressions from many of the
> Independent [sic] Workers of the World which proved
> them to be treasonable.... The most superficial investiga-
> tion in Arizona at this time will convince any fair-minded
> man of the truth of this statement. It is not a labor problem
> or an issue between employer and employee in any sense;
> it is a deep-laid plot against the government.[3]

And so began a debate that would flounder in polemics,
contradiction, ambivalence, civil suits and out-of-court settlements, and finally, drained of its energy, would sputter and
trail off, like most controversy, into obscurity. The Bisbeeites
took a strong defensive position immediately. In addition to
their message to Senator Ashurst, they wired President Wilson
and Secretary of War Baker claiming that: (1) the strike had
been called by a few IWW agitators; (2) violence and intimidation by IWWs attended the strike; (3) "seventy-five percent of
the I.W.W. pickets were strangers to the community"; (4) 90
percent of those deported were strangers, and four hundred
men were sleeping on the floor of the IWW hall when arrested;
(5) many of those deported were Austrians and other enemy
aliens; (6) the men on the train were provided with sufficient
food and water; (7) any loyal American would be given work in
Bisbee. In another telegram to Washington, Bisbee Mayor
Erickson; Sheriff Wheeler; J. R. Henderson, president of the
Citizens' Protective League; Miles W. Merrill, president of the
Workman's Loyalty League; and Charles W. Allen, president of
the Warren District Commercial Club, asserted that William
Cleary's statement to the press in Hermanas was not true.
While in Bisbee Cleary had been outspoken in his objection
to the purchase of Liberty Bonds, conscription and working
conditions, which "actually are the best in the country";
they also insisted that IWW activities were directly financed by
Germany and that the whole proceeding was "unavoidable
to avoid" sedition and open treason. The Warren district, they
added, was not peaceful and quiet.[4]

The Western Union Telegraph Company refused to be quiet. Almost immediately it announced an investigation into the censorship of its lines. Western Union named Robert Rae and H. H. Stout, Copper Queen general auditor and smelter superintendent, respectively, as being involved in the communication interruption of July 12.[5] In reaction to all the criticisms of the deportation day censorship, the editor of the *Bisbee Daily Review* wrote that "the necessity for action came too abruptly." The virtual *non sequitur* characterized much of the verbosity with which the Phelps Dodge Corporation bathed the condemnations of the deporters.[6]

In Bisbee, everyone took an absolute position. Brother had arrested brother, father had deported son. Ethnic identities had no strict loyalties, national backgrounds meant nothing and old-time Bisbeeites enjoyed no preferential treatment. Thomas English, born in Phoenix in 1880, was deported, as was John R. Chase, a resident of the Warren District since 1900 who was arrested "by a Bohunk and a Cousin Jack." Deportee William Blackburn was born in Tombstone and had lived in Bisbee almost all his thirty-two years. The town—and the state—was now deeply split only by the attitudes its citizens had regarding company loyalty and unionism.[7]

Shortly after the deportation, Arizona Governor Thomas E. Campbell made clear his position regarding the Arizona labor scene. In a letter to *The Outlook*, Campbell accused the IWW of conspiracy to create a "Nation-wide tie-up of industries." He mentioned the confict between the IWW and the IUMMSW but claimed, with full knowledge to the contrary, that "at present all the important mines and smelters in the Globe and Miami districts are closed down, due to Industrial Workers of the World agitation." He did concede the strikes in Clifton-Morenci had been called by the Mine, Mill and Smelter workers.[8]

Governor Campbell, together with several other western governors disturbed by the Bisbee Deportation, then asked President Wilson to intern the IWW radicals in "camps at some distance from the place of apprehension. This place would effectively mistify [sic] and frighten them; would avoid making heroes of them; and would deprive them of their best material for propaganda—besides avoiding rash action by citizens." The governor added that "there would be no more illegality involved than there was in the action of the Arizona citizens."[9]

On July 15 Governor Campbell wired President Wilson to request an audience for George L. Bell, the representative of the western governors. Bell, an attorney and executive officer of the California State Immigration and Housing Committee, was en route to Washington to present the details of the governors' proposal to Wilson. "Bell's mission has my unqualified approval," said Campbell. "May I respectfully bespeak your indulgence in awaiting the unfolding of these plans and proposals before directing Federal action in connection with the I.W.W. disturbances."[10] Emmett D. Boyle, governor of Nevada, had wired Wilson two days earlier requesting that the President listen to Bell.[11]

The recommendation of the western governors probably contributed to the influences that brought about the Wilson administration's decision to crack down on the IWW two months later.

On July 23 six representatives of the Bisbee and Douglas Protective Leagues met with Governor Campbell at the governor's office in Phoenix to give him "first-hand" information. The group included Calumet & Arizona's Dr. Nelson Bledsoe and Bisbee Loyalty League Organizer Miles Merrill. They denied reports that women and children had been injured and said that the deportees' families were being cared for by the League. They insisted that the Wobblies "would not again be admitted to the district." Moreover, they reported, the round-up and deportation had been observed by a representative of the federal government. To the committee, the presence of Lt. Col. Hornbrook at the Warren ball park had implied government sanction of the affair. One committee member, Thomas Hughes, mentioned that Governor Campbell's brother-in-law, Fred Juliff, a shift boss at Calumet & Arizona, had identified and vouched for several men at the ball park. Campbell showed no sign of response to this remark.[12]

The governor, maintaining a cool distance from his audience, said he knew about the affairs in Bisbee, and he instructed his visitors that deportation was not the proper way to handle the situation. Campbell, in a judicious form, told the committee that in spite of their claims, he was confident that some innocent persons had been deported.[13]

The governor asked the committee if it could prove the existence of German money behind the strikers. "This state is permeated with Secret Service men," said Campbell, and he informed his visitors that Mr. McCaleb, chief of the federal agents, had said that no evidence could be found of any pro-German influence in the state.[14] For public record, he was responding to President Wilson's admonition to "look upon such actions with grave apprehensions."

Off the record, Campbell had no intention of getting overweening. He hastened to reassure the real forces which instigated the directions and decisions in Arizona that he still maintained an awareness of his public servant status. The day after his meeting with the Loyalty League representatives, he wrote an off-the-record letter to Charles W. Clark, general manager of the United Verde Copper Company in Jerome and Clarkdale:

> Thanks for your letter of July twenty-third, especially for your appreciation of the embarrassment caused me by recent deportation of alleged undesirables from Jerome and Bisbee.
> I realize the impulses under which our citizens acted, and while I cannot countenance such forcible and unwarranted public expressions as Executive, I am not inclined to cry over the milk that has been spilt.[15]

Governor Campbell turned in still another direction that day. An indignant Phoenix citizen, Thomas H. Bell, had written Campbell on July 21 protesting in a somewhat circumspect way the Loyalty League, the Bisbee Deportation and the general rash of extralegal behavior around the state. On the twenty-fourth Campbell wrote back rather stiffly and equally cautious: "I ... feel inclined to concur in the majority of contentions set forth therein."[16]

Certain other public officials felt no more lachrymose than did Governor Campbell. In Washington, on July 25, Anthony Caminetti, Commissioner General of the Bureau of Immigration, wrote a letter to Assistant Secretary of Labor Louis F. Post:

> There are, perhaps, reasons for believing that the present activities of the I.W.W.'s are due to German influence and possibly backed with German funds.... Doubtless a successfully conducted campaign against the foreign leaders among these people would produce valuable and far-reaching salutary effects.[17]

A descendant of the "New Immigration," Caminetti appeared to be a classical model of the *arriviste* going to extremes to please his American nativist colleagues and his occupational superiors to prove his loyalty and strengthen his credentials for vertical ascent.

With the press, Bisbee became a *cause célèbre*. An immediate avalanche of response covered the nation. The newspapers of New York set the 2 to 1 ratio of approval and condemnation. The *New York Times* waxed righteously ambivalent. On July 12, commenting on the Jerome deportation, an editorial entitled "Workers of Mischief" read: "The Arizona mining town, Jerome, has deported its I.W.W. contingent. If the whole gang could be deported from the United States, the United States would be greatly improved." But two days later the *Times* had second thoughts: "The Sheriff of Bisbee ... would look well in a Bret Harte story or a history of Vigilance Committees, but a Sheriff who makes his own law is on dangerous and indefensible ground; and inhumanity is worse than the I.W.W. ... Bisbee had a right to defend itself against violence, not to do violence."[18] The *New York World* believed "We have nourished ... a nest of vipers."[19] But the New York *Commercial* dared to suggest, "It flavors too much of lynch-law."[20] Another New York paper, the *Globe*, opined the same under the heading "Lynch Law in Arizona": "The Bisbee plan does not work. It is foolish and fatal and is planting the seeds of trouble."[21]

A smaller midwestern town found the deportation technique too tame: "Any endeavor by the I.W.W. to prejudice the cause of the United States by fomenting strikes in the ore fields should be met by hanging a few ring leaders to the nearest tree."[22] The *Chicago Tribune* considered the same recourse but remembered its cosmopolitan responsibility and equivocated: "We are not counseling lynch law, but we think deportation is too mild a punishment."[23] But generally, midwest America, less feverish about the war, offered strong criticism of the deporters.* The Bisbee Deportation, felt the St. Louis *Republic*, was a "conspicuous exhibition of bad leadership." In Springfield, Illinois, the *Republican* commented that the Bisbee mining officials provoked criticism "by their

---

*Several of the newspaper articles quoted here have been taken, secondhand, from the *Review* to illustrate the Bisbee newspaper's awareness of and sensitivity to national opinion. Obviously never quite certain of the national acceptance of the deportation, the *Review*, of course, reprinted only those comments of a laudatory nature.

reckless and insolent conduct in imposing an unlawful embargo on news-dispatches over the telegraph-wires from the town to the outside world."[24]

In Boston, hub of American literature, philosophy and reform, the *Transcript* extravagantly extended its scope of nationhood: "As the crow flies, Bisbee is a long way from Boston, but as Americanism goes, Arizona and Massachusetts are next door neighbors." Employing its traditional prerogative to identify landmarks in national history and literature, the *Transcript* called the event the "Bisbee Tea Party." The paper deemed that Sheriff Wheeler's proclamation "will go down in the history of the German-American war as a great document.... its every word rings with the determination of the people to steady the palsied hand of the Government from the mines of Arizona to the trenches in France." The Boston paper went on: "What happened in Bisbee earlier in the week is what will happen in Boston and in every other American community when the Federal Government fails to afford the people protection from a foreign foe."[25] Thus did the *Transcript* articulate that compulsion Easterners have always had to find a reaffirmation and distillation of the American *élan vital* in the American West.[26]

Out West, the *Los Angeles Times* attributed catechistic qualities to the deportation. "The citizens of Cochise county, Arizona, have written a lesson that the whole of America would do well to copy."[27] Being less sensitive to the sedition theme, the larger newspapers of Arizona, as could be expected, emphasized the union-smashing effect of the deportation rather than commenting on the deporters' patriotism. "The breaking of the back of the I.W.W. at Bisbee has been of service to the whole country," said Phoenix' *Arizona Republican*. "Jerome and Bisbee have so freed themselves," said the *Republican*, "and we believe that their course will be followed by every other camp in the state."[28] The *Phoenix Gazette*, avoiding sexual prejudice and at the same time getting closer to the feelings of Phelps Dodge, stated that the strikes were "made possible by such people as Haywood, Mother Jones, Emma Goldman, Hunt and Moyer."[29]

American journals joined the newspapers in blessing the event. Only a few, notably the "liberal," "progressive" or "radical" ones, condemned it. *The Nation* found it "unlawful" and "practically foolish."[30] *The New Republic* castigated the

IWW for playing into the hands of the capitalists by guaranteeing the failure of the movement toward collective bargaining. This unofficial organ of the Progressive period provided the most objective and penetrating analysis among the immediate responses. But it concluded—with dutiful idealism —that "operators must allow responsible unions to organize or face anarchy." *The New Republic* apparently understood little about the social and political reality of western copper mining camps.[31] Citing the IWW as acting in a way that "is of great assistance to the enemy," *The Survey* also condemned the deportation. Disapproving of the Bisbee vigilantes, *Survey* columnist Edward T. Divine remonstrated that America had the "difficult task of stamping out the spirit of violence."[32]

More Deportations

There was little of that kind of stamping. More undesirables found themselves on the wrong end of a vigilante's gun. President Wilson's fear that Bisbee might set a precedent was realized. Although the earlier, smaller deportations in the West had denied Bisbee a unique or original experience, the success, support, publicity and absence of enforced restraint involved in the Bisbee Deportation inspired and licensed more of the same.

With the Bisbee model in the van, a mob of native Americans, on July 14—two days following the Bisbee episode— forced seven hundred aliens to leave the lead mining districts of Flat River, Missouri. The vigilantes said the employers had been discharging Americans and putting aliens in their places at lower wages.[33] The "aliens" included Italians, Russians and Poles, national backgrounds identified as allies with the United States.[34] On July 25, thirteen men and one woman, "all said to be members of the I.W.W.," were corralled by one hundred fifty citizens armed with clubs and sent out of town on a westbound train from Bemidji, Minnesota. This number of deportees later rose to thirty.[35]

Over in New Mexico, the sanctuary of the Arizona deportees, they had a deportation of their own on July 31. A truck with a machine gun mounted on it escorted thirty-two alleged IWW coal miners in Gallup to the railroad station. They were sent to Belen, New Mexico, where additional Gallup deportees later raised the total to eighty. When he discovered that most of these men belonged to the United Mine Workers of America,

Samuel Gompers became indignant and brought the fact to President Wilson's attention.[36] More fearless with New Mexico coal mine owners than with Phelps Dodge, Wilson interceded. After only four days in Belen and following receipt of a telegram from New Mexico Governor Lindsey, they received permission to return to Gallup.[37]

The precedent Wilson feared was set. In scope, size and planning, nothing paralleled it in the history of America, legal or extralegal. In August, another deportation took place in Fairbury, Nebraska.[38] In 1919, authorities cited Bisbee as a precedent for a deportation in California of orange grove workers from the Pomona Valley.[39]

Columbus

Once the deportation plan had gone into effect, it had proved remarkably well designed. Considering the number of people and the logistics involved, the presence of loaded weapons and the emotional tensions of everyone, that no more than two deaths occurred is surprising. From the same perspective, this contention of the *Review* seems valid:

> And in the end we know, and this is the finest thought of all, that if we were firm we were also humane, and that, if we took extreme measures, we took them in a way true to the best traditions of American citizenhood.[40]

While the train ride to Columbus and back to Hermanas became an agonizing, interminable series of unexplained delays, everyone survived the stifling boxcars. To the deportees the indignity of being forcibly expelled from their homes and community seemed far more painful than any physical discomfort.

Army red tape delayed the rations that the War Department ordered Colonel Sickel to provide for the men at Hermanas. To prevent starvation, army officials had dispatched a truck load of supplies from Columbus and authorized the shipment of two boxcar loads of provisions from Camp Bliss near El Paso, Texas. Meanwhile, Governor Lindsey ordered the arrest of the men, but the Luna County sheriff and district attorney guaranteed the deportees protection.[41]

By 5:00 A.M., Saturday, July 14, all the deportees in Hermanas were up looking for old oil cans and food tins in which to boil coffee. But they were interrupted by Lt. Col.

Hornbrook who had arrived in Hermanas with a small detachment of cavalrymen from Douglas. He telegraphed back to his Arizona District office at Douglas that everything was "orderly and quiet." Hornbrook counted 1,152 "strikers"; he could not see any women or children. By 6:25 A.M. the soldiers had loaded everyone back on the railroad cars.[42] Then, following the War Department orders to guard the men carefully, Hornbrook and the cavalrymen escorted the deportees via train from Hermanas to Columbus. At 10:10 A.M. Hornbrook turned the "prisoners" over to Colonel H. G. Sickel, 12th Cavalry, the commanding officer of Camp Furlong, Columbus, New Mexico. The 12th was composed primarily of black soldiers, who reportedly treated the deportees with sympathetic courtesy. At Camp Furlong the men ate their first real meal in two days.[43]

When the provisions from El Paso failed to arrive, the El Paso and Southwestern Railroad furnished the food. In addition, the railroad offered $90 worth of tobacco to the men who could pay for it. July 14 was said to be the hottest day of the summer of 1917 in Columbus. That day twenty men and twelve women, including Arizona State Representative Rosa McKay, arrived from Bisbee. A strong favorite with workingmen, Mrs. McKay was loudly cheered. The caravan from Bisbee included ten automobiles loaded with supplies.[44] From this point on the men experienced little physical danger and no extreme discomfort.

Since Pancho Villa had raided Columbus in 1916, the U.S. Army had assigned a garrison to Columbus to guard against further attacks by Mexican bandits and revolutionaries. Sheltered in a stockade built for Mexican refugees, the men could not know that it was to be their home for the next two months.[45] After splitting them into seventy-five-man companies, army officials assigned the deportees chores and then continued to treat them as military subjects.

Colonel Sickel immediately wired the Army adjutant general's office and gave notice that he had received the deportees. He said the men would be "organized into eight companies" and that the camp was "being prepared by utilizing every variety of tentage available for shelter." Sickel requested additional tents from Camp Bliss, and he asked the adjutant general's office for authority "to use lumber and other material on hand" to "construct mess shelters and other temporary buildings." He informed the Washington office that "three fourths of these men are without coats." The men had no blankets or other bedding, he added, and he asked if his charges should be "regarded as prisoners and closely guarded against escape." No one, Sickel said, had tried to leave. The colonel received no answer to this inquiry for several days, but the army soon installed showers, toilets and telephones in the camp. Later, white soldiers replaced the kindly blacks who had received the deportees.[46]

On July 15 the military leaders adopted a ration cost limit of twenty-three cents per man per day—two-thirds the value of the regular army ration, and every day they took a ration count.[47] This limit included "the cost of articles usually drawn on ration returns but not included in the cost of rations such as soap, candles, matches, toilet paper and ice." Hardtack made up a substantial amount of the food.[48]

Colonel Sickel kept the deportees in the compound under guard until he received orders "to remove restraint." The men obtained their release on July 22 when a bulletin from the War Department was posted notifying them that they could "stay or leave as they pleased." Immediately they held a meeting to discuss their next move. Even though various people came from Bisbee every day to plead with the men to return to work, most remained committed to the "strike." Since they could not return home without promising to go back to work, most of them chose to remain in camp.[49] Several men testified under oath later, however, that they had not learned they were free to leave for several weeks past July 22.[50]

Statistics concerning the deportees vary. The most reliable reports say 1,186 men left Bisbee on the train, but Lt. Col. Hornbrook counted only 1,152 two days later at Hermanas. Apparently some had slipped away. Colonel Sickel reported that 1,150 deportees were turned over to him at Columbus a few hours later. A count made by the army on July 30, eight days after the men had been given their freedom, indicated 1,053 deportees remained in camp.[51]

Bill Haywood claimed in Chicago the first week in August that "most of them are citizens, 456 of them are heads of

families, and many are owners of homes in Bisbee."[52] In May
of 1918 George W. P. Hunt, reinstated as governor of Arizona,
argued in an address to a special session of the Arizona legislature that a "searching investigation" had proved that only four
hundred twenty-six of the deportees were IWWs, three
hundred eighty-one were members of the American Federation
of Labor and three hundred sixty-one belonged to no union at
all. In addition, Hunt's figures showed that four hundred
seventy-two of the men were registered under the draft law,
sixty-two were former soldiers or sailors, two hundred five
were holders of liberty bonds and five hundred twenty had
made subscriptions to the Red Cross.[53]

Angered by these purported "facts," the copper companies compiled their own statistics and Bisbee lawyer Fred
Sutter, a copper interest member of the Arizona senate, offered
a rebuttal to Hunt's remarks. Combined evidence provided
by Phelps Dodge, Calumet & Arizona, and Shattuck-Denn
showed, according to Sutter, that only one hundred eleven of
the deported men ever subscribed for Liberty loans and only
seven had made the payments necessary to become bond-
holders. Sutter, enjoying the advantage of the accounting
departments of the copper companies, contended that of a
total payroll of 4,718 men in the Warren District, only 481
were included in the roundup and deportation, or, as
Sutter noted, 10.2 percent. This would mean that of the 1,186
deported men, 702 or 59.4 percent were not in the employ of
any of the Warren District copper companies.[54]

In his account of the Arizona labor problems in 1917, Governor Campbell included some figures from an army census
taken at Columbus. Since some of the men began to leave the
group before they ever arrived at Columbus, it is difficult to
know what percentage of the total original number of deportees was polled. The army found 433 married men, 199 native
born, 468 citizens of the United States and 47 registered under
the draft law. But these figures seem much too low.[55]

Apparently the screening out process conducted at the
Warren ball park had not discriminated carefully enough; some
of the wheat had been thrown out with the chaff. Bisbee officials reconfirmed that any men who wished to work were welcome in Bisbee but agitators could not return. Within a few

days several miners and shift bosses, their loss evidently felt back at Bisbee, received telephone calls from their employers asking them to come back to work. At least two deportees, Alfred Valenzuela and Andres Mendoza, received tickets sent to them by Sheriff Wheeler who asked them to return to Bisbee. But the deportees had adopted a stand-pat resolution, and no men were to go back to Bisbee until instructions arrived from Washington. The consensus appeared to be that the men felt safer in Columbus and, also, IWW or not, many shared the Wobbly "solidarity" spirit of "all for one and one for all."[56]

On July 24 the deportees sent telegrams to Governor Campbell, President Wilson and Secretary of Labor Wilson demanding to be returned to Bisbee. Campbell, obliging the resolve of the local authorities, pleaded helplessness: "I have no state funds or state forces now at my command. In my opinion federal action only can enforce your demands." This letter professing impotency was written the same day Campbell informed Charles W. Clark that he was "not inclined to cry over the milk that has been spilt." Moreover Bisbee authorities made it clear that undesirables would not be tolerated unless the federal government compelled the Bisbeeites to back down.[57]

The deportees at Camp Furlong tried to have the federal government guarantee their return to Bisbee. On July 31 several representatives of the men at Columbus sent a telegram to Bill Haywood in Chicago. They asked him to notify President Wilson, "If action is not taken by Federal Government forthwith in sending deported men back to homes in Bisbee, [the] men themselves will take action in returning with arms if necessary." The spokesmen's threat reasoned: "If corporations have [a] right to maintain armed forced, then labor unions have such a right." The telegrram ended by stating that the men believed "immediate action [is] absolutely necessary." Colonel Sickel intercepted this message and relayed it to the El Paso Army District headquarters. The commanding officer of the district, Brigadier General George Bell, Jr., in turn forwarded it to Headquarters, Southern Department, Ft. Sam Houston. There it was sent on to the adjutant general's office. But Washington delayed action for several weeks.[58]

That day two of the telegram's senders, deportee leaders A. S. Embree and Sam Brooks, requested the army to supply the men with blankets since the preceding three nights had been quite cool and the local army officers still had not been authorized to issue the men blankets. Earlier in the morning Colonel Sickel gave the owner of a local building permission to rent the building to the deportees in order that they might hold a meeting. "But," Colonel Sickel assured his commanding officer, "I will have an officer present in order to secure a report of what takes place." Adding to this prison camp atmosphere was the fact that many men discovered their mail from Bisbee had been steamed and opened and sealed up again. The deportees enjoyed neither real comfort nor freedom at Camp Furlong.[59] At least one deportee did not seem to mind his fate. From Camp Furlong M. C. Sullivan wrote to Grover Perry: "This is the life for me. Everything is fine and dandy."[60]

In reporting the arrival of the deportees at Camp Furlong on July 14, Colonel Sickel concluded by saying, "One of their number named Cleary [is] said to be a lawyer. [He] appears to be a leader and to have absolute control over them."[61] For many years Bill Cleary had been a prominent attorney in Bisbee. A defender of the workingman and his organizations, Cleary repeatedly opposed Walter Douglas and the Copper Queen power. Following the 1907 strike, Cleary and attorney A. A. Worsley, after "throwing in their fortunes with the strikers," defended numerous miners who had been charged with vagrancy, illegal assembly and other trumped-up offenses. Because of Cleary, the copper companies failed to secure a single conviction.[62]

Defense attorney Cleary had been scheduled to appear in Bisbee Police Court on July 12, 1917, the day of the deportation. As he had done ten years earlier, he represented pickets and other strikers who had been charged with vagrancy and loitering. Frank Thomas, Bisbee Police Court Judge, later said Cleary would probably have obtained acquittals in each of five cases.[63] That he could successfully defy corporate rule in Bisbee was one more reason the copper companies called the deportation and put Cleary on the train.

During the roundup it was Cleary who sneaked over the border to alert George W. P. Hunt and then return to give himself up to the vigilantes. In Hermanas it was Cleary who gave a lengthy press release giving the deportees' side of the picture. Also in Hermanas, it was Cleary who stood on top of a boxcar, explained the situation to the men and encouraged

William Cleary, Bisbee workingmen's lawyer, with deportees at
Camp Furlong, Columbus, New Mexico, in late summer of 1917

them not to despair. He stayed with the men in Columbus
for several days, and then, it was rumored, he "left the camp
of his friends for a hotel room and bath."[64]

Two weeks later Cleary headed for Globe to assist attorney
Frank McCann in defending alleged rioters there. Upon hearing the attorney was on his way to their city, Globe Loyalty
Leaguers announced that he was not wanted and two automobiles were waiting "to take Cleary for a ride." On August
11 Cleary showed up in El Paso getting a haircut. While openly
"shadowed" by detectives, he told reporters he had come to
El Paso to get the Southern Pacific train for Los Angeles
via Phoenix. He also told them that if the government would
take over the control of the mines and fix prices where they
were a year before, the miners would return to work at the old
scale of wages.[65]

Cleary gave his home address as "Bisbee, Arizona," when
he served as one of the defense counsels in the famous IWW
trial in Chicago in April 1918. But apparently he never returned.[66]

The *Bisbee Daily Review* summarized its view of Cleary in this doggerel from the July 18, 1917, edition:

The Ravings of Bill Cleary

Erstwhile Wobblie King, Crowned at
Hermanas, N.M., by the Wobblies,
Deported from the Bisbee
District.

(F. B. Camp in Douglas
International)

On a day for them quite dreary
A man named William Cleary
    Addressed a crowd of Wobblies from
    a soap box near the store.
He raved, and swore, and spouted
He cussed, and damned, and shouted
    As he had in patient Bisbee several
    nights before.

He spoke of things high-handed
To the Wobblies there disbanded
    And the deeds of Bisbee's people
    who had done them awful wrong.
While the Wobblies cheered and shouted
And the whole darn country flouted
    As they sang the cursed rhythms of
    their rabid Wobblie song.

There was cussing and much fussing
And an awful, awful mussing
    Of thoughts when King Bill and his
    bunch of Wobblies learned
And their freedom thoughts were shaken
When the whole darn bunch was taken
    To Columbus, New Mexico, and in
    the pen interned.

They were brought without a riot,
And they're mighty, mighty quiet,
*   In the stockade 'neath the*
*   eye of Uncle Sam*
And in the place they should be kept
'Til the country's cleanly swept
*   Of these Wobblie agitators who rave*
*   and curse and damn.*

"I Won't Work," the daily creed
Of this shiftless, useless breed
*   They're a menace to the*
*   country now at war*
When the truth is told and learned
The whole bunch'll be interned
*   And the country will have*
*   peace for ever more.*

Why did the mine operators pick Columbus for the destination of the deportees? No doubt they had learned from the Mojave County and Jerome deportations that officials in other states, particularly California, had no great fear of corporate power and would not permit the horrid Wobblies being dumped in their states. Sending them to Mexico would have created an international incident, and so that was out of the question. Columbus seemed ideal; a long way from El Paso, Bisbee and the New Mexico capital at Santa Fe, it was isolated and on the main line of the El Paso and Southwestern Railroad, a Phelps Dodge subsidiary. Walter Douglas, recognized as early as July 13 as the official who determined the transportation arrangements, was said to have ordered Columbus as the deportees' destination with the intention of forcing their care on the military authorities there.[67]

Mop-up

In their telegrams of July 15 to President Wilson and Secretary of War Baker, Bisbee's Citizens' Protective League and Workmen's Loyalty League insisted that the Warren District was now "peaceful and quiet." Their activities suggest something else. Anxiety and doubt gripped Bisbee. Rumors that the

IWWs were returning to Bisbee caused "great nervousness." On the day after the deportation, upon hearing that Wobblies were approaching Osborn Junction, eight miles out of town, "scores of automobiles, loaded with armed men, hurried to the scene."[68] Oscar Wager, a deputized miner, was then stationed at Osborn Junction along with ten other men to keep undesirables from returning. Wager accepted the IWW menace unquestioningly. When Frank Zietz returned to his Bisbee ranch from a business trip, he met the road guards. They tried to force him to wear a white arm band if he wanted to go on into Bisbee. He refused.[69]

But miners were wanted in Bisbee. "Men Who Want to Work Will Not Be Barred Here," invited a *Review* headline on July 14. By the twenty-second, hundreds of men had arrived in Bisbee from Globe, Miami and other mining districts.[70] However, everyone coming into town was subject to close scrutiny. All persons desiring to live or do business in Bisbee who were suspect had to appear for questioning before the Bisbee Vigilance Committee, formed shortly after the deportation. Presided over by Miles Merrill, president of the Workmen's Loyalty League, the committee conducted an extralegal "kangaroo court" in the Phelps Dodge medical dispensary until late August. Merrill along with A. C. Riefsnyder and local police court judge Frank Thomas served as the chief inquisitors on this despotic Bisbee bench. Aware of Judge Thomas' earlier sympathetic attitude toward workingmen, Bisbee officials perhaps felt that the judge's presence on this extralegal "court" gave it a touch of legality. Strangers and unemployed men in Bisbee found themselves asked whether they participated in the strike, whether they sympathized with the strikers and whether they were ready to go to work on such terms as the "court" might designate. Unsatisfactory answers resulted in an order to move on, a forcible deportation, or imprisonment and work on a convict road-repair gang.[71] Property owners unwelcome in Bisbee had to sell what they had for anything they could get. Thus did the Vigilance Committee pursue the mining companies' mop-up program.

Only one man was arrested on July 14. An Austrian, he was accused by the committee of having "been implicated in a dynamite plot."[72]

After Constable Percy Bowden released him from the Warren ball park, Mike Pintek returned home. Seeing several men, apparent victims of beatings, sitting in discomfort on a street corner near his home, Pintek filled a bucket with water and took it to them. About 7:00 P.M. gunman Donald Stetson, Pintek's neighbor, stood outside Pintek's house and called for him to come. Pintek answered from inside saying he had done nothing and asking Stetson to go away. The vigilante, with four or five men beside him, shouted: "Well, you red-blooded Socialist, I will get you tomorrow." Harassed further by Stetson and others, Pintek went to Naco, Mexico, where he stayed a week. When he returned to Bisbee a second time, an anti-union bully tore the AFofL membership sticker off his taxi's windshield saying, "You know we don't allow no unions in the Warren District."

When Pintek returned to Bisbee from Naco, he was arrested and taken to kangaroo court. The Vigilance Committee told Mike to "lay low." So, until things grew quiet, he decided to spend a month working at his molybdenum claims in Mexico. During the weeks of Pintek's absence, his wife Katie lived in fear and bewilderment as Billy Woods, always on horseback, watching from a distance, trailed her everywhere.[73]

The city of Douglas kept tight security, too. Five Slavonian restaurant workers who had been deported were seen on a train coming into town. Deputies and town police took the men from the train, gave them a meal and put them in jail. One man said he had but fifteen cents.

Drifters read in the *Review* that a "vag" (vagrant) roundup was on. "There is no place in Bisbee for men who are not working and who have no visible means of support." In the same issue, Bisbee citizens could read reminders that "the time of greatest peril to the Warren District is right now." Folks were exhorted to keep vigilant and "to keep the broom in constant use." "DO YOUR PART," warned the *Review*.[74]

Bisbeeites who did not "do their part" got more than an exhortation. The kangaroo court tried Dr. Pressly, "a reputable physician of Bisbee." On July 27 it gave him a jail sentence of ninety days for criticizing the deportation.[75] A few days later the Vigilance Committee forced a member of the Arizona State Legislature from Bisbee, Tom Foster, out of town because he was a Hunt supporter. Foster moved to Phoenix while his wife remained in Bisbee to sell their property. Later she joined her exiled husband in Phoenix, a haven, according to Foster, "which is in the United States of America."[76]

One man told of a night of horror at the hands of Vigilance Committee goons. For a short while during Bisbee's wartime boom, Louis Grass, a Bisbee miner, had tried to operate a pro-labor newspaper, the *Bisbee Square Dealer*, with an office near the Bisbee Miners' Union Hall on O.K. Street. When the Wobblies took over the hall, Grass sold the paper to the IWW, which for a few weeks published the *Bisbee Ore*. Although Grass had never joined any union, had never left his job during the strike and had never been considered for deportation during the "Big Drive," he was marked for trouble. Being literate and sensitive to injustice as well as being able to spot an opportunity for a marketable story, he began to keep a journal which he hoped to sell for publication. Since, as he put it, his "typewriter was being run all hours of the day and night," he became suspect in the eyes of the Bisbee inquisitors.[77]

On Thursday, August 2, Grass was arrested without a warrant on "a very serious charge" and jailed. Miles Merrill brought Grass' wife and nine-year-old daughter to see him. Merrill told them all that luckily Grass "would not be killed" but merely forced to leave town. At eight that night a deputy sheriff turned him over to the Loyalty League to be taken to the county jail at Tombstone. According to Grass, the two then got into an automobile driven by Phil Tovrea, son of prominent local meat merchant Ed Tovrea, and another man named Ludwick, a Bisbee tailor and cleaner. The men seized Grass and blindfolded him. They rode for an hour out on the desert and stopped, where young Tovrea balked at the prospect of becoming a murderer; he said, "then we will do the other." Grass described "the other.":

> They threw me on my face in the desert sand. Pulled my clothes off. I was tied, blindfolded [again] and gagged. One held my face in the dirt and the other held my feet and the third began to flog me with a leather belt. Blood came from every pore and all the time they were cursing me.

The beating eventually stopped, but before the men left, Grass said they told him: "Tomorrow a man will be set on your trail you son-of-a-bitch." Grass passed out, but a falling rain revived him. He lay still until daybreak, when he began to walk in an unknown direction. Finally he got his bearings. He told of being trailed by a car as he struck for the border. According to his story, Grass staggered and fainted several times in his flight, each time to be revived by stinging rain or jarring thunder.

> I looked back from whence I came, a shudder seized me as I saw a rider looking here and there, doubling back and forth, like a hound on the trail. I climbed the mountain, and from a craig [sic] or shelf I watched this rider going and coming, up and down the desert. I crept and crawled further back in the mountain, avoiding all habitation and people.

Eventually Grass made it into Douglas. A sip of coffee at a lunch counter choked him, and he vomited. A stranger told him to get out of town at once. As Grass started toward the nearby army encampment, he was stopped by three or four men in a car which pulled up to the curb.

> I ran into a private yard, over two back fences and jumped into a big tool box or garbage can. I could hear a machine charging up and down the alley for about twenty minutes. I crawled out from my shelter and zig zagged through private yards until I reached the soldiers' camp.

Befriended by a soldier in the camp who gave him asylum for the night, Grass started out on foot on the morning of August 4 for Columbus. His pursuers continued their search:

> I could see without being seen, a machine which would drive to the turn at Lee station and return towards Douglas. This was done four times. As I was entering the gap, I came in plain view of the railroad track and road way. A rifle was fired, the two bullets struck within twenty feet of me. I hurried on down the other side of the gap and cut further up into the mountains. It was like the tale of the Danites or Destroying Angels.

Grass walked all that day and at sunset reached a train stop, Bernardino, about twenty miles north of Douglas. It was Saturday night and he had not eaten since breakfast Thursday. Grass "induced a rancher" to feed him and then boarded the 11:30 El Paso and Southwestern train for Rodeo, New Mexico. There he met friendly strangers who drove him in their car to the Columbus deportee camp. When he arrived at Camp Furlong, Grass' face, the deportees could see, was badly swollen, his eyes practically closed and many teeth missing.

One Wobbly noticed, "He was a nervous wreck."[78] And this was not the end of Grass' humiliating and painful treatment by Bisbee goons. His wife, one report states, ran off with a Phelps Dodge gunman.[79]

All of these intimidations did not stop some determined deportees from returning to Bisbee. Within a few weeks, a number of men, some invited by the companies, tired of the Columbus camp and quietly returned to their jobs. By August 11 the *Review* decided to admit the obvious, and it reported that some men had returned from Columbus and had gone back to work. As the number of returning deportees swelled, the county clerk prepared warrants for Sheriff Wheeler to serve any returnees who refused to work; they were to be charged with "vagrancy and inciting to riot." One day later, on August 18, Wheeler served warrants to eleven returned deportees. Two owned property and were acquitted, four took draft examinations and five found themselves sentenced to ninety days or to leave town.[80]

Why did so many men try to return to Bisbee or refuse to leave for other parts? They probably had resolved that whatever hardships they might be forced to endure, the fact of their families remaining in Bisbee left them with no place else to go. Concern for their families, more than anything, drew them back or precluded their dispersal.

Without funds, estranged from the community, the families of the deportees did suffer. In one instance, J. L. Dechery had been seized at his root beer stand in Bisbee and sent to Columbus. Letters from his wife told of repeated insults by gunmen. Mrs. Dechery had practically no money and could not sell her husband's small business. Louis Asic, nursing a wounded head in Columbus, heard that his wife (also bruised by a blow from gunmen) and his three children had no resources. Asic's family faced imminent eviction from their home since the house stood on copper company-owned land. Deportee William Blackburn, a resident of Bisbee from childhood, had left in town a dependent mother and a father who was ill and without money.[81]

In response to anxious inquiries from the Columbus stockade, Bisbee Mayor Jake Erickson notified Colonel Sickel at Camp Furlong that the deportees' families were not being neglected. A citizens' relief organization (the Warren District Relief Association) had been formed and was taking care of every person asking aid. "Mexicans not barred," announced the mayor in a display of the southwestern sense of *noblesse oblige*; Phelps Dodge kept a careful count of aid given to Mexican families.[82]

Reports vary, but apparently the copper companies provided somewhere between $60,000 and $80,000 for a relief fund. Miss Ethel Cummings, county probation officer, had charge of disbursing the money to the approximately two hundred fifty families left behind. In addition, Bill Haywood told the deportees at Columbus that Grover Perry had sent $3,000 from the Salt Lake City IWW office to help Arizona strikers and their families.[83]

While this and other largesse found its way to the desperate folks in Bisbee, the *Review* perversely asked much mind-poisoning questions as "How do they do it?, Who feeds the family?, Who pays the rent?, Where do the strike funds come from?" Bisbee patriots were being tempted to believe, by inferring from the paper's hints, that the money spent by the families of the deportees, most of it given to them by the copper companies, actually came from some nefarious source.[84] Bisbee citizens undoubtedly were ignorant of the fact that by this time the United States Attorney General's office had announced that no German funds had aided strikers. The copper companies also knew that strike funds had been almost nonexistent by July 18.

Rumors of permanent and tragic rendings of families such as found in Longfellow's "Evangeline" grew up. But the evidence is slim. Some families were temporarily broken. After Samuel Brooks was shipped out of town, his wife and child went to stay with Mrs. Brooks' mother in Colorado. (While arresting Brooks, gunmen had leveled rifles at Brooks' wife and child and ordered them not to leave the house.) Following her husband's deportation, Mrs. James Cowan went to stay with her mother in Butte, where she got assistance from the local of the Metal Mine Workers Union. Hoping to destroy the lure of home and family that might draw the deportees back to Bisbee, the copper companies, as part of their "charity," urged women and children in a mandatory way to go and stay with relatives and friends in some other place. In order to accomplish this many dependents of deportees were finally given money for transportation and expenses.[85]

Despite the generosity toward the stricken families, charges that the dependents of deported men were destitute reached the ears of military authorities. General H. A. Greene, commander of the Arizona Military District, dispatched Captain M. E. Palen to investigate. The *Review* welcomed Captain Palen. After completing his investigation, the captain said that he failed to find any destitute families.[86] Bisbee citizens could then read about their own benevolence: "The *Review* claims that there are no kinder, finer, fairer, more generous, humane citizens in the world than those who are proud to live in this beautiful valley where the wind from the high places stings the face and brightens the eye and thrills the heart." This defensiveness appeared to betray a kernel of self-doubt that still existed in the mining town.[87]

Phelps Dodge Defends Itself

Bisbee may have experienced a twinge of conscience even though most of the newspapers around the state of Arizona and around the nation were giving strong support to the deportation. A few publications, it is true, had condemned the act. For some reason the Phelps Dodge people found it difficult to ignore their few detractors. In the days that followed the deportation, the *Review* did not relax its barrage of propaganda. While attempting to convince everyone that quiet and peace and satisfaction characterized Bisbee, the *Review* continued its assault on the IWW. Almost painfully self-conscious, the Phelps Dodge newspaper explained, boasted, congratulated and condemned. Not at all Olympian and indifferent to public opinion, the editorials, at times aggressive, at other times uncertain, took on a paranoid tone in their efforts to justify the July 12 event. "If they didn't want to work here, why did they keep on hangin' 'round?" the *Review* asked itself. The act of the vigilantes, it said again, "was not only just and right, it was patriotic."[88]

The treason aspect got more attention. The Prussian "engine of war" incorporates the IWW, said another *Review* editorial. "These strikes are a Prussian plot," it went on, including one of its few references to the Zimmerman note. Aiming its message at the uncommitted and uncertain middle class of Bisbee and of Arizona, the paper sensationalized a reported IWW conspiracy to destroy crops in Arizona's Salt River and Maricopa valleys. The *Review* pointed out that Wobblies got a "cold welcome" in the non-mining northern Arizona town of Flagstaff.[89]

In the *Review* every untoward incident around the land stemmed from IWW influence. When "hundreds of Negroes,

Indians and farmers" staged anti-draft demonstrations in Oklahoma, the "hand of the I.W.W." was seen in the trouble. A plumber, patching a roof on a hotel in Lowell, threw the Lowell people "into a fit" when they suspected a Wobbly bombing attempt. Over in McNeal, a small farming town in the Sulphur Springs Valley of Cochise County north of Douglas, the residents started a petition to recall Sheriff Wheeler. The farmers, no great supporters of the mining companies, felt their interests had been ignored by Wheeler who spent all of his time in the service of the Bisbee mine managers. Naturally the *Review* described the recall attempt as part of the "Wobbly movement."[90]

The squeeze was on in Bisbee for everyone to get on the vigilante bandwagon. Several ads sponsored by the Citizens' Protective League began to appear in the *Review*. One box announced that all people wishing to join the League could telephone 497 or write to P.O. Box 1719. Another box, addressed "To the Public," offered moral and financial support to boarding houses and restaurants in the Warren District which were providing lunches for loyal men in the mines. A page-long notice, two columns wide, listed more than two hundred fifty "business and professional members of the Citizens' Protective League." Next to this roster, in a much smaller black-bordered box, appeared forty-five names under the heading "Business Men and Firms Non-Members of Citizens' Protective League."[91]

Bisbee garage owner, W. P. French, was asked repeatedly to join the Citizens' Protective League. When he refused, the Vigilance Committee tried to pressure him. French's steadfast attitude brought him a notice from his landlord, whose building was on company property, that the garageman had twenty days in which to leave. French went to Los Angeles.[92]

For those who had resolved to take complete control of Bisbee, patriotism continued to be of great concern. Nothing short of open, wholehearted loyalty to America on the part of everyone would do. In particular, Bisbee authorities expected young men to show their pride and support and sense of responsibility. One way in which a young man could accomplish this was to go to war — eagerly and without dissent.

Not everyone in the state shared this attitude. In Washington, D.C., on August 7, 1917, in the Congress of the

United States, the lone representative from Arizona, Carl
Hayden, took the floor. Modestly eloquent, incisive, cool and
clear in an atmosphere of hysteria, he argued in favor of the
conscientious objection to warfare and urged the Congress to
consider the motives of men who were impelled to resist the
draft. The problem was not a new one, he argued. He spoke of
the IWWs and conceded there was "some measure of logic
in their opposition to the draft." But, Hayden added, the
Wobblies' views had no divine sanction and they had to be
classed as "social," not "conscientious."[93]

The *Review* felt no such tolerance for "slackers," as it called
men who attempted to avoid the draft, whatever their reasons.
A four-column list of Cochise County slackers appeared in
the August 19 edition of the paper. As part of its program
of vigilance and patriotism, the *Review* saw fit, as did the
Citizens' Protective League, to advertise the identity of those
who failed to meet Bisbee's standards of loyalty.[94]

On September 28 the *Review* ran a revised list of Cochise
County slackers. By now the number was down to thirty-nine.
Two of the reluctant young men the paper identified as the
sons of Lemuel Shattuck, president of Bisbee's third largest
mining operation. The boys were reportedly infuenced by a
pacifistic mother and left the country for Mexico where they
remained for several years. Apparently the *Review*, since it was
an organ only of Phelps Dodge, felt no compunction about
exposing the cowardice of the family members of a local and
friendly competitor. Also interesting is the fact that the first
man drafted from Cochise County happened to be Alexander
Duarte, an alien and IWW member. The irony continued with
draftee number two: I. C. Padilla, a Mexican national.[95]

In September, Phelps Dodge announced record dividends.
But in the stock market quotes of the *Bisbee Daily Review*,
figures for Phelps Dodge were conspicuously absent.[96]

9

ARIZONA KNUCKLES UNDER

A few days following the Bisbee Deportation, the Columbus, New Mexico, weekly newspaper contained this statement: "Striking miners are more welcome than would be 1,200 Cochise county corporation deputies." Two columns of the little paper then took the occasion (in the words of the *Bisbee Daily Review*) "to roast the Warren district citizens and uphold the action of the deported I.W.W." Although the *Review* told its readers that this was "the first paper thus far to take such a view of the situation," it appeared unnecessarily defensive about this miniscule challenge.[1]

Corporate Resolve

In truth there was more mopping up to be done than merely countering the opinion of some remote outpost's weekly. Although the press of the big cities around the country defended the vigilantes two to one, a substantial part of the citizenry of the West had not yet made up its mind. The popular mood of America—and of Arizona—had not swung as far to the right as Phelps Dodge wanted. Bisbee had been the climax of a corporation crusade, but securing statewide support still depended on convincing the citizens of the menace of radical labor groups and getting rid of those elected officials and their appointees who would not wear the "copper collar." The copper interests also wanted to restrain the statewide influence of those communities where labor strength was too strong to be neutralized in the way Bisbee had accomplished it.[2]

The greatest resistance met by the copper companies in their attempt to establish control of Arizona labor remained in Globe. A bastion of well-organized IUMMSW power, the Globe-Miami district also resisted the infiltration of the IWW with relatively little effort. Although the general manager of the Inspiration Copper Company, C. E. Mills, responded to the IUMMSW demands on June 29 saying, "We reserve the right and privilege to conduct our own affairs," the Globe operators did not appear indomitable.[3]

Globe, more accessible and more hospitable than Jerome or Bisbee, hosted several governmental authorities during its summer labor strike of 1917. Conciliator McBride, special investigator Hunt, Arizona Governor Campbell and other referees made difficult the kind of extreme action taken by the copper companies in Jerome and Bisbee. On July 22, Governor Campbell directly warned the citizens of Globe not to deport any strikers. A week later, some time after operations had returned almost to normal throughout the rest of the state, conferences between McBride and the Globe mine managers were still going on.[4] The Globe miners stayed on strike until October 22, when without gaining recognition of any specific union, they agreed not to walk out again for the duration of the war.[5] Despite their ability to keep copper production in Globe tied up for several months, the miners settled for an insignificant concession from the operators: a grievance committee with very limited authority. Corralled but not broken, the Globe mavericks kept their union alive longer than any place else in the state. An industrial medical investigator, Alice Hamilton, said of a trip to Globe in January 1919: "I was glad to find that in both Globe and Miami the union still survived and headquarters were still open."[6]

Mining company officials, particularly headstrong people like Walter Douglas, must have found the tenacity of labor in Globe-Miami vexing. Just as frustrating—even worse—was the meddling of the federal government. Whether it involved mediators or army troops, the Phelps Dodge people found federal intervention ineffectual, disturbing and a violation of the copper company territorial sovereignty. Of mediation, Phelps Dodge stated:

> The bad faith in the Jerome strike settlement leaves us no room for doubt but that settlements which may be made through mediation directed by the federal government have no [sic] standing with the strike promoters and their followers only as ruses under which they can gain time to renew and broaden trouble zones.

With a bald *non sequitur*, the *Review* concluded: "The Jerome violation of the June settlement and its terms of patriotism is accepted as convincing evidence that the strike movements are unquestionably in the aid of Germany."[7]

During the months of labor strife in Bisbee, however, mine operators experienced little federal meddling. When government representatives did come to town, the copper companies discovered them to be properly innocuous. After conducting the deportees from Hermanas to Columbus on July 14, Lt. Col. James Hornbrook returned to Bisbee. He found that the town was as quiet as it had been the first week of the month. But in his July 16 report to the adjutant general, Hornbrook recommended that the deportees not be returned to Bisbee. "They do not want to work, and they influence others for the bad," Hornbrook wired.[8]

For Lt. Col. Hornbrook, the *Review* had nothing but praise. The paper spent two substantial paragraphs eulogizing the Colonel's dignity, modesty, sense of duty and, most importantly, "his reticence." "Colonel Hornbrook," declared the *Review*, was "an officer and a gentleman."[9] This praise, in light of a letter written by Copper Queen mine superintendent Joseph P. Hodgson, seems understandable. About the military's view of the deportation, Hodgson wrote: "The only comment the military officers made to the people of this district was that they considered it 'a good job, well done.'"[10]

Not all army authorities reacted so complaisantly. The reports on the Arizona strike situation by Colonel Charles W. Harris, adjutant general of the Arizona National Guard, condemned the copper industry and the one-sidedness of the federal troops. Harris had been appointed to the office by Governor Campbell's predecessor and political adversary, George W. P. Hunt. Terming Harris' reports "seditious,"

Campbell asked the adjutant general to quit. Harris' reply
was "I will not resign."[11]

Phelps Dodge called for Harris' removal. His job had
"been a sinecure . . . the principal reason for its existence being
the necessity of keeping the national guard at its lowest efficiency."[12] (The guard had been used in Clifton-Morenci to
maintain impartial order, much to the mine owners' dismay.)
Since the National Guard was to go into national service on
August 6, Campbell was under pressure to obtain Harris' release quickly. On August 4 State Attorney General Wiley Jones
gave an opinion that the governor could not remove Colonel
Harris until a qualified successor was elected or appointed. But
Harris was replaced.[13]

Continuing with their efforts to assure control of the state,
the copper mine owners decided to expand their own private
paramilitary organization, the Loyalty League. By July 22 the
mining companies had influenced Arizona's general public
enough to enable their announcement in non-mining oriented
Phoenix a plan for a statewide Loyalty League.[14]

In Phoenix, on August 6, the day the Arizona National
Guard became absorbed into the United States Army, Miles
Merrill, Phelps Dodge shift boss, organizer of the Bisbee's
Workmen's Loyalty League and president of the Bisbee Vigilance Committee, formed and was named president of the
"Loyalty League of America." The new organization's avowed
purpose was "to exterminate the I.W.W."[15] Some people close
to the situation claimed the Bisbee Workmen's Loyalty League
had met secretly in Bisbee on July 28 and adopted a resolution
calling for the statewide organization. The resolution included
incorporating the "Loyalty League of America" for $100,000.

According to the resolution, a united group of Arizona
businessmen and mining officials was to back the organization.
Its organizers intended the league to operate "along the lines"
of the Bisbee Vigilance Committee, that is, to pass on the fitness of prospective employees around the state. The failure of a
worker to gain the unanimous approval of the league's state
officials would result in a statewide boycott of the worker.
IUMMSW members charged that the National Association of
Manufacturers endorsed and encouraged the league as part of a
broad employer program to destroy American unionism. The
"unsettled conditions" in Arizona permitted the program's
inauguration in that state on a large scale.[16] Old-fashioned

frontier vigilantism had supplanted the modern military as the protector of the people of the state of Arizona. Through its own well-organized program, Phelps Dodge had established an alternative to federal intervention. In doing so, the copper corporation gained control of labor as well as broad cooperation by much of Arizona's middle class.

Continued Response

National interest concerning the deportation stayed alive through August and September. As the weeks went by, certain New York–based newspapers and journals kept an eye on the Arizona events. The prominent and controversial Progressive philosopher, John Dewey, said in his inimitable syntax, "Various would-be leaders and noisy leagues are not morally innocent of promoting disunion through the distrust which they have sown of all who have dared to differ with them in matters of policy."[17] *The New Republic* editorialized:

> The press had shown an increasing disposition to stamp all manifestations of labor unrest with the outlawed brand of the I.W.W. and to gloss over both the unpatriotic conduct of certain employers and the legitimate grievances of wage earners who have not the remotest connection with the advocates of sabotage.[18]

The Nation, in its August 23 issue, called the practices at Bisbee "high-handed."[19] "A bad precedent...but it was the only way," remarked the promotional monthly magazine *Arizona*.[20]

At the nation's capitol on August 7, Representative Jeanette Rankin pleaded that President Wilson take over and operate the copper mines. To a crowded chamber which applauded approvingly, the lady from Montana assailed the "Copper Trust" and accused John D. Ryan, president of the Anaconda Copper Company, of bearing the "chief responsibility for labor unrest" in Montana.[21]

On August 6 President Wilson received a telegram sent to him by angry president of the Arizona Federation of Labor, John L. Donnelly. Donnelly, who was attending the Sixth Annual Convention of the Federation at Clifton, probably wrote in response to the founding of the Loyalty League of America that day in Phoenix. The message protested the Bisbee situation as "a beckoning finger to revolution" and an example of "legally elected authorities throwing down the law."[22] Donnelly asked Wilson if he intended to restore law and order in Cochise County and "return to their homes the deported men of Bisbee.... Are we to assume that Phelps-Dodge interests are superior to principles of democracy?"[23]

Donnelly's insinuation in this last sentence hurt the President. Immediately Wilson wrote to Samuel Gompers to complain that the message was "unjust and offensive."[24] Despite his pledge of wartime cooperation, Gompers had for several weeks resented what he considered to be the arrogant and illegal acts of the "capitalistic anarchists" in Arizona. Although he agreed Donnelly's telegram was harsh, he asked Wilson if it was "not right that we sometimes place ourselves in the position of others and take into account their feelings and their indignant resentment of a terrible outrage?" In what must have been one of Gompers' more impassioned statements of the war, he went on:

> You know that the men in the American trade union movement have nothing in common with [the] so-called I.W.W. ... And yet, when we have seen what we have seen, that hundreds of men, citizens of Arizona, nearly all of them law-abiding, rounded up by a group of capitalistic anarchists who have not only taken the law into their own hands, but even went far beyond any warrant of law and at the point of gun and bayonets driven into cattle cars, deported from their home, city, and state, into a foreign state, carried in such condition for days without food, or drink, or care, or opportunity for rest, and left stranded among strangers.[25]

The manifest anger of Gompers may have had a strong impact on Wilson. The President quickly informed the Arizona State Federation that the federal government could do little, though he declared he would do all in his power to safeguard the rights of the people. In November 1917, Wilson appeared at the AFofL convention in Buffalo and declared that the prosecution of war should not obstruct the "instrumentalities by which the conditions of labor are improved." But inadequate laws and the reality of the nation's political mood limited him. For the time being words were all he had to offer as consolation for those under the thumb of Phelps Dodge and its satellite copper firms.[26]

Gomper's letter to Wilson had been dated August 10. *The Survey*, in its August 11 edition, quoted the comments of IWW chief Bill Haywood, whose anger showed less restraint than did Gompers'. Promising that the IWW would take care of its men in Columbus, Haywood threatened that the Bisbee men "will go back to their homes if they have to shoulder arms and fight their way back."[27]

A flood of letters, many almost identical in phraseology and format, deluged Wilson during the month of August. They came from various union officials around the country, and they all protested the "outrageous" nature of the deportation. Each letter attempted to remind Wilson that the working-men of America expected Wilson to speak up in their behalf, not to quietly indulge the profiteering and high-handedness of American capitalists.[28] Wilson referred many of these letters to the War Department. Short, factual replies from Adjutant General Edward T. Donnelly explained that there was "no distress in Bisbee." But these responses did not answer the question, "What does the government intend to do?"[29]

All of this indignation, however, did not reflect the broader, fast-growing national mood. That mood was represented by the *Tulsa Daily World* which stated, "If the IWW ... gets busy in your neighborhood, kindly take the occasion to increase your supply of hemp."[30]

Bisbee Remains Closed and Defiant

In Arizona the copper companies were prepared to supply boxcars if not hemp for the anti-Wobbly cause. And they provoked more worries which could be attributed to IWWs. Scare stories continued to show the Wobbly hand in everything. One *Review* headline assured the reader that "Elimination of I.W.W. Intimidation Will Allow Mines of State to Resume Broad Plans of Development."[31]

In this same edition of the paper, the editors were doing a delicate balancing act. Trying to placate and please, frighten and coerce at the same time, the paper announced on the one hand that the "Cost of Producing Copper Today is Greatest Since the Civil War," and on the other hand the *Review* revealed that "Copper Dividends in U.S. During July Total Ten Million Dollars." Dividends had risen from $6,323,534 in July 1916, and $7,875,834 in April 1917. In addition, the *Review* on August 16 exposed a Wobbly conspiracy to attack Bisbee.

According to the news story, a few Mexican informers had reported that 1,000 men, mainly Mexicans led by Austrians and Germans, had organized a plot to seize the arms of the garrison at Columbus and "start a movement on Bisbee." Although the *Review* conceded that "Army and law officers [were] inclined to doubt the report," the scare potential of the story had been fully exploited.[32]

This steady verbal stream informing Bisbee's citizens of the residual menace of Wobblyism in Arizona had its effects. The Vigilance Committee pursued its duties zealously. Fred Moore, an IWW lawyer from Chicago, came to Bisbee armed with two letters of introduction from Governor Campbell. His references failed to impress the Committee; the vigilantes ran him out of town. He told about it:

> I came to Columbus, New Mexico, Saturday, July 21, direct from Chicago, and while there [at Columbus] talked with many of the deported men. A number of them gave me letters from their wives asking for assistance and information. I promised that when I was in Bisbee I would see their wives and families.
>
> On July 26 I interviewed Governor Campbell in Phoenix and received two letters of introduction, one to Harry C. Wheeler, sheriff of Cochise County, the other to Jacob Erickson, mayor of Bisbee. The letters were substantially the same.
>
> After informing him who I was, the letter to the sheriff said:
>
> "In behalf of Mr. Moore, I know I can command your best cooperation as to the purpose of his visit and I beg to thank you in anticipation of affording him all the privileges of the Warren district, which are his due as a law-abiding citizen."
>
> I did not arrive in Bisbee until about 10:30 this morning [July 30]. I registered at the Copper Queen Hotel from Chicago. I was told that Sheriff Wheeler's office was in Tombstone. I made inquiry for the mayor at the city hall and was told that he was at work but would be in his office at 4:30. I introduced myself to the city judge and was talking to him when a Mr. Vucovich came in. He told me his brother had been among the deported men, but had returned and had been ordered to appear before the committee and then was before the committee. I decided to go before the committee to advise them of my presence and to see what could be done in behalf of Vucovich.

On arriving at the committee room I asked for some member of the committee and one of them coming out I told him who I was and what my business was. After some delay, I was ushered into the presence of between 25 and 50 men. Most of the talking was done by four or five. I repeated to them who I was. One of them questioned the existence of the governor's letters and I showed them. Both letters were read by the chairman of the committee. Then I was informed the sheriff was out of the state. I also was told laughingly, when I said I expected to see the mayor at 4:30, that I wouldn't meet him, that they would take care of him. I could get no information about Vucovich or Rachel Johnson, a woman who had telegraphed me while in Phoenix, asking my good offices. Then I was told my presence in Bisbee was highly undesirable; that they feared my presence would give moral support to the men and women who sympathized with the deported men. The committee was very frank, one member saying my presence was a menace to them. I was told to return before the committee at 4:30.

I went to the telephone office and called the governor. I succeeded in getting him at 4:30. I told him of developments and asked that he call the committee before which I was to appear as I believed if he called he probably could reach the committeemen before I got there. On stepping out of the telephone booth, I was met by a man who told me the committee wanted me.

When I walked into the committee room the chairman was talking over the telephone with someone, his conversation consisting chiefly of monosyllables. Just as he hung up the telephone he said he had not seen the party and knew nothing about him. I thought he was talking with the governor, but he denied this to me. Shortly afterward he left the committee room. I then was advised to leave on the five-thirty train. I insisted that out of common courtesy to the governor they should telephone him, but they refused. They again advised me to leave as they could not answer for the consequences should I remain. They offered to accompany me and help pack my grip, but I refused, telling them my plans were not decided.

On reaching my hotel I was met by Mrs. Rosa McKay, a member of the state legislature, who was waiting for me. I talked with her only two or three minutes when three men, one of them armed, entered the hotel and informed me I would have to go. They shoved me toward my room and after I had packed my suitcase, accompanied me downstairs. As I passed through the lobby I called the attention of the clerk to the fact that I was a guest and being forcibly ejected without reason. He made no comment. I then was taken to Osborn, where I bought a ticket for Douglas.[33]

In pursuit of his "Executive" responsibility (that particular role which *did*, one assumes, demand that he "cry over milk that had been spilt"), Governor Campbell responded to such reports as this one concerning Fred Moore. He wrote Arizona State Attorney General Wiley Jones asking Jones to investigate the stories and conditions associated with the Bisbee Deportation. He instructed Jones to verify allegations of "illegal actions by certain officials and citizens" of the Warren District. Campbell proposed that Jones himself journey to Bisbee in order to get the facts first-hand.[34] Jones' report from Bisbee, dated August 9, 1917, informed the governor:

After calm discussion and an impartial presentation of the serious phase of the situation as to continued unlawful deportations by Bisbee's controlling committee, I was courteously informed by committee in presence of Sheriff that determination is fixed that daily practice of committee hearings and deportations will continue *regardless of law* [italics mine]. Therefore, I officially report that only armed forces of state under Governor's constitutional and statutory powers or Federal force through Governor's request under United States Constitution will overcome these unlawful deportations as well as denial of entrance into Bisbee as now conducted.[35]

Thus did the agents of the Phelps Dodge Corporation welcome official authorities of the state of Arizona to the Bisbee barony.

On the same day that Attorney General Wiley Jones wrote his report for Governor Campbell, he made a statement for the press:

No Industrial Workers of the World ought to have labor in this district or any other district. They cannot be tolerated. There is no room for such doctrine as theirs under the American flag.

He then told the wives of the deportees not to expect their husbands to return to Bisbee, for they would never obtain employment.[36]

This anti-radical sentiment on the part of Attorney Jones might have been intended as a palliative for his harsh report to the governor. If so, his attempt to ingratiate himself with the citizenry of Bisbee backfired. Bisbeeites immediately alleged that Attorney General Jones had reported to the governor that the Citizens' Protective League and the Workman's Loyalty League were in opposition to all organized labor. Indignantly these groups denied the rumor. Jones, in turn, denied that he had accused the two groups of trying to drive the AFofL out of Bisbee.[37]

Attorney General Jones enjoyed more hospitality in Bisbee than official representatives of American Federation of Labor. A committee designated by the membership of the Arizona State Federation of the AFofL, at that time holding its annual convention in Clifton, was sent to Bisbee. On August 7 the five-man committee, headed by state AFofL President J. L. Donnelly, was turned back at Forrest Ranch twelve miles east of Naco. The guards' excuse to the committee was that "the government had several agents" in Bisbee investigating conditions there.[38]

Irked by all this discord, the governor himself came to town. Along with four hundred Bisbee women, the governor and the attorney general listened to State Representative Rosa McKay excoriate corporate behavior. When Mrs. McKay complained of the "barbarous" deportation and said she had sent her nephew along with the deportees, the ladies hissed and hooted. Mrs. McKay then addressed the governor directly and insisted that troops were needed in the Warren District to protect women and children. A woman in the audience, the wife of a deported miner, said *she* believed the *IWW* were the worst offenders. After the meeting many wives of the deported men called on Campbell at the Copper Queen Hotel.[39]

Perhaps prompted by her strong sense of theatrics, State Representative Rosa McKay fled Bisbee for Tucson on August 14. In a telegram to President Wilson, Mrs. McKay claimed she "was afraid to remain longer without protection." "Gunmen and mob law" created conditions which were not safe. The legislatress told the President that three of the women who visited Governor Campbell heard the governor say he believed there was no danger. "I hated to leave those women in the state of mind they are in," she said, "but I did not feel safe to remain another night."[40]

After meeting with the Bisbee women, the two state officials left the Warren District; several days passed while Campbell prepared his report and wrote letters to Sheriff Wheeler, Cochise County Attorney Ross and Bisbee Mayor Erickson. Both the letters and the report, being products of Campbell's "executive" persona, had a strong, reproving tone. Although he admitted in the letters that the IWW tactics were "a stench in the nostrils of decent Americans," he insisted it was a disgrace to admit that administration of law and order had broken down. The methods of deportation, he had decided, were entirely without justification. No matter how much he shared the Bisbee citizens' attitude toward the Wobblies, the deportations were illegal and must stop. The people of the district had to begin to show caution and restraint.[41]

Campbell's report soft-pedaled. It stated: (1) the union's demands were unfair; the strike was called too soon; (2) the IWW tactics brought about a reign of lawlessness; (3) the sheriff had found the situation too dangerous; he had received no state aid; the absence of adequate "legal machinery" and the fact of limited jail capacity had made this action (deportation) necessary; (4) some persons not IWW or IWW affiliated were deported; (5) constitutional rights were ignored and not provided by law since July 12 ("passing of judgment by a tribunal without legal justification"); (6) letters of safe conduct from the governor were ignored or met with refusal; (7) there was little violence in the deportation; (8) the Warren District Relief Association had been thorough and comprehensive; and (9) regularly organized unions were not the objectives of mine operator and vigilante sentiment.[42]

Out of these facts the governor drew the following conclusions: (1) arrests should have been made and trials conducted legally; (2) the deportations were illegal; deported people were entitled to the constitutional rights of due process; (3) the examining board for entrance into Bisbee was "without legal status and must immediately cease"; and (4) the duties of the sheriff must be executed according to law.[43] But his hindsight meant little; Bisbee's notorious acts were *faits accomplis*.

On July 31 Colonel Sickel, after intercepting the telegram to Bill Haywood in which the deportees threatened to return to Bisbee with arms, told his commanding officer that his charges at Camp Furlong were "beginning to show restlessness." "I recommend," summarized the colonel, "that the whole matter be brought to the attention of the War Department."[44]

Colonel Sickel's request for War Department concern complemented another telegram A. S. "Sam" Embree, spokesman for the deportees, sent on July 31 from Columbus. Embree's message went to Secretary of Labor William B. Wilson. The telegram complained that the nights were cold and the deportees had no blankets; local military authorities had not been authorized to do anything about the problem. Also, Embree complained, the relief of families at Bisbee was inadequate. Along with a short, explanatory cover letter, Secretary of Labor Wilson relayed the deportees' telegram to Secretary of War Newton D. Baker.[45]

Baker did not share Wilson's concern for the deported miners, but he, in an effort to maintain harmony within the administration, took action immediately by notifying Acting Chief of Staff Major General Tasker N. Bliss on August 2 that the army should do more to placate the deportees at Columbus. General Bliss sent a memorandum to the adjutant general saying that the Secretary of War "desires proper provision [be] made for the protection of the people" at Camp Furlong. Referring to Secretary Wilson's letter, General Bliss advised that measures should be merely temporary "until some means are devised for getting rid of" the deportees.[46]

As he gave it more thought, General Bliss began to grasp the nature of the problem, for on August 6 he sent a memorandum to Secretary of War Baker:

> It seems to me very desirable for the Army to get rid of these people. Every day that we hold them will make it more difficult to release them. Why wouldn't it be a good idea to begin reducing their number by releasing individuals (a few at a time so that they cannot travel in considerable groups) who are able to look out for themselves. If this should result in a material reduction in their number it will be easier to handle the question of the disposition of the remainder.[47]

His essentially pragmatic solution—befitting a competent military commander—ignored the political dimensions of the problem.

This suggestion of General Bliss must have gained the quick approval of Baker; coded orders phrased in almost the same words as Bliss' memorandum went from Adjutant General Henry P. McCain to General Parker, commanding general of the army's Southern Department, on August 9. The instructions advised:

Take precautions to see that those released do not remain in Columbus nor in its vicinity. Native born Germans will not be released under the above authority until their individual cases have been passed upon by the War Department. In order that these cases may be investigated by our Intelligence Section, their names, together with all available information regarding them will be forwarded to this office.[48]

Within a few days, the trickle of men out of Camp Furlong increased to a steady flow. They scattered in all directions; some went to Mexico, several joined the Canadian army. In a telegram to his mother in Ohio, deportee Fred Watson asked for money. She sent $150, and Watson left Camp Furlong, "riding the 'rods'" of the El Paso and Southwestern Railroad to Rodeo, New Mexico. After some soldiers gave him a ride to Douglas, he called his girl friend in Bisbee, Dorothy Muat. She brought him some clothes, and he immediately left for Ohio.[49]

Some of the released men returned to Bisbee. Of these, several quietly—and gladly—returned to work. Others found themselves whisked to the Copper Queen dispensary to face Miles Merrill and the Bisbee Vigilance Committee. Those who were fortunate received a few hours to get out of town; others, convicted by the kangaroo court of trespassing or vagrancy, went to jail or to the county road gang.

Even though the Vigilance Committee made it difficult to return to Bisbee, the population of the Wobbly camp at Columbus had declined considerably. George W. P. Hunt went to talk with those who remained on August 20 and found them high-spirited but ready to go home. Fewer than 500 men remained at Columbus when a count was made on August 29. Tired of its paternalistic role, the government cut the rations of the deportees on September 8.[50] The army posted a notice in the camp stating:

Beginning Tuesday morning September 11th the allowance of rations for members of this camp will be reduced to one-half the present amount. Later further reductions will be made or issues entirely suspended.[51]

Before the notice appeared, A. S. Embree, chairman for the deportees, wired President Wilson a cryptic request: "Will federal government restore and make secure constitutional rights of men deported from Bisbee?"[52] Upon seeing the ration reduction announcement, Embree composed a night letter inquiring of the President if the posted notice was Wilson's answer to his earlier telegram. Did it mean, Embree went on sarcastically, that "common citizens have no rights worthy of consideration by men elected and sworn to uphold the constitution?" Embree requested "the courtesy of an answer."[53]

Wilson chose not to get into a dialogue with the outcasts; he failed to answer either telegram. Further angered by the President's silence, Embree and the "Executive Committee" sent Wilson a four-page, typewritten letter on September 10 proclaiming their innocence and their indignation. They emphasized Governor Campbell's failure either to protect them or to challenge the martial control of Bisbee by Sheriff Wheeler and his deputies. The deportees did not elect to become wards of the federal government, the letter stated. If the President would only guarantee the men's constitutional rights (the letter referred to Article XIV, Section I, specifically), the men could go home and not have to "remain here in discomfort, accepting the alms of the Government." (Yet there is no indication the deportees ever applied for court writ of restraint.) After reminding Wilson of the huge wartime profits being earned by the mining companies, the letter asked him if the decision to "scatter [the men] over the country" came from the White House. Again the deportees begged for a reply. Wilson referred the letter to the Department of Justice.[54] On September 12 the remaining men complained of the half-rations in telegrams to Governor Campbell and President Wilson. The deportees threatened to return *en masse* to the Warren District. Campbell responded only by relaying their message to Sheriff Wheeler.[55]

The deportees never received any answer of any kind from President Wilson. Ten days after Camp Furlong had closed, Samuel J. Graham, assistant attorney general, acknowledged the deportee committee's letter to Wilson. The statements, said Graham, had "received careful consideration. This Department does not believe, however, that there is any Federal law referred to by you which would justify action by the Department of Justice." A few weeks later, prompted by the findings of an investigating commission, the department changed its mind.[56]

Meanwhile, Bisbeeites had been notified that the deportees would not be allowed to come back. For two months the copper companies had maintained a united, unwavering front. But the ostracized men prevailed. By the middle of September, time and federal tact had diluted the Vigilance Committee's determination. On September 12, two months to the day after being run out of town, thirty-four deportees en route to Bisbee on the train from Columbus were arrested in Douglas. Guards escorted them the remainder of the way home. In an article headlined "Wobblies Given Great Reception in Bisbee Today," the *Review* quickly reassured the fearful citizenry that six of the men were "married with property." Eight others formed into a group for immediate induction examinations. Their leader A. S. Embree was arrested, charged with felonious inciting to riot and had bail set at a preposterous $3,000. Upon failure to post bond, he was jailed. Later his case was transferred to Tucson.[57]

September 17, 1917, marked the official end of the Bisbee Deportation camp at Columbus, New Mexico. Tents went down, supplies ceased.[58]

The Principals Disperse

Considering the gradual diminution of the numbers in the Columbus IWW pen, the willingness of the Bisbee authorities to dissolve extralegal law in Bisbee made sense. By October several summons, including the call to arms, dispersed many Bisbee deporters of July 1917. The corporation principals of the Arizona strike went off in new directions, a sign that their services at home were no longer in demand. The state had been secured.

On September 1 "Rawhide Jimmy" Douglas, Walter's brother, sailed from New York to work for the American Red Cross in France. That same week Rawhide Jimmy's son, Lewis, received a commission in the United States Army field artillery.[59]

In what must have been a stunning surprise for many, on September 13, the *Review* announced the resignation of Stuart W. French, the general manager of the Phelps Dodge Corporation. French had tendered his resignation to the board "some time before." Although French's office was in Douglas, his name rarely was mentioned in any connection with the vigilante action of July and August. More than any other Phelps Dodge official in Arizona, French had avoided participation in the offensive against labor.[60]

In the federal suit against the deporters brought later by the United States District Attorney, French, along with Walter Douglas, was named as a co-defendant. But French had left the

Warren District for the East Coast a few days after Phelps Dodge president Walter Douglas arrived in Bisbee in his private railroad car. French had joined Phelps Dodge in 1899 and had been general manager only since July 1916. The *Review* reported that Mr. and Mrs. French, originally from Chicago, "had always been prominent in the higher strata of social Douglas." With that eminent credential, Stuart French went East, but the *Review* had no knowledge of his plans for the future.[61]

French's resignation raises a question or two: Did Phelps Dodge president Walter Douglas feel that French had not dealt with the strikers severely enough and so sent him away, maybe even demanded his resignation? Perhaps the two men, upon Douglas' arrival in Arizona, had words, thus causing the manager to leave in anger. Or maybe French's gentility limited his tolerance for and implementation of the outrageous Phelps Dodge policies of vigilantism and deportation, and his self-respect compelled him to leave in disgust. French eventually moved to San Marino, where he died of Parkinson's disease in 1946.[62]

French's Calumet & Arizona counterpart, General Manager John C. Greenway, in late October gave up his reported fifty thousand-dollar-a-year job for a major's commission in the United States Army. The former member of Roosevelt's Rough Riders also went to France.[63]

Another Arizona Rough Rider veteran, Sheriff Harry Wheeler of Cochise County, wanted to go overseas. He applied for an army commission in September 1917, whereupon an immediate outcry went up from the ranks of Arizona labor. The Warren District Trades Assembly issued a set of resolutions protesting, in view of Wheeler's participation in the Bisbee Deportation, his fitness for military service. The Trades Assembly sent a copy along to Wheeler. In defense, Wheeler issued a public answer. He spoke of the "treasonable and unpatriotic" nature of the IWW. Then he made clear his own humility and desire to serve his country "freely, and, if accepted, even the supreme sacrifice of a soldier would be met gladly." But the opposition of labor to Wheeler's appointment did delay his entrance into the army for several months.[64]

In the meantime Wheeler was reprimanded by the federal commission sent to investigate the deportation. In a letter addressed to him, the commission told Wheeler that his past actions were "subversive of industrial peace and denials of lawful rights." The commission's report did not say he was the deportation's author.[65]

To show their support for the sheriff, Bisbee's citizens made him the guest of honor at a banquet. Wheeler expressed his appreciation:

> My friends, you pay me too much honor in this matter. There were scores of men in that drive the morning of July 12 who are entitled to more honor than I, who did more than I did on that day for the district and the home fires. I merely did my duty. I couldn't shirk. You could. But you didn't.[66]

The *Bisbee Daily Review* described the banquet as "a splendid gathering of high-class, patriotic" people of the district.[67]

Wheeler continued his effort, it was reported, to be accepted into military service. He went to officers' training camps at San Francisco, San Antonio "and other places." "He also attempted to enlist in the Canadian Army but was rejected because of wounds he received during his ranger career." Finally, on Thursday, March 22, 1918, Wheeler announced that he had been commissioned a captain in the 308th United States Cavalry.[68] The news of Harry Wheeler's acceptance into the United States military upset President Wilson. "I am a bit shocked," wrote Wilson to Secretary of War Baker, "to find the Sheriff of Cochise County is now in the Reserve Corps."[69]

The *Bisbee Daily Review*'s energetic editor Cullen H. Cain, who came to Bisbee in the hectic days of June 1917, left in the fall of 1918 to become publicity director of the National League of Professional Baseball Clubs. It was Cain's colorful and detailed journalism that would remain the best record of Bisbee's most historic event. A Bisbee under firm control had no further use for his disquieting skills.[70]

A violent, freak accident claimed United States Labor Mediator John McBride in Globe on October 9, 1917. While standing on the sidewalk of the main street of town, McBride was kicked through the front plate glass window of a downtown store by a runaway bronco. Severely cut, McBride bled to death within a short time.[71]

Over the months following Bisbee's Deportation, it became obvious that many of the people who had figured prominently in the affair were no longer needed. Bisbee and Arizona had been well secured for the mining interests. What remained to be done demanded less direct leadership and more subtle tact and manipulation. To properly complete the affair, the mining men needed the indulgence if not the approval of the state and federal governments. This was to be achieved, but it would take some time.

10

CLEAN HANDS
AND A BLESSING

185. Every person who forcibly steals, takes or arrests any person in this state, and carries him into another country, state or county, or into another part of the same county, or who forcibly takes or arrests any person, with a design to take him out of this state, without having established a claim according to the laws of the United States or of this state, or who hires, persuades, entices, decoys, or seduces by false promises, misrepresentations, or the like, any person to go out of this state, or to be taken or removed therefrom for the purpose and with the intent to sell such person into slavery or involuntary servitude, or otherwise to employ him for his own use, or to the use of another, without the free will and consent of such persuaded person, and every person who, being out of this state, abducts, or takes by force or fraud any person contrary to the laws of the place where such act is committed, and brings, sends, or conveys such person within the limits of this state, and is found within the limits thereof, is guilty of kidnapping.

Revised Statutes of Arizona, 1913,
Penal Code, Title 8, Ch. 44.

Investigation

Deputy Frank Johnson of Bisbee, Arizona, called socially on Felix Frankfurter. A member of President Wilson's Mediation Commission, Frankfurter had been sent to Arizona in the fall of 1917 to investigate the labor problems in the mining camps. The federal government was particularly interested in the Bisbee Deportation of July 12, 1917. According to an account by Frank Cullen Brophy, Johnson entered Frankfurter's private railroad car with a six-gun in his belt and said, "'Well, Mr. Frankfurter, you Jewish son-of-a-bitch, I just called to tell you, you had better be out of this town by six o'clock tonight.'" Brophy claims Frankfurter complied and "a second deportation" had taken place. "Bisbee," Brophy added, had "little use for Wobblies or presidential investigators."[1] Considering the temperament of the time and the place, Brophy's story is probably more authentic than apocryphal.*

Discussing Bisbee many years after the investigation, Frankfurter said that the deportation was carried out by "otherwise perfectly nice, decent people." Frankfurter had either a generous attitude or a weak memory. His added comments suggest the latter; like most people, Frankfurter suffered the myopia of retrospect. He remembered the "chief difficulty in this contest . . . was in the claim of the workers for status, . . . that they weren't just 'hands,' but men."[2] Had he reviewed his own report to President Wilson, he might have remembered that the problem as he saw it in 1917 was somewhat different than he reported it forty-four years later.[3]

President Woodrow Wilson had learned of the deportation from his appointed investigator, George W. P. Hunt, on the day it occurred. From that time on, in the midst of the overwhelming demands related to America's entrance into World War I, Wilson found himself deluged by telegrams, letters, visits and phone calls from those who demanded punitive or restrictive federal action and from those who defended themselves regarding the deportation. The governors of the western states, including Arizona Governor Campbell, requested Wilson in late July to crack down on the IWW.

---

*Frank Cullen Brophy was raised in Bisbee, Arizona, and graduated from Yale. In 1961 he acknowledged that he, along with another Arizonan, Judge M. T. Phelps, was a member of the National Executive Council of the John Birch Society.

Although Samuel Gompers usually frowned on governmental interference, he, understandably, reacted strongly to the unrest in the mining West. Gompers, meeting with Wilson in August, urged governmental action. In turn, the President asked the National Council of Defense to consider the problem. The Council proposed that Wilson set up a commission to investigate the labor turmoil in all the industries of the West. Owing to the wartime emergency demand for copper, the Council advised haste in forming a mediation commission.[4]

Acting on the Defense Council's recommendation, Wilson immediately appointed a five-man commission. On September 18, 1917, in a memorandum to Secretary of Labor Wilson, the President announced the names of the commission members. To represent management's interests, Wilson included Colonel Jackson L. Spangler, a coal operator from Pennsylvania, and Verner Z. Reed, silver-mine owner and sheep rancher from Colorado. For labor's side, the President appointed Ernest P. Marsh, chairman of the State Federation of Labor in the state of Washington, and John H. Walker, president of the Illinois Mine Workers. The fifth member was Secretary of Labor William B. Wilson.[5] As advisor and as Secretary of the Commission, Wilson named Felix Frankfurter who was Assistant Secretary of Labor at the time. The commission left Washington on September 30.[6]

In his memorandum Wilson charged the commission to visit the governor of each state advising him of its sympathetic intent to give counsel and aid in creating greater harmony in the state between labor and management. The members were to "deal with employers and employees in a conciliatory spirit" and to "compose differences and allay misunderstandings" in a way "just to both sides." More importantly, the memorandum instructed the commission to "endeavor to learn the real causes of any discontent which may exist on either side, not by the formal process of public hearings, but by getting in touch with workmen and employers by the more informal process of personal conversation."[7]

While all of this official preparation was going on, the National Labor Defense Council, a private organization, had initiated its own investigation of the Bisbee Deportation. Acting for the Council, Harold Callender went to Bisbee. Inexplicably, he was able to make extensive inquiries without being molested by the vigilantes. His one-sided report deploring the outrage appeared in print in the second week in September.

"The National Labor Defense Council" existed primarily as a legal counsel service to defend workers in their conflicts with employers. It also investigated and publicized these conflicts. Considered a "radical" organization, the Council had a legal staff which included Amos Pinchot, Clarence Darrow and the controversial firebrand Frank P. Walsh. John Reed, Lincoln Steffans and Carl Sandburg were among the members of the editorial staff.[8]

It is significant, given the urgency displayed by the administration, that the first concern of the federal commission was the situation at Globe-Miami where an effective strike was still in progress. The team arrived in Globe the first week in October.

But before going to Globe, the team held a two-day conference with Arizona labor leaders in Phoenix. These "legitimate" union representatives, all members of the AFofL, told the commission with "quiet and cogent earnestness" that IWWs had been imported by the copper companies to fan and feed the flaming anti-radical hysteria in the state. The labor leaders complained that the three letters "I.W.W." had, as one reporter told it, "come to stand in the popular mind as a symbol of something bordering on black magic; they were repeated over and over again by the press like the surd tappings of an Oriental drum." Thus the copper companies had been able to work up ordinarily rational people and their communities into a frenzied, unreasonable pitch. This hysterical attitude resulted in labeling all labor leaders, all strikers and everyone sympathizing with the labor movement as Wobblies. No copper company representative appeared in Phoenix to welcome the commission.[9]

After its short session in Phoenix, the commission went on to Globe. The Globe conferences lasted ten days, during which time Wilson's representatives took informal testimony from representatives of the various groups: miners, operators, union leaders, businessmen and townspeople. Each person appeared separately so that each testified without knowing what the other had said. IUMMSW President Charles Moyer came to Globe to be a union spokesman. While in his rooming house, Moyer survived an attempt to kill him. The commission gave him refuge in its private railroad car.[10] The panel found the mine operators to be the least cooperative; most were evasive, defensive, defiant and generally uncongenial. Some even showed discourtesy and hostility.[11]

Hopeful to improve the commission's success at their next stop, Clifton-Morenci, Frankfurter decided to do what he could to obtain cooperation from higher sources. Accordingly, while still in Globe he requested the War Department to prevail upon the British government to influence the Edinburgh-based Arizona Copper Company. Washington complied. In turn, British Ambassador to the United States Sir Stevenson Kent asked the British owners to cooperate with the commission. As a consequence of both this foresight and the experience obtained in Globe, the Clifton-Morenci hearings went more quickly and smoothly. [12]

Then the investigation moved to Bisbee where it took informal depositions from November 1 to November 5. The Warren District was still under strict vigilante control with armed guards inspecting people and their credentials throughout the day. Even the commission members were stopped and subjected to scrutiny one night. Sheriff Wheeler requested the commission to limit the number of deportees that would be asked to return to Bisbee for testimony. He felt a maximum of "fifty I.W.W. witnesses per day" would be "more than possibly could be heard." The commission refused Wheeler's request saying that unless all deportees were permitted to return "when and as they pleased," federal force would be used to assure the sheriff's compliance. Wheeler thereupon wired President Wilson. He told Wilson he had informed the commission of Bisbee's intention to "render every aid possible." But "repeated threats by I.W.W. ... [that] Bisbee would be sacked and various persons murdered" made this demand by the commission unreasonable. Wheeler's telegram stated that Bisbeeites could not "believe the government of the United States would compel us to submit to an organization of disloyal men." Only four or five deportees actually testified before the commission. [13]

Many of the other available personalities who figured in the deportation action testified. Anti-corporate witnesses appeared, and they did not fear to tell their side of the story. [14] The testimony of numerous people corroborated the claims made by the AFofL leaders in Phoenix. Witnesses told the commission that Walter Douglas hired *agents provocateurs* from a California detective agency (probably Thiel) and fired conservative union men. A local police-court judge, Frank A. Thomas, affirmed the peaceful nature of the strike and reported that the miners remaining in Bisbee were "very bitter" about the deportation. He said he knew many of the men were deported because they belonged to the IUMMSW. [15]

Unlike the other witnesses, the Bisbee mine managers appeared as a group. They presented long, prepared testimony. Their attitude was amiable, self-confident and, at times, patronizing. When the commission questioned the mine operators' actions, the witnesses became stern and defensive. None of their comments dealt with the basic issues; most of what they had prepared was trite and irrelevant. The commission members allowed themselves to become involved in long, personal, pointless discussions of social and economic opinions. Compared with the other witnesses, the mine men appeared to enjoy deference and partiality from the commission. Commission members even attempted to ingratiate themselves with the mine managers. A debate filled with their apologies for giving the impression they believed Sheriff Wheeler was "influenced by the mining companies" covered seven or eight pages of testimony. [16]

When the Bisbee hearings had been concluded, Max Lowenthal, a commission assistant, had to "take to bed" with shock. This breakdown, according to Frankfurter, resulted from hearing about the brutal behavior of Bisbeeites whom Frankfurter later called "perfectly nice, decent people." [17]

From Bisbee, on November 6, Frankfurter filed the commission's reports on its findings in the Warren District. Considering the congeniality that characterized the commission's relationship with the mine managers during the investigative sessions in Bisbee, the report was surprisingly severe in its condemnation of the operators' acts related to the Arizona labor conflict and, in particular, to the deportation. Although its members realized, Frankfurter wrote, that President Wilson had not charged it "to sit in judgment of the errors of the past," the commission felt that in the future recurrences of "such instances as the Bisbee deportation" had to be avoided. Avoiding further such events demanded "candor," said the commission, and candor it was prepared to give. The panel did not find that the grievances of labor in the district justified a strike. Since "no machinery for the adjustment of difficulties" existed in the Arizona mining communities, the commission worked out a plan to that end.

The commission determined that many men had gone out on strike to avoid being labeled as "scabs." What was more, the military had determined that troops were unnecessary. As all other reports indicated, the commission could find no evidence of violence or disorder in Bisbee prior to the deportation. After describing the deportees' roundup and exodus, Frankfurter's report mentioned that comparatively few deported men came from nations currently at war with the United States. Although it attributed the roundup execution to Sheriff Wheeler, it assigned responsibility for the deportation to Phelps Dodge Corporation and Calumet & Arizona Mining Company officials. (The identity of the responsible parties appears so often and so clearly it is puzzling to read interpretations blaming the affair on other sources.)

The mine managers' contention that striking miners had jeopardized life and property in Bisbee failed to impress Wilson's investigators. They dismissed this charge as having "no justification in the evidence in support of it presented by the parties who harbored it." Their report then emphasized the failure of local authorities to inform Governor Campbell of any danger and to apprise Lt. Col. Hornbrook that conditions had changed. Then, in direct language, the commission report stated that "the deportation was wholly illegal," as were Bisbee's subsequent vigilante activities. This violation of constitutional rights and usurpation of due process had "no authority whatever in law."[18]

Appreciating, no doubt, the precarious political position of President Wilson regarding labor, radicalism, the war, big business and the current American wave of patriotism, Frankfurter realized little administrative action, if any, would derive from the commission's findings. So he made the statement as strong as he dared, hoping to give some satisfaction to the embittered laboring men. Since the report was to be made public, its strong rhetoric hopefully would help to ease the tensions in Bisbee and Arizona even if no federal redress were ever forthcoming.

The commission report from Bisbee concluded with five strongly worded recommendations: (1) "All illegal practices and the denial of rights safeguarded by the Constitution and statutes must at once cease." (2) Arizona state and Cochise County officials should seek legal "vindication" for violation of state laws. (3) If the United States draft law had been interfered with, the United States Attorney General should be notified. (4) The Interstate Commerce Commission should prosecute anyone who interfered with interstate communications. (5)

Congress should make deportations a violation of federal criminal law "to the full extent of the constitutional authority of the Federal Government."[19] Only one commission member — Colorado mining operator Reed — failed to endorse the report.

This official report of the commission to President Wilson became public the last week of November. Scattered response was generated. *The New York Times*, coolly detached, quoted some of the more indictful passages concerning the mining officials. "The facts ... in the report to the President," wrote *The Survey*, "couched in the coolest and most unimpressive language, constitute a scathing arraignment" of the copper company officials. The progressive-minded *New Republic* praised it.[20]

Before it had made its report public, the commission wrote to Sheriff Wheeler condemning the deportation and the "subsequent practices." The practices, which the commission described to Wheeler as "subversive of industrial peace," had to be abandoned. The sheriff gave his response at his banquet of honor: "President Wilson's Commission reported to him things about this district and the deportation of the Wobblies that were not true."[21]

Sheriff Wheeler wasn't the only ex-Rough Rider who found the commission's report distasteful. Indignant at the suggestion that the deportation was not necessary for wartime security was former United States President — and "Progressive" — Theodore Roosevelt. Roosevelt's daughter, Mrs. Alice Longworth, shared her father's point of view. Felix Frankfurter later claimed he was able to show Alice (at a party on August 18, 1918) that the IWW movement was a response to unsatisfactory, remediable social conditions. According to Frankfurter, she finally agreed that the deportation of people from Bisbee represented the "disregard of fairness and decency in the treatment of people in the mines and in the mills."[22]

Commission Chairman Wilson wrote also to Arizona Governor Thomas Campbell on November 6, informing the governor that the commissioners had concluded their investigation of the Warren District. After describing the proposals their report had made for "the adjustment of grievances," Wilson apprised Campbell that his commission had "found practices which you have heretofore declared illegal still existing." He included a copy of his letter to Sheriff Wheeler in his letter to Campbell, and he emphasized the importance of bringing about "the prompt termination of all existing illegal practices." The letter assured Campbell that the governor could count on the full cooperation of the federal government.[23]

At about the same time, President Wilson's commission wrote the Phelps Dodge Corporation insisting that the company bargain collectively with its employees and that it not discriminate against the men for having union membership. Phelps Dodge wrote back to the commission saying it considered such practices unnecessary and contrary to the corporation's judgment. "'But,'" said the copper company, "'since we have no alternative in the matter, we shall endeavor to carry out your wishes in the spirit as well as the letter.'"[24] As the deportation had destroyed all effective unionism in the district, the promise meant little.

Upon receiving the recommendations of the mediation commission together with other demands for more efficient administration of labor conditions, President Wilson, in January 1918, established a vague and tentative administration policy. In a statement that must have appeared acceptably obscure for management and frustratingly empty for labor, Wilson demanded a more suitable system for providing a labor supply, machinery for the adjustment of labor disputes, plus administration of labor safety. These suggestions amounted to less than token crumbs for labor; they made clear Wilson's unwillingness to challenge meaningfully the status quo in the mining industry.[25]

After the United States Department of Justice had seen the November 6 report of the President's Mediation Commission, it started an investigation of the Bisbee Deportation. A flurry of letters was exchanged by Assistant Attorney General W. D. Fitts and numerous government officials and legal advisors. Fitts wanted to determine whether section 19 of the United States Criminal Code had been violated. The general meaning of this law involved infringement of constitutional rights, and it stated that prosecution could follow a charge that "two or more persons [did] conspire to injure, oppress, threaten, or intimidate any citizen in the free exercise or enjoyment of any right or privilege secured to him by the Constitution or laws of the United States, etc."[26]

Fitts corresponded with Special Assistant Attorney General Frank R. Nebeker (the chief prosecutor in the Chicago IWW trial) and with Attorney General T. W. Gregory during the last week of November 1917. After reading the President's Mediation Commission Report, the men discussed the advisability of prosecuting the deporters. Gregory had received a copy of the report from President Wilson. Along with the report, Wilson sent Gregory a letter (dated November 22) which referred to recommendation number five in the report. This item urged that Congress make deportations a violation of federal criminal law. Implying that the Justice Department might already have grounds for prosecution, Wilson suggested that the attorney general take "any action . . . you may think is wise or feasible."[27]

Fitts went to Tucson and, together with United States Attorney Oliver E. Pagan, attempted to build the government's case and proceed with such action as the "law and the facts" justified. The two prosecutors later learned that whatever course they felt the facts might justify, the courts would fail to favor.[28]

A telegram to Attorney General Gregory from Secretary of Labor and Mediation Commission Chairman William B. Wilson advised prosecution for reasons more political than judicial. The telegram, sent on December 4 from Seattle where the commission was still conducting its investigation of labor difficulties in the lumber camps of the Northwest, informed Gregory that the Bisbee Deportation had caused "a feeling of disquietude" in western labor circles. Wilson observed that since the

> . . .incident has been much exploited among laboring people. . . it is necessary to counteract its bad effects by action on the part of the Government which will leave labor and liberal opinion without any basis for the thoughts that the Government in the slightest sanctions such illegal acts as took place in Bisbee.[29]

In other words, Secretary Wilson felt that prosecution itself (he made no mention of conviction or punishment) would act as a buffer to absorb the outrage of labor and to still complaints by liberals. This may have been a maneuver on the Secretary's part to illuminate a provocative motive that would jar a Justice Department which, apart from prosecutor Fitts and one or two others, had maintained a complacent position. On the other hand, the Secretary of Labor may have been revealing his own basic aversion to the disruptive attitudes of labor's more liberal element. Like Samuel Gompers, Wilson hoped to undercut the more troublesome liberal element in the labor movement. Gompers, himself, wrote to the Attorney General on January 19, 1918, urging prosecution of the deporters.[30]

President Wilson's Policy

Early in September of 1916 President Wilson spoke approvingly of "labor's gains" and said that the workingman had been emancipated by government action. But wartime brought a new perspective on labor to the President. His oratory in the fall of 1916 praised the Clayton Act for restricting judicial harassment of labor. The courts, Wilson claimed, had treated members of unions "like fractional parts of mobs and not like accessible and responsible individuals."[31] As proof of his concern for labor, he signed the Railroad Eight-Hour law. This kind of legislation plus the apparent increase in take-home pay has prompted historians Richard Morris and William Greenleaf to record that "labor fared well during the war."[32]

But this evidence of support for labor is misleading. In 1921 Alexander Bing wrote:

> Many employers [and many historians] are under the impression that the Government truckled to labor during the war, and gave it everything it asked. A more careful study of just what labor did receive has confirmed and strengthened the opinion ... that this was not in any sense the case, and that the Government did not, except in isolated cases, give to labor any concessions which were not demanded both by justice and by expediency. It will also be realized that, taking into account the power which the abnormal economic conditions and the needs of the hour placed in labor's hands, its conduct was both conservative and patriotic.[33]

Bing found that Wilson's government had little comprehension of labor's problem in World War I. In its evaluation of labor problems, the administration as well as Congress usually blamed the workers. Also, hardly a single court case came up in which fault was found with the employer.[34]

Neither "justice" nor "expediency" made very great demands in favor of labor. The National War Labor Board, appointed by Wilson on April 8, recommended that strikes and lockouts be avoided during the war. Although the board endorsed the right of labor to organize and be recognized, it limited worker participation to "legitimate trade union activities." The War Department issued a statement on June 20, 1917, saying that the "government cannot commit itself in any way to the closed shop." The "agreement" between President Wilson and the labor leaders in September 1917 did not include any provision for the closed shop.[35]

During the industrial strife in the West, trade union officials said the trouble should be the cause of deep concern to those responsible for the conduct of the nation's affairs.[36] Big Bill Haywood claimed that after war was declared in 1917, Robert Bruere told him that

> Samuel Gompers had gone to Newton Baker, then Secretary of War, and had presented to him a plan to annihilate the IWW. Baker refused to take the suggestion of Gompers seriously; the latter then went to the Department of Justice where he met with more success.[37]

But when the western governors presented *their* plan to Wilson in July for dealing with the IWW, the government appeared to listen more closely. What Wilson saw in their proposal was the advantage of a police state over vigilantism. In the wartime situation, the Wilson administration became increasingly intolerant of radicalism. Perhaps Wilson saw the IWW prosecutions as a way of pleasing and promoting conservative unionism. In this way, he could gain organized labor's support of his war policy.[38] More likely, this severe policy gave fuller vent to the basic nativistic, moralistic and conservative nature of Wilsonian democracy.

The correspondence to and from the President and his administrative branches during the late summer of 1917 indicated the political nature of Wilson's policies in regard to labor and radicalism and the Bisbee Deportation. Despite Wilson's rhetoric and other gestures in support of American labor, the letters, memos and telegrams show clearly the administration's desire to avoid antagonizing America's increasing number of conservative voters by endorsing attitudes or actions favorable to the workingmen, particularly the more militant ones. For whatever the reason they had been invoked, repressive measures guaranteed for some time the preservation of the open shop in the West and the defeat of independent unionism.[39]

The equivocal action taken regarding the Bisbee Deportation, the biased attitude of federal troops stationed in labor-troubled communities and the violation of constitutional procedures in the government's handling of domestic disorders underlined the prejudicial qualities of Wilson's policy.[40] There is little doubt that even Wilson's Mediation Commission was sent to Arizona not to improve or assist organized labor but to bring industrial peace to the state. Frankfurter, for all his "sympathy," spent much time persuading AFofL organizers and many other union men to "relinquish and waive causes of legal action for damages against the corporations." In the name of harmony, he "pursued a neutral policy primarily in the interest of the government and its prosecution of the war."[41] United States Attorneys Fitts and Pagan enjoyed little administrative encouragement in their efforts to bring charges against the deporters. This substantiates the idea that the Wilson administration, despite Wilson's condemnation of the courts a year earlier, had a permissive attitude toward big business and the Phelps Dodge Corporation in particular.[42]

Indeed, Phelps Dodge may have received preferential consideration during Wilson's tenure as President. Although no specific documents can be found which prove this favoritism, considerable circumstantial evidence—including the correspondence of Wilson—suggests that the big copper company might have enjoyed special treatment by the federal government during Wilson's administration.

Cleveland H. Dodge, whose grandfather had helped to found the Phelps Dodge Corporation, was a partner in Phelps, Dodge & Company from 1889 until that organization was dissolved in 1908. He then became one of the nine original directors of Phelps, Dodge & Co., Inc., a position he held from 1908 until his death in 1926. Dodge was a vice-president of the company from 1909 until 1924. Cleveland Dodge graduated from Princeton University in 1879, and his classmates included Cyrus McCormick, scion of a midwest farm machinery dynasty, and a bright, promising young man born in Virginia, Thomas Woodrow Wilson. Dodge and Wilson formed a close personal bond which lasted for many years, and Dodge used his money and influence to support Wilson throughout his long career.[43]

This intimacy of Dodge and Wilson is sometimes mentioned in the major biographies of Wilson and histories of the period, but none ever focuses on this relationship. Yet the volumes of Wilson's correspondence edited by Ray Stannard Baker reveal a friendship which was broad and intense. The frequency of correspondence between Wilson and Dodge at times amounts to more than four or five letters a month. In addition, the two visited each other often. The nature of their writing leaves little doubt that Wilson considered "Cleve" Dodge to be his dearest, most trusted friend. Baker's collection contains letters which indicate Cleveland Dodge plotted and financed Woodrow Wilson's entire academic and political career. No one, it appears in the letters, influenced Wilson more than did Dodge. Conventional belief has it that Colonel Edward M. House served as Wilson's closest confidant. But many times Wilson solicited and heeded Dodge's advice first.[44]

Both McCormick and Dodge were among the twenty-five or so members of the Princeton board of trustees when Wilson first went to Princeton to teach in 1890. While at Princeton, Wilson became deeply in Dodge's debt. In 1898 Dodge and McCormick organized a private fund to raise Wilson's salary to keep him at the college. Other contributors to the fund were Moses Taylor Pyne and Percy R. Pyne, of the family that founded the National City Bank. (For many years Dodge was also vice-president and board member of the National City Bank.) In 1902 this same group arranged Wilson's election as president of the university. On June 9, the day of the decision, Dodge was one of three trustees who went to Wilson's home and surprised him with the news.[45]

During Wilson's stormy tenure as president at Princeton, Dodge led the coalition of trustees that supported Wilson in the controversies over administrative autonomy, academic emphasis and collegiate reform. Dodge provided the funds for Wilson's preceptorial experiment. In June 1910, before Wilson's graduate school program was defeated, Dodge was persuading him to run for governor of New Jersey. Not only did Dodge push Wilson into politics, he was the greatest contributor to Wilson's pre-nomination campaigns, for both the New Jersey governorship and the presidency.[46] While governor, Wilson discovered the tensions and pitfalls of political office. During the summer of 1911, in what he described as "his only moment of rest and delight," he went with Dodge for a short trip on Dodge's yacht, the *Corona*.[47]

Dodge collected $85,000 for Wilson's pre-convention campaign, and before Wilson's nomination for the presidency, Dodge introduced him to other officials of the National City

Bank including James Stillman and William Rockefeller. The connection of Wilson with the bank was close, and, according to muckraker Ferdinand Lundberg, had "an important bearing upon crucial decisions during Wilson's White House occupancy."[48]

Dodge contributed $51,000 to Wilson's 1912 presidential campaign fund, but when the donation was made public, he recalled the money. In the meantime, Dodge helped to subsidize the Trenton *True American*, a newspaper with national circulation which in reality was a campaign strategem for Wilson. As soon as he was nominated, on July 7, 1912, Wilson wrote a letter of appreciation to Dodge. ("I am so happy I can hardly think.") Three weeks later he was still sentimental; "You are an ideal friend; you do everything in the best and most generous way." Soon after his nomination, Wilson went on another yacht trip with Dodge but spent most of the time polishing up his acceptance speech, which he delivered from the porch of the governor's summer house at Atlantic Highlands, New Jersey, on August 7.[49]

Dodge's generous advice and financial aid followed Wilson into the White House. In March 1913, Dodge offered "up to fifteen or twenty thousand dollars a year" to implement the salary of Dean Fine if Fine would accept the appointment as United States Ambassador to Germany. Fine, a fellow Princetonian, declined. That month Wilson asked Dodge if he would "bring pressure to bear" on John R. Mott to be Minister to China. Mott, too, declined his appointment.[50] Then, on July 12, 1914, another situation arose. Wilson asked Dodge to donate $25,000 to keep Walter Hines Page at the Court of St. James. Page's expenses exceeded the salary authorized by Congress, and he threatened to quit. Disgruntled over the niggardliness of Capitol Hill, Wilson wrote:

> Will you forgive and understand me if I turn to you? I know that you will, and that you will come to my aid if you can. I know of no other friend like you, and of no other friend to whom I could afford to turn in such a matter and with such a request.[51]

Dodge responded the next day:

> Your beautiful letter ... is well worth the whole price of admission and I thank you from the bottom of my heart

for this new mark of your confidence.... I can attend to
this little matter without embarrassment.... I will not
mention the matter to a soul.[52]

About this "little matter" Dodge showed discretion: "I
should think it would be just as well not to have my name
appear in any way." He suggested possible intermediaries.[53] A
week later Wilson expressed *his* gratitude[54]:

> Certainly God has blessed me with one of the truest
> and most generous friends a man could have. Friendship
> such as yours, coming by fresh proof to me here in the
> midst of business at every turn of which it is necessary, in
> common caution, to scrutinize motives and reckon with
> what may be covertly involved is like God's pure air to a
> man stifled and breathing hard to keep his lungs going. I
> am deeply grateful and happy whenever I think of you.
> May God bless you and he has blessed me *in* you....
>
>   Your grateful and devoted friend
>   Woodrow Wilson

Later, after America's entry into the war, Page and Wilson
drifted apart in their views on England. But as Ferdinand
Lundberg has pointed out, Page, as America's wartime ambassador to Great Britain, was being financed by a man who was
the vice-president of a large copper company and a "big stock-
holder of the National City Bank who also happened to be one
of America's munitions magnates."[55]

In 1915 Cleveland Dodge contributed $7,000 to the "League
to Enforce Peace," an organization urging United States' entrance into World War I. (Bernard Baruch gave $47,500.) In 1916
Dodge, along with oilman Edward L. Doheny, was the biggest
contributor to Wilson's campaign fund ($25,000).[56] On April 21,
1917, Woodrow Wilson named a committee chaired by Cleveland Dodge to help lead the Red Cross fund-raising campaign.
The irony of a wartime profiteering copper magnate heading a
Red Cross committee did not deter Wilson.[57]

A pregnant gap exists in the Wilson-Dodge correspondence in the Baker collection. The letters between Friday, May
25, 1917, and Saturday, September 1—if there were any—have
been omitted. The Bisbee Deportation took place during this
time. But Wilson revealed something about himself to Dodge

in his September 1 letter. He said he needed Dodge's opinion on matters "because I never entirely trust my own instinct and conclusion." When Dodge wrote three months later that he hoped Wilson would not declare war on Turkey and Bulgaria, Wilson replied, "I sympathize with every word of your letter."[58]

Their correspondence included no mention of the Arizona labor difficulties or of the Bisbee Deportation, but the long, intense relationship of the two men provokes—inescapably— a question or two. Could Wilson, considering his dependence on and indebtedness to Dodge, pursue with any aggressiveness his executive responsibility to restrain the outrageous behavior that Phelps Dodge had shown in Arizona in the summer of 1917? And, in view of Wilson's loyalty to such a great figure of financial and industrial America, was he really very concerned—other than in token statements—about the American workingman?

Wilson's close relationship to Dodge might not have accounted substantially for his willingness to repress radical labor spokesmen and indulge wartime profiteers, but the possibility is too compelling to ignore. After Cleveland Dodge's death in 1926, executors valued his estate at twenty to twenty-five million dollars.[59]

Continued Hysteria

If President Wilson did feel indifferent or even antagonistic toward the "un-American" behavior of certain laboring groups, he shared these feelings with a growing number of his countrymen. Whatever fears, vague or specific, many Americans felt about their wartime enemies were rapidly congealing. Passed before the United States even entered the war, a federal statute of February 3, 1917, made aliens deportable if they were anarchists or if they believed in the overthrow of the government by force and violence. Usually aimed at the IWW, "criminal syndicalism" or "sabotage" laws were enacted in many states beginning in Idaho in 1917. Enforced most vigorously was the California criminal-syndicalism law. Of 530 persons charged, 500 were apprehended, more than 270 tried and 164 convicted. A sabotage bill passed the legislature in Arizona in 1918 but was vetoed by Governor Hunt. The veto failed to be overridden. By June of 1917 enough antagonism prevailed in Congress to enable the passage of the Espionage Act. Signed into law by President Wilson on June 15, it provided for penalties up to $10,000 and 20 years in prison for those found guilty of aiding the enemy, obstructing recruiting or causing disloyalty in the armed forces. Nationwide, the hostility toward suspected seditious elements in America continued to grow. The six governors of the western states who had in late July petitioned President Wilson to crack down on troublemakers in the Far West subsequently (on August 11) stated that a clear distinction must be made between "legitimate" labor organizations and the IWW. But the tendency of middle-class Americans was to find labor, in general, suspect.[60]

On August 15 Elihu Root and Theodore Roosevelt both denounced the IWW.[61] The Commissioner General of the Bureau of Immigration felt that a "campaign against the foreign leaders among these people would produce valuable and far-reaching salutary effects."[62] Shortly after the Bisbee Deportation one United States district attorney recommended that any alien enemy who was "unreliable" should be subject to internment. "It is apparent that this is not the time for the I.W.W.s and their kind to be shifting around from place to place."[63] Throughout America the mood was building for some broader crackdown than merely deportation out of a particular community.

Quietly operating behind all this sound and fury, the United States Department of Justice could find no substance to support the claims of sedition, espionage activities or German influence and financial support. Within four days after the Bisbee Deportation, an apologetic Justice Department meekly announced that it could not find evidence of German gold financing IWW activities.[64] Later, the IWW trials of 1918, despite the terrible sentences meted to the defendants, showed that IWW revenue from April 1, 1917, to September 1, 1917 "clearly...had come from normal, not covert, sources."[65] During the Red Scare, in 1920, *The New Republic* quoted Judge George W. Anderson concerning his activities as a United States attorney from November 1914 to October 1917, and as a member of the Interstate Commerce Commission from October 15, 1917, until the armistice, November 11, 1918. During those periods he was in "intimate association with the Attorney General and with the men charged with responsibility as to discovering, preventing, and punishing pro-German plots." Judge Anderson said, "Now, I assert as my best judgment, grounded on the information that I can get, that more than ninety-nine per cent of the advertised and reported pro-German plots never existed.... I doubt the Red menace having more basis in fact than the pro-German peril."[66] But the general public paid little attention to reality.

Numerous inquiries in the weeks and months that followed the deportation resulted in no concrete proof of treasonable conspiracy or outside financial aid to the Bisbee strikers and deportees.[67] It had been alleged in several press dispatches on August 1 that the United States government was in possession of a mass of evidence showing seditious and treasonable activities in America financed by agents using German money. When asked if the dispatches were true, Assistant Attorney General William C. Fitts replied:

> If we had evidence of violation of federal law, we would instantly take steps to apprehend the violators of the law. We have not made arrests, and we will not make arrests until federal laws have been violated. Of course, we are keeping a close watch on persons who may be suspected of planning to commit such violations. If fires are set, or property is destroyed, or men are killed, within a state, those are matters covered by state law.[68]

Apparently state laws were not adequate for some people who resented IWW attitudes. So they employed, Bisbee-style, "extralegal" methods. The precedent of the July deportation expanded. Masked vigilantes in Butte before dawn of August 1 went to the hotel room of IWW organizer Frank Little. Only a few days earlier Little had arrived in Butte from Globe, Arizona, from where, in response to the Bisbee Deportation, he had sent Arizona Governor Campbell a telegram saying, "I don't give a damn what your country is fighting for; I am fighting for the solidarity of labor."[69] The thugs took Little, who was recovering from a broken leg, from the room. Still in his underwear, he was tied to a car's rear bumper and towed to a railroad trestle outside of town. His body was torn and broken from the brutal dragging. Little was then lynched; a note, pinned to his bloodied union suit, read: "Others Take Notice — First and Last Warning."[70]

A huge crowd turned out for Little's funeral, but whatever martyrdom might have been attributed to Little's death was imperceptible and short-lived, while the routine criminal investigation produced no suspects. There was almost no journalistic opposition to the Little lynching; some Congressmen even supported it. *The Literary Digest* summed up the general response: "A service to the State and the United States."[71]

While the IWW odium of treason made the lynching acceptable on the popular level, most people close to the situation assumed that Little's death had been part of the effort by the copper companies to destroy unionism. The *New York Call*, one of the few emotionally restrained newspapers in the land, averred that along with the Bisbee Deportation, the lynching of Frank Little "would indicate that there is a concerted movement afoot, backed primarily by the Copper Trust and auxiliary big business, to crush the very life out of this organization."[72] When asked if Little was not lynched because he was believed to be unpatriotic, Big Bill Haywood replied that "Little was murdered because there is a strike in Butte, and he was helping to win it."[73]

Some cynicism developed during the journalistic *post mortum* on Frank Little. Several sources alleged that when Little's body was cut down, papers were found in a pocket of his underwear identifying Little as an operative for a detective agency. From this purported evidence arose two main speculations: (1) Little had been killed by fellow IWWs who had discovered his identity and (2) a mistake had been made by company goons who were unaware of his true connection. In view of Little's dedication to the Wobbly cause, both suggestions, though plausible in light of the rampant infiltration of the IWW by company detectives, are unlikely.[74]

Generally speaking, the Little lynching did nothing to assuage the rising malice toward the IWW. Inflammatory editorials intensified. Congressmen and Senators from states untouched by Wobblyism received a gratuitous education on the evils of the organization. Arizona Senator Henry Fountain Ashurst spouted forth a torrent of anti-Wobbly invective: "With the I.W.W.s perjury is a fine art...murder is reduced to a science...I.W.W....means simply, solely, and only, 'Imperial Wilhelm's Warriors.'"[75]*

---

*Later, in December, Arizona's lone Congressman, Carl Hayden, braved the tide to introduce an "anti-deportation" bill. Nothing came of it. (*Arizona Republican*, December 14, 1917, p. 1.)

This particular speech of Ashurst's, delivered in the nation's Capitol on August 17, represented the acme of the public anti-IWW sentiment. Americans were now ready for a nationwide Bisbee-like Wobbly drive. In the states of Washington and Montana, during the week following August 17, the United States Army, authorized as a *posse comitatus*, raided IWW halls, broke up meetings and jailed dozens of Wobblies. Soldiers patrolled towns and initiated a system of forced labor for Wobblies, and authorities often jailed Wobblies indefinitely, "for their own protection" from "dangerous citizens." On August 20, police arrested twenty-seven IWWs at their Spokane headquarters and held them incommunicado. [76]

These broadened repressive acts against the Wobblies brought virtually no protests from most Americans. Instead, American attitude appeared to be one of general approval. This public approval the Wilson administration took as a mandate for more massive attacks. Bill Haywood's words seem appropriate: "The country was going mad about the war." Two weeks after the raid on the Spokane IWW office, on the 5th of September, agents from the Department of Justice "swooped down on the IWW like a cloud of vultures." Across America IWW headquarters, local union branches and even members' homes were invaded. Books, ledgers, records, literature, typewriters, furniture, pictures, duplicating equipment and even spittoons were seized. The accumulated evidence amounted to several tons, and a number of special agents were assigned to investigate the material. Their findings resulted in five counts, all based on new laws, which made up the indictments brought against the arrested men. Most of those arrested were IWW leaders. The charges against them involved conspiracy related to the Espionage and Selective Service Acts. [77]

Then, when everyone felt the storm had passed, another general raid took place on September 29. This time wider arrest was conducted, and thousands of Wobblies were crowded into jails all over the country. Eventually those prisoners not released were concentrated in Sacramento, California; Wichita, Kansas; and, the largest group, in Chicago, Illinois. By April 1918 more than one hundred fifty men had been charged with various and multiple forms of conspiracy. Among them were such well-known leaders as IWW President "Big Bill" Haywood, sometime Executive Secretary Vincent St. John, *Solidarity* editor Ralph Chaplin, Arizona IWW President Grover

H. Perry and national organizer and Jerome deportee, James P. "Red" Thompson.[78]

Trials: Traitors and Patriots

The Chicago IWW trial began on April 1, 1918. It was to become, up until its time, the longest criminal trial in American history. Presided over by Judge Kenisaw Mountain Landis, the courtroom throughout the hot five summer months became a scene of casual disregard for traditional judicial decorum. Prisoners were allowed to loll or even sleep on their courtroom benches, while Judge Landis eschewed the uncomfortable robes of his office. To save time and trouble Landis had the noon meals brought into the courtroom and personally provided cigarettes for those men who wanted to smoke.[79]

No question existed about what was really on trial. The indictment only personified the real objects of the prosecution's argument—the IWW, radicalism and nonconformity to the popular will. The IWW defendants were not treated so much as traitors but as freaks, and "flippancy rather than prejudice characterized the daily reports of the court proceedings."[80]

Led by a Utah corporation lawyer, Frank N. Nebeker, the prosecution did not fix the guilt for specific crimes. Rather it emphasized the general notoriety of the IWW as an organization. Nebeker reasoned that if the organization was subversive, then its members were subversive. The defense in Chicago seemed eager to get the trial over with. It was headed by George F. Vanderveer, who took charge when Clarence Darrow declared he was tied up with war work in Washington. Vanderveer had the assistance of several other lawyers including Fred Moore and William Cleary, both of whom had figured in the Bisbee affair back in July.[81]

The Wobbly defense argued: (1) no interference with the prosecution of the war could be shown, (2) the IWW had engaged in no anti-war sabotage and (3) all strikes called had been for legitimate labor grievances. As the weeks wore on, the defendants attempted to verify that their reputation was derived mainly from boastful talk and inflammatory literature, by deliberate propaganda issued from big business and from slander generated by the antagonism between themselves and the AFofL together with other trade unions.[82] But the Wobblies found little sympathy inside the courtroom or out. Public animosity had reached a broad, popular level. A handful of intellectuals and fashionable radicals did attempt to solicit support for the defendants. Through an appeal placed in *The New Republic*, such well-known liberal Progressives as John Dewey, John A. Fitch, Robert W. Bruere, Thorstein Veblen, Helen Keller, and historians Carlton J. H. Hayes and James Harvey Robinson urged donations to defray court costs of the Wobblies on trial.[83] Besides a shortage of funds, the defense ran into other difficulties: Fred Moore suffered a nervous disorder, and Vanderveer began to drink heavily.[84]

The last week of August the case went to the jury. It took but fifty-five minutes to reach a decision; all defendants were found guilty on all counts. Immediately Judge Landis, whose courtroom conviviality had lifted the hopes of many defendants, changed his mien. He dropped his earlier "objectivity" and passionately denounced the IWW and then threw the book at ninety-three prisoners. Though not one man had been proven guilty of any overt act against the government or another person, Landis assigned prison terms ranging up to twenty years and fines up to $30,000. No specific evidence had been introduced against Vincent St. John, but he received both of the maximum penalties. Five of the convicted men were legal residents of Arizona. One of those convicted, Stanley J. Clark, a former member of the Socialist Party but not a Wobbly, had gone to Bisbee after the deportation and spoken out on behalf of the wives and children of the deportees. For this treasonous transgression and open "seditious utterances," Clark got twenty years and a $30,000 fine. The Jerome deportee, organizer "Red" Thompson, was given the same maximum sentence.[85]

In Sacramento on January 16, 1919, all forty-six of the IWWs on trial there were found guilty of violating the United States Espionage Act. However, Judge Rudkin excused three of them and gave the rest sentences much lighter than those given by Judge Landis in Chicago—one to ten years in prison.[86]

After the war, in April 1919, Alexander Sidney Lanier wrote a sane and sensitive open letter to President Wilson. The letter appeared in *The New Republic* and pointed out that no conspiracy had been proven in the Chicago IWW trial. But the Red Scare of the time undoubtedly intimidated Wilson. Not until Warren Harding took office were pardons forthcoming.[87]

All IWWs convicted under federal law were released within six years and four months after their arrest. While out awaiting appeal after his conviction, Bill Haywood skipped bail and took asylum in Soviet Russia where he died in 1928 in lonely exile.[88]

As a gauge of America's prevailing concept of justice and its swing away from the earlier Progressive mood, the IWW conspiracy convictions can be more fully appreciated when contrasted with the attempt to prosecute those responsible for the Bisbee Deportation. In Chicago, Wichita and Sacramento ineffectual hoboes and social visionaries received extreme sentences for only their braggadocio and radical dreams; in Tucson, San Francisco and Washington, D.C., the federal courts indulged powerful corporation leaders and their agents and eventually acquitted them of charges based on behavior violent, substantial and overt.

On his tour through Arizona in 1864, J. Ross Browne found, in addition to the murderous Apaches,

> ...the most desperate race of renegades from Texas and California....Tucson became the headquarters of vice, dissipation and crime...[and] probably the nearest approach to Pandamonium [sic] on the North American continent. Murderers, thieves, cutthroats, and gamblers formed the mass of the population.

Instead of offering protection, "the [military] garrison at Tucson confined itself to its legitimate business of getting drunk or doing nothing." He noted:

> Arizona was perhaps the only part of the world under the protecting aegis of a civilized government in which every man administered justice to suit himself, and where all assumed the right to gratify the basest passions of their nature without restraint.[89]

United States government policy changed little in the next fifty-three years. No doubt federal prosecutors W. C. Fitts and Oliver E. Pagan overlooked the basic truism of Arizona-style jurisprudence when they set out to make a case against the perpetrators of the Bisbee Deportation. What J. Ross Browne could not know in 1864 was that in 1920 the Supreme Court of the United States would protect this unique and insular sense of justice. Prosecutors Pagan and Fitts, too, failed to account for this modern permissiveness.

After spending six months preparing their case, the two federal attorneys obtained federal warrants resulting in the arrest on May 15, 1918, of twenty-one of Bisbee's leading mining company officials, employees and businessmen. A federal grand jury in Tucson the week before had returned indictments, based on an investigation which included evidence presented by Fitts and Pagan, charging the Bisbee men with "conspiracy to injure, oppress, threaten and intimidate citizens in the exercise of the right to peaceably reside in the state of Arizona." The alleged conspiracy, the indictment said, was in violation of section 19, United States penal code. During the week of testimony the grand jury questioned more than one hundred witnesses from Douglas, Bisbee and Warren.[90]

Included among those indicted were Phelps Dodge Corporation president Walter Douglas and Phelps Dodge officials Joseph P. Hodgson, H. H. Stout and Gerald H. Sherman.* Grant H. Dowell, Copper Queen general manager, was the first person arrested. Lemuel Shattuck, president of Shattuck & Denn, and Miles Merrill, Loyalty League organizer, were included. United States Marshal Dillon served the warrants, and the arrested men met at the law offices of Ellinwood and Ross in Bisbee. United States Commissioner H. C. Beumler fixed their bonds at $5,000 each. According to one report, every member of the Cochise County Bar Association rushed to offer his services gratis to the defendants.[91]

In Tucson Federal Judge William H. Sawtelle said he would allow no inspection of the specific charges until all those indicted had been taken into custody. Several key principals for whom indictments had been prepared were not available. Sheriff Harry Wheeler, John Greenway, James Douglas and W. H. Brophy, manager of the Phelps Dodge Mercantile Company, were all serving in France with either the American Expeditionary Force or the Red Cross. Later in the day United States Commissioner Beumler and United States Marshall Dillon issued additional warrants to a number of miners, cattlemen and others who had been found culpable by the jury.[92] Sheriff Harry Wheeler's absence did not prevent the case from being labeled *United States v. Wheeler et al.* Upon hearing of the indictment, Wheeler cabled from France:

---

*Interestingly, the federal government awarded the job of printing the formal indictment to the *Arizona Daily Star,* Walter Douglas' own newspaper. (Indictment, *U.S.A. v. H. C. Wheeler, et al.*)

Wish my friends to know am anxious to protect them by
again assuming all responsibility for deportation. Would
do same thing over again under same circumstances. No
traitors or I.W.W. sympathizers over here, only American
soldiers. My country needs me here, but when I can be
spared, if still alive you will find me ready to go home and
stand with my friends and fellow Americans to undergo
any tribulations the politicians, the I.W.W. sympathizers
and other traitors can inflict. The Eagles feel only contempt for those vultures at home, but do not fear them.[93]

On Saturday, May 18, the defendants were arraigned at
the United States Court House in Tucson. Included with the
conspiracy charge was an indictment for kidnapping. Walter
Douglas, a primary defendant, did not appear in court. The
United States Attorney General's office had heard Douglas
was in New York attending to his sick father; Douglas was
not asked to be present. Immediately defense attorney E. E.
Ellinwood filed for a demurrer on grounds that no federal laws
had been violated. The court, accepting the request, postponed
the case until the indictments could be reviewed. Six months
passed, and on December 2, 1918, Judge William Morrow of
San Francisco upheld the defense counsel's contention and
sustained the demurrer filed for the defendants saying that
the offense, if there was any, should be presented in the state
and not the federal court.[94] In his opinion, Judge Morrow
remarked:

> The situation is indeed a lamentable one and one to be
> greatly deplored; but it ought not to influence this court to
> enlarge the statute to include an offense not within its
> constitutional authority.[95]

The indictment had been quashed.

While this decision was pending, Governor Hunt prevailed upon federal prosecutor Fitts to initiate action against the
Jerome deporters. Hunt had begun to suspect that the federal
government was purposely dilatory in this effort. Fitts told the
attorney general's office that no state lines had been crossed in
the Jerome affair, and he advised against prosecution. (State
lines, of course, had been crossed.) "There is no good reason,"
stated Fitts, referring to the prosecution of the Bisbee deporters, "to ride the same horse a second time around the ring."[96]

The Nation, shocked by Judge Morrow's decision, commented that the deportation was "a gross and scandalous outrage...committed against the miners" for which some responsibility must be fixed. Contrasting the dismissal of the charges against the mining officials with the outrageous convictions and sentencing of the IWWs in Chicago, *The Nation* remarked that the disparity between the two actions was "utterly offensive to a natural sense of justice." Any condoning of the Bisbee affair by the courts, it believed, could only breed resentment, sedition and revolution. The article pointed out that while the Chicago Wobblies had been sentenced to an aggregate of 800 years and $2,500,000 in fines, the Bisbee deporters had gone free. The leading citizens of Bisbee, Arizona, claimed *The Nation*, comprised the "anarchist mob."[97]

That Judge Morrow would rule as a "strict constructionist" did not surprise federal attorney Fitts. He expected the judge to support a "states' rights" position and to sustain the demurrer. Fitts wrote Assistant Attorney General Claude R. Porter on December 4 and said that the decision "may be just as well" since now the case could go to the Supreme Court under the Criminal Appeals Act. Solicitor General Alexander A. King sent Porter a memorandum ten days later supporting Fitts' desire to appeal. In addition to agreeing with Fitts that the government had a good case, King said he felt an appeal was necessary since "public policy demands consistency."[98]

The Justice Department then appealed the lower court decision to the Supreme Court. Barristers argued the case on April 28, 1920. Seven months later, the court announced its decision. Citing the Articles of Confederation, Article IV of the Constitution, and precedent (*U.S. v. Harris*), the majority opinion of the high court found in favor of the defendants and sustained Judge Morrow's ruling. Only one man, Justice Clarke, dissented.[99] By endorsing a "states' rights" attitude, the federal judiciary had in effect deferred to the sovereignty of absentee capitalists. The decision confirmed the earlier (August 6, 1917) apprehension of Arizona Federation of Labor president John L. Donnelly in his telegram to President Wilson; Arizona labor now could surely "assume that Phelps Dodge interests are superior to interests of democracy."[100] The federal case was officially closed.

Criminal law failing them, victims of the Bisbee Deportation sought legal redress in other ways. Within two years after the deportation, deportees and their families brought civil suits totaling more than $6,150,000 in the state courts. In negotiations arranged primarily out of court, Phelps Dodge Corporation, Phelps Dodge Mercantile Company, Calumet & Arizona Mining Company, El Paso and Southwestern Railroad and a few minor parties tentatively agreed to pay more than a million dollars in damages. In some cases $1,250 was mentioned as suitable for men with children, $1,000 to married childless men and $500 to single men for "pain, inconvenience and loss of income suffered." Difficulty was encountered in locating some deportees. Given the situation, that was understandable. The Bisbee mining companies continued to withhold *all* payments until *all* deserving recipients could be found.[101] Phelps Dodge made no attempt to conceal the names of those deportees who filed damage suits. To the other copper mining companies in the state it sent press-printed black lists identifying more than 500 plaintiffs.[102]

The United States Supreme Court had pronounced the Bisbee Deportation a matter fit for only the state of Arizona to try, but state criminal charges were delayed for several years. The Cochise County attorney in 1917 through 1919 was John F. Ross (not to be confused with John Mason Ross, a partner in the law firm of Ellinwood and Ross, legal counsels for the Phelps Dodge Corporation, or with John Wilson Ross, who was appointed to the Arizona State Supreme Court by Governor Hunt in November 1918). Together with his successor, Robert N. French, Ross began to collect evidence and testimony in the summer of 1919. In order that the state might institute proceedings, Justice of the Peace William C. Jack held preliminary hearings from July to September 1919 in Douglas Precinct No. 4 justice court. For the defense, W. H. Burges, Cleon T. Knapp, Fred Sutter and other attorneys including Ellinwood and Ross took depositions in Chicago and Rockport, Illinois, Salt Lake City, Utah, and Butte, Montana, during October–November 1919.[103]

The Phelps Dodge people and the other alleged lawbreakers seemed overjoyed to be on trial. They knew acquittal of a criminal charge would make their payments of civil damages unlikely. They immediately dropped the out-of-court settlement negotiations. Those company employees who had signed criminal complaints or who appeared as witnesses to testify against the companies were fired. During the week of February

7, 1920, two hundred ten Bisbee citizens were arraigned at the Cochise County Courthouse in notoriously lawless Tombstone on charges of kidnapping.[104]

Tombstone, benign and moribund as it declined from a heyday, rejuvenated—and experienced its greatest excitement since the town's early mining boom. Reporters from all over the country flocked to see what they hoped would be a spectacle; every voter in Cochise County was summoned for possible jury duty. As a result, some people had to go to other towns to find lodging.[105]

A representative for the *en masse* trial had to be picked. Sheriff Harry Wheeler, back from the less dramatic setting of wartime France, was selected by the other defendants. But County Attorney French, sensing Wheeler's wide popularity, asked Presiding Judge Samuel J. Pattee of Pima County (liberal Judge A. C. Lockwood of the Superior Court of Cochise County had been disqualified under state law) to dismiss Wheeler's indictment. Judge Pattee obliged and Wheeler was replaced by Harry E. Wootton, Phelps Dodge employee, Loyalty League member and deputy.[106]

Counsel for the defense, Frank E. Curley, told the court that he expected to show: (1) a conspiracy by the IWW to overthrow the government of the United States, (2) the conspirators had "proceeded to apply the axe at the very roots of civilization" and subvert the religious and patriotic beliefs of unsuspecting people and (3) the demands of the IWW were a screen to hide their efforts "to bring about the defeat of the United States in its war against Germany and the ultimate overthrow of the United States government." Not forgetting its loyal supporters, Phelps Dodge put up the money for the legal defense.[107]

Witnesses vied for the honors of serving their country. Once upon the stand, Wheeler claimed the entire responsibility for Bisbee's deportation. His claim was topped by Miles Merrill, however, who said *he* was the *author* of the deportation plan, and that he perfected it after consulting with Walter Douglas. Most of the exhibits the defense submitted in this state trial consisted of IWW literature which the Bisbee deportees had never seen. In fact, most of the exhibits were made up of materials United States marshals had taken from IWW offices including the Chicago headquarters during the raids of September 1917. Photocopied records and correspondence together with printed IWW literature constituted almost all the evidence used to justify the deporters' action. (In Chicago, the *prosecution* employed this technique.) A contention in the opening statement by Defense Counsel Curley that the IWW brought weapons and dynamite into Bisbee for the purpose of destroying the mines was not mentioned again.[108]

Both during the preliminary hearings and the Tombstone trial, plaintiffs' attorneys French and Guy M. Walker constantly sounded objections to the defense argument. The testimony in behalf of the defendants, they protested, was "wholly illegal and unconstitutional" and "irrelevant and immaterial." The defense strategy "merely is an effort to introduce into the trial of these cases the defense of IWWism, propaganda and actions as well as the trial and convictions of W. D. Haywood." The prosecution insisted the arguments and exhibits introduced by the deporters' lawyers were "merely for the purpose of influencing public opinion and prejudicing possible jurors, and thus defeating the ends of justice."[109]

After three months the trial went to jury; Wootton was acquitted on the first ballot. All of the jurors agreed that the deportation had been a good thing. Speaking for the others, Jury Foreman J. O. Calhoun said: "The verdict of the jury is a vindication of the deportation." It would be "morally wrong for the county attorney's office to bring up another of the deportation cases for trial."[110] This was the last of any legal action against the deporters; the vigilantes and their chiefs had been conclusively exonerated. A handful of aggrieved deportation victims did eventually collect pittances; Katie Pintek got $60.[111]

A great ado echoed around the country at the time over what the defense claimed was its central justification for executing the Wobbly drive and deportation: the "law of necessity," a dubious legal argument based on a vague contention of "self-defense." The "law of necessity" appeared to more detached minds as nothing more than a rationalization for vigilantism. The "law of necessity," as it was explained by Attorney Curley, was *not* to be confused with the necessity of self-defense. Jury Foreman Calhoun summarized: "The essence of the law of necessity . . . as laid down . . . by Judge Pattee, is that it protects a man in his invasion of the rights of others when his fear for his own safety or welfare is great enough to force him to a drastic step, and this fear does not have to be a fear of really existent dangers but only of apparent danger when the appearance of that danger is so compelling as to be real to him who views it."[112] This convoluted logic, in effect, authorized paranoidal behavior—as long as the paranoia expressed itself in the interest of the mining companies of Arizona.

Shortly after the conclusion of the trial, a strange publication appeared around the state of Arizona. Entitled *The Law of Necessity as Applied in State of Arizona vs. H. E. Wootton, the Bisbee I.W.W. Deportation Case*, it was published by an unknown source called "Bureau of Information."[113] While Defense Counsel Frank E. Curley was given as author, no date or place of publication was mentioned. The pamphlet attracted the attention of George Soule, who discussed it in the August 31, 1921, issue of *The Nation*. Soule found the booklet suspect since it contained only the case given by the defense counsel. None of the argument and none of the evidence presented by the prosecuting attorney appeared in the pamphlet. Soule believed the copper interests printed and circulated it. The printer's identity—"Star Job Print—Tucson"—offers a strong clue to identification. The *Daily Star,* a Tucson newspaper, was owned, of course, at that time by Walter Douglas and his brother James.[114]

Unquestionably Phelps Dodge did publish *The Law of Necessity* as part of its statewide defensive propaganda program. No doubt, even though it had handily shed in the courts all charges of criminal and civil dereliction, Phelps Dodge felt some need to sharpen its state and national image of probity. The copper company was not without its detractors. Reporters from outside Arizona inquired around Bisbee and other mining towns during the trial looking for more than the one-sided courtroom testimony. One over-zealous newsman, in Bisbee to interview the families of deportees, reportedly "received a wholesome whipping" for his nosiness.[115] Outraged, he "camped on Tombstone and howled at the moon."[116]

At least one serious law book, *American State Trials*, incorporated the Tombstone case into its 1936 collection of precedents. Newman F. Baker of the Northwestern Law School failed to perceive the context of the trial and stated in the book's preface: "While there is no showing that the I.W.W. brought about the Arizona copper mine strikes [in 1917], it was generally so thought. If there was no actual danger to the community, there was undoubtedly a vast potential danger." Phelps Dodge's propaganda program had far-reaching, long-lasting success.[117]

PART IV

THE
QUIET KINGDOM

11

ARIZONA DONS THE COPPER COLLAR

The deportation "trials," if they had not erased the national high-handed image of Phelps Dodge, had enfranchised the copper company's political freedom in Arizona; most Arizona citizens responded positively to the "law of necessity" argument. Although a "radical" New York journalist such as Robert Bruere might claim that the Bisbee Deportation and the three-month reign of lawlessness which followed had been "trumpeted throughout Europe by the anti-capitalist revolutionists" of Russia and that this publicity had damaged America's reputation, national observers, including academicians, came around to an "understanding" point of view.[1] Perhaps Utah Senator William H. King summed up the public attitude in a statement to his fellow Senators about the Bisbee Deportation: "It was a drastic step. It was perhaps without legal sanction. But the frightful condition brought on by the reign of the organization which knows no law became intolerable to those who had homes and property and who were denied peace and opportunity to labor."[2]

Triumph of the Mining Companies

In the mining camps small pockets of resistance still needed mopping up. An independent Jerome newspaper, for example, found that a tightening up of the camp by the United Verde Copper Company resulted in a "if you're not with us you're against us" condition. The *Jerome Sun*, founded in the wild boom of late 1916, felt the tyranny of copper camp rule. Nettled by pressures subtle and overt, editor Lindley C. Branson wrote on December 17, 1917:

> Agree with Mr. Tally and do his dirty work for him and you are a patriot and a conservative citizen; disagree with him and you are a "Wobbly." ... every person who does not wear a copper collar is a "Wobbly."[3]

For refusing to don the copper collar, Mr. Branson found his advertisers and subscribers quickly abandoning him. At the same time, Eugene Barron, a stooge of the United Verde Copper Company, acquired with United Verde financial aid the loan on the *Sun's* press. When Branson's loss of revenue caused him to miss payment, the sheriff replevied the equipment. By April 1918 the *Sun* had set.[4]

Even T. A. Rickard, editor of the prestigious San Francisco-based *Mining and Scientific Press*, bent his knee to the Arizona copper kings. After receiving an indignant protest from Charles Clark concerning Rickard's mild and impartial account of the Jerome strike conditions in May 1917, Rickard contritely commented: "We accept Mr. Clark's correction, with pleasure."[5]

While opposition to the mining companies collapsed within the state of Arizona, some federal criticism of the policies and practices of Arizona mine operators did take place. After President Wilson's Mediation Commission had returned to Washington from the fields of labor strife in the Far West, its members prepared a comprehensive report for the President. The report, submitted on January 9, 1918, reviewed the labor-management difficulties in the mines, lumber camps, oil fields and packing industries. Discarding the sedition factor as inconsequential, the commission attributed labor unrest in the mines to autocratic rule and lack of labor representation. The cure they recommended lay in some form of substantial collective bargaining. The report was strongly sympathetic with labor and condemned profiteering, injustice, repression and suspicion.[6] Writing for *Survey*, John Fitch said the report was "a document of surpassing importance.... It ought, therefore, to be accepted in a serious spirit by employers and workers the country over."[7] Evidently his vantage point did not give Fitch a realistic view of America's labor situation. The subordination of labor organizations would in the next few years not decline but intensify.

Perhaps knowledgeable of President Wilson's close ties with Phelps Dodge, the commission took it upon itself to notify the copper company directly of its recommendations. The company's officials agreed to do what they could even though such a proposal was "contrary to their best judgment."[8] But the mine operators had their own concept of "organized labor" and "collective relationship." It did not include the recognition of any independent labor union. Indeed, the mining men had recently spent a great amount of effort in ridding Arizona of such organizations.

There had never been any doubt about the copper companies' desire to break the political hold unionism had on the state of Arizona. Also, there is no doubt about Walter Douglas' crusade against Arizona unionism itself. In 1907 he pledged to defeat labor; he reaffirmed that vow at Clifton-Morenci in 1915 and at Globe on the day preceding the Bisbee Deportation. For years it was "a common saying in Bisbee that there would be grass growing on the streets before they would unionize the town."[9] Now there was no doubt the corporations had succeeded. Not a single shift was lost in Arizona after November 1, 1917.[10] The Bisbee Deportation resulted in guaranteeing an open-shop mining camp and helped to destroy the political influence of labor at the state level. After the deportation the IUMMSW declined rapidly throughout the country. Within a few years it had almost completely collapsed.[11]

Only about one hundred true IWW members were in Bisbee on July 12, 1917. (Three hundred more were "two-card" men.) Of these, only about twenty-five were considered to understand anything about IWW philosophy; not one Bisbee Wobbly who later testified against the deporters could demonstrate any knowledge of the IWW tenets. None of the older IUMMSW members who converted to the IWW participated as a soapbox activist, while the most outspoken of these (such as James Chapman) were probably company-hired detectives.

What is more, except for the organizers, the Bisbee IWW membership developed only after Charles Moyer's revocation of the Bisbee IUMMSW charter on July 3—only a week and two days before the deportation.

For the most part, Bisbee IWWism represented the most dedicated—and frustrated—conventional unionists. Nothing, however, could have worked more to company advantage. By using the IWW radical charge as a blanket label for all the strikers, the copper companies had rid Bisbee and Arizona of the nucleus of political-labor leadership. AFofL leaders Frank Harmon, Charles Cavis, J. F. Jones, Fred Brown and Frank Vaughan were among those deported. Thirty of thirty-nine members of the local Painters' Union were shipped out—not one was an IWW. Two-card men such as A. S. Embree and Charles Tannehill, also deported, certainly were pragmatic unionists, not doctrinaire Wobblies. Phelps Dodge's records show that of a total of 2,201 hourly wage earners at the Copper Queen on June 26, the day the strike began, only 168 were deported on July 12. This number included most of Bisbee's IUMMSW membership and all of the union's leaders. The bulk of the men deported on July 12 had been unemployed before the strike began.[12] The copper companies could easily comply with the recommendation of President Wilson's Commission to bargain collectively—now that no labor organization was left with which to bargain.

Not everyone remained blind to the copper corporations' tactic. Bitterly, the secretary-treasurer of the Arizona State Federation of Labor stated that the Bisbee Deportation was an example of the "established rule with corporations to use members of the I.W.W. for the purpose of confusing the minds of the public and thus discrediting the bona fide labor organizations in the public mind."[13] IUMMSW president Charles A. Moyer repeated the charge: "Through their lying statements and poisonous work [the IWW] have created such dissension among a number of our locals as entirely to destroy them."[14] In an immediate response to the sensational and fictitious allegations which prompted the deportation *The New Republic* criticized the IWW for allowing itself to become a pawn of big business.[15] One analyst, transcending the haze of wartime hysteria for a clearer view, called attention to the fact that in America autocratic industries dominated the political situation, and he said that current labor unrest was a result of industry manipulating "constructive" worker energy and diverting it into "destructive" channels.[16] In a nation convulsed by irrationality, this point of view was rare.

But developments indicated the strategy worked. On August 3, 1917, the Phoenix Chamber of Commerce passed a resolution showing that merchant class sympathies were moving rapidly away from labor. The resolution urged "the need of a census of labor," and it recommended "that an industrial drafting service be devised to be in operation during the war." Further, the Phoenix organization recommended that "legislation be enacted which will prohibit in every form advocation of crime, sabotage, violence, and any unlawful methods of securing industrial or political reforms." Phoenix's support of Miles Merrill's "Loyalty League of America" underscored the Chamber of Commerce resolve. Even such people as former liberal territorial governor Joseph H. Kibbey signed the Loyalty League's constitution, a document which called in its preamble for the "extermination" of the IWW.[17]

A few weeks later Walter Douglas continued his public assault on the IUMMSW. In a paper presented to his fellow mining engineers, Douglas showed that a negative correlation existed between increased wages and increased efficiency in the Clifton-Morenci district. Included in his argument was the contention that IWW doctrine had come to permeate the Arizona Federation of Labor. The miner, implied Douglas, had been infected by dreams of a syndicalist society, and thus his productivity, company loyalty and sense of pride had deteriorated. Douglas was attempting to convince people at every level that conventional unionism differed in no way from the IWW.[18] In Montana, Senator William A. Clark amplified the voice of the mine owners and reiterated their position when he said: "I would rather close them [the mines] down, flood them and never take another pound of ore out" than recognize the union.[19]

The pre-World War I momentum carried national union membership to a peak in 1920. That year's total membership of 5,047,800 fell to 3,622,000 by 1923. The Red Scare as well as post-war economics had undermined pro-union sentiment. In Arizona, as throughout the country, the depression of 1921 was an abrupt setback for labor.[20]

Students of labor economics belatedly observed organized labor's collapse. A few token gains by labor were enough to offset labor's more substantial setbacks in the eyes of most analysts. A United States Supreme Court decision in early 1919 upheld a law making employers in so-called "hazardous occupations" liable in damages for all accidents which could not be attributed to the worker's negligence. Some states' work weeks were shortened from forty-eight to forty-four hours, while women and child labor laws as well as workman's compensation legislation passed in a few states. AFofL membership, a deceptive criterion of "success," continued to rise.[21]

Even at the end of the war, labor economist Gordon S. Watkins was optimistic about labor's future. He found encouragement in the fact that the war had revealed labor-management weaknesses and that the government had adopted a new, compassionate labor policy. Speaking of the wartime situation, Watkins said that it was the first time capital, management, labor and government had accepted fundamental standards of work. These "harmonious relations" meant that "labor and capital have finally appeared to each other in a truer light than before."[22] Meanwhile Arizona labor strength continued to deteriorate.

The End of Middle-Class Liberalism

As part of its effort to finish off the Arizona labor movement after the blow of July 1917, the copper industry began to flood the Arizona labor supply by actively recruiting miners from other states. In November 1917 S. E. Rau-Roesler, owner of a small gold mine in Bagby, California, protested active recruitment at his mine by a representative of the Inspiration mine in Miami, Arizona. The recruiter, C. F. Arnold, promised higher pay, safer mines and more pleasant living conditions to the Bagby miners.[23]

Many more complaints followed. Federal Conciliator Joseph S. Myers wrote Secretary of Labor Wilson about the Globe-Miami problem. On January 24, writing from Globe, Myers said men were being recruited from other states by General Manager C. E. Mills of Inspiration Consolidated Copper Company while numerous unemployed workers roamed the streets of Globe. Myers reported that he was "reliably informed" that "higher officials and directors of the company" were "very dissatisfied" with Mills. Only because Mills did not report "the real facts," said Myers, was the mine manager able to retain his position.[24]

So insistent became the cry of "labor importation," that a special agent, Frank Brown, of the United States Office of Employment set up an office in Phoenix. His investigation showed that in their efforts to break the strong grip labor had on the particular mining district of Globe-Miami, operators from that district had sought workers from outside sources. Declining to put proven dissidents back on their payrolls, the mine managers ran advertisements in several large out-of-state mining and industrial centers. The announcements implied — or even stated — that jobs were to be had in abundance in Arizona. This was not at all true. Agents were sent out; some, like recruiter Arnold, went to small mines.[25] Brown wrote to Secretary of Labor Wilson:

> Many men have been shipped and are still being shipped into this State to Miami by the Inspiration Consolidated Copper Co., from Texas, California, Nevada, Colorado and Missouri in spite of the fact that hundreds of men are now idle in this district.

2,500 men were unemployed in Arizona mining camps, reported Brown, seven hundred of them in the Globe-Miami district.[26]

The Inspiration Copper Company immediately denied the charge. But several convincing sources supported the alleged recruitment. Governor Simon Bamberger of Utah sent a letter to the governor of Arizona dated February 26, 1918. Bamberger said C. E. Arnold had shown up in Utah and tried to induce miners there to go to the Globe-Miami District. After a quick investigation to confirm the report and also to confirm that Arizona was filled with idle men, Utah Industrial Commissioner William Kerr appealed to the United States Secretary of Labor William B. Wilson. Even more importantly, many charges included the contention that some of the imported workers were well-known IWW activists.[27]

IWW membership in Arizona increased sharply after the Bisbee Deportation, and detective company "operatives" continued to suggest that the IWW was still dangerous. No significant labor unrest developed despite the agents' report that "7000 rounds of ammunition" had been brought by the radicals into the state. The Department of Justice files contain many documents of a cautionary nature which suggest that IWW activity provoked much trouble in Arizona after the summer of 1917. All of this was, however, *alleged* activity or *suspected* activity. Mine managers were far too perspicacious—and secure—to be taken in by detective agency alarmism.[28]

Both sides reacted strongly to the charges of labor importation. When the controversy reached a distracting cacophony, the Arizona Council of Defense decided to investigate. The Labor Committee of the Arizona Council of Defense, dormant since the May 10, 1917, debacle at the Arizona capitol, reorganized in January 1918 with Thomas Croaff as chairman; he attempted to form a meeting of inquiry.[29] Coincidental with the Defense Council's entrance into the dispute was the bimonthly meeting of the mine operators' organization, the Arizona Chapter of the American Mining Congress. In the second week of April 1918 the chapter met for two days in Tucson. On Monday, April 8, during the opening session, Secretary of the Arizona Chapter Joseph E. Curry received a telephone call from Phoenix. The call was from Croaff who said he did not want to discuss his topic over the telephone. But he requested Curry to put an important matter before the chapter. Curry told Croaff that if he wanted to reach the members before the meeting adjourned, he had best telegraph his message immediately. Croaff's telegram, received in Tucson Tuesday morning, asked the chapter to send a committee of representatives to meet with labor representatives and the Labor Committee of the Council of Defense. The message did not mention a specific subject, only a general proposal that the two sides and the labor committee "work out a program" to insure fair profits, just wages and good working conditions.[30]

That day Curry responded to Croaff saying the chapter was "most anxious to co-operate" and that the Executive Board of the Arizona Chapter would "be glad to meet with the Executive Committee of the Arizona Council of Defense." The message from Curry was clear; the operators had no intention of recognizing either the labor representative or the labor committee. During the sessions of this second day, Arizona Chapter directors made emphatic denials that IWW were being actively sought and knowingly employed in Arizona mines. Absurdly wrapping themselves with the flag, the operators also agreed to cooperate in the "detection of all disloyal citizens," to oppose putting the United States Bureau of Mines under the War Department and to support the establishment of a department of mines with full cabinet status as "a member of the President's official family."[31] The latter resolution obviously reflected the mining men's strategy to get more direct political control of their industry. They thereupon adopted a resolution demanding that the Council of Defense investigate the charges.[32]

The following week, on Wednesday, April 17, sixteen Arizona mining officials went to the governor's chamber at the state capitol in Phoenix. The meeting, unlike the affair of the previous May, did not involve either a "labor committee" or a broad representation of Arizona labor organizations. Instead, the Council of Defense Executive Committee met the mining potentates just as the copper men had prescribed.* The mining operators had succeeded in dictating the terms of the conference; two "spokesmen" for the miners of Arizona were allowed in the room. Prior to the meeting the Council of Defense, in a gesture toward balance, had passed a resolution recognizing the allegations by several sources that "members of the I.W.W. organization are being brought into Arizona and employed in the mines, for the purpose of disturbing labor conditions in the state."[33]

After the Bisbee Deportation, this meeting was the deadliest stroke to Arizona labor. It was, in fact, the *coup de grace*. In terms of Arizona political reality, the Council of Defense represented the increasing but relatively powerless non-mining middle-class population of the state. Yet this group had become the swing or balance factor in the class and economic war that had by now reached its climax. Chairman Dwight Heard of the Council's Executive Committee was the spokesman for the previously small but rapidly growing Maricopa County agrarian-commerical bloc. Heard had played a role in the statehood movement and, along with a strange bedfellow, Calumet & Arizona General Manager John C. Greenway, had supported the Progressive movement of Theodore Roosevelt. Heard, everyone knew, represented the Arizona bourgeois. To some degree he still reflected the pre-war suspicion and resentment

---

*Years later Dean Scarlett said that the Council of Defense Labor Committee "had accomplished nothing." (Bishop Scarlett to Matt Hanhila, Hinton tapes.)

the Arizona middle class felt for the mining companies.*
This fact had strengthened the hand of labor from 1910 to 1916.
A switch of middle-class support to the copper interests would
leave labor helpless.[34]

The mining company officials came into the governor's
chamber "on their ire." Affecting to construe the resolution of
the Council of Defense as an accusation of the copper mine
operators, the mine men demanded the Council rescind the
resolution. Put on the defensive, the members of the Council's
Executive Committee insisted their intent had been mis-
understood. During the "hearing" IUMMSW organizer Henry
S. McCluskey (one of the two labor "spokesmen" permitted in
the room by the mine operators) said he felt that the mine
operators of Arizona had been "in cahoots" with the IWW,
if not purposely then at least unwittingly. Grant Dowell of
Bisbee's Copper Queen did hedge when McCluskey asked
him to deny that some men employed by Phelps Dodge were
both detectives and IWW members. C. E. Mills of the Miami
Copper Company and Louis Cates of Ray Consolidated, angered by the charge, challenged McCluskey to provide some
proof for his statement that the copper companies had knowingly hired an IWW member. Mills declared that any man so
stating, "is a liar."[35]

McCluskey backed down. He had, of course, confused the
issue by introducing the IWW factor, and the copper men had
made a big play on it. He would have been able to prove,
easily, the importation charge, but over-zealous in his attempt
to claim the mining men had tried to wreck the IUMMSW by
importing Wobblies to malign the whole Arizona labor movement, McCluskey lost his case. Now unsure, the Council of
Defense backed away from its concern for Arizona labor.[36]

The controversy over the importation of labor had been
killed. Along with it had died middle-class support for labor in
Arizona. The triumph of the mining companies in their sys-
tematic destruction of bona fide unions was at hand. Whatever
other little mop-up jobs the mine operators did got no criticism
from the Arizona public.[37]

Two separate but extremely similar incidents illustrated
both the public indifference to and the continued coordination
of Arizona mine management's constraint of union activity. On

*Heard's personal relationship with the Douglases, which had cooled after
the Bisbee Deportation, was not rekindled. (Bishop Scarlett, March 13, 1972.)

Tuesday evening, March 26, 1918, three masked, armed men kidnapped William Waldroop, a hoisting engineer for the Verde Combination Copper Company and chairman of the Arizona Executive Committee for the IUMMSW, from in front of the drugstore on Jerome's Main Street. They took Waldroop out in the country, where he was stripped, smeared with crude oil, feathered and left. About 3:00 A.M. he appeared at the UVX Texas shaft and begged for hot water. Several men helped clean him up. After borrowing some clothes, he returned to his room in Jerome. That same night in Bisbee a man accused of being an IWW organizer, Walter N. Johnson, suffered identical treatment.[38]

George W. P. Hunt (who had been reinstated as governor in December 1917) sent a letter to Sheriff Joe Young of Yavapai County on March 27 requesting an investigation of the kidnapping and abuse of Waldroop. Young responded perfunctorily.[39] Hunt also wrote to Cochise County Attorney John F. Ross protesting Walter Johnson's treatment.[40] On the twenty-seventh, Hunt informed his state attorney general, "I cannot help but feel that there is a sinister connection between the affair at Bisbee and the one at Jerome. They were identical in their nature and time, but for the good name of Arizona and its industrial peace I hope this was only a coincidence."[41] Hunt's "hope" could have been nothing but polite rhetorical protocol. By this time he understood full well the nature of Arizona's industrial war.

A complaint from Governor Hunt about the Waldroop incident to the War Department elicited federal orders on April 1 outlawing Loyalty Leagues.[42] But mine managers felt little concern. Assistant General Manager of the United Verde Copper Company Robert E. Tally, in a letter to General Manager Charles W. Clark, remarked serenely that labor conditions in Jerome and Clarkdale were "apparently quiet." "The Waldroop affair," wrote Tally, "has caused very little excitement in the district." Referring to his miners, Tally told Clark, "It is impossible to figure out what these dogs will do, but I am not in any way alarmed over the matter."[43] Mine managers throughout the state shared Tally's confidence.

The Progressives' Last Spasm

One last death rattle remained in the Arizona liberal movement. The decision in the contested 1916 gubernatorial election which the Maricopa County Superior Court awarded

to Tom Campbell in May 1917 was overruled by the Arizona
Supreme Court on December 22. George W. P. Hunt's attorneys, using the same evidence produced in the lower court,
convinced the Supreme Court that only the invalid individual
ballots of a voting precinct should be considered void. Former Territorial Supreme Court Judge and Governor Richard
Sloan, a long-time friend of the copper companies, served as
Campbell's chief counsel. His influence and argument, however, did not sway the court. Reversing the ruling of the lower
court which had voided many other Hunt votes in precincts in
which irregularities had been found (albeit caused by pro-
Campbell intrigue), the high court members unanimously endorsed Chief Justice Franklin's opinion which found Hunt to be
the winner by a margin of forty-three votes. On Christmas
Day, 1917, Campbell turned the office back to Hunt. "Copper
Tom" had been in long enough to enable the great deportation.
On January 8 Campbell instituted an appeal for a rehearing, but
nothing came of it. Within a year he was elected to return to the
governor's seat. [44]

In a message to a special session of the Third State Legislature on May 21, 1918, Governor Hunt summoned up all his
resentment and presented a bitter denunciation of Arizona's
mine managers, particularly those responsible for the Bisbee
Deportation. Without mentioning the names of Walter Douglas
or the other deportation instigators, Hunt described their
kind as

> ... a certain thing in human shape ... but yet is a craven
> cur; whose mind is a sink of infamy; whose character is as
> devoid of principle as that of a mowing ape in an African
> jungle...Such a thing is the "profiteering patrioteer."
> the detestable hypocrite, who with sanctimonious de-
> meanor goes through the mummery of patriotic service,
> though arriving all the while to profit by his country's dire
> stress....There is no word in all the range of human
> tongues, from Sanskrit to Anglo-Saxon, with which to de-
> scribe this creature, so I abandon the effort in despair. [45]

Hunt went on, in the same style, to deplore the brutality of the
deportation, the shameful nature of it, the copper companies'
misrepresentation of the deportees, the attempt to label all
unions "IWW," the kidnappings of March 27 and the general
autocracy of the mining men. Quoting journalist Robert Bruere,
Hunt said,

"I am certain that it [the IWW] was not a determining factor in the strikes that have tied up the copper mines. ... These strikes grew out of a long-standing struggle between the forces of legitimate organized labor and the forces of organized business, dominated by the copper companies. So far as there was a concerted attack by the I.W.W., it was principally directed against the unions affiliated with the American Federation of Labor. Crimes have been committed in Arizona, but they are not chargeable to the I.W.W. So far as lawlessness is concerned, the chief role of the I.W.W. has been to serve as camouflage."[46]

Four days after Hunt's tongue-lashing, Norman Carmichael, general manager of the Arizona Copper Company at Clifton, wrote the governor a lengthy, indignant retort. Carmichael spoke in strong terms and denounced Hunt's administration as well as his address. Referring to both the Clifton-Morenci strike and the Bisbee Deportation, he blamed Hunt for encouraging unlawful behavior and failing to defend "the right against the wrong, the cause of the weak against the oppressor." "The public of Arizona," Carmichael warned, "have not such short memories that these things have already been forgotten."[47]

Hunt answered the mine operator. He regretted Carmichael's continued bitterness and referred to the Clifton-Morenci mine managers' refusal to negotiate the labor difficulties of 1915–16. That Carmichael would serve as a dutiful "spokesman for the copper companies of this state," Hunt found less than honorable or patriotic. The reply, though flattering, patronizing, sarcastic and self-righteous, at times showed a genuine conciliatory tone and ended with a plea for harmony. The correspondence continued. On July 7, Carmichael wrote back another long, defensive letter concerned with the same subjects and displaying the same point of view as his first. Hunt this time sent a more stern and reproving answer.[48] But Carmichael's contention that the "Arizona public" was "grossly outraged" by Hunt's May 21 speech proved valid. So indignant were Arizona citizens over the governor's intemperate remarks that more people than ever swung around to support the copper companies. Enraged by the governor's charges that the deportation had been conducted with the purpose in mind of destroying the Arizona labor movement, the *Bisbee Daily Review* bristled: "Bisbee struck in the open against the I.W.W. and nothing else."[49] The governor's earlier friends were silent; his honeymoon with "the people" was over. A "work or fight bill" was passed by the now-conservative legislature. This "industrial draft" resolution which had grown out of a Phoenix Chamber of Commerce patriotism meeting in August 1917 reached Hunt's desk on June 18, 1918. He promptly vetoed it.[50] But he could do little else.

Back on March 2, 1917, an editorial had appeared in the Bisbee *Square Dealer*, the short-lived pro-labor newspaper that sprang up in the war-boom period prior to the deportation. The editorial said:

> It is to be doubted that the people of Arizona will ever vote to return to the "good old days" when the Southern Pacific attorneys and Ned Creighton could say how the laws were to be enforced and who was to be executed by the hangman.[51]

The *Square Dealer* underestimated the nostalgic temperament of Arizona's voters. Just as Miami's *Arizona Silver Belt* and other newspapers moved away from support of liberal reform during the spring and summer of 1916, so did many voters previously in support of Hunt embrace a renascent conservative attitude. Even those few publications around the state which did not "wear the copper collar" began to view Hunt and the liberal Democrats with reserve.

Up in Jerome, mine managers enjoyed a renewed self-assurance about their ability to determine the outcome of the approaching primary and general elections. In a letter to Charles W. Clark written on June 4, United Verde operator Robert E. Tally suggested getting "an outside man" to be Marshal of Jerome in order to avoid "causing any temporary friction or give the other side a chance to say that this was a Copper Company Council, with a Copper company's gun man in charge of the police force." But Tally's planned subterfuge did not involve getting anyone from very far "outside." "Taking everything into consideration," Tally went on,

> ... and realizing the importance of having no friction on account of the fall election, I finally decided upon, and recommended, J. G. Crowley for marshall....He is an old personal friend of mine, and one in whom I have every confidence. At present he is employed as a miner at the

U.V. Extension, which will have a tendency to disconnect him from the [United Verde] Copper Company. He was one of the ring leaders, at my request, in the Wobbly deportation, and also helped fight our battles as a union man.[52]

Arizona mine managers felt the same kind of certainty about the gubernatorial race. Since Hunt had decided not to run for governor in 1918, the Democrats nominated Fred T. Colter from Apache County. Colter's credentials as a conservative were faultless. He had served as a delegate to the Constitutional Convention in 1910 where, along with Phelps Dodge attorney Everett Ellinwood, he fought to exclude the recall of judges provision. As everyone expected, Tom Campbell ran on the Republican ticket. The mining companies appreciated Colter's conservatism, but they stayed loyal to their "Copper Tom," a tried and true performer.* Shortly after Campbell's election in the primary, Tally wrote Charles Clark saying, "It is now important that a whirl-wind campaign for Campbell be conducted."[53] A week later he predicted the governor's race would be close. Colter, a non-mining county man, may have been conservative enough, but his loyalty to the copper interests was questionable.[54] At the Constitutional Convention, Colter, an agriculturally oriented Mormon, had proposed including a provision borrowed from the Utah constitution that would define priorities concerning the use of Arizona's limited water supply. It gave preference to stock and agricultural water usage over mining.

For a while it appeared that Colter might be disqualified. As a member of the previous session of the state legislature, he had voted with the majority to increase the governor's yearly salary from $4,000 to $6,000. While the law could have been construed to deny Colter's eligibility for the office, no serious attempt was made to disqualify him.[55]

The race was close; Campbell won by less than four hundred votes.[56] Arizona's political shift from Progressivism was complete.

---

*In this primary a United Verde Mining Company candidate from Jerome for county supervisor, Tom Miller, was defeated. "The Prescott crowd double crossed us," Tally grumbled. Arizona's middle class still had a mind of its own.

Truax v. Corrigan

Only one major development remained in the process of securing Arizona for the copper corporations. This development involved the controversial "anti-injunction" law and it became, in some circles, a *cause célèbre* greater than was the Bisbee Deportation.

For many years American business and industrial management enjoyed judicial assistance in its campaign to check organized labor's efforts to improve the workingman's condition. The Sherman Anti-Trust Act, passed by Congress in 1890 ostensibly to control business trusts, was cited frequently as the authorization for issuing injunctions to break strikes or to forbid picketing by striking workers. The Clayton Act of 1914 was passed as a corrective to the abuses of the Sherman Act, and it specifically forbade the use of the injunction in labor disputes "unless absolutely necessary." Like much other pro-labor legislation of the period, the Clayton Act fell short of its promise when administered or interpreted in the courts.[57]

In 1913 the First Arizona State Legislature passed an anti-injunction bill which gave Arizona labor the right to peaceful picketing and assembly. The law, Paragraph 1464 of the 1913 Arizona State Code, prohibited court issuance of injunctions in labor disputes "unless necessary to prevent irreparable damage to property or to property right of the party making the application [for an injunction], for which injury there is no adequate remedy by law...." This law, along with the eighty percent hiring act, had been proposed at the liberal-dominated Constitutional Convention; both had failed to pass. Their passage in the first legislature came only a few months after the impudent restoration by popular referendum of the recall-of-judges provision. These two "radical" laws undoubtedly caught the attention of former President William H. Taft since Taft had denied statehood to Arizona until the recall of judges had been removed. But Taft was to have the last word.

The quiescence of the Arizona labor-management conflict between 1913 and 1915 provided no opportunity to invoke the anti-injunction provision. During the Clifton-Morenci strike from September 1915 to January 1916, Governor G. W. P. Hunt sent troops to the strike zone with instructions to keep strike-breakers out, while the companies paid deputized strikers to guard their property. The mine managers attempted to create the illusion that their lives and property were imperiled, but no injunctions were sought. Thus thwarted, the copper companies felt a need for a test case.

Little time passed before a test of the law took place. Early in April 1916, father and son William and William A. Truax, the two colorful Bisbee restaurateurs, announced their intention to cut the wages and increase the working hours for their "English Kitchen" employees. On April 10 the ten cooks and waiters, all members of the AFofL-affiliated Cooks' and Waiters' Union of Bisbee, walked out. They immediately began to picket the cafe.

Considering the prosperity of the nation and particularly of Bisbee, it is difficult not to conclude that the Truaxes wished to provoke a strike. The two men were ardent Phelps Dodge sympathizers and had figured in the test case in which the eighty percent hiring law, challenged by corporation lawyers, was found unconstitutional in 1915.

Far from demonstrating any disorder, the striking restaurant workers employed publicity methods more familiar to festive holidays than to the serious matter of employee-employer warfare. Donkeys, draped with banners expressing sarcastic sentiments about the Truaxes, paraded around the streets for several days. Handbills and circulars cast doubt on the quality of the English Kitchen's food and the fairness of its prices. No violence occurred, but the picketing hurt the Truaxes; their daily receipts dropped by more than 50 percent.[58]

Since the Arizona anti-injunction law did permit court restraints to be issued when "necessary to prevent irreparable damage to property or to property right," the restaurant owners brought suit on April 24 against the Cooks' and Waiters' Union. Claiming that the strike was a conspiracy to hurt their business and that the picketing had "damaged" their "property right," the Truaxes sought an injunction. Cochise County Superior Court Judge Alfred C. Lockwood—elected by the Warren District's liberals—sided with the defendants and interpreted strictly the anti-injunction law. He dismissed the case on July 22, 1916.[59]

The strike continued. On October 24 the Truaxes signed another complaint. For the defendants, William Cleary filed a demurrer on January 17, 1917, which was upheld by Judge Lockwood on April 28. With a bond of $1,000 put up for them by Phelps Dodge Mercantile Company administrator, A. J.

Cunningham and Bisbee meat merchant Phil Tovrea, the Truaxes appealed to the Arizona Supreme Court on June 8, 1917. (No appellate court had yet been created in Arizona.)[60]

The Truaxes' argument did not convince the state's high court. On December 14, 1918, Chief Justice D. L. Cunningham gave the court's opinion which denied the contention that the anti-injunction statute was unconstitutional. The ruling held further that peaceful picketing did not interfere with business, did not invade the plantiff's legal rights and the effect of the statute did not deprive them of their property without due process of law nor did it deny them the equal protection of the law. Peaceful picketing, held the justice, was a means of peaceful communication and was, therefore, a fundamental civil right. The court concluded that the Arizona law was not in conflict with the Fourteenth Amendment as the plaintiffs' attorneys had contended. The Truaxes' application for an injunction was again denied.[61]

Truax and son appealed to the United States Supreme Court which now was headed by Chief Justice William Howard Taft. On April 29 and 30, 1920, the case was argued. It was reargued on October 5 and 6, 1921. Insisting that the Arizona law was "class legislation," the Truaxes' counsel claimed the law made "arbitrary and capricious" distinctions among persons and property. The union's conduct, the counsel contended, was coercive and, therefore, unlawful. Picketing and publicity were injurious and effected an "unlawful secondary boycott."[62]

On December 19, 1921, by a five to four split court decision, the Supreme Court ruled in favor of the Truaxes. In a minority opinion, Justice Oliver Wendell Holmes observed that the right to do business was not a property right and that business conduct, like any other conduct, was subject to restraint. He opposed the use of the Fourteenth Amendment to "prevent the making of social experiments that an important part of the community desires." Dissenting also, Justice Louis D. Brandeis stressed the need for flexibility in industrial relations, while Justice Mahlon Pitney and John H. Clarke, in their dissent, emphasized the "states' rights" nature of prescribing rules for doing business. All the dissenting Supreme Court members criticized the majority opinion.[63]

But the logic of the minority failed to persuade the others. The recall-of-judges indignity suffered earlier by Chief Justice Taft at the hands of the Arizona liberals was, in effect, to be avenged. Taft, delivering the majority opinion, agreed with the plaintiff that the strikers had used illegal methods, that business *was* a property right, that picketing plainly constituted a conspiracy and that the Arizona law denied equal protection under the Fourteenth Amendment and other guarantees of the United States Constitution. The Chief Justice concluded by saying the injunction should have been granted as requested; the state law prohibiting court interference with peaceful picketing was declared unconstitutional.[64]

That same year, 1921, the court narrowly construed the Clayton Act in such a way as to deny labor the protection intended by the law's makers. Thus labor in 1921 met the same defeat in the courts that it had experienced in the past.[65]

For the Arizona corporations and the opponents of the closed shop, the decision amounted to a great victory. For the American workingman, it was evidence that ultimately the forces in support of the *status quo* would triumph. For Arizona labor, it signified the denouement following the Bisbee Deportation. If the Council of Defense meeting in April 1918 had been the *coup de grace* of the Arizona liberal movement, William Howard Taft's ruling in *Truax v. Corrigan* became its epitaph.[66]

Kindly Observe
Following Regulations:

DO NOT SHIMMY,
DO NOT DANCE
CHEEK TO CHEEK.

THE DANCE COMMITTEE

(Sign at Bisbee Dance Hall)

12

AS TIME PASSED

After the deportation Bisbee was never the same again. One old-time Bisbeeite, George J. Keahey, looked back and remembered that many of the deportees were friends of his and "sound citizens." Many people, though cautious about saying so, knew "Phelps Dodge had been behind it because it wanted to gain complete power" over the town, the workers and the politics of the state. The deportation, Keahey and many others felt, was a big turning point in the social life of the community.

Bisbee and Arizona Afterwards

Before July 1917, Bisbee pulsated with four dance halls, six or seven theaters and a well-patronized red-light district. Opera stars, minstrel shows and such popular entertainers of the day as Fatty Arbuckle came to town. On Saturday nights, one could barely move through the downtown streets. Sports-minded Bisbeeites supported four baseball clubs, while soccer matches and prize fights were regular events. Before the deportation the town had been buoyant, casual, friendly and somewhat democratic. (The elections of liberals T. Foster and R. McKay attested to the latter.) After the deportation Bisbee was characterized by bitterness, suspicion, low morale and paternalistic, authoritarian and arbitrary control by Phelps Dodge. "Bisbee," lamented Keahey, "was ruined."[1]

A scholarly study done in 1966 on the "historical geography" of Bisbee supports the observations of Keahey. William W. Newkirk, in what appears to be a thoughtful, thorough piece of scholarship, discovered that the period of greatest expansion in Bisbee had ended by 1917. After that date, Newkirk's study reveals, Bisbee saw a decline in population and civic vitality. A gradual stagnation of the Bisbee townsite set in.[2]

Almost as if it had detected this trend immediately after the deportation, Phelps Dodge, through its influence, had the Arizona State Bureau of Mines make a "sociological survey" of the Warren District. Dated December 31, 1917, the survey included a detailed study of recreational facilities, wages, "scientific management," store "cooperatives," and health and safety precautions. Referring to the bonus plan adopted by Phelps Dodge, the report stated that Bisbee was taking "steps in the right direction" to reduce labor turnover. The report admitted the loss of "personal bonds between employee and employer" but said the mine managers hoped to improve this situation by installing an employment office. It is difficult to believe that Phelps Dodge's report represented anything other than token window-dressing.[3]

An advertisement paid for by Phelps Dodge appeared in the *Arizona Labor Journal* in June of 1920. It praised the social improvements and advantages of Bisbee by describing the community's transportation facilities, up-to-date city conveniences, good and safe working conditions, high wages, low cost of living, utilities, pension system, hospital and health service, excellent schools, playgrounds, library and YMCA. But it had the same image-building propaganda tone of the "sociological survey," the *Daily Review* editorials and *The Law of Necessity*.[4]

Not all the citizens of Bisbee agreed that the deportation had ruined the community. One person claiming to be a "working man" reportedly said:

> It [the deportation] is the most beautiful thing I have ever seen. It has united the entire camp. We are like one big family. It has removed the social and religious [?] bars. The rich and the poor, the society people, and the laboring people are absolutely united. We mingle together as never before. We feel that our interests are one.[5]

Reverend A. D. Raley ("field representative of the Arizona and New Mexico Sunday School Association") visited Bisbee during the kangaroo court period of vigilantism in August 1917. Using his power of ecclesiastical insight and compassion, Raley concluded that the deportations were a good thing. Referring to the vigilantes, he wrote the *Arizona Mining Journal*: "I am quite sure that there are no better people in the State of Arizona." In so saying, Rev. Raley was simply perpetuating the traditional alliance of press and pulpit regarding impudent workingmen.[6]

Later, in January of 1919, federal health and safety investigator Alice Hamilton went to Arizona. She observed that the "shadow of the deportation still lay heavy" on the state. She found a state of armed truce existing in most camps with everyone lined up on one side or the other "eyeing his adversaries with suspicion and hatred, peaceful for the moment, but ready to fight again at the drop of a hat. There were no neutrals anywhere."[7]

Once the Bisbee labor unions had been smashed, the Phelps Dodge Corporation made good on its promise to the Mediation Commission to "carry out your wishes in the spirit as well as the letter" of the Commission's demand that the company bargain collectively with the workers. Since no union existed with which to bargain, the Phelps Dodge Corporation began a program of building company loyalty. The "company" itself (not to be confused with a "company union" which was set up in 1921) became the "miners' organization."

On March 26, 1918, Walter Douglas described a new Phelps Dodge "company bonus plan" to the New York section of the American Institute of Mining Engineers. The Copper Queen program, Douglas reported, was designed to attract and retain workers, and it included a reduction of prices at Phelps Dodge's company store.[8] In July of 1918 Copper Queen Manager Grant Dowell presented this "bonus plan" in which men would be rewarded for loyalty to the company. Employee "loyalty," of course, would be reflected in service longevity, that is to say, by how well a man succeeded in avoiding discharge.[9]

The plan as originally announced included a $100 bonus at the end of the first full calendar year of service. An additional $10 would be added to the $100 each year for consecutive years of service up to $250 a year.[10] In fact, in January 1918 the Copper Queen had voluntarily paid $181,120 in bonuses to

2,286 employees, presumably for their loyalty during the crisis of the summer of 1917. This bonus for longevity, which by now had already been in effect for more than six months, was increased in Dowell's announcement.[11] A few days later the United Verde Extension Company in Jerome, Rawhide Jimmy Douglas' company, announced the adoption of the same bonus plan.[12]

This independent move on the part of the Douglases reflected these copper barons' diminishing desire to maintain harmony among the various mining corporations within the state. Now that labor, the corporations' common foe, had been neutralized, Phelps Dodge could resume its old arbitrary and competitive ways. Upon hearing of the Copper Queen bonus plan, United Verde Assistant General Manager Robert Tally wrote to General Manager Charles W. Clark. Tally told Clark the pay increase at Bisbee had been announced without the knowledge or approval of the other mine manager. Obviously concerned about expenses, Tally said: "We must discontinue the building of elaborate houses for our workmen, and decide on something that can be rented cheaply and without loss."[13] Profoundly angered by Tally's news, Clark wrote back:

> It is perfectly outrageous that we should be placed in the position of submitting to Copper Queen regulations in labor and wage matters. I am also very much incensed at the attitude taken by Jimmie Douglas in all of this, as he has not shown the decency to cooperate with us in a camp where our interests are identical.[14]

Inter-copper company relations were rapidly returning to their normal pre-labor-management-war conditions.

In November 1918 federal authorities suspended the Loyalty League's "employment bureau." Through a routine inquisition, the "employment bureau" had tested a worker's patriotism by uncovering his attitude toward trade unionism.[15] But the tribunal was no longer necessary. The war being over, copper prices tumbled and returning veterans swamped the labor market. From Calumet & Arizona four hundred men had gone to war, while from Phelps Dodge the number was six hundred. The workers had no leverage; men were laid off to make room for the returning veterans. Phelps Dodge continued its program of buying fidelity to the company by building new change rooms and showers. A few months later the company enlarged its new patronizing policy when it established an annuity pension fund. After fifteen years or more of continuous service, men were entitled to annuities of 2 percent of their average wages of the most recent three years previous to retirement times their number of years in the service of Phelps Dodge.[16]

Industrial "peace" was evident throughout the West. A report from Federal Labor Conciliator Hywel Davies on October 20, 1919, stated that no strikes or disturbances were occurring in Montana, Nevada, Utah or Arizona on that date. Davies continued by explaining, "A better industrial relation is being gradually widened with the larger contact of management and employees through the various workmen's committees, now recognized in almost every mine, mill, and smelter in Arizona."[17] The tactics of deportation, importation, paternalism and propaganda had worked for the mining operators. Bisbee had been the leader; districts throughout the state followed suit.

Two years later Phelps Dodge came straight out with it: in July 1921 it announced an outline of a company union. Containing a "constitution" written up by the company, the plan offered employees "democratic participation" insofar as the plan could be terminated after six months by a two-thirds vote of the miners or "action by the Board of Directors of Phelps Dodge."[18] This ignominy together with the anguish that attended the national depression of the same year ended the funeral dirge of the early twentieth century labor movement in Arizona.

The Copper Queen, unmolested, poured forth her treasure. The richest mine in Arizona for many years, from 1916 to 1929 she yielded $220,554,434, more than 22 times the price paid for the entire Gadsden Purchase. Most of the profits went to stockholders who, like Cleveland Dodge and Walter Douglas, lived on the East Coast—or somewhere other than Arizona.

Wobblies' Collapse

A few scholars have attempted to depict the IWW as a significant force in American life. One has even tried to show that IWW activity *after* World War I was more aggressive, more productive for its own ends and more bothersome to capital than it had been in early 1917.[19] Except for scattered moments of IWW brazenness, the evidence to support this contention is hard to find. Repression resulting from federal legislation shows that "the I.W.W. was the decisive influence in the evolution of federal policy."[20] The general impact, in other words, of the IWW movement was more repression for any radical or reform group. The Sabotage Act, signed by President Wilson April 23, 1918, was a direct result of IWW-induced fears. According to the Department of Justice, this was the most important and sweeping of all war statutes relative to hostile or anti-war activities.[21] Subsequent national deportations and the Palmer raids found their models in the IWW roundup of 1917, the most dramatic being the Bisbee Deportation.

In 1964 even a Marxist historian observed that the IWW had been reduced to "a legal aid society" by the indictment of the Wobbly leaders.[22] The same writer, Michael Johnson, concluded that once the Wobblies were cut down, the momentum carried the nation on to condemn not only IWWism but "every nuance of dissent.... A suspicious, intolerant and frightened national administration turned from arresting Wobblies to deporting immigrants, harassing pacifists, and imprisoning socialists."[23]

Contrary to some fears, jail failed to make martyrs of the IWW leaders. The prisoners at Sacramento were described as a "typical cross section of American life." They showed little sullenness or defiance or dramatics; "on most faces one reads kindliness, commonsense and American humor."[24] (The public took little interest in this trial.[25]) Once locked away in Fort Leavenworth Prison, Harrison George, sentenced in the Chicago trial, bitterly lamented the curse of being afflicted "with a social vision." George added that mere liberals were not strong enough for radicalism; they had "saccharin souls" and their weak ideals had soon been broken by prison life.[26] Several of these men died or went insane while awaiting trail or while in prison.[27]

Although their leaders might have been locked up, enough Wobblies remained active in 1918, '19, '20 and '21 to keep the pot of hate and fear in America boiling.[28] On November 11, 1919, an Armistice Day parade in Centralia, Washington, ended with a raid by American Legionnaires on the Centralia IWW hall. Three Legion members were killed outright and another was shot while in pursuit of one of the fleeing Wobblies. The Wobbly, Wesley Everest, a World War I army veteran in uniform, was then beaten, castrated and lynched and became, along with Joe Hill and Frank Little, a member of the IWW trinity of martyrs.[29] During a Butte IWW strike in April 1920, mine company officials ordered their guards in huge headlines in the Butte *Daily Bulletin*: "SHOOT THE SONS OF BITCHES." Anaconda guards complied, and twenty picketing miners were gunned down on a public highway. Two of them died.[30]

But something was happening. IWWs imprisoned during an orange pickers' strike in Southern California in 1920 had some sympathy. One writer believed that earlier prosecution of the IWW had weeded out the adventurer, the weak, the wild, and the unsteady. The IWW had become, through some form of natural selection, a stable and dignified labor organization. It is more likely, though, that public sentiment rather than the Wobblies had changed.[31]

An even more compassionate tone appeared by 1923. The Wobblies were no longer ogres; they now were mainly hoboes who needed steady work. "The great majority are simply ordinary working men," *Harper's Magazine* pointed out, "jobless, moneyless, homeless; more to be pitied than feared."[32] Now that hysteria had subsided, Carleton Parker's opinion of 1917 was acceptable. *Sunset* magazine, which had switched its opinion from sympathy to hatred so quickly in 1917 swung back around full circle. Its November 1924 issue claimed, "The I.W.W. as a revolutionary organization has proved a ludicrous, pitiful failure."[33] *Current History*, published by the *New York Times*, still revealed in 1922 "definite facts about an organization whose avowed purpose is to destroy the wage system and the government of the United States...I.W.W.ism is a virulent thing." The polemical denunciation went on to call the IWW "utterly depraved."[34] Two and half years afterward, in a belated eulogy to the lifeless Wobblies, *Current History* said, "What the uninformed American does not understand, he magnifies into a monstrous menace." While the magazine pointed out that the IWW had had a deep belief in honest virtues, *Current History* failed to mention its own contributions to "magnifying a monstrous menace."[35]

On January 2, 1924, United Verde Copper Company Assistant General Manager Robert E. Tally wrote to United States Attorney General Harry M. Daugherty expressing his appreciation for the "splendid results accomplished by the Department of Justice in Arizona, particularly in its relation to radicalism." As elsewhere in America, Arizona had not seen any "radical" activity for some years.[36]

By 1925 Wobblyism had virtually died. Failing rapidly after the Chicago, Wichita and Sacramento convictions of 1918, an internal split in 1924 left it penniless, leaderless and direction-less. Spotty and minor eruptions of IWW activity were man-ifest in Colorado, Michigan, Ohio and Washington during the next twenty-five years. In the 1930s "I.W.W.'s" struck at con-struction sites as diverse as Hoover Dam, the Mississippi Bridge near New Orleans and a New York water tunnel.[37] But the niggling nature of IWW reality was greatly overshadowed by the growing substance of IWW legend.

EPILOGUE

Each of the earlier interpretations of the Bisbee Deportation—
pragmatic, ideological or behavioral—gave a singular explanation to the event. But, as in other historical developments,
there are multiple branches in the Bisbee Deportation's causal
tree. Confused motives and ambivalent concerns clouded
everyone's vision of the scene. Even corporate officials vacillated. Arizonans of the time struggled—as is often universally
the case—to discern their true interests. While ideological
rhetoric flourished, ideological identity wavered. Internal conflicts abounded. Intra-corporate, intra-union, and intra-
political party rivalries flourished. People switched allegiances,
spied on their own friends and betrayed political promises.
"Stoolies," scabs, *agents provocateurs* and goons swarmed over
the scene. Paradox prevailed.

Howard Zinn, in his assessment of the 1914 Ludlow, Colorado, Massacre, offers a set of conclusions that are appropriate
to the Bisbee Deportation. Zinn emphasizes "the firm connection between entrenched wealth and political power, manifested in the decisions of government, and in the machinery of
law and justice," and "the teamplay of the federal system, in

which crass action by local police on behalf of the rich and powerful is modified—especially after resistance develops—with a more masked but still biased intervention by the national government." Zinn also points out "the selective control of violence, in which government power is fumbling and incompetent in dealing with corporate and local police violence, sure and efficient in dealing with the violence of protest movements," and he observes "the somewhat different style of the national government (without difference in substance) in dealing with those outside its bounds who are helpless to resist and impotent as an internal political force ... " and "the opiate effect of commissions and investigations."

In addition to confirming Zinn's observations, this study of Arizona suggests that clearly and specifically, rather than by way of circumstance and suggestion, a heretofore unmentioned pattern of historical development took place in Arizona between 1901 and 1921. The Bisbee Deportation in 1917 was the climax of that development. The Bisbee events reveal that a powerful colonial relationship existed between the East and the West, the old and new. Crude habits and sensational events veiled the sponsorship and manipulation of the American frontier by East Coast political and economic figures. But the Arizona experience shows that instead of independent, individualistic pioneers who founded a new and liberated western society, there existed, standing behind each frontiersman—trapper, railroadman, soldier, or miner—a speculating financier or an ambitious entrepreneur or an exploitive politician. For every dutiful United States Land Office agent on the frontier there was a representative of a speculating eastern real estate venture. For every dogged and altruistic New England preacher on the western scene there was an ambitious eastern-educated mine manager—in daily telegraph contact with his New York office. Grubstaking each significant newcomer to Arizona was a quiet patron who kept western settlers of importance tied to eastern interests. Moreover, the colonial ties between the East and Bisbee were quite close and western mining communities enjoyed anything but "independence."

The exploitability of "radicalism" in Arizona labor relations enabled employers to screen their own profit-making ambitions with violent but socially acceptable union-smashing methods. At no time prior to the Bisbee Deportation was the IWW a threat to the Arizona mining industry; in fact, evidence indicated that most Westerners felt relatively little real fear specifically about the war or the possibility of subversion. Not until they had been inundated with company-sponsored propaganda did Arizonans indicate a malicious attitude toward so-called "enemy agents." In a constant state of hypertension, mining camps welcomed any opportunity to release their anxieties and channel their hostile energies. By deliberately avoiding the use of federal troops—troops for which Colonel Hornbrook could see no need—Bisbee's mine managers took care of their problem in their own way. By falsifying existing conditions, they persuaded many townspeople and much of the nation to share company antipathy toward labor. The Bisbee Deportation was the climax of a successful, concerted effort by eastern corporate interests to destroy the political power of labor in Arizona.

Other national traits characterized the region, too. In the history of Bisbee, one can see the general early twentieth century American transition from an entrepreneurial, experimental, technically unsophisticated, individualistic economy and society to the rentier-centered, scientific, specialized, "expert," corporate form which characterizes America today. More specifically, the Bisbee Deportation, as a test of public opinion in 1917, was a precedent for the massive national IWW arrests and trials and the later Palmer raids. Bisbee in addition became a nationwide object lesson, a warning to everyone to "toe the mark" and "stay in line." Bisbee was a sharp symbol of the national popular swing back to conservatism from pre-World War I Progressivism, and it signaled the "return to normalcy" of the 1920s.

Everything considered, by 1917 the reputed "ethos" of the nineteenth century American West should have been anachronistic in Bisbee. Bisbee's form of dirtiness, dreariness and violence after 1900 seemed to more closely parallel Pittsburgh's than Tombstone's, and Bisbee had economic problems more in common with those of Chicago than those of Phoenix. Yet, in 1917, for all of its apparent modernity, Bisbee, closely viewed, still had many frontier traits. Its citizens, notwithstanding their twentieth century concerns, were strongly possessed by the frontier mentality. This mentality enabled a twentieth century application of the old Western American legacy—vigilantism. The mine operators, by using vigilante methods in an industrial situation, established their supreme position and stifled union activity in Arizona until the New Deal. While their resident managers, with little effective dissent, ruled the desert colonies, absentee owners continued to cash generous dividend checks in Nassau or Southampton. Tarnished by the wartime blanket identification of "seditious," bona fide Arizona labor organizations struggled lamely and from 1917 until the late 1930s accepted their role as virtual company unions.

Arizona mining companies fought the enforcement of the country's National Labor Relations Act of 1935, and in 1946 Arizona's anti-labor forces succeeded in enacting a "Right-to-Work" law making union shops and closed shops within the state illegal. The post-World War II years, because of a prodigious growth in population, saw an increasing dominance of conservative middle-class Republican power in Arizona. The state never has had a potent and enduring populist tradition, and it never has been free of the bitter heritage that has characterized many other American industrial regions, a heritage of militant labor-management relationships and hostile political tensions as sophisticated and rancorous as any in the land.

REFERENCE MATERIAL

CHAPTER NOTES

The Bisbee Deportation of 1917

1. Gordon S. Watkins, "Labor Problems and Labor Administration in the United States During the World War, Part II," *University of Illinois Studies in the Social Sciences*, Vol. VIII, No. 4 (December, 1919), p. 154.

2. Alexander M. Bing, *War-Time Strikes and Their Adjustment* (New York: E. P. Dutton and Co., 1921), p. 264.

3. Mary Austin, "Arizona: The Land of the Joyous Adventure," *Nation*, Vol. 116, No. 3013 (April 4, 1923), p. 387.

4. For more on this, see G. Edward White, *The Eastern Establishment and the Western Experience* (New Haven: Yale University Press, 1968); Roderick Nash, *Wilderness and the American Mind* (New Haven: Yale University press, 1967); Henry Nash Smith, *Virgin Land* (Cambridge: Harvard University Press, 1950) and, especially, Edwin Fussell, *Frontier: American Literature and the American West* (Princeton: Princeton University Press, 1965).

5. James Oneal, "The Socialists in the War," *American Mercury*, Vol. X, No. 40 (April, 1927), pp. 418, 425.

6. Mary Ritter Beard, *The American Labor Movement* (New York: The MacMillan Co., 1928), p. 156.

7. Andre Siegfried, *America Comes of Age* (Harcourt, Brace and Company, New York, 1927), pp. 241–43.

8. John S. Gambs, *The Decline of the I.W.W.* (New York: Columbia University Press, 1932), p. 30.

9. Thomas E. Campbell, "The I.W.W. in Arizona," *Typescript Concerning Reconstruction of Labor Troubles in Arizona*, San Fernando, California, 1962. Arizona Pioneers' Historical Society, Tucson, n.p.

10. Writers' Program of the Work Projects Administration. *Arizona: A State Guide*. (New York: Hastings House, 1940), pp. 99–100.

11. Fred Thompson, *The I.W.W.: Its First Fifty Years* (Chicago: Industrial Workers of the World, 1955), p. 119.

12. *Arizona Republic*, October 8, 1948, p. 6.

13. Robert Glass Cleland, *A History of Phelps Dodge* (New York: Alfred A. Knopf, 1952), p. 175.

14. *Arizona Republic*, July 17, 1955, p. 7.

15. *Ibid.*, July 24, 1955, p. 6.

16. Phelps Dodge Council of the IUMMSW Bisbee Miners Local 501, "This is the Face of Phelps Dodge" (pamphlet, n.d., n.p.)

17. Alice Hamilton, *Exploring the Dangerous Trades* (Boston: Little, Brown and Company, 1943), pp. 210, 215.

18. John C. Dickinson, interview with J. Byrkit, April 11, 1966.

19. J. G. Berlindis, taped interview, Harwood Hinton Collection.

20. Si Morris, taped interview, Harwood Hinton Collection.

Chapter 1: The Setting

1. F. E. Richter, "The Copper-Mining Industry in the United States," *The Quarterly Journal of Economics*, Vol. 41 (February 1927), pp. 236, 247.

2. James Douglas, "Historical Sketch of Copper Queen Mine," *Mining and Engineering World*, Vol. XXXVIII, No. 11 (March 15, 1913), pp. 525–27.

3. Glenn Chesney Quiett, *They Built the West: An Epic of Rails and Cities* (New York: D. Appleton-Century Company, Inc., 1934), p. 7; Odie B. Faulk, *Too Far North ... Too Far South* (Los Angeles: Western Lore Press, 1967), p. vii; Paul Neff Garber, *The Gadsden Treaty* (Philadelphia: Press of the University of Pennsylvania, 1923); Douglas D. Martin, *An Arizona Chronology* (Tucson: The University of Arizona Press, 1963), no pagination; and Rufus K. Wyllys, *Arizona: the History of a Frontier State* (Phoenix: Hobson & Herr, 1950), pp. 110–18.

4. Thomas E. Farish, *History of Arizona*, Vol. I (Phoenix: T. E. Farish, 1915), pp. 278–79.

5. J. Douglas, *loc. cit.*

6. Charles H. Dunning, *Rock to Riches* (Phoenix: Southwest Publishing Company, Inc.), pp. 72–76; Robert G. Raymer, "Early Copper Mining in Arizona," *Pacific Historical Review*, Vol. IV, No. 2 (1935), pp.

123–30; Odie B. Faulk, *Land of Many Frontiers* (New York: Oxford University Press, 1968), *passim*; Frank J. Tuck, *History of Mining in Arizona* (Phoenix: State of Arizona, Department of Mineral Resources, 1955), p. 3. For a description of early mining and other resources in Arizona, see Patrick Hamilton, *The Resources of Arizona* (Tucson: Pinon Press, 1881).

7. J. Ross Brown, *A Tour Through Arizona: 1864* (Tucson: Arizona Silhouettes, republished 1951), pp. 20–22.

8. James Brand Tenney, "History of Mining in Arizona, Vol. I," Unpublished notes compiled 1927–29 (Special Collections, University of Arizona Library, Tucson), pp. 27–29; Annie M. Cox, "History of Bisbee: 1877 to 1937" (unpublished M.A. thesis, University of Arizona, 1938), *passim*; Richter, "The Copper Mining Industry . . . ," pp. 252–54.

9. Tenney, *loc cit.*; Opie Rundle Burgess, "Bisbee," *Arizona Highways*, Vol. XXVIII, No. 2 (February 1952), pp. 12–13, 32–35.

10. J. Douglas, *loc. cit.*; Burgess, *loc. cit.*

11. *Ibid.*; George Wharton James, *Arizona, The Wonderland* (Boston: The Page Company, 1917), p. 410.

12. Tenney, p. 28; Cleland, p. 87; J. Douglas, *loc. cit.*

13. *Ibid.*; J. Douglas, *loc. cit.*

14. Cleland, pp. 98–99; H. H. Langton, *James Douglas: A Memoir* (Toronto: University of Toronto Press, 1940), pp. 54–78; Tenney, p. 29; "Description of Property," Prospectus issued by Copper Queen Mining Company, New York, 1881 (Special Collections, University of Arizona Library, Tucson); J. Douglas, *loc. cit.*

15. Tenney, *loc. cit.*; Raymer, p. 129. See Arthur Notman, "Geology of the Bisbee, Ariz., Ore Deposits" (*Mining and Engineering World*, Vol. XXXVIII, No. 12 [March 22, 1913], pp. 387–391) for the geology of the Bisbee ore deposits, and James Douglas (*loc. cit.*) for an account of recovery methods and problems. For the Reilly-Zeckendorf story, also see Dunning, pp. 70–72.

16. Cleland, pp. 120–125. However, these properties paled beside the Copper Queen. For an example of the veneration accorded the Douglases see Charles A. Nichols, "Four Generations of the Douglas Family in America" (Unpublished typescript, Douglas, Arizona, 1965, copy in Special Collections, University of Arizona Library, Tucson).

17. "The Warren District, Arizona," *Engineering and Mining Journal*, Vol. LXXVIII, No. 14 (October, 1904), pp. 545–546.

18. Browne, *passim*; Frank C. Lockwood, *Pioneer Days in Arizona* (New York: MacMillan Co., 1932), p. 215; Writers' Program of the Works Projects Administration, *Arizona: A State Guide* (New York: Hasting House, 1940), pp. 171–175.

19. Langton, p. 78.

20. James, p. 410.

21. Writers' Program . . . , *loc. cit.*

22. Browne, P. 149; Writers' Program . . . , p. 175.

23. Cleland, pp. 109–110.

24. Writers' Program . . . , *loc. cit.*; Martin, n.p.

25. In 1900 Phelps Dodge decided to build a new smelter on a plain at 3,966 feet near the Mexican border about 25 miles east of Bisbee. On a tip from company officials, two minor Phelps Dodge administrators, W. H. "Billy" Brophy, manager of the Phelps Dodge company store, and A. J. Cunningham decided on the location for the townsite. They laid out the plot for "Douglas" (in honor of Dr. Douglas) on what had been open cattle range and along with six other men, including Dr. Douglas's son Walter, enjoyed the advantages of enlightened speculation (Will C. Barnes, *Arizona Place Names* [Tucson: University of Arizona, 1935], p. 134; Robert S. Jeffrey, "The History of Douglas, Arizona" [unpublished M.A. thesis, University of Arizona, 1951], p. 8). For an "objective" narrative, see Glenn S. Dumke, "Douglas, Border Town" (*Pacific Historical Review*, Vol. 17, No. 3 [August 1948], pp. 283–98.

Bisbee, in 1917, had a population of 14,500. But the proximate towns of Warren and Lowell increased that figure to 21,000. By comparison, the cities of Phoenix and Tucson had 25,000 and 22,000 people, respectively. Douglas, Bisbee's Cochise County industrial companion, was fourth largest in the state with 16,000. (*Ibid.*)

26. *Arizona State Business Directory: 1916–1917* (Denver: The Gazetteer Publishing & Printing Co., 1916), pp. 122, 162, 361, 473.

27. *Tucson Citizen* quoted in Joseph Miller, *Arizona: The Last Frontier* (New York: Hastings House, 1956), p. 32.

28. C. P. Connolly, "The Fight of the Copper Kings," *McClures Magazine*, Vol. XXIX, No. 3, p. 223.

29. Waino Nyland, "Western Mining Town," *Scribner's Magazine*, Vol. XCV, No. 5 (May 1934), pp. 365–69.

30. Richter, pp. 273–74; Thomas M. Erving, taped interview, Harwood Hinton Collection.

31. "Bisbee and the Warren District," *Arizona Labor Journal*, Vol. I, No. 17 (August 21, 1913), p. 45.

32. J. H. Gray, "Bisbee's Future Greatness," *Arizona*, Vol. IV, No. 9 (July 1914), p. 5.

33. Fred Sutter, "Senator Sutter Makes Reply," *Arizona Mining Journal*, Vol. II, No. 1 (June 1918), p. 48.

34. James, P. 417.

35. Herb Burrows, Interview, Tucson, June 27, 1968.

36. Mine managers watched their ethnic ratios carefully. In 1904 Will Clark, the United Verde administrator, received a nationality census from a subordinate, Frank Clement. The report listed, among the workers in the mine, eighty-eight Italians, thirty-six Irish, twelve Swedes, one Russian, two Turks and eighty-nine miners lumped together under "other nationalities." (Frank Clement, letter to Will

L. Clark, March 7, 1904 [United Verde Copper Company files, Jerome, Arizona. Courtesy of Herbert V. Young].)

37. Writers' Program ... , p. 175; Will H. Robinson, *The Story of Arizona* (Phoenix: The Berryhill Company, 1919), p. 397.

Chapter 2: Labor and Politics in the West and in Arizona

1. For a fine description of 19th C. western mining camp life see Richard E. Lingenfelter's *The Hardrock Miners* (Berkeley: University of California Press, 1974).

2. Rodman Paul, *Mining Frontiers of the Far West: 1848–1880* (New York: Holt, Rinehart & Winston, 1963), p. 196.

3. Howard Roberts Lamar, *The Far Southwest, 1846–1912: A Territorial History* (New Haven: Yale University Press, 1966), pp. 415–31.

4. The history of this phenomenon can be found in Melvyn Dubofsky, ''The Origins of Western Working Class Radicalism'' (*Labor History*, Vol. VII, No. 2 [Spring 1966], pp. 131–54).

5. ''Development of Collective Bargaining in Metal Mining,'' *Monthly Labor Review*, Vol. 47, No. 3 (September 1938), p. 591; Paul Frederick Brissenden, *The I.W.W.: A Study of American Syndicalism* (New York: Columbia University, 1920), pp. 116–215.

6. Philip Taft, *Organized Labor in American History* (New York: Harper and Row, 1964), p. 238.

7. Melvyn Dubofsky, *We Shall Be All* (Chicago: Quadrangle Books, 1969), p. 37.

8. Richter, p. 257.

9. Abe C. Ravitz and James N. Primm, eds., *The Haywood Case* (San Francisco: Chandler Publishing Co., 1970), *passim*. See this source for a collection of documents and articles relating to the famous 1907 trial in Boise, Idaho.

10. Taft, pp. 259–309.

11. Howard Zinn, *The Politics of History* (Boston: Beacon Press, 1970), pp. 79–101. Zinn sees the Ludlow Massacre as ''the culminating act of perhaps the most violent struggle between corporate power and laboring men in American history.'' Zinn's account and interpretation of the Ludlow affair are outstanding. For a comprehensive examination of the Ludlow Massacre see U.S., Congress, Senate, Commission on Industrial Relations, *The Colorado Coal Miners' Strike*, S. Doc., Vol. 25, 64th Cong., 1st sess., 1916.

12. Thomas R. Brooks, *Toil and Trouble* (New York: Dell Publishing Co., 1964), pp. 128–31.

13. Taft, p. 256.

14. Vernon H. Jensen, *Heritage of Conflict* (Ithaca: Cornell University Press, 1950), pp. 325–68; Selig Perlman and Philip Taft, *History of Labor in the United States, 1896–1932* (New York: The MacMillan Company, 1935), p. 401; Paul F. Brissenden, ''The Butte Miners and the

Rustling Card," *American Economic Review*, Vol. 10, No. 4 (December 1920), p. 757. Phelps Dodge historian Cleland states unequivocally that the IWW dynamited the union hall in Butte.

15. "Development of Collective Bargaining . . . ," p. 592; Brissenden, "The Butte Miners . . . ," *loc. cit.*

16. Richter, p. 256.

17. Dubofsky, "The Origins . . . ," *loc. cit.*

18. Arthur L. Walker, "Recollections of Early Day Mining in Arizona," *Arizona Historical Review*, Vol. VI, No. 2 (April 1935), p. 35.

19. Victor DeWitt Brannon, "Employers' Liability and Workmen's Compensation in Arizona" (M.A. thesis, University of Arizona, 1932), p. 1.

20. Jensen, p. 17; Wyllys, p. 291; Robinson, p. 287.

21. Madeline Ferrin Paré, *Arizona Pageant* (Phoenix: Arizona Historical Foundation, 1965), p. 305; Writers' Program . . . , p. 97.

22. Dulles, pp. 186–97; U.S., Congress, House, Industrial Commission Report, *Capital and Labor Employed in Mining Industry*, H. Doc., Vol. 75, 57th Cong., 1st sess., 1901–02.

23. Will L. Clark, letter to W. C. Bashford, July 26, 1904 (UVCC files).

24. Martin, n.p.

25. *Ibid.*; Writers' Program . . . , *loc. cit.*

26. Jensen, p. 357.

27. Cleland, p. 110; "Labor Conditions in the Southwest," *Engineering and Mining Journal*, Vol. LXXVI, No. 13 (March 3, 1904), p. 510.

28. *Bisbee Daily Review* quoted in Cleland, p. 109; "Labor Conditions . . . ," (*loc. cit.*) emphasizes the Bisbee labor-management harmony up until this time.

29. Frank Cullen Brophy, *Though Far Away* (Glendale: The Arthur H. Clark Co., 1940), p. 167.

30. Cleland, pp. 100–01; Richter, pp. 245, 275. For a general history and production record of the Bisbee mining district, see Morris Jesup Elsing, "The Bisbee Mining District: Past, Present and Future" (*Engineering and Mining Journal-Press*, Vol. 115, No. 4 [January 27, 1923], pp. 177–84). Good bibliography on Bisbee on page 184. On Bisbee at that time, also see Dwight E. Woodbridge, "The Copper Queen Consolidated Mining Company" *Engineering and Mining Journal*, Vol. LXXXI, No. 24 [June 16, 1906], pp. 1134–35).

31. Nels Anderson, *The Hobo* (Chicago: The University of Chicago Press, 1923), *passim*.

32. Cleland, p. 110.

33. Jensen, p. 357.

34. "The Bisbee Miners," *Arizona Labor Journal*, Vol. I, No. 17 (August 21, 1913), p. 46.

35. *Bisbee Daily Review* quoted in Jensen, p. 358.

36. "The Bisbee Miners," *loc. cit.*

37. The Panic of 1907 had enabled Bisbee copper companies to reduce production without worry of profit loss.

38. "The Bisbee Miners," *loc. cit*; Pare, p. 305.

39. Jensen, p. 360.

40. George Soule, "Law and Necessity in Bisbee," *Nation*, Vol. 113, No. 2930 (August 21, 1921), p. 225; Pare, *loc. cit.*; "Cochise County," *Arizona Mining Journal*, Vol. I, No. 12 (December 8, 1909), p. 9.

41. "The Bisbee Miners," *loc. cit.*

42. Martin, n.p.

43. Jensen, p. 364.

44. Writers' Program . . . , p. 98.

45. Davies, p. 246.

46. Herbert V. Young, *Ghosts of Cleopatra Hill* (Jerome: Jerome Historical Society, 1864), pp. 73–74.

47. *Ibid.*

48. Harvey J. Lee, letter to H. J. Allen, June 16, 1900 (UVCC files).

49. Young *loc. cit.*

50. Martin, n.p.

51. Howard A. Hubbard, "The Arizona Enabling Act and President Taft's Veto," *Pacific Historical Review*, Vol. III (1934), p. 318; Howard A. Hubbard, "Political History," *Arizona and Its Heritage* (Tucson: University of Arizona Press, 1936), p. 154; Victor DeWitt Brannon, "Employers' Liability and Workmens' Compensation in Arizona" (M.A. Thesis, University of Arizona, 1932), p. 7.

52. Taft, *Organized Labor* . . . , p. 234; Dulles, pp. 196–200; Henry Pelling, *American Labor* (Chicago: University of Chicago Press, 1960), p. 116; Marc Karson, *American Labor Unions and Politics: 1900–1918* (Carbondale: Southern Illinois University Press, 1958), p. 29.

53. Paré, p. 238. The Arizona Rangers had been formed in 1901 with ex-Rough Rider Harry Wheeler as third captain. On February 28, 1907, Arizona Ranger Wheeler engaged in a gun battle on the main street of Benson, Arizona. Although twice wounded, Wheeler killed an assailant threatening a double murder. (Martin, n.p.) These wounds later delayed his entrance into the army during World War I.

54. "The Bisbee Miners," *loc. cit.*; Jensen, p. 404; Paré, pp. 194, 238, 305. Arizona, *Session Laws of the Twenty-fifth Legislative Assembly of the Territory of Arizona* (Phoenix: The H. H. McNeil Co., 1909), p. 3.

55. "The Bisbee Miners," *loc. cit.*

56. U.S., Committee on Public Information, "Report and Recommendations of President's Mediators on the Underlying Causes and Remedy for Labor Unrest," *Official Bulletin*, Vol. II, No. 231 (February 11, 1918), p. 9.

57. For documented accounts of Hunt's rise to success, see Marjorie Haines Wilson, "The Gubernatorial Career of G. W. P. Hunt of

Arizona" (Ph.D. thesis, Arizona State University, 1973), pp. 1–16; and John S. Goff, *George W. P. Hunt and His Arizona* (Pasadena: Socio-Technical Publications, 1973), pp. 3–13.

58. Wilson, *loc. cit.*; Goff, *loc. cit.*; Writers' Program ... , p. 200; Effie R. Keen, "Arizona's Governors," *Arizona Historical Review*, Vol. III, No. 3 (October 1930), p. 17.

59. *Ibid.*

60. Alan V. Johnson, "Governor G. W. P. Hunt and Organized Labor," (M.A. thesis, University of Arizona, 1964), pp. 20–22, 38; John Rapp, interview, August 16, 1968; Writers' Program ... , p. 53. Bishop Wm. Scarlett, interview, March 13, 1972.

61. The unofficial movement began as early as the 1870s.

62. Howard R. Lamar, "The Reluctant Admission: The Struggle to Admit Arizona and New Mexico to the Union," *The American West: An Appraisal* (Santa Fe: Museum of New Mexico Press, 1963), p. 165; Wyllys, p. 300; John Braeman, "Albert J. Beveridge and Statehood for the Southwest, 1902–1912," *Arizona and the West*, Vol. 10, No. 4 (Winter 1968), pp. 327–34.

63. *Ibid.*; Wyllys, p. 304. One writer says this new anti-business attitude was "a major turning-point in Albert Beveridge's shift from stand-pattism to Progressivism" (Braeman, *loc. cit*).

64. Wyllys, *loc. cit*. For a history of territorial Arizona, see Jay J. Wagoner, *Arizona Territory, 1863–1912* (Tucson: University of Arizona Press, 1970).

65. Braeman, *loc. cit*.

66. Jack L. Cross, *et al.*, eds., *Arizona: Its People and Resources* (Tucson: University of Arizona Press, 1960), p. 186.

67. Young, p. 75.

68. Will L. Clark, letter to Charles Clark, August 27, 1910 (UVCC files).

69. Donald Robinson Van Petten, *Constitution and Government of Arizona* (Phoenix: Tyler Printing Company, 1960), pp. 17–27; Cross, p. 185.

70. Writers' Program ... , p. 98; Wyllys, pp. 305–06.

71. Lockwood, p. 337.

72. Will L. Clark, letter to Charles Clark, September 21, 1910 (UVCC files).

73. *Tucson Citizen*, August 22, 1910, p. 1; Everett E. Ellinwood, "Making a Modern Constitution," speech delivered at Bisbee Opera House, August 27, 1910.

74. *Tucson Citizen*, *loc. cit*.

75. "George W. P. Hunt and the Constitution of Arizona," typescript in Special Collections, University of Arizona Library, Tucson, n.d.

76. Van Petten, *loc.cit*. Elected vice-president of the convention was liberal Yavapai Democratic delegate, Morris Goldwater, Prescott

merchant and uncle of 1964 Republican Presidential candidate, Barry Goldwater.

77. *Ibid.;* Wyllys, *loc. cit.;* Cross, p. 186.

78. Robinson, p. 180.

79. Lockwood, p. 377.

80. Most accounts of the convention for some reason or other play down or ignore the capital-labor conflict as the essential controversy of the convention. But a survey of basic documents offers little else to explain the issues that arose. Tru Anthony McGinnis ("The Influence of Organized Labor on the Making of the Arizona Constitution," M. A. thesis, University of Arizona, 1931, p. 96) probably puts the influence of labor at the Constitutional Convention in its most appropriate perspective.

81. Writer's Program . . . , p. 98.

82. The anti-injunction measure and the 20 percent alien labor proposal were passed in 1913 in the state's first legislature, a body even more left-leaning than the Constitutional Convention. After being made into law, both provisions were ultimately found unconstitutional by the United States Supreme Court. The Maricopa County delegation, on the other hand, did not hesitate to initiate anti-corporate proposals that favored Phoenix citizens. Employer liability was introduced by the Maricopa people (Will Clark, letter to Senator William Andrews Clark, October 20, 1910 [UVCC files]). It is likely that some "radical" legislation was supported by conservatives (such as E. E. Ellinwood) in the hope that they could sabotage the Constitution by guaranteeing its rejection when reviewed by Congress and President Taft.

83. W. Clark to Sen. W. A. Clark, Oct. 20, 1910, *loc. cit.*

84. *Ibid.*

85. "The Peoples' Rights," *Arizona Gazette*, August 8, 1910, p. 2.

86. "Who Are the Sane?" *Arizona Gazette*, August 9, 1910, p. 2.

87. Will L. Clark, letter to Senator William Andrews Clark, November 5, 1910 (UVCC files).

88. *Ibid.*

89. Yolanda LaCagnina convincingly shows this filiation of the recall provision in her master's thesis, "The Role of the Recall of Judges Issue in the Struggle for Arizona Statehood" (University of Arizona, 1951), p. 129 and *passim*.

90. Wyllys, pp. 307–08.

91. Cross, p. 187.

92. Arizona, *Constitution*, p. 4; Van Petten, *passim*.

93. Wyllys, p. 309; Van Petten, p. 27. Wyllys and Van Petten give the count as 12,584 for, 3,920 against. The official source says 12,187 for, 3,302 against (Wesley Bolin, "Facts and Figures," *Constitution of Arizona* [Phoenix: Secretary of State, 1961], p. 1).

94. Will L. Clark, letter to Senator William Andrews Clark, February 10, 1911 (UVCC files).

95. Hubbard, "The Arizona . . . ," p. 322.

96. Writers' Program . . . , p. 98; Hubbard, "The Arizona . . . ," p. 320.

97. John R. Murdock, *Constitutional Development of Arizona* (Tempe, Arizona: Arizona State Teachers' College, 1930), p. 46.

98. Cross, p. 188.

99. "George W. P. Hunt and . . . ," p. 11.

100. 14,863, yea; 1,890, nay (Bolin, p. 1).

101. Lamar, "The Reluctant . . . ," p. 163.

102. Taft, though, would have the last word. See pp. 314–15. Only once has the recall provision been invoked against an elected judge in Arizona. In 1924 Superior Court Judge Stephen H. Abbey of Pinal County had a petition filed against him. A recall election including two opponents was held, and Judge Abbey placed second. An appeal to the State Supreme Court by Abbey resulted in a decision upholding the recall provision and the ouster of the judge.

103. Bolin, *loc. cit.*; Wyllys, p. 316.

104. Wyllys, p. 315.

105. W. Clark to Sen. W. A. Clark, Oct. 20, 1910, *loc. cit.*; W. Clark to C. Clark, Aug. 27, 1910, *loc. cit.*; W. Clark to Sen. W. A. Clark, Oct. 20, 1910, *loc. cit.*; W. Clark to Sen. W. A. Clark, Feb. 10, 1911, *loc. cit.*

106. Will L. Clark, letter to Charles W. Clark, July 21, 1910 (UVCC files).

107. Official Ballot, Town Election, Jerome, Arizona, May 23, 1910, marked to show results of election (UVCC files).

108. Pelling, p. 123.

109. W. Clark to Sen. W. A. Clark, Oct. 20, 1910, *loc. cit.*; W. Clark to Sen. W. A. Clark, Feb. 10, 1911, *loc. cit.*

110. Samuel Yellen, *American Labor Struggles* (New York: The Harbor Press, 1956), p. 171; Pelling, p. 117.

111. For representative samples of the "objective" if not "sympathetic" studies of labor and unions which were beginning to appear in print during this period see George C. Groat, *An Introduction to the Study of Organized Labor in America* (New York: The MacMillan Co., 1917).

112. "Blinders," *New Republic*, Vol. II, No. 15 (February 13, 1915), pp. 33–35.

113. "The Law Relating to Trades-Unions and Industrial Disputes," *Monthly Review of the Bureau of Labor Statistics*, Vol. I, No. 5 [November 1915], pp. 58–59; "Report of the Commission on Industrial Relations," *Monthly Review of the Bureau of Labor Statistics*, Vol. L, No. 5 (November 1915), pp. 48–76.

114. Robinson, pp. 353–60. Also see Arizona, *Acts, Resolutions and Memorials of the Regular Session, First Legislature* (Phoenix: The McNeil Printers, 1912), pp. 24–25.

115. Soule, p. 225; *Tucson Citizen*, January 7, 1915, p. 1.
116. "The Arizona Alien Labor Law," *Outlook*, Vol. 109 (January 20, 1915), pp. 109–10.
117. *Ibid*.
118. *Ibid*.
119. *Raich v. Truax, et al.*, 219 Fed. 272 (Ariz.).
120. *Tucson Citizen*, January 7, 1915, p. 1; "The Arizona Alien ... ," *loc. cit.; Raich v. Truax;* "Arizona's Anti-Alien Law Unconstitutional," *Survey*, Vol. XXXV, No. 7 (November 13, 1915), p. 155; Soule, p. 225.
121. "Editorial Notes," *New Republic*, Vol. VI, No. 53 (November 6, 1915), p. 4.
122. For a more detailed account of the history of the Arizona anti-injunction law, see pp. 312–15.
123. *United States v. Phelps Dodge Mercantile Co., et al.*, 209 Fed. 190 [Ariz.]. *Arizona Daily Star*, October 23, 1913, p. 1; *Arizona Republican*, October 24, 1913, p. 1; *Arizona Republican*, December 3, 1913, p. 1; *Arizona Republican*, December 11, 1913, p. 1; *Messenger*, July 28, 1917.
124. George W. P. Hunt, "The Coming Citizen," address delivered to the Arizona Federation of Women's Clubs, Nogales, Arizona, January 21, 1914; Robinson, p. 363.
125. James R. Kluger, *The Clifton-Morenci Strike* (Tucson: University of Arizona Press, 1970), *passim*; John A. Fitch, "Arizona's Embargo on Strike-Breakers," *Survey*, Vol. XXXVI, No. 6 (May 6, 1916), pp. 143–44.
126. For this and other company expenditures during the strike, see *Journal M* (Vol. 13), The Arizona Copper Co., Ltd., Records, 1882–1921 (October 1912–May 1916 records in Special Collections, University of Arizona Library, Tucson).
127. Cleland, pp. 98, 111, 207–09; Kluger, pp. 18, 20. For a tame sketch of the Clifton-Morenci district history dating back to 1873 see "The Story of the Clifton-Morenci District," *Arizona*, Vol. VIII, No. 5 (August 1918), pp. 8–9, or Roberta Watt, "History of Morenci, Arizona" (M.A. thesis, University of Arizona, 1956).
128. Kluger, pp. 18–31; Fitch, p. 143; Jensen, p. 367.
129. *Arizona Gazette*, September–October, 1915.
130. Bowie *Enterprise*, September 3, 1915, p. 2
131. *Tucson Citizen*, September 10, 1915, p. 1.
132. *Arizona Republican*, September 24, 1915, p. 1.
133. *Arizona Record*, September 28, 1915, p. 1; *Ibid.*, September 29, 1915, p. 1.
134. Governor George W. P. Hunt, address to strikers in Clifton, September 30, 1915 ("Clifton-Morenci Strike, 1915–1916," Special Collections, University of Arizona Library, Tucson); "Excerpt from Statement of Gov. Hunt After Visiting the Clifton-Morenci District," n.d. (Special Collections, University of Arizona Library, Tucson).
135. *Ibid*.
136. *Arizona Gazette*, September 30, 1915, p. 1.

137. Fitch, pp. 143–46; Jensen, *loc. cit.*

138. *Arizona Gazette*, October 3, 1915, p. 1.

139. Typescript account of Clifton-Morenci Strike, no title, no date ("Clifton-Morenci Strike, 1915–1916," Special Collections, University of Arizona Library, Tucson).

140. "The Tables Turned," *Dunbar's Weekly*, Vol. II, No. 39 (October 9, 1915), p. 6.

141. Fitch, *loc. cit.*; letter signed by Norman Carmichael, general manager of the Arizona Copper Co., Ltd.; M. H. McLean, general manager of the Detroit Copper Mining Company of Arizona and J. W. Bennie, general manager of the Shannon Copper Co., to "The Committees Representing the Former Employees of Their Companies," n.d. (in file, "Clifton-Morenci Strike, 1915–1916," Special Collections, University of Arizona Library, Tucson).

142. Kluger, pp. 49–60.

143. Charles W. Harris, adjutant general of Arizona State Militia, "A Statement," n.d. (in file "Clifton-Morenci Strike, 1915–1916," Special Collections, University of Arizona Library, Tucson).

144. *Arizona Daily Star*, October 24, 1915, p. 1.

145. "Conciliation Work of the Department of Labor, March 4, 1913 to June 6, 1916," *Monthly Review of the Bureau of Labor Statistics*, Vol. III, No. 1 (July, 1916), pp. 30–31.

146. Walter Douglas, "The Strike in Arizona," *Mining and Scientific Press*, Vol. III, November 20, 1915, pp. 771–772.

147. "Miners Resume Work," *Arizona Labor Journal*, February 3, 1916 (clipping in George W. P. Hunt Scrapbooks, Special Collections, University of Arizona Library, Tucson).

148. Kluger, p. 71 and *passim*.

149. Fitch, *loc. cit.*

150. George W. P. Hunt, "The Strike Situation Reviewed," n.d. (in files "Clifton-Morenci Strike, 1915–1916," Special Collections, University of Arizona Library, Tucson).

151. Kluger, pp. 49–60.

152. Hywel Davies and Joseph S. Myers, letter to G. W. P. Hunt, February 10, 1916 (copy in file "Clifton-Morenci Strike, 1915–1916," Special Collections, University of Arizona Library, Tucson).

153. Kluger, pp. 52–53. The study of the Clifton-Morenci Strike by James Kluger makes almost certain that the strike was the "turn-around" event in Arizona Progressive period history. (Kluger, *passim*.)

Chapter 3: Arizona Turn-Around

1. "A Strike Without Disorder," *New Republic*, Vol. V, No. 64 (January 22, 1916), pp. 304–06.

2. "Walter Douglas," *Who's Who in Arizona*, 1916; Douglas Martin, "The Douglas Dynasty," typescript (Special Collections, University of Arizona Library, Tucson), 1961; Nichols, "Four Generations . . . ."

3. "Personal," *Mining and Scientific Press*, Vol. 113, July 29, 1916, p. 183. Dr. James Douglas died in New York on June 25, 1918, at the age of eighty-one. ("Personal," *Mining and Scientific Press*, Vol. 116, June 29, 1918, p. 905.)

4. *Tucson Citizen*, May 2, 1918, p. 1; "Walter Douglas," *loc. cit.*

5. Walter Douglas' clubs were: St. Andrews Society, DownTown Association, Century Association, New York Yacht Club, Columbia University Club, Grolier Club, St. Andrews Golf Club of Hastings, New York, and the American Yacht Club of Rye, New York. Later in his life and for many years, Douglas served on the Board of Managers for the Memorial Hospital of New York City. He was Board President, 1924–1933, and Board Chairman, 1933–1943. A Republican and an Episcopalian, Douglas had five children. ("Walter Douglas, Industrialist," *National Cyclopedia of American Biography*, Vol. XXXVI [New York: James T. White & Company, 1950], p. 310.)

6. Martin, "The Douglas Dynasty," pp. 25–26; "Walter Douglas," *loc. cit.*; *New York Times*, October 4, 1946, p. 23.

7. Martin, "The Douglas Dynasty," pp. 28–29; "Nineteenth Annual Convention of Mining Congress was Great Success," *Mining Congressional Journal*, Vol. II, No. 12 (December 1916), pp. 523–24.

8. Langton, p. 85.

9. William W. Newkirk, "Historical Geography of Bisbee, Arizona" (M.A. thesis, University of Arizona, 1966), p. 119.

10. H. S. McCluskey, letter to J. Byrkit, April 21, 1966.

11. Cleland, p. 188.

12. "Organization of Anarchy," *New Republic*, Vol. XI, No. 142 (July 21, 1917), p. 321.

13. Robert W. Bruere, "Copper Camp Patriotism: An Interpretation," *Nation*, Vol. CVI, No. 2748 (February 28, 1918), p. 302.

14. *New York Sun* quoted in "The Arizona Copper Strike," *Outlook*, Vol. 116, No. 13 (July 25, 1917), p. 466.

15. W. Douglas, "The Strike in Arizona," *loc. cit.*

16. Walter Douglas, "The Arizona Strike," *New Republic*, Vol. VI, No. 72 (March 18, 1916), pp. 185–86.

17. *Ibid.*, "Note."

18. "From Governor Hunt," *New Republic*, Vol. VI, No. 76 (April 15, 1916), p. 293.

19. Walter V. Woehlke, "The Greatest Mining Boom in History," *American Review of Reviews*, Vol. LIV, No. 4 (October 1916), pp. 429–32.

20. Howard A. Hubbard, "Political History," *Arizona and Its Heritage* (Tucson, University of Arizona, 1936), p. 157; Martin, *An Arizona ...* , n.p. For the first half of 1909, Phelps Dodge declared record dividends of $2,224,730. (Martin, *loc. cit.*)

21. Cross, p. 248. G. M. Butler gave the figures as $37,800,000 for 1910, $80,500,000 for 1915 and $194,400,000 for 1917 in his article. ("Mineral Industries," *Arizona and Its Heritage*, p. 160.)

22. Tenney, p. 404; Phelps Dodge Corporation, *Annual Report*, 1914–1918.

23. "Changes in Wholesale Prices in the United States," *Monthly Review of the Bureau of Labor Statistics*, Vol. VI, No. 6 (June 1918), p. 291. In 1912 copper sold at 16½ cents a pound; in 1916, 28½ cents a pound; and during the week of July 13, 1917, 29½ cents a pound. (U.S., Bureau of Census, *Historical Statistics of the United States, 1789–1945* [Washington: United States Department of Commerce, 1949], p. 150.) By March of 1917 it reached its monthly wartime peak of 35.74 cents a pound. (Paul Willard Garrett, *Government Control Over Prices* [Washington: Government Printing Office, 1920], p. 273.) The daily high for the period was 38 cents a pound, on March 21, 1917. (*New York Times*, March 21, 1917.)

24. *New York Times*, July 21, 1917, p. 12; Report of Phelps, Dodge & Co. for fiscal year ending December 31, 1916, "Annual Reports," *Commercial and Financial Chronicle*, Vol. 104, No. 2700 (March 24, 1917), p. 1139; *New York Times*, March 20, 1917, p. 15; "Vast Profits for the Mines," *American Review of Reviews*, Vol. LIII, No. 5 (May 1916), p. 535; *New York Times*, March 14, 1917, p. 12; "General Investment News," *Commercial and Financial Chronicle*, Vol. 104, No. 2712 [June 16, 1917], p. 2456.

25. An investigation after World War I by the Graham Committee showed that the Calumet and Hecla Mining Companies made a profit of 800 percent. (U.S., Congress, House, *Select Committee on Expenditures in the War Department*, H. Rep. No. 1400, Vol. 2, 66th Cong., 3rd sess., 1921.)

26. *Bisbee Daily Review*, July 1, 1917, sect. 2, p. 1; William P. DeWolf, "Reopening Old Mines in Arizona," *Mining and Engineering World*, Vol. 45, No. 8 (August 19, 1916), pp. 329–31. For information on wartime growth of smaller Arizona copper mines see Charles F. Willis, "Mining in Arizona," *Mining and Scientific Press*, Vol. 112, January 29, 1916, pp. 171–72.

27. T. A. Rickard, "Editorial," *Mining and Scientific Press*, Vol. 112, January 8, 1916, p. 32.

28. James, p. 417.

29. U.S., Bureau of Labor Statistics, "Index Numbers of Changes in Cost of Living, 1913, to December, 1919," *Monthly Labor Review*, Vol. X, No. 6 (June 1920), p. 79; Gordon S. Watkins, "Labor Problems and Labor Administration in the United States During the World War," *University of Illinois Studies in the Social Sciences*, Vol. VIII, No. 4, Part 1 (Urbana: University of Illinois, December 1919), p. 92; Paul H. Douglas, *Real Wages in the United States: 1890–1926* (Boston: Houghton Mifflin Company, 1930). Purchasing power of the working man during this period is the subject of a classic debate among economic historians of this period. See Albert Rees, *Real Wages in Manufacturing: 1890–1914* (Princeton: Princeton University Press, 1961).

30. Bur. of Labor Stats., "Index Numbers ... ," *loc. cit.*; U.S., Bureau of Labor Statistics, "Changes in Union Wage Scales and in Retail Prices of Food, 1907 to 1917," *Monthly Review of the Bureau of Labor Statistics*, Vol. VI, No. 6 (June, 1918), pp. 1508–1509.

31. "The Cause of High Prices," *Literary Digest*, Vol. LIV, No. 11 (March 17, 1917), p. 703; "American Labor in the World War Period, 1914 to April, 1917," *Monthly Labor Review*, Vol. 49, No. 4 (October, 1939), pp. 785–795; Bur. of Labor Stats., "Index Numbers ... ," *loc. cit.*; "Relative Retail Prices of the Principal Articles of Food in the United States, January, 1913, to June, 1919," *Monthly Labor Review*, Vol. IX, No. 2 (August, 1919), pp. 90–91. In 1915 one-fourth to one-third of the male workers in United States factories and mines earned less than $10 a week. Women in industrial occupations made less than $8 a week. Despite the passage of numerous eight-hour-day and six-day-week laws, the rule of twelve hours a day, seven days a week still prevailed in a substantial number of places. (Bing, p. 2.)

32. Watkins, "Labor Problems ... ," pp. 92, 96.

33. Actually, Bisbee workers did much better than the national average. In 1913 a mucker in the Copper Queen earned $3.75 a day; by 1917 the daily rate had climbed to $5.35, an increase of almost 43 percent. ("Rates of Wages Per Day in Certain Branches of Metal Mining Where Gold is a Direct By-Product, September, 1913 to 1918," *Monthly Labor Review*, Vol. VIII, No. 4 [April 1919], pp. 177–78.) This was far from matching dividend growth. A $10 per week minimum wage for women act passed in the Arizona legislature in May 1917 meant nothing to the Bisbee miners. ("Minimum Wage Established in Arizona," *Survey*, Vol. XXXVIII, No. 6 [May 12, 1917], p. 149.) They remained unhappy with existing conditions.

34. Robert W. Bruere, "Copper Camp Patriotism," *Nation*, Vol. CVI, No. 2747 (February 21, 1918), pp. 202–03.

35. *Messenger*, May 26, 1917.

36. McGinnis, *passim*.

37. Brannan, p. 7.

38. George H. Kelly, ed., *Legislative History: Arizona, 1864–1912* (Phoenix: Manufacturing Stationers, 1926), p. 96.

39. *Ibid.*, pp. 168–69, 193–96.

40. *Ibid.*, pp. 195–96, 206–18.

41. Wagoner, *Arizona Territory* ... , pp. 397–403; Kelly, pp. 222–23.

42. Kelly, pp. 222–23.

43. *Ibid.*, pp. 225–26.

44. *Ibid.*, pp. 250–51.

45. *Ibid.*, pp. 236–37.

46. Wagoner, *Arizona Territory* ... , pp. 442–43.

47. Kelly, pp. 250–253.

48. Wagoner, p. 443.

49. D. C. O'Neil, "Forty Years of Mine Taxation in Arizona, 1907–1946," Typescript in Special Collections, University of Arizona Library, Tucson, p. 2; Kelly, pp. 252–54.

50. Arizona, *Session Laws of the Twenty-fourth Legislative Assembly of the Territory of Arizona* (Phoenix: The H. H. McNeil Co., 1907), pp. 20–26; "Go To It," *Dunbar's Weekly*, Vol. IV, No. 30 (August 4, 1917), p. 3; Hubbard, "The Arizona . . . ," p. 318; Hubbard, "Political History," p. 154.

51. Operators did endure local setbacks. A school election in June, 1910, went badly for the United Verde Copper Company. Will Clark wrote that despite his efforts citizens voted for a new $15,000 school building. "The only saving arrangement we could make," moaned Clark, "was to have our Engineer, C. V. Hopkins, appointed a member of the board." (Will Clark, letter to Charles Clark, June 21, 1910 [UVCC files].)

52. Kelly, pp. 259–71; Wagoner, p. 446; Van Petten, p. 22; Arizona, *Constitution*, Article IX ("Public Debt, Revenue, and Taxation") and Article XVII ("Labor").

53. Martin, *An Arizona . . .* , n.p.; Arizona, *Acts, Resolutions . . .* , pp. 24–25; O'Neil, p. 2; Arizona, *Special Reports of the State Tax Commission of Arizona on Mining Taxation*, Special Report to the Governor, March 17, 1913, pp. 5–7.

54. "Mine Taxation in Arizona is Entirely in Hands of State Tax Commission," *Mining Congress Journal*, Vol. I, No. 9 (Sept., 1915), p. 447. For more information on Arizona taxation during this period see Arizona, *Report of the Conference of the Tax Commission, Board of Supervisors and County Assessors of the State of Arizona*, 1913, 1914, 1915, 1916, 1917, 1918.

55. "Do You Know?" *Arizona State Herald*, September 1, 1916, p. 12.

56. George W. P. Hunt, "So the People May Know" (pamphlet privately published, Phoenix, December 16, 1915), pp. 4 and 5; for the minutes of this session see Arizona, *Senate Journal of the Second Special Session of the Second Legislature of the State of Arizona, 1915* (Phoenix: The McNeil Co., 1915), pp. 38–51.

57. Kluger, pp. 52–53; O'Neil, p. 2.

58. Van Petten, p. 22; Arizona, *Constitution*, Article IX ("Public Debt, Revenue and Taxation") and Article XVII ("Labor").

59. "Arizona Is the Premier Copper State . . . ," *Mining and Scientific Press*, Vol. 113 (August 26, 1916), p. 298; *Southwestern Stockman-Farmer*, August 4, 1916, *loc. cit.*

60. O'Neil, p. 2.

61. Statistics supporting these statements can be found in the *Biennial Reports of the State Tax Commission of Arizona*, 1912–18.

62. *Arizona Daily Star*, September 29, 1915, p. 2; Garrett, p. 273; "Changes in Wholesale Prices . . . ," p. 91.

63. "Nineteenth Annual Meeting American Mining Congress," *Mining and Engineering World*, Vol. 45, No. 22 (November 25, 1916), p. 906. At this same convention Walter Douglas was elected president of the national organization for 1917. ("Nineteenth Annual Convention . . . " [*Mining Congress Journal*, Dec., 1916], *loc. cit.*)

64. Kluger, pp. 52–53.

65. It appears that Hunt's taxation and expense program might have been exemplary. Badly needed highways, bridges, schools and other institutions were built between 1912 and 1916. Yet Hunt maintained a frugal administrative budget and he cut back many extravagant expenses of the territorial days. In addition, during Hunt's administration, the militia was doubled and the governor's prison reform became a model for the nation. ("Do You Know?" *loc. cit.*)

66. *Arizona Republican*, October 27, 1915, p. 1. The *Arizona Gazette* called sending the National Guard to Clifton-Morenci an "imbecile act." (*Arizona Gazette*, October 3, 1915, p. 2).

67. Kluger, pp. 52–55; *Arizona Gazette*, November 29, 1915, p. 1; *Arizona Republican*, November 30, 1915, p. 1.

68. Editorial, "Just a Political Move," *Arizona Labor Journal*, October 25, 1915, p. 3.

69. Editorial, "Recalling Gov. Hunt," *Winslow Mail*, October 29, 1915, p. 2.

70. Hunt, "So the People . . . ," p. 3.

71. Gilson Gardner, "Mine Owners Want Governor Recalled" *Worcester Evening Post*, January 7, 1916 (Gardner was a syndicated Washington correspondent; the article appeared in several Eastern newspapers).

72. Hunt, "So the People . . . ," *loc. cit.*

73. *Ibid.*, pp. 4–5.

74. "Arizona's Political Trouble Caused by Unsympathetic Landlords," *Arizona Silver Belt* (reprinted in Bowie, Arizona, *Enterprise*, April 7, 1916, p. 2).

75. *Arizona Silver Belt*, May 29, 1916, p. 2.

76. *Ibid.*, March–September, 1916, *passim*.

77. *Arizona Republican*, October 22, 1915, p. 3.

78. *Arizona Silver Belt*, June 3, 1916, p. 2.

79. *Ibid.*, June 24, 1916, p. 6.

80. *Ibid.*, July–November, 1916, *passim*.

81. B. F. Fly, "Non-Resident Copper Barons Advance Candidate for Governor," *Dunbar's Weekly*, Vol. III, No. 7 (February 24, 1916), p. 3; Robinson, p. 360. For Olney's connections with the Arizona power elite, see Ernest J. Hopkins, *Financing the Frontier* (Phoenix: The Arizona Printers, 1950), pp. 6, 21, 24, 25, 144, 168, 170.

82. Editorial, "The Poor Fool," *Dunbar's Weekly*, Vol. III, No. 9 (March 11, 1916), p. 2.

83. *Arizona Silver Belt*, September 9, 1916, p. 4.

84. "Do You Know?" *loc. cit.*

85. *Dunbar's Weekly*, Vol. III, No. 16 (April 29, 1916), p. 2.

86. *Arizona Daily Star*, April 2, 1916, p. 2; *Ibid.*, April 4, 5, 1916.

87. Editorial, "Carpet Baggery and Class Rule," *Ibid.*, May 17, 1916, p. 2.

88. Editorial, "Primaries vs. Publicity," *Arizona Silver Belt*, May 21, 1916, p. 2.

89. "The Horseshoe in the Glove," *State Herald*, September 1, 1916, p. 12. The short-lived *State Herald* claimed to be a Republican publication.

90. *Arizona Silver Belt*, September 9, 1916, p. 4; unidentified newspaper clipping, George W. P. Hunt Scrapbooks, Vol. 22 (Special Collections, University of Arizona Library, Tucson), unclear pagination.

91. *Arizona Silver Belt*, September 14, 1916, p. 4.

92. Fiorello La Guardia, another popular politician, graduated from the same school three years later. ("Fiorello Henry La Guardia," *The National Cyclopedia of American Biography*, Vol. XXXVI [New York: James T. White & Company, 1950], p. 9.)

93. Keen, p. 18; Robinson, pp. 361–62; Young, pp. 85–91.

94. *Arizona Silver Belt*, October 20, 1916, p. 1; *Arizona Daily Star*, November 14, 1916, p. 1; "Campbell Carries Water on Both Shoulders," *Dunbar's Weekly*, Vol. III, No. 39 (October 7, 1916), p. 10. Watson, July 19, 1972.

95. Robinson, *loc. cit.*; Young, *loc. cit.*; H. S. McCluskey, letter to J. Byrkit, *loc. cit.*; "A State With Two Governors," *The Independent*, Vol. 89, No. 3554 (January 15, 1917), p. 96; Keen, *loc. cit.*

96. *Arizona Republican*, November 7, December 16, 30, 1916, January 3, 25, 27, 30, 1917; Arizona, *Abstract of Record, Appeal to the Supreme Court of the State of Arizona from Superior Court of Maricopa County, George W. P. Hunt v. Thomas E. Campbell* (1588), filed August 16, 1917. This abstract contains the entire 3366 page transcript from the lower court.

97. Kluger, p. 73; *Abstract* ... , *Hunt v. Campbell*, pp. 10–300 and *passim*.

98. Only a few precincts are discussed here. See transcript of Maricopa County Superior Court trial.

99. Editorial, "Douglas No. 1," *Arizona Labor Journal*, Vol. V, No. 3 (March 33, 1917), p. 2.

100. *Arizona Republican*, March 15-30, 1917, *passim*.

101. "Douglas No. 1," *loc. cit.*; *Abstract* ... , *Hunt v. Campbell*, *passim*.

102. "Bisbee Precinct No. One Now Under the Microscope," *Dunbar's Weekly* (this clipping in George W. P. Hunt Scrapbooks, Vol. 21 [Special Collections, University of Arizona Library, Tucson], unclear pagination). *Abstract* ... , *Hunt v. Campbell*, pp. 3300–65.

103. *Messenger*, May 5, 1917, p. 1; Robinson, pp. 361–62. For details of testimony in this governorship litigation, see *Arizona Republican*, March 15–30, 1917, and *Abstract . . . , Hunt v. Campbell*.

Chapter 4: Enter Organized Resistance

1. W. L. Clark to Sen. W. A. Clark, Oct. 20, 1910 (UVCC Files); *Ibid.*, Feb. 10, 1911.

2. F. Ernest Richter, "The Copper-Mining Industry in the United States," *Quarterly Journal of Economics*, Vol. 41 (August 1927), p. 716.

3. Watkins, "Labor Problems . . . ," Part I, p. 105.

4. "The Copper Market," *Arizona Mining Journal*, Vol. I, No. 4 (September 22, 1909), p. 3.

5. Martin, *An Ariz. Chronology*, n.p.

6. F. Ernest Richter, "The Amalgamated Copper Company: A Closed Chapter in Corporation Finance," *Quarterly Journal of Economics*, Vol. 30, February 1916, p. 407.

7. Jensen, pp. 289–324.

8. Kluger, p. 20.

9. Writers' Program . . . , p. 91; Steward H. Holbrook, *The Age of the Moguls* (Garden City, N.Y.: Doubleday, 1953), pp. 277–302; "Problems of Labor," *Mining and Scientific Press*, Vol. 110, January 30, 1915, pp. 170–71.

10. According to one copper company executive, Phelps Dodge had an inflexible anti-Semitic attitude that was implemented in company policy (retired Phelps Dodge Official "Y", interview, December 28, 1965). The same was true at Senator Clark's United Verde. As early as 1901, Henry J. Allen wrote from Jerome that a "Miss Laube called to-day with her father . . . and her appearance indicates she has some 'sheeny' blood in her, as she certainly had a Hebrew face. Her father looks like a Rabbi. I do not understand why they should come in here unless it is to look over the property with a view of sometime in the future being interested." Allen reported he told the two "that the property was not on the market," and asked the addressee to "kindly treat this as strictly confidential." At least his prejudice had the refinement of discretion. (Henry J. Allen, letter to James A. Macdonald, May 18, 1901 [UVCC Files].)

11. Harlan B. Phillips, *Felix Frankfurter Reminisces* (New York: Reynad & Company, 1960), pp. 117–18.

12. Jensen, p. 417. Frankfurter discovered somewhat less open-mindedness and congeniality in Bisbee. See pages 265 and 268–69.

13. Langton, pp. 114–15.

14. George Hunter, "John C. Greenway and the Bull Moose Movement in Arizona" (M.A. thesis, University of Arizona, 1965), p. 100 *et passim*.

15. One source speculates that Greenway "saw in the platform of the Bull Moosers a means of achieving desirable pro-business reforms through the vehicle of government regulations" (Davies, p. 249).

16. Pelling, p. 117.

17. Albion G. Taylor, *Labor Policies of the National Association of Manufacturers* (Urbana: University of Illinois, 1928), p. 13; Dulles, p. 193.

18. "Employers' Organizations: A Survey," *International Labor Review*, Vol. VI, No. 6 (December 1922), p. 941.

19. Gordon S. Watkins, *Labor Problems* (New York: Thomas Y. Crowell Co., 1935); "Employers' Associations in the United States," *International Labour Review*, Vol. VIII, No. 3 (September 1923), pp. 367–79.

20. For an extensive discussion of the history of the Sherman Act and its use to legally control boycotts and strikes, see Louis B. Boudin, "The Sherman Act and Labor Disputes: II" *(Columbia Law Review*, Vol. XL, No. 1 [January, 1940], pp. 14–51).

21. Russell A. Smith, "Significant Developments in Labor Law During the Last Half-Century," *Michigan Law Review*, Vol. 50, No. 8 (June, 1952), p. 1267; Taft, p. 361.

22. "The Employers' I.W.W.," *The New Republic*, Vol. XI, No. 134 (May 26, 1917), pp. 98–99. This on the same day—March 12, 1917— that the AFofL declared a "patriotic truce."

23. Watkins, "Labor Problems ... ," Part I, p. 110; Joyce L. Kornbluh, *Rebel Voices: An I.W.W. Anthology* (Ann Arbor, 1964), p. 295; Bing, p. 225.

24. Soule, p. 226.

25. George W. P. Hunt, "The Strike Situation Reviewed" (file, "Clifton-Morenci Strike, 1915–16," Special Collections, University of Arizona Library), n.p.

26. "The Kaiser of Cochise," *Messenger* (in Hunt *Scrapbooks*, Vol. 22, Special Collections, University of Arizona Library, Tucson), n.d., n.p.

27. F. M. Murphy, "Thanks American Mining Congress for Arizona Work," letter published in *Mining Congress Journal*, Vol. I, No. 9 (September 1915), p. 443.

28. "American Institute of Mining Engineers to Meet in Arizona," *Mining Congress Journal*, Vol. II, No. 9 (September 1916), p. 414.

29. Charles F. Willis, "The Institute Meeting," *Mining and Scientific Press*, Vol. 113, October 7, 1916, p. 535.

30. "Nineteenth Annual Convention ... ," pp. 523–24.

31. Cover, *Mining Congress Journal*, Vol. II, No. 12 (December 1916).

32. "Nineteenth Annual Convention ... ," p. 534. For a brief history of the evolution of the American Mining Congress' conventions, see "American Mining Congress, Nineteen Years Old, Has Had Eventful Career" *(Mining Congress Journal*, Vol. II, No. 11 [November 1916], pp. 481–89).

33. *Mining Congress Journal*, Vol. 3, No. 1 (January 1917), *passim*; Martin, "The Douglas Dynasty," n.p.' "Nineteenth Annual Convention ... ," pp. 523–24.

34. "Arizona Chapter of Mining Congress Shows Long List of Achievements," *Mining Congress Journal*, Vol. III, No. 5 (May 1917), pp. 170–173.

35. *Ibid*.

36. "Editorial Comment," *Dunbar's Weekly*, Vol. IV, No. 36 (September 15, 1917), p. 7.

37. *Arizona Republican*, 1910–1917.

38. Management statement, *Arizona Daily Star*, April 1, 1916.

39. George W. P. Hunt, typewritten note on unidentified clipping of a newspaper editorial, "Arizona's Shame," October 5, 1915 (Hunt Scrapbooks, Special Collections, University of Arizona Library, Tucson), n.p. An article appeared in *Bisbee Daily Review* on April 1, 1948, observing the fiftieth anniversary of the paper. Written by Editor Folsom Moore, the article confirmed Phelps Dodge ownership, at one time or another over the years, of the *Star*, the *International*, the *Dispatch* and the *Review*. (*Bisbee Daily Review*, April 1, 1948, pp. 1–3.) See also Ferdinand Lundberg, *America's Sixty Families* (New York: The Vanguard Press, 1937), p. 274, on this. Hunt, himself, received support in 1916 from out-of-state newspapers throughout the nation. Among them: *The San Diego Sun*, *The San Francisco Daily News*, *The Denver Labor Bulletin*, *The Kansas City Post*, *Des Moines News*, *Women's National Weekly*, *Worcester Evening Post* and *The Milwaukee Leader*. (Hunt *Scrapbooks*, *passim*.)

40. *Dunbar's Weekly*, Vol. 4, Nos. 28 and 29 (July 21 and 28, 1917), p. 2. Ned Creighton, letter to *Santa Cruz Patagonian*, October 22, 1915 (file, "Clifton-Morenci Strike, 1915–16," Special Collections, University of Arizona Library, Tucson).

41. "Editorials," *Dunbar's Weekly*, Vol. IV, No. 27 (July 14, 1917), p. 1; Hunt, "So the People ... ," p. 10.

42. "A Strike Without Disorder," p. 305.

43. W. Douglas, "The Arizona Strike," p. 186.

44. Ned Creighton, copy of letter sent to Arizona newspapers, October 15–16, 1915 (file, "Clifton-Morenci Strike, 1915–16," Special Collections, University of Arizona Library, Tucson).

45. N. Creighton to *Santa Cruz Patagonian*, Oct. 22, 1915.

46. *Copper Era*, April 14, 1916, p. 1.

47. Ernest Douglas, "'Douglas' Review of Clifton Strike," *Arizona Republican*, November 1, 1915, p. 10; *Jerome News*, 1916–17.

48. "Branding a Liar and Issuing a Challenge," *Dunbar's Weekly*, Vol. III, No. 23 (June 10, 1916), p. 2.

49. "Editorial Comment," *Dunbar's Weekly*, Vol. III, No. 28 (July 15, 1916), p. 3.

50. "Arizona Chapter of Mining Congress Shows ... ," p. 171.

51. *Ibid*.

52. *Mining Congress Journal*, 1917–19.

53. "The Mining News," *Engineering and Mining Journal*, Vol. 99, No. 6 (February 6, 1915), p. 300.

54. "Those Copper Quotations," *Mining and Scientific Press*, Vol. 113, October 14, 1916, p. 550.

55. *Ibid.*, "Copper Quotations," *Mining and Scientific Press*, Vol. 113, September 30, 1916, pp. 482–83; Editorial, *Arizona Silver Belt*, September 18, 1916, p. 4; Harold Callender, "True Facts About Bisbee" (Report published by the National Labor Defense Council), *Dunbar's Weekly*, Vol. 14, No. 36 (September 15, 1917), p. 10; "Editorials," *Dunbar's Weekly*, Vol. IV, No. 27 (July 14, 1917), p. 1.

56. "Copper Questions," pp. 482–83. Not for several years did a representative of the small mine operators speak up. See Ben Heney, "The Trust Price of Copper" (*Mining and Scientific Press*, Vol. 118, February 22, 1919, pp. 241–42).

57. The *Bisbee Daily Review* originally published the letter, and then newspapers such as the *Arizona Silver Belt* picked it up.

58. *Arizona Silver Belt*, August 18, 1916, p. 2.

59. "Copper Quotations," p. 483.

60. "Those Copper Quotations," p. 550.

61. Phelps Dodge did not possess a record clear of this kind of alleged legerdemain. The United States government sued the company for $1,000,000 in the early 1870s for defrauding United States Customs. By casting zinc and lead into thousands of crude Dianas and Venuses and Mercurys in Europe, Phelps Dodge imported them as "works of art" and enjoyed a reduced tariff rate. Once in the United States, the disguised ingots were melted and sold as regular metal bars. The scandal was well publicized and the evidence overwhelming, but Phelps Dodge settled out of court for $271,017.23. (Gustavus Myers, *History of the Great American Fortunes* [New York: Random House, Inc., 1909] pp. 428–31.)

62. Carl A. Bimson, *Transformation in the Desert* (New York: pamphlet published by the Newcomer Society, 1962, address delivered at a banquet in Phoenix, March 20, 1962), p. 12.

63. Alice Hamilton, *Exploring the Dangerous Trades* (Boston: Little, Brown and Company, 1943), pp. 210–211.

64. W. K. Meade to atty. gen., Dec. 7, 1917.

65. "Arizona Chapter of Mining Congress Shows . . . ," p. 172.

66. LDS members usually supported corporate policy enthusiastically.

67. See pp. 99 and 349 (note 10) on Phelps Dodge anti-Semitism.

68. A. Hamilton, p. 211.

69. Bishop William Scarlett, letter to H. S. McCluskey, June 28, 1963 (McCluskey Papers, Special Collections, Arizona State University, Tempe). In an earlier letter, Bishop Scarlett wrote McCluskey: "Mac, I

have often thought that some day I would write up the story behind the Bisbee deportation. I think it has never been done properly and yet it is a bit of valuable American history. I probably will be sued if I do this, but that is all right, too. They threatened to do that before! Have you any material on that in the form of papers of that date. My file seems to have disappeared and I suspect the Phelps-Dodge Corporation!" (Bishop William Scarlett, letter to H. S. McCluskey, January 8, 1953 [McCluskey Papers].)

70. *Biennial Report of the State Tax Commission of Arizona*, 1913–18.

71. Edward Levinson, *I Break Strikes! The Technique of Pearl L. Bergoff* (New York: Robert McBride and Company, 1935), *passim*; and Louis Adamic, *Dynamite: The Story of Class Violence in America* (New York: The Viking Press, 1935), p. 97.

72. Levinson, p. 235.

73. H. Young, Dec. 20, 1966; McCluskey, April 21, 1966.

74. Robert W. Bruere, "The Industrial Workers of the World," *Harper's Magazine*, Vol. CXXXVII, No. DCCCXVIII (July 1918), pp. 250–57.

75. Robert Reill, *Copper Mine Strikes in 1917, Globe, Arizona* (typed statement, n.d., No. 57, Harwood Hinton files, University of Arizona).

76. Soule, p. 220.

77. *Bisbee Daily Review*, July 1, 1917, p. 4.

78. Jensen, p. 400; William Holther, testimony, *Abstract . . . , Hunt v. Campbell*.

79. McCluskey, April 21, 1966; Joseph Oates, letter to Grover Perry, July 6, 1917 (*Simmons v. El Paso & Southwestern R.R., et al.*).

80. John H. Lindquist, "The Jerome Deportation of 1917," *Arizona and the West*, Vol. XI, No. 3 (Autumn 1969), p. 244.

81. G. Myers, p. 352.

82. Frank Donner, "The Theory and Practice of American Political Intelligence," *New York Review of Books*, Vol. XVI, No. 7 (April 22, 1971), pp. 27–39; Levinson, p. 233.

83. Levinson, p. 233.

84. Jensen, *passim*; Edward Massey, testimony in "Transcript . . . taken . . . at Bisbee . . . ," p. 58.

85. Bruere, "The IWW," p. 255.

86. Carlos Aldai and others, affidavits dated June, July, September, 1918 (McCluskey Papers).

87. Campbell, "The I.W.W. in Arizona," n.p.

88. "Operatives" reports, August 1917 (UVCC files).

89. Robert Bruere quoted in John S. Gambs, *The Decline of the I.W.W.* (New York: Columbia University Press, 1932), p. 44.

90. G. Watkins, "Labor Problems . . . ," Part I, p. 110.

91. Kornbluh, p. 292.

92. *Ibid.*; Brissenden, "The Butte Miners . . . ," p. 757.

Chapter 5: The Illusion of Change

1. Foster Rhea Dulles, *Labor in America* (New York: Thomas Y. Crowell, 1949), pp. 184–88; Henry Demerest Lloyd, "Lords of Industry," *North American Review*, Vol. CXXXVIII, No. 331 (June 1884), p. 552.

2. The degree to which this effort succeeded is a growing historical debate. See Gabriel Kolko, *The Triumph of Conservatism* (New York: The MacMillan Company, 1963), a revisionist work as opposed to such standard accounts of the period as Harold U. Faulkner, *The Decline of Laissez Faire: 1897–1917* (New York: Rinehart & Company, Inc., 1952).

3. Richard O. Boyer and Herbert M. Morais, *Labor's Untold Story* (New York: Cameron Associates, 1955), p. 180.

4. Aaron I. Abell, "Labor Legislation in the United States," *Review of Politics*, Vol. X, No. 1 (January 1948), pp. 35–60.

5. Karson, *American Labor Unions . . .* , pp. 280–91.

6. See W. Y. Elliott, "The Political Application of Romanticism" (*Political Science Quarterly*, Vol. 39, No. 2 [June 1924], pp. 234–64) for a comment on the political use of Sorel's syndicalism. For a study of the socialist and radical influences in the American labor movement, see John H. Laslett, *Labor and the Left* (New York: Basic Books, Inc., 1970), and Robert Hunter, *Violence and the Labor Movement* (New York: The MacMillan Company, 1914).

7. Selig Perlman, *A History of Trade Unionism in the United States* (New York: The MacMillan Company, 1922), p. 266. For an example of the tortuous and painful rhetoric and rationale of the labor theorists of the period see Selig Perlman, *A Theory of the Labor Movement* (New York: Augustus M. Kelly, 1928). For a later survey of the academics of labor theory see Mark Perlman, *Labor Union Theories in America* (Evanston, Illinois: Row, Peterson & Co., 1958).

8. See Harvey Goldberg, ed., *American Radicals: Some Problems and Personalities* (New York: Monthly Review Press, 1957).

9. This nickname has a multiple speculative etymology. On this see Fred Thompson, *The I.W.W.: Its First Fifty Years* (Chicago: Industrial Workers of the World, 1955), p. 66. For other comment and an IWW glossary see Stuart H. Holbrook, "Wobbly Talk" (*American Mercury*, Vol. VII, No. 25 [January 1926], pp. 62–65.) Another good dictionary of IWW vernacular can be found in Kornbluh, pp. 405–08.

10. John Spargo, "Why the I.W.W. Flourishes," *World's Work*, Vol. XXXIX, No. 3 (January 1920), pp. 243–47.

11. Robert L. Tyler, "The I.W.W. and the West," *American Quarterly*, Vol. XII, No. 2 (Summer 1960), pp. 185–87. Also ironical is the fact that those rare situations where the IWW gained some recognition were not in the West, but in Massachusetts and New Jersey. For an

analysis of the contradictions, fluctuations, ideology, effectiveness and directions of "radical" unionism, see Sidney Lens, *Left, Right & Center* (Hinsdale, Illinois: Henry Regnery Company, 1949).

Most historians of the IWW recognize the ephemeral and futile nature of the IWW. Some emphasize that the glamour of its reputation was (and is) derived from the fact that it has become part of the "Western myth." (Louis Levine, "The Development of Syndicalism in America," *Political Science Quarterly*, Vol. XXVII, No. 3 [September 1913], pp. 451–79.) For bibliography of IWW see Eldridge Foster Dowell, "A History of Criminal Syndicalism Legislation in the United States" (*The Johns Hopkins University Studies in Historical and Political Science*, Vol. LVII, No. 1 [1939]), and Kornbluh, pp. 409–19. Other accounts include Brissenden; Gambs; John Graham Brooks, *American Syndicalism: The I.W.W.* (New York: The MacMillan Company, 1913); Robert L. Tyler, *Rebels of the Woods: The I.W.W. in the Pacific Northwest* (Eugene: University of Oregon, 1967); and Bruere, "The Industrial Workers of the World."

12. Brissenden, *The I.W.W. . . .* , pp. 57–65.

13. *Ibid.*, pp. 32–37.

14. Dulles, p. 219.

15. *Ibid.*, p. 209.

16. Brissenden, *The I.W.W. . . .* ; Dubofsky, *We Shall Be All; passim*. The best account and analysis of the radical labor movement in the West is found in Dubofsky, "The Origins of Western Working Class Radicalism."

17. Brissenden, *The I.W.W. . . .* , pp. 55–57, 105–06.

18. Kornbluh, pp. 290–91.

19. G. Watkins, *Labor Problems*, p. 434.

20. Brissenden, *The I.W.W. . . .* , p. 83.

21. Quoted in J. Brooks, *Amer. Syndicalism*: . . . , p. 82.

22. Brissenden, *The I.W.W. . . .* , pp. 85, 416–17.

23. Taft, pp. 322–23; Patrick Renshaw, *The Wobblies* (Garden City, New York: Doubleday & Company, Inc., 1967), pp. 58–62.

24. Renshaw, pp. 278–82. See David J. Saposs, *Left Wing Unionism* (New York: Russell & Russell, 1926), on dual unionism and "boring from within" technique.

25. Brissenden, *The I.W.W. . . .* , p. 282. Young radical Walter Lippmann provided, in 1913, a sympathetic attempt to put the IWW in some acceptable Socialistic perspective. (Walter Lippmann, "The I.W.W. — Insurrection or Revolution?" [*New Review*, Vol. I, No. 19 (August 1913), pp. 706–07].)

26. Renshaw, pp. 156, 164.

27. For the frontier character of IWW see J. Brooks, *Amer. Syndicalism*: . . . , Preface.

28. Renshaw, pp. 265–70.

29. *Ibid.*, p. 269.

30. For a description of the more adventurous "advance guard of revolutionary unionism" see Levine, "The Development..."

31. *Post-Intelligencer* cited in "The I.W.W. Develops into a National Menace" (*Current Opinion*, Vol. LXIII, No. 3 [September 1917], p. 154).

32. Renshaw, *passim*; Anderson, *passim*; Bruere, "The Industrial Workers of the World," pp. 250–57.

33. George W. Pierson, "A Restless Temper ... ," *American Historical Review*, Vol. LXIX, No. 4 (July 1964), pp. 969–89.

34. Carleton H. Parker, "The I.W.W.," *Atlantic Monthly*, Vol. CXX (November 1917), pp. 654–56.

35. Bruere, "The Industrial Workers of the World," p. 250.

36. John Graham Brooks, *Labor's Challenge to the Social Order* (New York: The MacMillan Co., 1920), pp. 362, 393.

37. Several sympathetic, patronizing accounts of this "hobo" nature of the western IWW appeared at the time. The compassion and sensitivity of their genteel, Progressive authors failed to compensate for the articles' weaknesses. All of the accounts were somewhat detached and superficial; each failed to articulate the grim futility of the situation. Perhaps this failure was explained by one of the writers who said: "It is extremely difficult for the ordinary, respectable, conventional type of individual to understand this class of men." Charles H. Forster, "Despised and Rejected Men: Hoboes of the Pacific Coast" (*Survey*, Vol. XXXIII, No. 25 [March 20, 1915], pp. 671–72). Peter Alexander Speek, "The Psychology of Floating Workers" (*Annals of the American Academy of Political and Social Science*, Vol. LXIX, No. 69 [January 1917], pp. 72–78), and Leon Stern, "The Drifters" (*Survey*, Vol. XXI, No. 5 [November 1, 1913], pp. 136–138), are two other examples. Carleton H. Parker was a glaring exception. For a detailed, personal account of a classic drifter, see Alfred Kendrick's testimony, *Original Blanket Hearings*, Book 2, Justice Court of Precinct No. 4, Douglas, Arizona, July-September 1919, pp. 322–24.

38. Industrial Workers of the World, *Proceedings of Tenth Convention* (Chicago, Illinois, November, 1916), pp. 61, 99.

39. Walter E. Weyl, "The Strikers at Lawrence," *Outlook*, Vol. 100, February 10, 1912, pp. 309–12; Robert F. Hoxie, "The Truth About the I.W.W.," *Journal of Political Economy*, Vol. 21, No. 9 (November 1913), p. 797.

40. Levine, "The Development ... ," pp. 451–79.

41. John A. Fitch, "Baiting the I.W.W.," *Survey*, Vol. XXXIII, No. 23 (March 6, 1915), pp. 634–35.

42. Brissenden, *The I.W.W.* ... , p. 9; G. Watkins, *Labor Problems*, p. 434; C. Parker, "The I.W.W.," p. 651.

43. Ralph Chaplin, *Wobbly* (Chicago: University of Chicago Press, 1948), p. 203. For examples of the impressions of the IWW as reflected in the press, see Dowell, "A History of Criminal Syndicalism ... ," pp. 40–43.

44. Ole Hanson, *Americanism vs. Bolshevism* (New York: Doubleday, 1920), p. ix. For an example of extreme hate literature, see Joseph J. Mereto, *The Red Conspiracy* (New York: The National Historical Society, 1920), and T. Everett Harre, *The I.W.W.: An Auxiliary of the German Espionage System* (pamphlet, no place, no publisher, 1918).

45. C. Parker, "The I.W.W.," pp. 651–62.

46. Walter V. Woehlke, "The I.W.W.," *Outlook*, Vol. 101, July 6, 1912, pp. 531–36.

47. Hoxie, "The Truth . . . ," p. 785.

48. G. Watkins, *Labor Problems*, p. 428. In 1917 the AFofL had 2,350,000 members; the IWW had 60,000 members. (*Ibid*.)

49. Hoxie, "The Truth . . . " p. 797.

50. J. Brooks, *Amer. Syndicalism*: . . . , p. 250.

51. Pelling, p. 112.

52. Brissenden, *The I.W.W.* . . . , p. 264.

53. *Ibid.*, p. 9.

54. *Ibid.*, p. 11.

55. Harvey Duff, *The Silent Defenders, Courts and Capitalism in California* (Chicago: Industrial Workers of the World, pamphlet, no date), pp. 8, 12.

56. *Bisbee Daily Review*, July 13, 1917, p. 2.

57. Gambs, pp. 81–82.

58. Philip Taft, "The Federal Trials of the I.W.W.," *Labor History*, Vol. III, No. 1 (Winter 1962), p. 42.

59. William D. Haywood, *Bill Haywood's Book* (New York: International Publishers, 1929), pp. 294–95.

60. U.S., Congress, Senate, Senator Thomas, *Congressional Record*, Sixty-fifth Congress, First Session, June 28, 1917, Vol. LV, Part 5, p. 4395.

61. Bisbee IWW minutes quoted in Samuel Morse, *The Truth About Bisbee* (typewritten manuscript, 1929), p. 3, which appeared in Jerome A. Vaughan, "All Women and Children Keep Off Streets Today" (typescript article, Arizona Pioneers' Historical Society, n.d.), p. 4.

62. I.W.W., *Proceedings of Tenth* . . . , pp. 42–43.

63. Chaplin, p. 206.

64. Samuel P. Orth, *The Armies of Labor* (New Haven: Yale University Press, 1919), p. 215; Frank Little, telegram to Bill Haywood, April 10, 1917 (*Simmons v. El Paso & Southwestern R.R., et al.*).

65. *Solidarity*, April 21, 1917.

66. Gambs, p. 43.

67. Orth, p. 219; Lewis Allen Browne, "Bolshevism in America," *Forum*, Vol. 59, June 1918, pp. 703–17; Gambs, p. 43.

68. Renshaw, p. 269.

69. U.S., Congress, House, Rep. Gard, *Congressional Record*, Sixty-fifth Cong., First Session, April 11, 1917, Vol. LV, p. 610; Brissenden, *The I.W.W.* . . . , p. 347.

70. William Preston, Jr., *Aliens and Dissenters* (New York: Harper & Row, 1963), p. 123.

71. H. C. Peterson, *Propaganda for War* (Norman: University of Oklahoma Press, 1939), pp. 163, 324; U.S., Congress, House, Rep. Johnson, *Congressional Record*, Sixty-fifth Congress, First Session, June 25, 1917, Vol. LV, Part 8, Appendix, p. 594; U.S., Congress, Senate, Sen. Ashurst, *Congressional Record*, Sixty-fifth Congress, First Session, August 17, 1917, Vol. LV, p. 6104.

72. "Organization or Anarchy," p. 321.

73. Gov. Stewart quoted in "The Week," *Nation*, Vol. 105, No. 2721 (August 23, 1917), p.191.

74. "Bills Drafted to Curb the I.W.W.," *Survey*, Vol. 38, No. 21 (August 25, 1917), pp. 457–58.

75. Preston, pp. 98–99; Gambs, pp. 52–53.

76. Walter V. Woehlke, "The I.W.W. and the Golden Rule," *Sunset*, Vol. 38, February 1917, p. 65.

77. Walter V. Woehlke, "The Red Rebels Declare War," *Sunset*, Vol. 39, September 1917, pp. 20, 75.

78. "Raiding the I.W.W.," *Literary Digest*, Vol. LV, No. 12 (September 22, 1917), p. 17.

79. Will L. Clark, letter to Walter Douglas, July 22, 1911 (UVCC files).

80. Bing, pp. 53, 241.

81. Jensen, pp. 378–80.

82. Fred Brown, "Transcript of the Testimony Taken Before the President's Mediation Commission at Bisbee, Arizona, November 1–4, 1917" (Record Group 174, General Records of the Department of Labor), pp. 24–30.

83. Jensen, p. 380.

84. McCluskey, April 21, 1966; Kornbluh, p. 293.

85. Renshaw, pp. 176–79.

86. Jensen, pp. 373–74; retired Phelps Dodge executives "X" and "Y."

87. Jensen, pp. 374–76.

88. Grover H. Perry, letter to William D. Haywood, February 2, 1917 (*Simmons v. El Paso & Southwestern R.R.* exhibits, Special Collections, University of Arizona Library, Tucson); Metal Mine Workers Industrial Union #800 (I.W.W.), *Bulletin Number One*, Phoenix, Arizona, February 24, 1917, and *Bulletin Number Two*, April 4, 1917 (Department of Justice files).

89. Jensen, pp. 379, 424.

90. Writers' Program ... , p. 98; Jensen, pp. 379–424.

91. "Labor Unrest in the Southwest," *Survey*, Vol. 38, No. 19 (August 11, 1917), p. 429.

92. Editorial, "A Piece of Corporate Depravity," *Jerome Sun*, February 9, 1918, p. 2.

93. This source corroborates contemporary reports. (F. Thompson, *The I.W.W.* ... , p. 118; *Jerome Sun*, May 28, 1917, p. 3.)

94. Cleland, pp. 110–11; Bruere, "Copper Camp Patriotism," p. 203.

95. Bill Cleary, statement at Hermanas, July 13, 1917 (*New York Times*, July 14, 1917).

96. Glisio Chukovich, taped interview, Harwood Hinton Collection.

97. John H. Walker, "Transcript ... of Testimony Taken ... at Bisbee ... ," p. 545.

98. Jensen, pp. 381–410.

Chapter 6: Moving Toward a Showdown

1. B. S. Rountree, "Labour Unrest," *Contemporary Review*, Vol. CXII, October 1917, pp. 368–79.

2. *Ibid.*, pp. 373–374.

3. G. Watkins, "Labor Problems ... ," p. 105.

4. F. Harcourt Kitchins, "The Troubles and Desires of Labour," *Fortnightly Review*, Vol. CII, No. DCX (October 1, 1917), pp. 582, 583.

5. G. Watkins, "Labor Problems ... ," pp. 111, 117.

6. Irving Bernstein, "Growth of American Unions," *American Economic Review*, Vol. XLIV, No. 3 (June 1954), pp. 302–09; Dulles, p. 224; "Strikes and Lockouts in the United States, 1916 to 1927," *Monthly Labor Review*, Vol. 27, No. 1 (July 1928), pp. 82–96.

7. Bing, p. 6; Pelling, p. 104.

8. "American Labor in ... ," p. 794; G. Watkins, "Labor Problems ...," pp. 104–05.

9. "Strikes and Lockouts ... ," pp. 84, 89; Bing, p. 265; G. Watkins, "Labor Problems ... ," p. 80.

10. "Deportations from Bisbee and a Resume of Other Troubles in Arizona." Reprinted in "The Arizona Strike," *Arizona Mining Journal*, Vol. I, No. 2 (August 1917), p. 7; Campbell, "The I.W.W. in Arizona," n.p.

11. *Bisbee Daily Review*, July 1–6, 1917; *New York Times*, June 27–July 6, 1917; *Los Angeles Times*, June 27–July 6, 1917; Jensen, pp. 389–400.

12. *Ibid.*

13. *Los Angeles Times*, July 4, 1917, p. 1; "Demands of Metal Mine Workers' Industrial Union No. 800" from "Transcript of the Testimony Taken Before the President's Mediation Commission at Bisbee, Arizona, November 1–4, 1917" (Record Group 174, General Records of the Department of Labor), pp. 351–52.

14. "The Strike at Jerome," *Arizona Mining Journal*, Vol. I, No. 1 (June 1917), p. 6. This turned out to be a foolish point of view for the new magazine. It soon complained of being boycotted by most of the big mining companies. Not much later its tone became more politic and changed to a strong support of the mine owners.

15. *New York Times*, July 1–14, 1917; *Ibid.*, July 12, 1917, p. 5.

16. *Bisbee Daily Review*, July 1, 1917, p. 1.

17. *Los Angeles Times*, July 1, 1917, p. 4.

18. *New York Times*, July 1, 1917, p. 17.

19. *Bisbee Daily Review*, July 3, 1917, p. 4.

20. G. Watkins, "Labor Problems ... ," p. 30.

21. Taft, *Organized Labor*, p. 327.

22. Robinson, p. 291.

23. *Bisbee Daily Review*, July 5, 1917, ed., p. 4; Soule, p. 226; Brissenden, "The Butte Miners ... ," p. 772. For an excellent article on propaganda, public opinion and the restriction of liberties in World War I, see O. A. Hilton, "Public Opinion and Civil Liberties in Wartime, 1917–1919" (*Southwestern Social Science Quarterly*, Vol. XXVIII, No. 3 [December 1947]), pp. 201–24.

24. Taft, *Organized Labor*, p. 310; Anthony Bimba, *The History of the American Working Class* (New York: Greenwood Press, Publishers, 1968), *passim*; "A Program for Labor," *New Republic*, Vol. X, No. 128 (April 14, 1917), pp. 312–13.

25. Jensen, p. 384. For labor's eventual pledge to cooperate, see Roland Hill Harvey, *Samuel Gompers, Champion of the Toiling Masses* (Stanford, California: Stanford University Press, 1935), pp. 220–22.

26. Preston, p. 93.

27. U.S., Department of Labor, Secretary of Labor and Bureaus, *Sixth Annual Report of the Secretary of Labor, 1918* (Washington, D.C.: Government Printing Office, 1918), p. 26; Gambs, p. 44.

28. Preston, p. 113.

29. Taft, *Organized Labor*, p. xvi.

30. Retired Phelps Dodge officials "X" and "Y".

31. Fitch, "Baiting the I.W.W.," p. 634.

32. Brissenden, *The I.W.W.* ... , p. 321.

33. Kornbluh, pp. 295–296.

34. Brissenden, "The Butte Miners ... ," p. 769; Jensen, p. 424; Sec. of Labor, *Sixth Annual Report* ... , p. 26.

35. U.S. Committee on Public Information, "Report of President Wilson's Mediation Commission on the Bisbee, Arizona, Deportations, Including its Recommendations as Made on Findings of Facts," *Official Bulletin*, Vol. I, No. 170 (November 27, 1917), pp. 6–7.

36. For early Jerome labor history see J. Carl Brogden, *The History of Jerome, Arizona* (M.A. thesis, University of Arizona, 1952). For a more intimate popular account of Jerome's personalities, see Herbert V. Young's *Ghosts of Cleopatra Hill*.

37. T. A. Rickard, "The Story of the U.V.X. Bonanza—I," *Mining and Scientific Press*, Vol. 116, January 5, 1918, pp. 9–11; Cleland, p. 238; H. Young, p. 5. For an early map with descriptions and locations of Jerome claims see John F. Blandy, "The Mining Region Around Prescott, Arizona" (*Transactions, American Institute of Mining Engineers*, Vol. XI, February 1883, p. 290).

38. However, Phelps Dodge eventually obtained this mine. In 1935, taking advantage of the ignorance and doubt about the depression-devalued mining property, Phelps Dodge bought out the Clark heirs. The mine eventually closed in 1953, and today the skeleton of Jerome creaks along as a commercial "ghost town." Over a period of seventy years the mine produced more than a billion dollars worth of copper, gold and silver. (H. Young, *passim*.)

39. H. Young, p. 6; Cleland, pp. 238–39.

40. Joseph D. Cannon, letter to Charles H. Moyer, July 5, 1909 (H. S. McCluskey papers, Special Collections, Arizona State University Library, Tempe); Jensen, p. 361.

41. Richter, "The Copper Mining Industry ... ," p. 283; Rickard, "The Story of ... ," pp. 9–17.

42. Jensen, p. 391; "The Jerome Strike," *Arizona Mining Journal*, Vol. I, No. 1 (June, 1917), p. 16. Two "votes" were taken. The election at IUMMSW headquarters registered 545 to 25 in favor of the strike. But some United Verde employees were polled that same day as they received their paychecks. The result was announced as 767 against striking and 445 for.

43. Jensen, pp. 383–84, 387, 388, 391. McCluskey never ascertained the specific motives of the men who kidnapped him. Neither did he learn the identity of those who ordered his abduction. (H. S. McCluskey to J. Byrkit, April 21, 1966.)

44. "Report of Proceedings of Meeting Held by Committee Representing Jerome Miners' Union and Mr. W. A. Burns with Mr. R. E. Tally Regarding Demands Made by the Union Against the United Verde Copper Company," May 23, 1917, n.p. (UVCC files).

45. Jensen, p. 385.

46. "Report of Proceedings ... ," n.p.

47. *Ibid*; Robert E. Tally, "The Labor Situation of the United Verde," n.d., n.p. (UVCC files).

48. "The Jerome Strike," p. 16.

49. *Ibid*.; Jensen, pp. 383–90.

50. *Jerome Sun*, February 9, 1918, p. 2.

51. "The Jerome Strike," p. 10; *Jerome Sun*, May 28, 1917, p. 3; Jensen, pp. 388–390.

52. *Jerome Sun*, May 28, 1917, p. 4.

53. Robert E. Tally, letter to John G. McBride, May 31, 1917 (copy in UVCC files).

54. "The Jerome Strike," p. 16.

55. Jensen, pp. 391–92; Fred Watson interview, July 19, 1972.

56. Helen Marot, *American Labor Unions* (New York, Henry Holt and Company, 1914), p. 261.

57. Callender, "True Facts About Bisbee," p. 10.

58. Bulletin from Grover Perry, June 1, 1917 (*Simmons v. El Paso & Southwestern* exhibits, Special Collections, University of Arizona).

59. Jensen, pp. 400–03; Grover Perry, telegram to William Haywood, June 25, 1917 (*Simmons v. El Paso and Southwestern* exhibits, Special Collections, University of Arizona).

60. "Demands of Metal Mine Workers' . . . ," pp. 351–52.

61. *Los Angeles Times*, July 4, 1917, p. 1; Grover Perry, letter to Bisbee Executive Committee, July 10, 1917 (*Simmons v. El Paso & Southwestern* exhibits, Special Collections, University of Arizona).

62. "Preliminary Hearings of Defendants in the Bisbee Deportation Trials," *Individual Transcripts*, Book 1, p. 18 (Arizona, Justice Court [Cochise Co. Precinct No. 4]); Jensen, pp. 401–03.

63. *New York Times*, June 29, 1917, p. 17.

64. *Ibid.*, July 1, 1917, p. 3.

65. *Ibid.*, June 29, p. 17, July 1, 1917, p. 3.

66. Letter from copper securities brokerage firm Chas. A. Stoneham & Co. quoted in *New York Times*, July 1, 1917, p. 11.

67. *Bisbee Daily Review*, July 1–4, 1917; Jensen, pp. 404–405; *Los Angeles Times*, June 27–July 4, 1917; *New York Times*, June 27–July 4, 1917; William S. Beeman, *History of the Bisbee Deportation by an Officer in Charge of the Loyalty League*, Unpublished Manuscript, Arizona Law Library and Archives, Phoenix, 1940; Soule, p. 226; Samuel Morse, *The Truth About Bisbee*, Typescript in Arizona Historical Society, Tucson, Arizona, n.d.; Cleland, pp. 197–98.

68. *Bisbee Daily Review*, July 1, 1917, p. 1. "At any cost" was to appear, with a number of variations, in the language of the *Review* for the next few weeks.

69. Ed., "In the Trenches," *Ibid.* and ed., p. 4.

70. William Curnow, *Ind. Trans.*, Book 1, pp. 32–34.

71. *Bisbee Daily Review*, July 1, 1917, p. 2.

72. *Ibid.*, sect. 2, p. 4.

73. *Ibid.*, p. 3.

74. *Ibid.*, April 1, 1948, p. 2.

75. *Los Angeles Times*, July 2, 1917, p. 1.

76. *Ibid.*, July 3, 1917, p. 4; "Recapitulation of Daily Labor Output," "Transcript . . . Taken . . . at Bisbee," pp. 289–90.

77. *Bisbee Daily Review*, July 1, 1917, sect. 2, p. 5.

78. T. E. Campbell, "The I.W.W. in Arizona," n.p.; Bruere, "Copper Camp Patriotism," Feb. 21, p. 203.

79. T. E. Campbell, "The I.W.W. in Arizona," n.p.

80. Lt. Col. James J. Hornbrook, telegrams to adjutant general, June 30, July 1, 3, 5, 1917 (War Department files A.G. 370.61, in Department of Justice files).

81. Affidavits in "Transcript . . . Taken . . . at Bisbee," pp. 358–67.

82. *Bisbee Daily Review*, June 26–July 12, 1917.

83. *Ibid.*, July 3, 1917, p. 1.

84. *Ibid.*, July 12, 1917, p. 1; J. G. Berlindis, taped interview, Harwood Hinton Collection; Erving, Hinton tapes.

85. Perhaps the people of Bisbee had a rather histrionic sense of conflict. The *Review* carried a story on July 3 about an incident in Globe. The headline read "American Brutally Beaten By Mob of Alien Enemies," and the story, lacking considerably in detail, went on to reveal that the man's "face was slightly cut before he escaped." He must have been a very tough fellow to survive such an ordeal with so little evidence. Here was a good example of over-reaction and hyperbolic headlining. (*Bisbee Daily Review*, July 3, 1917, p. 1.)

86. *Ibid.*, July 4, 1917, p. 1.

87. *Los Angeles Times*, July 4, 1917, p. 1.

88. *Bisbee Daily Review*, July 3, 1917, p. 1. Reciprocity as well as the miners' sense of community loyalty was involved here. See page 31. (Jensen, p. 360.)

89. *Bisbee Daily Review*, July 5, 1917, p. 1.

90. Bruere, "Copper Camp Patriotism," Feb. 21, 1918, p. 203.

91. *Bisbee Daily Review*, July 3, 1917, p. 2; *Los Angeles Times*, July 4, 1917, p. 1; *Bisbee Daily Review*, July 5, 1917, p. 1.

92. Jensen, p. 401; *Bisbee Daily Review*, July 3, 1917, p. 2; Cleland, p. 179.

93. *Bisbee Daily Review*, July 6, 1917, p. 1.

94. Frank H. Little and William Haywood, telegram to A. D. Kimball, July 6, 1917 (*Simmons v. El Paso & Southwestern* exhibits); *Bisbee Daily Review*, July 6, 1917, ed., p. 4; July 8, 1917, sect. 2, p. 5 and sect. 1, p. 1.

95. *Bisbee Daily Review*, July 11, 1917, pp. 1, 4.

96. *Ibid.*, July 7, p. 4.

97. Robert Tally, letter appearing in "The Arizona Strike," *Arizona Mining Journal*, Vol. 1, No. 2 (August 1917), p. 2.

98. *New York Times*, July 7, 1917, p. 1.

99. Herbert V. Young, "The Jerome Deportations of 1917" (typescript in J. Byrkit files), n.d., p. 2.

100. *Jerome Sun*, July 10, 1917, p. 1.

101. H. V. Young, "The Jerome . . . ," pp. 2, 4, 5.

102. *Jerome Sun*, July 10, 1917, p. 1.

103. *Ibid.*

104. H. V. Young, "The Jerome . . . ," pp. 6–8.

105. *Jerome Sun*, July 10, 1917, p. 1.

106. *Ibid.* "Red" Thompson, in Bill Haywood's words, "was a splendid specimen of manhood with mind clear as a bell." Haywood stated in his autobiography that Thompson's portrait hung in the hall of the Irish Workers in Dublin. In 1918 Thompson, along with Haywood and others, was a defendant in the famous Chicago IWW trial. Judged guilty on four counts, he was sentenced to twenty-eight years in federal prison and a $30,000 fine. (Haywood, pp. 320, 321, 368.)

107. *Jerome Sun*, July 10, 1917, p. 2.

108. H. V. Young, "The Jerome ... ," pp. 7–9.

109. *Verde Copper News*, July 10, 1917, p. 1; July 11, 1917, p. 1; Lindquist, "The Jerome Deportation ... ," pp. 242–44.

110. Robert Bruere, *Following the Trail of the IWW*, pamphlet published by *New York Evening Post*, 1918, p. 12.

111. *Verde Copper News*, July 12, 1917, p. 1; Lindquist, p. 244; *New York Times*, July 11, 1917, p. 18.

112. Bruere, *Following the Trail ...* , p. 12.

113. H. V. Young, "The Jerome ... ," p. 15; Lindquist, "The Jerome Deportation ... ," p. 244; Bruere, *Following the Trail ...* , p. 12; *New York Times*, July 11, 1917, p. 18.

114. Operative #13, "Complimentary Report re: I.W.W. Matters," July 30, 1917 (UVCC files). H. V. Young, "The Jerome ... ," pp. 15–16; Lindquist, "The Jerome Deportations ... ," p. 244; Thomas A. Flynn, letter to United States Attorney General, August 6, 1917 (Department of Justice files).

115. Telegrams quoted in Bruere, *Following the Trail ...* , p. 12.

116. Miami and Globe Branches, Industrial Union No. 800, I.W.W., telegram to President Wilson, July 11, 1917 (copy in Department of Justice files, 186813-4.)

117. "The Arizona Copper Strike," *Outlook*, Vol. 116, No. 13 (June 25, 1917), p. 466.

118. *Bisbee Daily Review*, July 11, 1917, p. 1.

119. *El Paso Times* quoted in Bing, p. 265. For the "spontaneity" and "local" nature of vigilantism, see John Caughey, *Their Majesties, the Mob* (Chicago: University of Chicago Press, 1960). For general narrative on the vigilante tradition, see Wayne Gard, *Frontier Justice* (Norman: University of Oklahoma Press, 1949).

120. Pelling, p. 110. For an early account of deporting IWWs by businessmen's protective associations and mine owners' cooperation in the frontier settings of Goldfield and Tonopah, Nevada, see Barton Currie, "How the West Dealt with One Labor Union" (*Harper's Weekly*, Vol. LI, No. 2635 [June 22, 1907], pp. 908–10).

121. Fitch, "Baiting the I.W.W.," p. 635.

122. Graham Romeyn Taylor, "Moyer's Story of Why He Left the Copper Country," *Survey*, Vol. XXXI, No. 15 (January 10, 1914), pp. 433–35.

123. Arthur Walworth, *Woodrow Wilson: Vol. II* (New York: Longmans, Green and Co., 1958), pp. 117–18; Arthur Link, *Wilson: Confusion and Crises, 1915–1916* (Princeton: Princeton University Press, 1964), pp. 338–39.

124. *Arizona Republican*, April 19, 1917, p. 1.

125. Soule, p. 226; Bishop Scarlett, interview, March 13, 1972.

126. *Arizona Republican*, April 19, 1917, p. 1.

127. Arizona State Council of Defense, *A Record of the Activities of the Arizona State Council of Defense, from Formation April 18, 1917, to Dissolution, June, 1919*, n.d., p. 44.

128. Dwight B. Heard, letter to Walter S. Gifford, June 29, 1917 (Department of Justice files).

129. "Transcript of the Testimony Taken Before the President's Mediation Commission at Clifton, Arizona, October 25–30, 1917," testimony of Judge Ernest W. Lewis (Record Group 174, General Records of the Department of Labor), p. 382.

130. Bruere, *Following the Trail* . . . , p. 7.

131. Soule, p. 226; Bishop Scarlett; Jensen, pp. 384–85.

132. *New York Times*, February 5, 1917, p. 8.

133. *Jerome Sun*, July 9, 1917, p. 1.

134. On October 16, 1918, sixty "undesirable" aliens were deported out of the country by the United States Attorney General. See Constantine M. Panunzio, *The Deportation Cases of 1919–1920* (New York: Federal Council of the Churches of Christ of America, 1921).

135. *New York Times*, July 8, 1917, p. 11.

136. *Bisbee Daily Review*, July 11, 1917, p. 1.

137. Jensen, p. 394.

138. *Bisbee Daily Review*, July 7, 1917, p. 1; *New York Times*, July 4, 1917, p. 5.

139. Jensen, p. 396.

140. Woodrow Wilson, letter to G. W. P. Hunt, July 2, 1917 (copy in file "Clifton-Morenci Strike, 1915–16," Special Collections, University of Arizona Library, Tucson).

141. Jensen, p. 396.

142. Typescript account of strike, n.d., p. 4 (in file "Clifton-Morenci Strike, 1915–16," U. of A. Library); *Bisbee Daily Review*, July 7, 1917, p. 1; Marcus A. Smith, letter to Citizens' Protective League of Douglas, July 17, 1917 (copy in file "Clifton-Morenci Strike, 1915–16," U. of A. Library).

143. John C. Greenway, telegram to Newton D. Baker, June 28, 1917 (copy in Adjutant General's file 370.61 [Department of Justice files]).

144. Thomas E. Campbell, telegrams (2) to Newton D. Baker, July 2, 1917 (Adjutant General's file 370.61 [Department of Justice files]).

145. T. E. Campbell, "The I.W.W. in Arizona," n.p.; Hugh W. Foster, telegram to Newton D. Baker, July 2, 1917 [Adj. Gen. file 370.61 (Dept. of Justice files)]; Walter Douglas, telegram to Newton D. Baker, July 3, 1917 (copy in Dept. of Justice files); Bernard Baruch, telegram to Newton D. Baker, July 3, 1917 (copy in Dept. of Justice files). All of the telegrams requesting federal help sent to Baker on July 2 and 3 used a slight variation of the same comments and prose style. Each emphasized the "Austrian and I.W.W. control and influence" involved in the state's labor strife.

146. Thomas E. Campbell, telegram to Newton D. Baker, July 3, 1917 (copy in Adj. Gen. file 370.61 [Dept. of Justice files]).

147. Brig. Gen. Henry P. McCain, telegram to Governor, State of Arizona, July 3, 1917 (copy in Adj. Gen. file 370.61 [Dept. of Justice files]); McCain, letter to Commanding General, Southern Department, July 5, 1917 (Dept. of Justice files).

148. Brig. Gen. James Parker, telegram to Adjutant General, July 4, 1917 (Dept. of Justice files).

149. Parker, letter to Adj. Gen., July 5, 1917 (Dept. of Justice files).

150. *New York Times*, July 4, p. 5, and July 6, p. 9, 1917; *Arizona Republican*, July 4, p. 1, and July 7, p. 1, 1917.

151. Thomas A. Flynn, letter to Attorney General, July 14, 1917 (Dept. of Justice files).

152. Parker, telegram to Adj. Gen., July 14, 1917 (Dept. of Justice files); Parker, telegram to Adj. Gen., July 12, 1917 (War Dept. files, Dept. of Justice files); Thomas E. Campbell, telegram to Woodrow Wilson, July 20, 1917 (Dept. of Justice file 186813.341); Official Army Correspondence and Orders, August 1918–July 1920 (Dept. of Justice files); George W. P. Hunt, letter to Newton D. Baker, February 9, 1918 (Dept. of Justice files); *Arizona Republican*, July 8, p. 1, July 9, p. 1, 1917; Parker, telegram to Adj. Gen., July 16, 1917 (Dept. of Justice files).

153. *Arizona Republican*, July 8, 1917, p. 1.

154. Preston, pp. 188–200; "Respecting Troops for Arizona," *Arizona Mining Journal*, Vol. 1, No. 9 (March 1918), p. 16.

155. Roger S. Culver, statement recorded, July 9, 1917 (Dept. of Justice files).

156. In his study of military repression in Arizona, William Preston, Jr., points out, "Although the federal government insisted that its troops should play an absolutely neutral role in any labor-capital dispute, there was no such fine impartiality in practice." The effect of the presence of troops on the striking miners was, in fact, repressive. But "repression" was not what Walter Douglas had in mind; the army only served to interfere with his plan to *eliminate* labor unions in Arizona. (Preston, pp. 108–10.)

157. *Bisbee Daily Review*, July 8, 1917, ed., sect. 2, p. 4; *Ibid.*, July 12, 1917, p. 1. This is not what the article said, however. The small print revealed that Conciliator John McBride merely wired the Department of Labor in Washington saying that at that hour there was "no hope of an early settlement."

158. *New York Times*, July, 1917, sect. 2, p. 5.

159. For border problems with Mexican revolutionaries, see Robert W. Jeffrey, "The History of Douglas ... ," pp. 51–88. In her book, *The Zimmerman Telegram*, Barbara Tuchman points out that the interception and decoding of the telegram (sent January 1917) produced a shock that only "penetrated to the mid-point of the continent." Although it probably helped to intensify the willingness of East Coast Americans to enter the war, it had scarce acknowledgment west of

the Mississippi. The Germans, she explains, had hoped to provoke American aggression against Mexico. (New York: The MacMillan Company, 1958, pp. 184–88.) By making war on the United States with Germany, Mexico, if the Central Powers triumphed, would receive territory lost by the Treaty of Guadalupe Hidalgo in Texas, New Mexico and Arizona. But Arizonans, including those near the border, showed little, if any anxiety or antagonism. On July 11, even the alarmist *Review* included a story headlined "Uncle Sam Not Anxious to See Mexico in War." The story below, with no apparent hysteria, endorsed the neutrality of Mexico. (*Bisbee Daily Review*, July 11, 1917, p. 2.)

160. Erving, Hinton tapes.

161. U.S., Congress, Senate, Senator Meyers, *Congressional Record*, Sixty-fifth Congress, First Session, 1917, Vol. LV, Part 5, p. 5029.

162. *Arizona Republican*, July 11, 1917, p. 1.

163. "Editorials," *Dunbar's Weekly*, July 14, p. 1.

164. "Editorial Comment," *Dunbar's Weekly*, Vol. IV, No. 29 (July 28, 1917), p. 6. For Cleveland H. Dodge's relationship with President Woodrow Wilson, see pp. 276–80.

165. T. E. Campbell, "The I.W.W. in Arizona," n.p. A pronounced gap exists in Governor Campbell's official records. Most of his known correspondence between July 2 and July 12 is missing. (Bruere, "Copper Camp . . . ," Feb. 21, p. 203.)

166. *Arizona Record*, July 11, 1917, p. 1. The *Review* carried this speech on July 11—omitting the last sentence. See the *Wall Street Journal* quoted in "Industrial Workers Who Won't Work," p. 20: "Why wait until . . . mines [are] flooded and destroyed? . . . [T] reason must be met with preventative as well as punitive measures. When you hear the copperhead hissing in the grass why wait until it strikes before stamping on it? Death might be the price of that delay. Copperheads, branded with the Iron Cross . . . are in the copper mines. . . . Instead of waiting to see if their bite is poison, the heel of the Government should stamp them at once."

167. *Tucson Citizen*, July 11, 1917, p. 1.

168. *Bisbee Daily Review*, July 12, 1917, ed., p. 4.

169. Operative No. 5, "Complimentary Report," pp. 1–3 (UVCC files).

Chapter 7: Big Day in Arizona

1. *Bisbee Daily Review*, July 13, 1917, p. 4.

2. William S. Beeman, "History of the Bisbee Deportations by an Officer in Charge of the Loyalty League" (Arizona Law Library and Archives, Phoenix, 1940), p. 3.

3. Letter from United States Attorney Thomas A. Flynn, Phoenix District, to the attorney general. Tucson, Arizona, May 23, 1918. (Dept. of Justice files, 186813-78.)

4. Beeman, *loc. cit.* Everett Ellinwood and John Ross opposed this early specific plan, not the general idea, of deportation. W. K. Meade, who had practiced law in Cochise County for forty years, wrote in 1917 that it was "well and fully known" that Ellinwood and Ross "helped plan and ... assisted in every possible way, the deportation." One of them, claimed Meade, took a gun in his hand and participated in the roundup. (Letter from W. K. Meade to the attorney general, Tombstone, Arizona, December 7, 1917 [Department of Justice Files]). Ellinwood's testimony before President Wilson's Mediation Commission verified this. (Testimony of Everett E. Ellinwood, "Transcript of the Testimony Taken Before the President's Mediation Commission at Bisbee, Arizona, November 1–4, 1917" [Record Group 174, General Records of the Department of Labor].)

5. Beeman, p. 4; Dr. Nelson A. Bledsoe, interview, August 15, 1968; George Soule, "Law and Necessity in Bisbee," *The Nation*, Vol. 113, No. 2930 (August 31, 1921), p. 226; Samuel Morse, "The Truth About Bisbee" (Arizona Pioneers' Historical Society, Tucson, n.d.), p. 7.

6. The record shows Phelps Dodge felt little anxiety about trouble from the Mexicans. Even its operations within Mexico experienced slight disruption as a consequence of the turmoil in that country during the early twentieth century. In April 1915 revolutionaries forced about five hundred Phelps Dodge employees to flee the Phelps Dodge property at Nacozari, Mexico; after several weeks the refugees returned. They found no serious damage. Phelps Dodge historian Robert G. Cleland wrote that except for a few temporary shutdowns and a few inconveniences "the Phelps Dodge properties below the border suffered relatively little from the years of banditry and revolution that took such a heavy toll of life and property in many other parts of Mexico between 1911 and 1920." (Robert Glass Cleland, *A History of Phelps Dodge* [New York: Alfred A. Knopf, 1952], pp. 197–98.)

7. Beeman, p. 4.

8. Soule, *loc. cit.*

9. Beeman, pp. 4–6.

10. Testimony of George F. Kellogg, "Transcript ... taken ... at Bisbee," pp. 3–8.

11. Beeman, p. 9.

12. Kellogg, *loc. cit.* At least one man, Colonel James H. McClintock, a journalist, "state historian" and sometimes Arizona politician, recorded he knew about the Loyalty League's intentions as early as July 9. (Arizona Pioneers' Historical Society, "Colonel McClintock and the 1917 Copper Strike," *Arizoniana*, Vol. III, No. 1 [Spring, 1962], p. 25.) This was unlikely.

13. Beeman, p. 7; interview with Dr. Nelson Bledsoe, August 15, 1968.

14. Kellogg, *loc. cit.* Edward Massey, an inspector for the Arizona State Department of Mines, later testified that Shattuck, unlike the officials of Bisbee's other two mining companies, never discriminated between union and non-union miners. While Phelps Dodge and Calumet and Arizona fought uncompromisingly to keep an open camp, Massey said, Shattuck-Denn maintained a more permissive policy. (Testimony of Edward Massey, "Transcript ... taken ... at Bisbee," p. 50.) *Dunbar's Weekly*, a Phoenix-based, passionately anti-copper company publication, said Lem Shattuck "showed his courage and his patriotism by refusing to be a party to the disreputable deportation scheme of the Douglas family, and we apprehend he has gained their enmity." ("Editorials," *Dunbar's Weekly*, Vol. IV, No. 37 [September 22, 1917], p. 1.) Yet Shattuck was an armed participant in the roundup and was included among the deporters indicted nine months later by the federal government.

15. Kellogg, *loc. cit.*

16. *Ibid.* Beeman recorded that only about forty men attended (p. 8).

17. Robert Bruere, "Copper Camp Patriotism," *Nation*, Vol. 106, No. 2747 (February 21, 1918), p. 203.

18. *Bisbee Daily Review*, July 1, 1917, p. 5; Bruere, *loc. cit.*

19. Thomas E. Campbell, "The I.W.W. in Arizona; Typescript Concerning Reconstruction of Labor Troubles in Arizona," San Fernando, California, 1962 (Arizona Pioneers' Historical Society, Tucson), no pagination.

20. Beeman, p. 10.

21. "Deportations from Bisbee and a Resume of Other Troubles in Arizona," reprinted in "The Arizona Strike," *Arizona Mining Journal* (August, 1917), p. 7; Beeman, p. 8.

22. Beeman, p. 8; Kellogg, *loc. cit.*

23. Bledsoe, *loc. cit.* It was later reported by an inside source that Grant Dowell had received two carloads of rifles and ammunition a few days before the deportation. According to this report, these arms were consigned directly to Dowell, not to the company store. (Harold Callender, "True Facts About Bisbee," Report published by The National Labor Defense Council, *Dunbar's Weekly*, Vol. 14, No. 36 [September 15, 1917], pp. 10–11.)

24. *New York Times*, July 13, 1917, p. 1.

25. *Bisbee Daily Review*, July 13, p. 1; Vernon Jensen, *Heritage of Conflict* (Ithaca: Cornell University Press, 1950), p. 405; Bruere, "Copper Camp ... " (Feb. 21), p. 203.

26. Beeman, p. 10.

27. Kellogg, *loc. cit.*

28. "Deportations from Bisbee ... ," pp. 4–7.

29. *New York Times*, *loc. cit.*

30. A dramatic, fictionalized account of the Bisbee Deportation can be found in Stephen Vincent Benet, *The Beginning of Wisdom* (New York: Henry Holt and Company, 1921).

31. *Bisbee Daily Review*, July 15, 1917, p. 7.

32. July 13, 1917, p. 4. The *Review* reported that the newsboys were "heroes" that "should not be overlooked."

33. *Ibid.*, July 12, 1917, p. 1.

34. Robert Glass Cleland, p. 186.

35. "Deportations from Bisbee . . . ," p. 6.

36. *New York Times*, July 13, 1917, p. 1.

37. *The Messenger*, July 21, 1917, p. i.

38. *State of Arizona v. Pat Andrews, et al.*, Transcript, Preliminary Hearings (Original Blanket Hearings) Vol. 1, Justice Court of Precinct No. 4, Douglas, Cochise County, Arizona, August 25, 1919, Book 1, pp. 161–71; Callender, p. 12; *The Messenger*, July 21, 1917, p. i.

39. John Ercek, Testimony, *State of Arizona v. Cass Benton*, Preliminary Hearing (Case No. 270), Justice Court, Precinct No. 4, Cochise County, State of Arizona, "Individual Transcripts," Book No. 1, July 17, 1919, pp. 182–83.

40. Nancy Thomas, Testimony, *St. of Ariz. v. P. Andrews*, Book 1, pp. 81, 133–37; Book 3, pp. 610, 638; Book 4, p. 1014, *passim*; William Eddy, *ibid*, Book 2, p. 322; Callender, p. 12.

41. Callender, p. 12; Nancy Thomas, *Original Blanket Hearings*, Justice Court of Precinct No. 4, Douglas, Arizona, July–September 1919, Book 1, pp. 161–71; Book 3, p. 322; Book 4, p. 1014; William Eddy, *ibid.*, Book 2, 322; Book 1, pp. 133–35, 81.

42. *The Messenger*, July 21, 1917, p. 4; *St. of Ariz. v. P. Andrews*, July–September, 1919, *passim*; Fred Watson, affidavit, Bisbee, Arizona, August 31, 1970; Fred Watson, interview, Bisbee, July 19, 1972.

43. Watson affidavit; Fred Watson, Membership Card, Western Federation of Miners, 1909–1917; Fred Watson, Membership Book ("Red Card"), Industrial Workers of the World, Gen. No. 272861, 1917; Watson, interview.

44. R. McKay, *loc. cit.*

45. Matt Hanhila, taped interview, Harwood Hinton Collection; Matt Hanhila, "The Bisbee Tea Party," *Maricopa Open Door*, Vol. 1, No. 1 (Fall–Winter, 1972), p. 13; Matt Hanhila, interview, March 13, 1972.

46. Mrs. Katie Pintek, interviews, April 8, 1966, July 19, 1972; testimony of Mike Pintek, *Original . . . Book* 1, pp. 161–71.

47. Bruere, "Copper Camp . . . ," (Feb. 21), pp. 202–03.

48. *Bisbee Daily Review*, July 12, 1917, p. 4.

49. K. Pintek, *loc. cit.*

50. "Mark Larkin," unidentified clipping. George W. P. Hunt Scrapbooks (Special Collections, University of Arizona).

51. Bishop William Scarlett, interview, March 13, 1972; Fred Watson and William Eddy interviews, July 19, 1972.

52. K. Pintek, *loc. cit.*
53. *Ibid.*, July 12, 1917, p. 8
54. *Ibid.*, July 13, 1917, p. 1.
55. *Ind. Trans.*, Book 3, p. 52; Testimony of Fred Brown, "Transcript...Taken...at Bisbee," p. 32.
56. John Pintek and Fred Watson, interviews, July 19, 1972.
57. Testimony of Anna Ballard, Tony Rodriguez, Richard Denning, Mike Pintek and others, *Prelim. Ind. Trans.*, Book 1, *passim*.
58. *Ibid.*
59. *Ibid.*, pp. 1–2; *Ind. Trans.*, Book 3, p. 34 and Book 2, p. 109; Watson, affidavit.
60. "Deportations from Bisbee ... ," p. 6; Watson, affidavit.
61. Leslie Marcy, "The Eleven Hundred Exiled Copper Miners," *The International Socialist Review*, Vol. XVII, No. 3 (September, 1917), pp. 160–62; *Bisbee Daily Review*, *loc. cit.*
62. Katy Pintek, *loc. cit.*; Mike Pintek, testimony, *Preliminary ... , Ind. Transcripts*, Book 1, pp. 219–26.
63. Deportations from Bisbee ... ," *loc. cit.*, Beeman, p. 10; John P. Chase, *Original Blanket Hearings*, Book 1, p. 33; Ballard, p. 166; *The Messenger*, July 21, 1917, p. 1; Dominic Catero, *Original Blanket Hearings*, Book 1, p. 54.
64. *Bisbee Daily Review*, July 13, 1917, p. 2; *Ind. Trans.*, Book 3, p. 222. The number of men deported varies in the numerous accounts. Both President Wilson's Mediation Commission's and the copper companies' statistics gave 1,186 as the figure. (U.S., Committee on Public Information, *Official Bulletin*, Vol. 1, No. 170 [November 27, 1917], "Report of President Wilson's Mediation commission on Bisbee, Ariz., Deportations, Including Its Recommendations as Made on Findings of Fact," p. 6; Fred Sutter, "Senator Sutter Makes Reply," *Arizona Mining Journal*, Vol. II, No. 1 [June 1918], p. 48; Phelps Dodge Corporation, Copper Queen Branch, "Employees to Columbus," "Transcript ... Taken ... at Bisbee," p. 287.)
65. *The Messenger*, *loc. cit.*
66. *New York Times*, July 13, 1917, p. 1; Testimony of Richard Denning, *Original ... ,* p. 1003; *Bisbee Daily Review*, July 13, 1917, p. 2; *Ind. Trans.*, Book 3, p. 32, p. 82; Stout's claim to "Captain" grew out of the smelter superintendent's past relationship with Copper Queen employees. The "Cousin Jacks" traditionally called their shift bosses, foremen and other occupational superiors "Captain" or "Cap'n" (Kellogg, *loc. cit.*).
67. Bruere, "Copper Camp ... ," (Feb. 21), pp. 202–03; Kellogg, p. 15.
68. R. McKay, *loc. cit.*
69. Rosa McKay, telegrams 1 and 2 to President Woodrow Wilson, July 12, 1917. (Copy in Department of Justice Files, 186813-4.)
70. Bruere, *loc. cit.*; Kellogg, *loc. cit.*
71. Callender, p. 12.

72. *New York Times*, July 13, 1917, p. 3.

73. Lt. Col. James J. Hornbrook, telegram to adjutant general, July 12, 1917. Adj. Gen. Files 370.61 (Bisbee, Ariz.). (Copy in Department of Justice Files.)

74. *Bisbee Daily Review*, *loc. cit.*; "Deportations from Bisbee ... ," pp. 6–7.

75. Campbell, "The I.W.W. in Arizona," n.p.

76. *New York Times*, July 13, 1917, p. 3.

77. *New York Times*, *loc. cit.*

78. *Ibid.*, July 14, 1917, p. 4.

79. United States Attorney Thomas A. Flynn, District of Arizona, telegram to the attorney general, July 12, 1917. (Copy in Department of Justice Files.)

80. Dominic Catero, *loc. cit.*

81. Brown, "Transcript ... Taken ... at Bisbee," pp. 37–43.

82. Watson affidavit, August 31, 1970.

83. *New York Times*, *loc. cit.*; Morse, p. 12; Beeman, pp. 10–11.

84. *Bisbee Daily Review*, July 13, 1917, p. 1; Brown, *loc. cit.*

85. Marlin Arms Corporation, "Bill of Sale to S. W. French, Gen. Manager, Phelps Dodge," April 10, 1917. (Copy in Department of Justice Files.)

86. *Bisbee Daily Review*, July 14, 1917, p. 4.

87. Brown, "Transcript ... Taken ... at Bisbee," pp. 37–43.

88. *New York Times*, July 14, 1917, p. 1; *Bisbee Daily Review*, July 13, 1917, p. 1.

89. Brown, *loc. cit.*

90. *Ibid.*

91. *New York Times*, *loc. cit.*, p. 4.

92. *Ibid.*; Brigadier General James Parker, Commanding Officer, United States Army, Southern Department, San Antonio, Texas, telegram to adjutant general, July 13, 1917. (Adj. Gen. Files 370.61, So. Dept., copy in Department of Justice Files.)

93. *New York Times*, *loc. cit.*

94. *Bisbee Daily Review*, July 14, 1917, p. 4.

95. *Ibid.*, July 18, 1917, p. 4.

Chapter 8: Securing Control

1. U.S., *Congressional Record*, Sixty-fifth Congress, First Session, 1917, Vol. LV, Part 5, p. 5028. *Jerome Sun*, July 14, 1917, p. 1.

2. *New York Times*, July 13, 1917, p. 3; William B. Haywood, *Bill Haywood's Book* (New York: International Publishers, 1929), p. 300.

3. U.S., *Cong. Record*, Vol. LV, p. 5154.

4. *Bisbee Daily Review*, July 16, 1917, sect. 1, p. 3.

5. "The Mining Summary," *Mining and Scientific Press*, Vol. 15, July 21, 1917, p. 102.

6. *Bisbee Daily Review*, July 22, 1917, sect. 2, p. 2.

7. John P. Chase, Book 1, p. 28 and Thomas English, Book 3, p. 711, *Original Blanket Hearings*. William Blackburn, *Individual Transcripts*, Book 1, p. 198.

8. Governor Thomas E. Campbell, letter printed in "The Industrial Workers of the World," *The Outlook*, Vol. 116, No. 13 (July 25, 1917), p. 468.

9. William Preston, Jr., *Aliens and Dissenters* (New York: Harper and Row, 1973), p. 124.

10. Thomas E. Campbell, telegram to President Wilson, July 15, 1917. (Copy in Department of Justice files.)

11. Emmett D. Boyle, telegram to President Wilson, July 13, 1917. (Copy in Department of Justice files.)

12. *Bisbee Daily Review*, July 24, 1917, p. 1; "Minutes of Conference, Thomas E. Campbell, Governor of Arizona, with Citizens' Committee from Bisbee, Arizona," July 23, 1917. (Department of Justice files.)

13. *Ibid.*

14. "Minutes of Conference, . . . "

15. Thomas E. Campbell, letter to Charles W. Clark, July 24, 1917 (UVCC files).

16. Thomas E. Campbell, letter to Thomas H. Bell, July 24, 1917. (Printed in *The Messenger*, August 4, 1917.)

17. U.S., Congress, House, *Exclusion and Expulsion of Aliens of Anarchistic and Similar Classes*, Document No. 7652, Doc. 504, 65th Congress, 2nd Session, H. R. 504, December 16, 1919, p. 4.

18. *New York Times*, July 12, 1917, p. 10; July 14, 1917, p. 6.

19. *New York World* quoted in *Bisbee Daily Review*, July 19, 1917, p. 5.

20. *Commercial* quoted in "Industrial Workers Who Won't Work," *The Literary Digest*, Vol. LV, No. 4 (July 28, 1917), p. 20.

21. *Globe* quoted in Alexander M. Bing, *War-Time Strikes and Their Adjustment* (New York: E. P. Dutton and Co., 1921), p. 249.

22. Freeport, Illinois, *Bulletin* quoted in Bing, pp. 247–48.

23. *Chicago Tribune* quoted in *Bisbee Daily Review*, *loc. cit.*

24. *Republic* and *Republican* quoted in "Industrial Workers Who . . . ," *loc. cit.*

25. *Ibid.*; *Bisbee Daily Review*, *loc. cit.* The *Literary Digest* called the *Transcript* "an authority on history and literature."

26. See Edwin Fussell and G. Edward White on the "eastern establishment and the western experience" on pages 6 and 331 (note 4).

27. *Bisbee Daily Review*, *loc. cit.*

28. "Industrial Workers Who . . . ," *loc. cit.*

29. *Bisbee Daily Review*, *loc. cit.*

30. "The Week," *The Nation*, Vol. 105, No. 2716 (July 19, 1917), p. 57.

31. "Organization or Anarchy," *The New Republic*, Vol. XI, No. 142 (July 21, 1917), pp. 320–33.

32. Edward T. Devine, "The Bisbee Deportations," *The Survey*, Vol. XXXVIII, No. 16 (July 21, 1917), p. 353.

33. "Enemies Within the Camp," *The Independent*, Vol. 91, No. 3582 (July 28, 1917), p. 122.

34. *New York Times*, July 15, 1917, Sect. I, p. 1.

35. *Bisbee Daily Review*, July 26, 1917, p. 1; "The I.W.W. Develops into a National Menace," *Current Opinion*, Vol. LXIII, No. 3 (September 1917), p. 153.

36. "Labor Unrest in the Southwest," *The Survey*, Vol. 38, No. 19 (August 11, 1917), p. 428; *New York Times*, August 2, 1917, p. 20.

37. *Bisbee Daily Review*, August 5, 1917, p. 1.

38. "The I.W.W. Develops . . . ," *loc. cit.*

39. Nelson Van Valen, "The Bolsheviki and the Orange Growers," *Pacific Historical Review*, Vol. 22, No. 1 (February 1953), pp. 45–56; Cleland, p. 191. A federal district court, in 1919, sustained as legal the deportation of two IWWs from the United States. ("Deportation of I.W.W. Members Sustained," *Law and Labor*, Vol. 1, No. 5 [May 1919], p. 6.) Federal deportations continued in 1920; see Louis F. Post, *The Deportations Delirium of Nineteen Twenty* (Chicago: Charles H. Kerr and Company, 1923); U.S., Congress, House, *Deportation of Certain Aliens* (H. Rpt. 7252, Doc. 127, 65th Cong., 1st Sess., 1917.); U.S., Congress, House, *Exclusion and Expulsion of Aliens of Anarchistic or Similar Classes* (H. Rpt. 7652, Doc. 504, 66th Cong., 2nd Sess., 1919) and U.S., Congress, House, *Hearings Before a Sub-Committee on Immigration and Naturalization* (66th Cong., 2nd Sess., 1920).

40. *Bisbee Daily Review*, July 13, 1917, p. 4.

41. *New York Times*, July 14, 1917, p. 1, and July 15, 1917, p. 12.

42. Brown, *loc. cit.*; Acting Arizona District Commander Welty, telegram to the Adjutant General, July 14, 1917 (Department of Justice files).

43. Colonel H. G. Sickel, letter to Adjutant General, July 14, 1917 (Adjutant General files, Department of Justice files).

44. *Arizona Record*, July 15, 1917, p. 1; Welty to Adj. Gen., July 14; *New York Times*, July 15, 1917, p. 12.

45. *New York Times*, July 15, 1917, p. 12; Watson, affidavit, August 31, 1970.

46. Sickel to Adj. Gen., July 14; *New York Times*, July 17, 1917, p. 7. The tone of this telegram tends to confirm deportee Fred Brown's later statement that Col. Sickel "used us as though we were buck privates" (Brown, "Transcript . . . Taken . . . at Bisbee," p. 42); Watson, affidavit.

47. Colonel H. G. Sickel, letter to Brig. General George Bell, Jr., July 31, 1917 (Department of Justice files).

48. Watson, affidavit. From July 15 to July 31, inclusive, the total cost to the government for maintaining more than 1000 deportees at Camp Furlong amounted to $3,422.23. (*Ibid.*)

49. Brown, "Transcript ... Taken ... at Bisbee," pp. 24–30; Sickel to Brig. Gen. Bell, July 31; J. MacDonald, letter to Grover Perry, July 23, 1917 (*Simmons v. El Paso & Southwestern R.R., et al.* exhibits, Special Collections, University of Arizona Library, Tucson); Watson, affidavit, August 31, 1970.

50. *Original Blanket Hearings*, Book 4, *passim*.

51. *Ibid.*; Welty to Adj. Gen., July 14.

52. "Labor Unrest ... ," p. 429.

53. Robert A. Watkins, "Respecting the Governor's Message," *Arizona Mining Journal*, Vol. II, No. 1 (June 1918), p. 10; "Message of George W. P. Hunt to the Special Session of the Third State Legislature" (Phoenix: privately printed pamphlet, n.d.), May 21, 1918, pp. 10–11; *New York Evening Post*, May 23, 1918, p. 1.

54. Senator Fred Sutter, address delivered in the Arizona Senate, June 4, 1918; "Sen. Sutter Makes ... ," p. 48.

55. Campbell, "The I.W.W. in Arizona," n.p.

56. *New York Times*, July 17, 1917, p. 4; "Mark Larkin," unidentified newspaper clipping, Hunt Scrapbooks, Vol. 22, n.d.; *Bisbee Daily Review*, July 22, 1917, p. 1.

57. *New York Times*, July 17, 1917, p. 4; *Bisbee Daily Review*, July 25, 1917, p. 1.

58. Sickel to Bell, July 31.

59. *Ibid.*; J. MacDonald to Perry, July 23, 1917; Secretary of Labor William B. Wilson, letter to Secretary of War Newton D. Baker, August 1, 1917 (Adj. Gen. file 370.61, Department of Justice files).

60. M. C. Sullivan, letter to Grover Perry, n.d. (*Simmons v. El Paso & Southwestern R.R., et al.* exhibits, [Special Collections, University of Arizona Library, Tucson].)

61. Sickel to Adj. Gen., July 14.

62. "The Bisbee Miners," p. 46; McCluskey to Byrkit, April 21, 1966.

63. Frank Thomas, "Transcript ... taken ... at Bisbee," p. 60; Bledsoe, "Transcript ... taken ... at Bisbee," pp. 315–35.

64. Brown, "Transcript ... taken ... at Bisbee," pp. 37–43; *Bisbee Daily Review*, July 18, 1917, p. 4.

65. *Bisbee Daily Review*, August 5, 1917, p. 1; August 12, pp. 1, 2.

66. Haywood, *Bill Haywood's Book*, p. 313.

67. *New York Times*, July 14, 1917, p. 1.

68. *Ibid.*, p. 4.

69. Roscoe Willson, "Sheriff's Aide Tells of Bisbee Deportation," *Arizona Days and Ways Magazine*, November 8, 1964, pp. 42–43; Minnie Adams, taped interview, Harwood Hinton Collection; Minnie Adams, interview, July 19, 1972.

70. *Bisbee Daily Review*, July 14, 1917, p. 2, and July 22, 1917, p. 1.

71. Campbell, "The I.W.W. in Arizona," n.p.; Soule, pp. 225–27; William Eddy, Minnie Adams, Fred Watson, July 19, 1972; Original Blanket Hearings, *passim*; Bruere, "Copper Camp Patriotism ... ," February 28, 1918, pp. 235–36.

72. *New York Times*, July 14, 1917, p. 4.

73. Katie Pintek, April 8, 1966, July 19, 1972; Mike Pintek, *Orig. Blanket Hearings*, Book 1, pp. 185–93.

74. *Bisbee Daily Review*, July 24, 1917, p. 2; July 27, 1917, p. 1; and July 28, 1917, p. 1.

75. *Dunbar's Weekly*, Vol. IV, No. 29 (July 28, 1917), p. 7.

76. "Editorials," *Dunbar's Weekly*, Vol. IV, No. 31 (August 11, 1917), p. 1.

77. Watson, July 19, 1972.

78. Louis Grass, "The Story of a Bisbee Crime" (letter to editor), *Dunbar's Weekly*, Vol. IV, No. 31 (August 11, 1917), p. 9; Watson affidavit, August 31, 1970. For location of Lee Station and Bernardino, see Barnes, pp. 44 and 253.

79. Watson, July 19, 1972.

80. *Bisbee Daily Review*, August 11, 1917, p. 4; August 17, 1917, p. 1; August 18, 1917, p. 2.

81. Callender, p. 12.

82. *Bisbee Daily Review*, July 22, 1917, p. 5. Phelps Dodge Corporation, "Records of Mexican Families Given Aid Through Warren District Relief Association," "Transcript ... taken ... at Bisbee," pp. 294–308.

83. Rev. A. D. Raley, "Deportations Justified," *Arizona Mining Journal*, Vol. 1, No. 2 (August 1917), p. 8; Morse, preface; report of investigating United States Army Captain M. E. Palen quoted in letter from Adjutant General Edward T. Donnelly to Leo Sigal, Chairman, Amalgamated Meat Cutters and Butchers Workmen of North America, August 15, 1917 (Adj. Gen. file 370.6, Department of Justice files); William Haywood, telegram to A. D. Kimball, July 26, 1917 (*Simmons v. El Paso & Southwestern R.R., et al.* exhibits, Special Collections, University of Arizona Library, Tucson).

84. *Bisbee Daily Review*, August 4, 1917, p. 4.

85. Callender, p. 12. For Phelps Dodge records of transportation expenses to families of deported men, July 24–September 25, see Phelps Dodge Corporation, "Records of Transportation Expenses to Families of Deported Men," "Transcript ... taken ... at Bisbee," pp. 291–94. Deportee representative A. S. Embree notified Secretary of War Baker that Phelps Dodge forced some women in Bisbee to accept "transportation assistance" against their husbands' wishes. (Wm. B. Wilson to Newton D. Baker, Aug. 1, 1917.) The Hanhila family handled things their own way. After the deportation of her husband Felix, Mrs. Hanhila and her son, eight-year-old Matt, decided to sell

their house. Since the three members of the family had only recently arrived in Bisbee from Finland, where they were all born, Mrs. Hanhila could not speak English very well. With young Matt's help she finally sold the house and the two went to live with Mr. Hanhila at Columbus. There Matt enjoyed the adventure of stockade life, and he made friends with the soldiers. Eventually the Hanhilas went to California, then to Minnesota where the father found work. The Hanhila family returned to Bisbee in 1920 where the father was reemployed under an assumed name. But the Hanhilas felt the employers actually knew his identity. (Hanhila, Hinton tapes and "The Bisbee Tea Party," pp. 13–15.)

86. Captain Palen's figures were quoted in Ed. T. Donnelly to Leo Sigal, August 15, 1917.

87. *Bisbee Daily Review*, August 7, 1917, pp. 3, 4.

88. *Ibid.*, August 14, 1917, pp. 1 and 4.

89. *Ibid.*, July 17, 1917, p. 4; July 13, 1917, p. 1. Until July 21 the newspaper did not include any photographs of the deportation. On that day Dix Studio of Bisbee advertised a set of twenty-four views of the IWW drive for $2.00. Three days later two pictures of the deportation appeared in the *Review*. (*Ibid.*, July 21, 1917, p. 6; July 24, 1917, p. 3.)

90. *Ibid.*, August 4, 1917, p. 1; July 29, 1917, sect. 2, p. 4; August 19, 1917, p. 3.

91. *Ibid.*, August 11, 1917, p. 3.

92. Callender, p. 12.

93. U.S., Congress, House, Representative Hayden, *Congressional Record*, Sixty-fifth Congress, First Session, August 7, 1917, Vol. LV, Part 6, p. 5898.

94. *Bisbee Daily Review*, August 19, 1917, p. 6.

95. Bledsoe interview, Aug. 15, 1968; *Bisbee Daily Review*, September 28, 1917, p. 3; September 22, 1917, p. 2; September 23, 1917, p. 3; July 21, 1917, p. 1.

96. *Ibid.*, September, 1917.

Chapter 9: Arizona Knuckles Under

1. Columbus paper quoted in *Bisbee Daily Review*, July 22, 1917, sect. 2, p. 3.

2. The *Review* did not appreciate a challenge to its authority. In one boxed front page complaint entitled "WHY?" on August 5, the *Review* asked: "Why is it possible to have a lively sale of El Paso papers on the streets of Bisbee every morning?" The El Paso papers, pointed out the *Review*, were printed the night before—*Review* news was seven hours fresher. "Why buy stale telegraph news from a paper printed in another state and devoted to the interests of another state?" A few

days later, when a Yuma paper reported that a Yuma man visiting his sick sister in Bisbee on the day of the deportation had been sent to Columbus, the *Review* insisted that the *Yuma Sun* had been a victim of IWW "press-agentry." (*Ibid.*, August 5, 1917, p. 1; August 18, 1917, p. 4.)

3. "The Mining Summary," *Mining and Scientific Press*, Vol. 115, July 7, 1917, pp. 29–30.

4. *Bisbee Daily Review*, July 22, 1917, p. 1; July 31, 1917, p. 2.

5. "Globe, Arizona," *Mining and Scientific Press*, Vol. 115, November 3, 1917, p. 659.

6. A. Hamilton, *Exploring the Dangerous Trades*, p. 218.

7. *Bisbee Daily Review*, July 22, 1917, sect. 2, p. 3.

8. Hornbrook to Adj. Gen., July 16, 1917.

9. *Bisbee Daily Review*, July 29, 1917, p. 4.

10. Letter from Hodgson quoted in Morse, "The Truth About Bisbee," preface.

11. *Bisbee Daily Review*, July 29, 1917, p. 1.

12. *Ibid.*, July 31, 1917, p. 4.

13. *Ibid.*, August 4, 1917, p. 1.

14. *Ibid.*, July 25, 1917, p. 1.

15. *Ibid.*, August 7, 1917, p. 1.

16. John Murray and R. G. Rigg, "Transcript ... taken ... at Bisbee," pp. 7–8.

17. John Dewey, "In Explanation of Our Lapse," *New Republic*, Vol. XIII, No. 157 (November 3, 1917), pp. 18–19.

18. "The I.W.W. Raids and Others," *New Republic*, Vol. XII, No. 150 (September 15, 1917), p. 176.

19. "The Week," *Nation*, Vol. CV, No. 2716 (July 19, 1917), p. 57.

20. "The Bisbee Episode," *Arizona*, Vol. VII, No. 8 (August 1917), p. 1.

21. *New York Times*, August 1, 1917, p. 4.

22. *Bisbee Daily Review*, August 7, 1917, p. 6.

23. Harvey, p. 223.

24. *Ibid.*

25. *Ibid.*

26. *Ibid.*, p. 224.

27. "What Haywood Says of the I.W.W.," *Survey*, Vol. 38, No. 19 (August 11, 1917), p. 429.

28. For numerous examples, see Department of Justice file 186813 in United States National Archives.

29. Ed. T. Donnelly to Leo Sigal, August 15, 1917.

30. *Tulsa Daily World*, November 9, 1917, quoted in Bing, p. 248.

31. *Bisbee Daily Review*, August 5, 1917, sect. 2, pp. 1–2.

32. *Ibid.*, August 16, 1917, p. 1.

33. *Ibid.*, July 31, 1917, p. 1, 2.

34. *Ibid.*, August 7, 1917, p. 5.

35. Bruere, "Copper Camp Patriotism," February 28, p. 236; *Tucson Citizen*, August 10, 1917, p. 1.

36. *New York Times*, August 10, 1917, p. 17.

37. *Bisbee Daily Review*, August 12, 1917, p. 1.

38. *Tucson Citizen*, August 8, 1917, p. 1; John Murray and R. G. Riggs, letter to Samuel Gompers, August 21, 1917, "Selected Documents Relating to I.W.W." (National Archives of the United States).

39. *Tucson Citizen*, August 11, 1917, p. 1.

40. Rosa McKay, telegram to President Woodrow Wilson, August 14, 1917. (Department of Justice file, 186813-41¼.)

41. *New York Times*, August 21, 1917, p. 4; *Bisbee Daily Review*, August 21, 1917, p. 2.

42. *Ibid.*, pp. 1–2.

43. *Ibid.*

44. Sickel to Bell, July 31, 1917.

45. Wm. B. Wilson to Baker, August 1, 1917.

46. Major General Tasker N. Bliss, memorandum to Adjutant General, August 3, 1917 (Adj. Gen. file 370.61, Department of Justice files).

47. Major General Tasker N. Bliss, memorandum to Secretary of War, August 6, 1917 (Adj. Gen. file 370.61, Department of Justice files).

48. Adjutant General Henry P. McCain, telegram to Commanding General, Southern Department, August 9, 1917 (decoded copy in Adj. Gen. files 370.61, Department of Justice files).

49. Fred Brown, "Transcript ... taken ... at Bisbee," pp. 42–43; Fred Watson, affidavit.

50. *Bisbee Daily Review*, August 21, 1917, p. 1; August 30, 1917, p. 1; September 9, 1917, p. 1; Unidentified clipping, Hunt Scrapbooks, Vol. 22, n.p.

51. Notice quoted in A. S. Embree, letter to President Woodrow Wilson, September 10, 1917 (Department of Justice file 186813-17).

52. A. S. Embree, telegram to President Woodrow Wilson, September 8, 1917 (Department of Justice file 186813-44).

53. Embree to President Wilson, Sept. 10, 1917.

54. A. S. Embree, letter to President Wilson, September 10, 1917 (Department of Justice file 186813-47).

55. *Bisbee Daily Review*, September 13, 1917, p. 1; A. S. Embree, A. D. Kimball, *et al.*, telegram to President Wilson, September 12, 1917 (Department of Justice file 186813-46).

56. Samuel J. Graham, letter to A. S. Embree, September 29, 1917 (Department of Justice file 186813-47 ¼).

57. *Bisbee Daily Review*, September 14, 1917, p. 1; *Jerome Sun*, September 14, 1917, p. 1 and September 15, 1917, p. 1.

58. *Bisbee Daily Review*, September 18, 1917, p. 1.

59. "Personal," *Mining and Scientific Press*, Vol. 115, September 8, 1917, p. 368.

60. *Bisbee Daily Review*, September 13, 1917, p. 1.

61. *Ibid*.

62. State of California, Los Angeles County, District 1929, *Certificate of Death*, "Stuart Whitney French," filed September 20, 1946. Of all the personalities involved in the deportation that he knew, Dr. Bledsoe could speak highly only of French. (Bledsoe, August 15, 1968.)

63. Beeman, p. 4; "Personal," *Mining and Scientific Press*, Vol. 115, October 27, 1917, p. 628.

64. "Sheriff Wheeler Answers His Defamers," *Arizona Mining Journal*, Vol. I, No. 5 (October 1917), p. 4.

65. Bruere, "Copper Camp Patriotism," Feb. 21, 1918, pp. 202–03. One eastern reporter interviewed Wheeler on November 4, 1917, and concluded that Wheeler had become truly convinced he was the originator of the Big Drive. (Bruere, *Following the Trail* ... , p. 13.) In view of the real nature of Sheriff Wheeler's "responsibility" in the matter, the commission's telling him that he should have done otherwise would be like the court jester's telling the masked executioner to notify Henry VIII that beheadings must be terminated.

66. Bruere, "Copper Camp Patriotism," Feb. 21, 1918, pp. 202–03.

67. *Ibid*.

68. "Wheeler as Cavalry Leader," *Arizona Mining Journal*, Vol. I, No. 9 (March 1918), p. 17; *Coconino Sun*, March 22, 1918, p. 1.

69. Jensen, p. 426.

70. *Bisbee Daily Review*, April 1, 1948, p. 2.

71. Unidentified clipping, Hunt Scrapbooks, Vol. 23, n.p. (Special Collections, University of Arizona Library, Tucson).

Chapter 10: Clean Hands and a Blessing

1. Brophy, *Though Far Away*, p. 168.

2. Phillips, F. *Frankfurter Reminisces*, pp. 119, 137.

3. U.S., Committee on Public Information, "Report of President Wilson's Mediation Commission On the Bisbee, Ariz., Deportation, Including Its Recommendations as Made on Findings of Fact," *Official Bulletin*, Vol. 1, No. 170 (November 27, 1917), pp. 6–7.

4. Gordon Watkins, "Labor Problems ... ," Part II, pp. 150–51.

5. Two years earlier, during the Clifton-Morenci strike, Secretary Wilson had written Governor George W. P. Hunt: "I have had in mind making a thorough investigation of the labor conditions in and around the mines in Arizona." Wilson told Hunt that it was not advisable for him to come to Arizona until "all hope of an amicable adjustment is at an end." (William B. Wilson, letter to Governor Hunt, December 19, 1915 [copy in file "Clifton-Morenci Strike, 1915," Special Collections, University of Arizona Library, Tucson].)

6. Gordon Watkins, *loc. cit.*; Phillips, pp. 115–17.

7. "Adjustment of Labor Difficulties in Arizona Copper Region," *Monthly Review of Labor Statistics*, Vol. V, No. 6 (December 1917), pp. 54–55.

8. Callender, p. 1.

9. Bruere, *Following the Trail* . . . , pp. 1–5.

10. Jensen, pp. 412–14.

11. *Ibid.*; "Transcript of the Testimony Taken Before the President's Mediation Commission at Globe, Arizona, October 9–16, 1917" (H. S. McCluskey papers, Special Collections, Arizona State University Library, Tempe, Arizona).

12. Jensen, pp. 412–14. "Transcript of the Testimony taken Before the President's Mediation Commission at Clifton, Arizona, October 25–30, 1917" (Record Group 174, General Records of the Department of Labor).

13. Harry C. Wheeler, letter to President Wilson, October 31, 1917 [copy in Department of Justice files].

14. Jensen, pp. 416–19; "Transcript . . . taken . . . at Bisbee," *passim.*

15. Testimony of Frank Thomas, "Transcript . . . taken . . . at Bisbee," p. 60; Jensen, pp. 416–419.

16. "Transcript . . . taken . . . at Bisbee," pp. 400–500.

17. Phillips, pp. 136–37.

18. "Report of . . . Commission On . . . Bisbee . . . ," pp. 6–7.

19. *Ibid*.

20. *New York Times*, November 25, 1917, sect. I, p. 22; "The Bisbee Deportations Illegal," *Survey*, Vol. 39, No. 10 (December 8, 1917), pp. 291–92; "The President's Commission at Bisbee," *New Republic*, Vol. XIII, No. 162 (December 8, 1917), pp. 140–41.

21. Bruere, "Copper Camp Patriotism," Feb. 21, 1918, p. 203.

22. Phillips, p. 138.

23. William B. Wilson, letter to Governor Campbell, November 6, 1917 (copy in Department of Justice file 186813-49).

24. Phelps Dodge letter to Secretary of Labor Wilson quoted in Bing, p. 227.

25. Gordon Watkins, "Labor Problems . . . ," Part II, pp. 158–59.

26. See correspondence in Department of Justice files. "Investigation of Bisbee (Ariz.) Deportations," *Monthly Review of the United States Bureau of Labor Statistics*, Vol. VI, No. 6 (June 1918), p. 57; Court of the United States of America, District of Arizona, "Indictment of Bisbee Deporters," Presented to Grand Jury, May term, 1918 (Department of Justice files).

27. See correspondence in Department of Justice files. Woodrow Wilson, letter to Attorney General Gregory, November 22, 1917 (Department of Justice file 186813-50).

28. "Investigation of Bisbee . . . ," p. 57.

29. William B. Wilson, telegram to Attorney General Gregory, December 4, 1917 (Department of Justice files).

30. Samuel Gompers, letter to Attorney General Gregory, January 19, 1918 (Department of Justice file 186813-55). See the Justice Department files of this period for documents and correspondence regarding federal action against the Bisbee deporters. These sources include several instances of advice *against* prosecution.

31. "Doing Things for 'Labor,'" *American Review of Books*, Vol. LIV, No. 4 (October 1916), p. 361.

32. Richard Morris and William Greenleaf, *USA: The History of a Nation* (Chicago: Rand McNally & Co., 1969), Vol. 2, p. 619.

33. Bing, pp. 151–52.

34. *Ibid.*, pp. 244–46.

35. Taft, *Organized Labor*, p. 317; "Adjusting Labor to War Demands," *Literary Digest*, Vol. LV, No. 11 (September 15, 1917), pp. 74–75. For brief accounts of the development of government wartime labor adjustment machinery, an outline of various wartime government labor boards and a summary of war labor policies, see Louis B. Wehle, "The Adjustment of Labor Disputes Incident to Production for War in the United States" (*Quarterly Journal of Economics*, Vol. XXXII, November 1917, pp. 122–33); "Labor Problems in the United States During the War" (*Quarterly Journal of Economics*, Vol. XXXII, February 1918, pp. 333–84) and "War Labor Policies and Their Outcome in Peace" (*Quarterly Journal of Economics*, Vol. XXXIII, February 1919, pp. 321–43).

36. Gordon S. Watkins, "Labor Problems . . . ," Part I, p. 79.

37. Haywood, *Bill Haywood's Book*, p. 299.

38. Preston, pp. 124–25, 129.

39. Department of Justice files, *passim*; Michael R. Johnson, "The I.W.W. and Wilsonian Democracy," *Science and Society*, Vol. XXVIII, No. 3 (Summer 1964), pp. 258–74. Marxist Johnson emphasized the "frightened" and "suspicious" nature of the Wilson administration's repressive wartime policies. (*Ibid.*, p. 273.) O. A. Hilton ("Public Opinion and . . . ") argued more realistically than Johnson that the restriction of civil liberties during and immediately after World War I was more a result of rabid public pressure on a weak government than an expression of a specific administrative policy.

40. Preston, pp. 109–16.

41. McCluskey, letter to J. Byrkit, April 21, 1968; "Report of . . . Commission on . . . Bisbee . . . ," pp. 6–7.

42. Of interest is the fact that at least one specific, tangible case of government discipline of industry did take place. In September 1918, Wilson directed Secretary of War Baker to commandeer the Smith and Wesson firearms company and operate it after the company refused to accept the instructions of the War Labor Board concerning discrimination against its organized employees. The war ended, of course, within two months. (Gordon S. Watkins, "Labor Problems . . . ," Part II, p. 170.)

43. Cleland, pp. 201, 274–278.

44. Ray Stannard Baker, *Woodrow Wilson: Life and Letters*, 8 Volumes (Garden City: Doubleday, Doran & Company, 1931).

45. Ferdinand Lundberg, *America's Sixty Families* (New York: The Vanguard Press, 1937), p. 114.

46. Baker, Vol. 2, p. 130 and *passim*. Ferdinand Lundberg said Dodge was the "inheritor of the invisible mantle that passed from Mark Hanna." (Lundberg, p. 113.)

47. Baker, Vol. 3, p. 238.

48. Lundberg, p. 114.

49. Lundberg, p. 109; Baker, Vol. 3, pp. 233, 365, 372, 373.

50. Baker, Vol. 4, pp. 30–31.

51. *Ibid.*, p. 33.

52. *Ibid.*, p. 34.

53. *Ibid.*

54. *Ibid.*

55. Lundberg, pp. 142–43.

56. *Ibid.*, pp. 132, 265.

57. Baker, Vol. 7, p. 32.

58. *Ibid.*, pp. 87, 392.

59. Myers, *History of the Great ...* , p. 432.

60. *Taft, Organized Labor*, p. 336–37; Gambs, p. 29; Brissenden, *The I.W.W. ...* , p. 347; Cole, p. 200; *Bisbee Daily Review*, August 12, 1917, sect. 1, p. 6.

61. *Bisbee Daily Review*, August 16, 1917, p. 1.

62. "Exclusion and Expulsion ... ," p. 4.

63. *New York Times*, July 14, 1917, p. 4.

64. *Ibid.*, July 17, 1917, p. 7.

65. Taft, "The Federal Trials ... ," p. 58.

66. "The Red Hysteria," *New Republic*, Vol. XXI, No. 269 (January 28, 1920), pp. 249–52.

67. Bruere, "Copper Camp Patriotism," February 21, 1918, pp. 202–03.

68. "Labor Unrest ... ," p. 429.

69. *Ibid.*; "Lynch-Law and Reason," *Literary Digest*, Vol. LV, No. 7 [August 18,1917], pp. 12–13.

70. *New York Times*, August 2, 1917, p. 20.

71. "Lynch-Law and Reason," pp. 12–13.

72. *Ibid.*

73. "What Haywood Says ... ," p. 430; "The Labor Troubles at Butte," *Mining and Scientific Press*, Vol. 115, September 1, 1917, pp. 305–08.

74. Jensen, pp. 438–39.

75. Ashurst, *Cong. Record*, Aug. 17, 1917.

76. *Bisbee Daily Review*, August 21, 1917, p. 1; Preston, pp. 106–107.

77. Haywood, *Bill Haywood's Book*, pp. 302–03.

78. *Ibid.*, pp. 307–08.

79. *Ibid.*, pp. 313–26; Renshaw, pp. 223–24; Lowell S. Hawley and Ralph Bushnell Potts, *Counsel for the Damned* (Philadelphia: Lippincott, 1953).

80. Victor S. Yarros, "The Story of the I.W.W. Trial," *Survey*, Vol. 40, No. 22 (August 21, 1918), pp. 603–605.

81. Renshaw, pp. 223–24; Victor S. Yarros, "The I.W.W. Trial," *Nation*, Vol. 107, No. 2774 (August 31, 1918), pp. 220–23.

82. National Committee, A.C.L.U., *The Truth About the I.W.W. Prisoners* (New York: American Civil Liberties Union, 1922).

83. There is a tendency for people to believe that artists and the literati comprise the activist radical support among middle-class intellectuals. This has been a common belief particularly associated with the nineteenth century and the first four decades of the twentieth. But the signatures on the advertisement supporting the IWW prisoners indicate that in 1918 social scientists dominated. A poll conducted among 60,000 professors from 307 colleges and universities by the Carnegie Commission on Higher Education showed the same loyalties prevailed in 1969. The humanities' faculty support of liberal causes ranked considerably lower than that of the social sciences'. (Seymour Martin Lipset and Everett Carll Ladd, Jr.,"...And What Professors think," *Psychology Today*, Vol. 4, No. 6 [November, 1970], pp. 49–51.)

84. Advertisement, "Never Mind What You Think About the I.W.W.," *New Republic*, Vol. XV, No. 191 (June 29, 1918), p. 242; Renshaw, pp. 215–42; "Ol' Rags an' Bottles," *Nation*, Vol. CVIII, No. 2795 (January 25, 1919), pp. 114–16.

85. Yarros, "The Story ... ," pp. 660–63; Robinson, p. 294; Herbert Young, "The Jerome ... ," p. 14.

86. Brissenden, *The I.W.W. ... ,*' p. 282.

87. Alexander Sidney Lanier, "To the President," *New Republic*, Vol. XVIII, No. 233 (April 19, 1919), pp. 383–84; Gambs, p. 23.

88. *Ibid.*

89. J. Ross Browne, p. 22.

90. "Federal Indictment of Bisbeeites," *Arizona Mining Journal*, Vol. 1, No. 12 (May 1918), p. 15; "Arizona Loyalty Leaguers Indicted," *Survey*, Vol. 40, No. 8 (May 25, 1918), p. 226; Court of the United States of America, District of Arizona, Indictment, *United States of America v. Harry C. Wheeler et al.*, May term, 1918 (Department of Justice files); "Indictment of Bisbee ... " (Department of Justice files).

91. "The Week," *Nation*, Vol. 107, No. 2783 (November 2, 1918), p. 501; "Federal Indictment ... ," p. 15.

92. "Federal Indictment ... ," p. 15; "Arizona Loyalty ... ," p. 226.

93. *Arizona Daily Star*, June 20, 1918, p. 1.

94. Thomas A. Flynn, letter to Attorney General, May 23, 1918 (Department of Justice file 186813-78); *Tucson Citizen*, May 29, 1918, p. 1; Robinson, p. 293.

95. *United States v. Wheeler, et al.*, 254 U.S. 625 (1918).

96. William C. Fitts, letter to Attorney General, August 20, 1918 (Department of Justice file 186813-96).

97. "The Week," *Nation*, Vol. CVII, No. 2789 (December 14, 1918), p. 717.

98. William C. Fitts, letter to Assistant Attorney General Claude R. Porter, December 14, 1918 (Department of Justice file 186813-113); Alexander C. King, memorandum to Assistant Attorney General Claude R. Porter, December 14, 1918 (Department of Justice file 186813).

99. "The Supreme Court Holds that the Bisbee Deportations do not Offend the Federal law," *Law and Labor*, Vol. 3, No. 1 (January 1921), pp. 11–13; *United States v. Wheeler, et al.*, 254 U.S. 281 (1920).

100. Donnelly quoted in Harvey, p. 223.

101. "The High Cost of Deporting," *Survey*, Vol. 42, No. 12 (June 21, 1919), p. 457; Taft, *Organized Labor*, p. 335.

102. "List of Bisbee Deportees Who Have Filed Damage Suits Against the Copper Companies" (UVCC files).

103. "Judges," *Pacific Reporter*, Vol. 176 (St. Paul: West Publishing Co., 1919), p. v; Crim. No. 2685, Cochise County, September 13, 1919; Arizona, Justice Court (Cochise Co. Precinct No. 4), "Preliminary Hearings of Defendants in the Bisbee Deportation Trials," 11 Vols. (*Individual Transcripts* [books 1–7] and *Original Blanket Hearings* [books 1–4], July–September 1919. John Wilson Ross also helped to bring these suits against the copper companies.

104. "Bisbee," *Survey*, Vol. XLIII, No. 16 (February 14, 1920), p. 571; *Preliminary Hearings ... Ind. Transcripts*, Book 2, pp. 8, 47; *Michael Simmons v. El Paso & Southwestern Railroad, et al.*, No. 2364.

105. "Bisbee," p. 57; Bishop Scarlett, interview, March 13, 1972.

106. *Arizona Republican*, January 21, 1920, p. 1, and January 22, 1920, p. 1; Morse, Preface; T. E. Campbell, "The I.W.W. in Arizona," n.p.; "Preliminary Hearings ... ;" John D. Lawson, ed., "The Trial of Harry E. Wootton for Kidnaping, Tombstone, Arizona, 1920," *Arizona State Trials*, Vol. 17 (St. Louis: Thomas Law Book Co., 1921), pp. 1–175.

107. Lawson, pp. 1–175; Frank E. Curley, *The Law of Necessity as Applied in State of Arizona vs. H. E. Wootton, the Bisbee Deportation Case* (Tucson: Bureau of Information, n.d.), pp. 1–18; Bledsoe, August 15, 1968.

108. Soule, p. 226; Curley, pp. 15–19; Lawson, *passim*.

109. *Simmons v. El Paso & Southwestern Railroad, et al.*, *passim*.

110. Lawson, pp. 165–170; Curley, p. 28.

111. K. Pintek, April 8, 1966, and July 19, 1972.

112. Soule, p. 255; Curley, pp. 25–30.

113. Curley, front cover.

114. Soule, pp. 225–37; Curley, *passim* and back cover.

115. Another journalist, Frederic Farquhar McLeod, put together as a rough play what is probably the most meaningful statement about

the outsiders' impressions. He called it *Old Man Necessity or Have You Talked With Allie Howe?*, "A Hell of a Drama in One Act and a Referee's Decision." (Allie Howe was one of the Bisbee deputies originally indicted by the federal government in 1918. He worked for *The Bisbee Daily Review* and from time to time wrote articles for that newspaper. [*Bisbee Daily Review*, April 1, 1948, p. 1.] No doubt there is some vicious intraprofessional sarcasm intended in the play's title.) A collection of nonsense by bored newspapermen staying at Tombstone during the deportation trial, the play ridiculed Arizona justice, local people, unions and the social scene in general. More than anything, McLeod and his cronies created, as they drank bootleg whiskey in their hotel rooms to while away the hot summer months, an elaborate doodle. With a tasteful format and a strong concern for poetic and dramatic style—at the expense of content—the concoction said something about the futility of making civilized sense out of the nature of Arizona law. Yet the writers seemed more disgusted by the ignorance, immaturity, crudity and buffoonery of the people of Arizona than they were repulsed by the gross manipulation of "justice." (Frederic Farquhar McLeod, *Old Man Necessity or Have You Talked With Allie Howe?*, "A Hell of a Drama in One Act and a Referee's Decision," Tombstone, 1920 [Special Collections, University of Arizona Library, Tucson].) This tone of absurdity was lost to later legal analysts.

116. Bledsoe, August 15, 1968.

117. Newman F. Baker, "Preface" in Lawton. Another article concerned with the "Law of Necessity" appeared years later in the *Arizona Law Review*. ("Law of Necessity as Applied in the Bisbee Deportation Case," Vol. 3, No. 2 [Winter, 1971], pp. 264–79.) The author dared to mildly call into question the arguments and decision of the case. He did not, however, dare to sign his name; the article was credited to "Editorial Board."

Chapter 11: Arizona Dons the Copper Collar

1. Bruere, "Copper Camp Patriotism," February 21, 1918, pp. 202–03. For a representative study of this kind see Wehle, "Labor Problems ... "

2. U.S., Congress, Senate, Senator King, *Congressional Record*, Sixty-fifth Congress, Second Session, May 6, 1918, Vol. LVI, Part 6, p. 6091.

3. *Jerome Sun*, December 17, 1917, p. 2.

4. *Barron v. Branson*, No. 7054, Superior Court, State of Arizona, Yavapai County, decided for plaintiff May 14, 1918; *Jerome Sun*, April 9, 1918, p. 1 (last issue).

5. Charles Clark, "The United Verde and Labor," *Mining and Scientific Press*, Vol. 116, May 25, 1918, pp. 709–10.

6. "Report and Recommendations ... ," pp. 9–14.

7. John A. Fitch, "A Report of Industrial Unrest," *Survey*, Vol. 39, No. 20 (February 16, 1918), pp. 545–46.

8. Phelps Dodge letter quoted in Bing, p. 277.

9. Kellogg, "Transcript . . . taken . . . at Bisbee," p. 19.

10. Sec. of Labor, *Sixth Annual Report* . . . , p. 29.

11. Massey, "Transcript . . . taken . . . at Bisbee," p. 50; "Development of Collective Bargaining . . . ," p. 593.

12. Brown, *loc. cit.*, pp. 24–30; Kellogg, *loc. cit.*, p. 19; numerous testimony, *Original Blanket Hearings*, all books, *passim*; Frank J. Vaughan, *loc. cit*, p. 46; Massey, *loc. cit.*, p. 50; Phelps Dodge Corp., "Employees to Columbus," "Transcript . . . taken . . . at Bisbee," p. 287.

13. Thomas A. French, "Arizona State Federation of Labor," *Arizona Labor Journal*, Vol. VIII, No. 6 (June 11, 1920, p. 4). At least one scholarly study of this period in Arizona history concludes that mining corporations used the IWW to weaken the power of legitimate mine unions. (Alan Johnson, p. 91.)

14. "The Arizona Copper Strike," p. 434.

15. "Organization or Anarchy," p. 321.

16. Robert Wolf, "Securing the Initiative of the Workman," *American Economic Review* (Supplement), Vol. IX, No. 1 (March 1919), p. 120.

17. U.S., Congress, Senate, *Congressional Record*, Sixty-fifth Congress, First Session, Vol. LV, Part 6, August 13, 1917, p. 5981.

18. Walter Douglas, "Increased Wages and Decreased Efficiency in the Clifton-Morenci District," *Mining and Scientific Press*, Vol. 115, September 8, 1917, pp. 339–40. One member of the Phelps Dodge president's audience, John B. Hastings, talked to Douglas immediately after the presentation. According to Hastings, Dodge admitted that his information did not reflect the situation at Morenci's Phelps Dodge mine. Douglas told Hastings that his argument was based on "what the other managers tell me; in our [Phelps Dodge's] case a bonus system was arranged which resulted in our getting more than the highest earnings, while the work cost less than in pre-war times." (John B. Hastings, "Mine Labor," *Mining and Scientific Press*, Vol. 118, May 24, 1919, p. 696.)

19. Charles Merz, "The Issue in Butte," *New Republic*, Vol. XII, No. 151 (September 22, 1917), pp. 215–17.

20. Irving Bernstein, *The Lean Years: A History of the American Worker, 1920–1933* (Boston: Houghton-Mifflin Company, 1960); Writers' Program, p. 100.

21. "U.S. Supreme Court Upholds Law Making Employers In So-Called Hazardous Occupations Liable in Damages for All Accidents Without Fault," *Law and Labor*, Vol. 1, No. 7 (July 1919), p. 19; Joseph G. Rayback, *A History of American Labor* (New York: The MacMillan Company, 1959), p. 279; Bernstein, "The Growth of . . . ,'" p. 313 and *passim*.

22. Gordon S. Watkins, "Labor Problems ... ,"' pp. 226–28. It took Watkins more than fifteen years to acknowledge the unpleasant reality of the labor-management relationship during this period. In 1935 he commented bitterly, "Ever since the close of the Great War in 1918, employers have made an unprecedented effort to marshall their forces in the fight against unionism and the union shop." (Gordon S. Watkins, *Labor Problems*, p. 562.) Other optimistic statements about labor in the post-war period can be found in J. M. Budish and George Soule, *The New Unionism* (New York: Russell & Russell, 1920), and J. G. Rayback, *A History of American Labor*. A study which shows the paralysis of the labor movement after 1918 is Irving Bernstein, *The Lean Years*.

23. S. E. Rau-Roesler, "Recruiting Labor from the Gold Mines," *Mining and Scientific Press*, Vol. 115, November 24, 1917, p. 747.

24. Joseph F. Myers, letter to Secretary of Labor Wilson, January 24, 1918 (Department of Justice file, No. 33/438-A6, in Department of Justice files).

25. "Importation of Labor," *Arizona Mining Journal*, Vol. I, No. 9 (March, 1918), pp. 16–17.

26. Frank Brown, letter to Secretary of Labor Wilson, February 4, 1918 (Department of Labor file, No. 33/438-A6, in Department of Justice files).

27. "Importation of Labor," pp. 16–17; Jensen, pp. 421–25.

28. Department of Justice files, especially reports of operatives working out of the Office of Department Intelligence Officer, War Department, Headquarters Southern Department, Fort Sam Houston, Texas.

29. *Tucson Citizen*, April 10, 1918, p. 1. "Report of Labor Committee," *Arizona Service Bulletin* (official bulletin of Arizona State Council of Defense), Vol. 1, No. 1 (May 1, 1918), p. 6.

30. "Importation of Labor," pp. 16–17; "Mining Men Confer With Council of Defense," *Arizona Mining Journal*, Vol. 1, No. 10 (April 1918), p. 6; Arizona State Council of Defense, "A Record of the Activities of the Arizona State Council of Defense from Formation April 18, 1917 to Dissolution, June, 1919," n.d., p. 44.

31. "Importation of Labor," pp. 16–17; "Arizona Chapter, American Mining Congress," *Arizona Mining Journal*, Vol. I, No. 10 [April 1918], p. 4.

32. *Tucson Citizen*, April 10, 1918, p. 1.

33. "Mining Men Confer ... ," p. 6.

34. In 1910 Maricopa County ranked second in population (34,488) to Cochise County (34,591). By 1918 Maricopa (with 73,042) had begun to far exceed the premier copper county (59,535). (*Fourth Biennial Report of the State Tax Commission of Arizona*, December 31, 1918.)

35. "Report of the Meeting of the Executive Committee of the Arizona State Council of Defense Held at the Office of Governor Hunt April 17th, 1918, For the Purpose of Discussing the I.W.W.

Movement in Arizona," 33 pages (typescript report in H. S. McCluskey papers, Special Collections, Arizona State University Library, Tempe).

36. *Ibid.; "Mining Men Confer . . . ," p. 6; Arizona Republican*, April 26, 1918, p. 1.

37. For a study of the final pre-Wagner Act breakup of the IUMMSW in Arizona between 1918 and 1921, see Jensen, Chap. 24.

38. *Verde Copper News*, March 27, 1918; *Jerome Sun*, March 27, 1918, p. 1; George W. P. Hunt, letter to Cochise County Attorney John F. Ross, March 27, 1918 (G. W. P. Hunt papers, Special Collections, Arizona State University Library, Tempe).

39. *Verde Copper News*, March 29, 1918, p. 1. This old-fashioned treatment got results; Waldroop left for Butte on March 28.

40. Hunt, letter to Ross, March 27, 1918.

41. George W. P. Hunt, letter to State Attorney General Jones, March 27, 1918 (G. W. P. Hunt papers, Special Collections, Arizona State University Library, Tempe).

42. "Loyalty Leagues Outlawed," *Arizona Mining Journal*, Vol. VI, No. 4 (April 5, 1918), p. 1.

43. Robert E. Tally, letter to Charles W. Clark, April 8, 1918 (UVCC files, Phelps Dodge Corp. office, Jerome, Arizona).

44. Abstract of Record . . . , *Hunt v. Campbell*, pp. 11, 18, 23, 251, 290; *George W. P. Hunt v. Thomas E. Campbell, Report of Cases Argued and Determined in the Supreme Court of the State of Arizona*, from May 19, 1917 to July 19, 1918 (Vol. 19) (San Francisco: Bancroft-Whitney Company, 1919), pp. 254–304; Robinson, p. 361; *Arizona Republican*, December 23, 1917, p. 1; *Chicago Post*, December 22, 1917, p. 1; Abstract of Record . . . , *Hunt v. Campbell*.

45. George W. P. Hunt, "Message to the Special Session of the Third Legislature," May 21, 1918 (Phoenix: privately printed pamphlet, 1918), pp. 6–15.

46. *Ibid*. Bruere wrote to Hunt after this speech and thanked the Arizona governor for endorsing the journalist's writings. He commended Hunt's stand and asked for more copies of the address. (Bruere's letter quoted in *Dunbar's Weekly*, Vol. 5, No. 23 [June 8, 1918], p. 2.)

47. "Norman Carmichael Replies to Governor Hunt," *Arizona Mining Journal*, Vol. II, No. 1 (June 1918), pp. 13–14.

48. "Governor Hunt's Reply," *Arizona Mining Journal*, Vol. II, No. 1 (June 1918), p. 14; "Mr. Carmichael's Rejoinder," *Ibid.*; "Hunt Replies to Carmichael," *Dunbar's Weekly*, Vol. 5, No. 24 (June 15, 1918), p. 7.

49. Robert A. Watkins, "Respecting the Governor's Message," *Arizona Mining Journal*, Vol. II, No. 1 (June 1918), pp. 9, 11; Editorial: "Next!" *Bisbee Daily Review*, June 30, 1918, p. 2.

50. Arizona, *Journal of the House of Representatives*, Third Legislature of the State of Arizona, First Special Session, June 18, 1918.

51. *Bisbee Square Dealer*, March 2, 1917, p. 2.

52. Robert E. Tally, letter to Charles W. Clark, June 4, 1918 (UVCC files).

53. Van Petten, p. 34; Robert E. Tally, letter to Charles W. Clark, September 13, 1918 (UVCC files).

54. Robert E. Tally, letter to Charles W. Clark, September 20, 1918 (UVCC files).

55. Van Petten, pp. 44–45; Tally, letter to C. W. Clark, September 13, 1918.

56. 25,927 to 25,588. (Wyllys, p. 317.)

57. Edward Berman, *Labor and the Sherman Act* (New York: Harper and Brothers Publishers, 1930), *passim*. Berman showed the use of the Sherman Act in issuing injunctions against labor unions. He emphasized the period after the Clayton Act which culminated in the Bedford Stone decision of 1927. Also see Gordon S. Watkins, *Labor Problems*, p. 474, for the use of the injunction to restrain unions in boycotting and picketing. (Bucks Stove and Range Case.)

58. Elias Lieberman, *Unions Before the Bar* (New York: Harper and Brothers, 1950), pp.119–22; *Truax et al. v. Bisbee Local No. 380, Cooks' and Waiters' Union, et al.* (No. 1544), 171 Pac 121 (Arizona); *Wm. Truax, et al. v. Bisbee Local No. 380, Cooks' and Waiters' Union, et al., Abstract of Record*, Arizona Supreme Court, Appeal from the Superior Court of Cochise County, filed 13th October 1916.

59. *Traux v. Bisbee Local No. 380, Abstract…*

60. *Wm. Truax et al. v. Michael Corrigan, et al., Abstract of Record*, Arizona Supreme Court, Appeal from the Superior Court of Cochise County, filed 8th June 1917; *Truax, et al. v. Corrigan, et al.* (No. 1580), 20 Ariz. 7 (1918).

61. Lieberman, pp. 122–26; "Peaceful Picketing Held to be Lawful and Validity of Anti-Injunction Statute Sustained in Arizona," *Law and Labor*, Vol. 1, No. 2 (February, 1919) p. 7; *Truax, et al. v. Corrigan, et al.* (No. 1580), 176 Pac. 570 (Arizona).

62. Lieberman, pp. 122–26.

63. *Ibid.*

64. *Ibid.*; Gordon S. Watkins, *Labor Problems*, pp. 475–76; "Anti-Injunction Law of Arizona Held Unconstitutional," *Monthly Labor Review*, Vol. XIV, No. 2 (February, 1922), pp. 124–128; "Equality Before the Law," *Independent and the Weekly Review*, Vol. 108, No. 3800 (January 14, 1922), pp. 30–31. For a naive commentary on the anti-injunction law, see Archibald MacLeish and E. F. Pritchard, Jr., eds., "The Same Mr. Taft" in *Law and Politics; Occasional Papers of Felix Frankfurter* (New York: Harcourt, Brace and Company, 1939), pp. xiii, 44, 45, 227. Also see Felix Frankfurter and Nathan Greene, *The Labor Injunction* (New York: MacMillan Company, 1930), pp. 152–154, 177–180. A more realistic study can be found in Russell Smith's "Significant Developments … ," pp. 1268–1271. Smith reveals how the

injunction negated the advances made by labor in obtaining legal recognition and other goals.

65. Lieberman, p. 126.

66. Numerous other rulings further disabled the American labor movement during this time. One study revealed that "no prior era in the history of the [Supreme] court approached the twenties in the number of statutes invalidated, most of them labor laws." (Bernstein, *The Lean Years*, p. 242.)

Chapter 12: As Time Passed

1. George J. Keahey, interviewed by J. Byrkit, August 15, 1968; Eddy and Watson, July 19, 1972; Hanhila, Hinton tapes; Burrows, June 27, 1968.

2. Newkirk, p. viii. "An abnormal psychological tension" between employers and employees existed in Bisbee after the deportation, claimed Robert Bruere. (Bruere, "The Industrial . . . ," p. 252.) He did not say if this were less desirable than the "normal psychological tension."

3. S. C. Dickenson, *A Sociological Survey of the Bisbee-Warren District*, typescript by Arizona State Bureau of Mines, Tucson, December 31, 1917 (Special Collections, University of Arizona Library, Tucson).

4. "The Warren Mining District," *Arizona Labor Journal*, Vol. VIII, No. 60 (June 11, 1920), p. 15.

5. Raley, p. 8.

6. *Ibid.*, p. 7.

7. Alice Hamilton, p. 210.

8. "Review of Mining," *Mining and Scientific Press*, Vol. 116, April 13, 1918, p. 523.

9. "The Mining Summary," *Mining and Scientific Press*, Vol. 117, July 20, 1918, p. 95.

10. *Ibid*.

11. A. M. Heckman, "A New Bonus Plan," *Mining and Scientific Press*, Vol. 117, August 24, 1918, pp. 249–50.

12. "The Mining Summary," July 20, 1918.

13. Robert E. Tally, letter to Charles W. Clark, July 26, 1918 (UVCC files).

14. Charles W. Clark, letter to Robert Tally, July 28, 1918 (UVCC files).

15. "The Week," Nov. 2, 1918, p. 501.

16. "Review of Mining," *Mining and Scientific Press*, Vol. 118, February 8, 1919, p. 194; "Review of Mining," *Mining and Scientific Press*, Vol. 118, June 14, 1919, p. 826.

17. U.S., Secretary of Labor and Bureaus, *Seventh Annual Report of the Secretary of Labor–1919* (Washington, D.C.: Government Printing Office, 1920), p. 33.

18. Phelps Dodge Corporation, Copper Queen Branch, "Employees' Representation Plan" (pamphlet dated July 1921). For a discussion of company unions, see Robert W. Dunn, *Company Unions* (New York: Vanguard Press, 1927).

19. Hyman Weintraub, "The I.W.W. in California: 1905–1931 (M.A. thesis, U.C.L.A., 1947).

20. Preston, pp. 2, 8 and *passim*.

21. Gordon S. Watkins, "Labor Problems . . . ," Part I, p. 40.

22. Michael Johnson, p. 274.

23. *Ibid.*, p. 273. Also see Saposs, *Left-Wing Unionism*.

24. Harrison George, "What a Political Prisoner Thinks About," *Nation*, Vol. 113, No. 2931 (September 7, 1921), p. 266.

25. Catherin Hofteling, "Sunkist Prisoners," *Nation*, Vol. 113, No. 2933 (September 21, 1921), p. 316; "Ol' Rags an' Bottles," p. 116.

26. Hofteling, p. 316.

27. Harrison George, p. 266.

28. See Lewis Browne, "Bolshevism in America" and Lynn Ford, "The Growing Menace of the I.W.W." (*Forum*, Vol. LXI, No. 1 [January 1919], pp. 62–70.)

29. Theresa S. McMahon, "Centralia and the I.W.W.," *Survey*, Vol. XLIII, No.6 (November 29, 1919), pp. 173–74.

30. Kornbluh, p. 296; Ray Ginger, *The Burning Cross* (New Brunswick: Rutgers University Press, 1949), p. 396.

31. Hofteling, p. 316.

32. D. D. Lescohier, "With the I.W.W. in the Wheat Lands," *Harper's Magazine*, Vol. CXLVII, No. DCCCLXXIX (August 1923), pp. 371–80.

33. "Why I Quit the I.W.W.," *Sunset*, Vol. 53, No. 5 (November, 1924), p. 92.

34. Harry Hibschman, "The I.W.W. Menace Self-Revealed," *New York Times Current History*, Vol. XVI, No. 5 (August 1922), p. 761–68.

35. James Oneal, "The Passing of the I.W.W.," *Current History Magazine*, Vol. XXI, No. 4 (January 1925), pp. 528–34.

36. Robert E. Tally, letter to Attorney General Daugherty, January 2, 1924 (copy in Department of Justice files).

37. Kornbluh, pp. 351–55.

BIBLIOGRAPHIC ESSAY

Although she pretended to veil her secrets, the Copper Queen wore her heart on her sleeve. Explicitly or between the lines, Phelps Dodge expressed its opinions in the pages of the *Bisbee Daily Review*. For its revelations, the *Review* ranks as the premier source for a study of Bisbee and Phelps Dodge. At times astonishingly frank and objective, the *Review* also demonstrates the mercurial moods and passions which were themselves representative of the ingenuous attitudes of a simpler time. Phelps Dodge did not open its Bisbee, Douglas or Jerome files to this study, but the old United Verde Copper Company records, provided by Jerome historian Herbert V. Young, proved to be a rich vein. In particular, the periodic reports of United Verde operators Henry Allen, Will Clark and Robert Tally to William Andrews Clark and his son Charles reveal the great concern mine owners and managers had for Arizona politics. The reports of the Thiel Detective Agency operatives found in the United Verde files emphasize this political awareness.

Because President Wilson's Mediation Commission failed to discern or, at least, probe the political motivations that underlay the labor turmoil in 1917 Arizona, the transcripts that came out of its investigating sessions at Globe, Clifton and Bisbee provide little more than narrative details and examples of specious testimony. Likewise, though they contain numerous telegrams and letters pertinent to the Arizona strife and to the Bisbee Deportation, the files of the United States Departments of Labor and Justice in the National Archives provide only details which corroborate more telling sources. For the same reason, the personal and public papers of George W. P. Hunt are disappointing.

Several contemporary observers did ascertain the issues, tensions, motivations and true contenders of the early twentieth century Arizona management-labor political war. Of these, no one cut through the murk and no one rejected the diversions better than the *New York Post* journalist Robert Bruere. His series on the wartime labor-management battles of the far west (*Following the Trail of the I.W.W.*) anticipated by more than fifty years most of the conclusions supported by this study. Two other observers of the time, Gordon S. Watkins (*Labor Problems*) and Alexander Bing (*War-Time Strikes and Their Adjustment*), shared to a considerable degree Bruere's keen, level-headed understanding.

In the category of courageous Arizona journalism of the period, one publication, *Dunbar's Weekly*, stands out. Among its insightful (if intemperate) comments it gave details and analyzed deeds more than any other national or statewide publication. Only one bound set—now badly crumbling—of *Dunbar's* remains.

Three important sources of twentieth-century Arizona history should be mentioned here. All of the abstracts of appealed Arizona Superior Court decisions are now on microfilm. Many of these abstracts include the entire lower court transcript. Secondly, the technical periodical collection of the University of Arizona Science Library contains a large body of historical information heretofore neglected. One outstanding journal, T. A. Rickard's *Mining and Scientific Press*, merits special attention for its richness of detail. Thirdly, Harwood P. Hinton, University of Arizona history professor and editor of *Arizona and the West*, is presently acquiring a valuable collection of taped oral history. Its use should be encouraged.

Several accounts and interpretations of the Bisbee Deportation have appeared over the years. The first scholarly version was an article by Meyer Fishbein in the *Southwestern Social Science Quarterly* in 1949. The following year Vernon Jensen published a fine study of western mining labor problems (*Heritage of Conflicts*). It includes one of the better narratives of the deportation. Saul Landau, in a 1959 Master's Thesis for the University of Wisconsin, gave the event a doctrinaire Marxist interpretation. In a more recent account (*We Shall Be All*, 1969), Melvyn Dubofsky, like Landau, emphasized the significance of the IWW. Only one published source concerns itself specifically and solely with the Bisbee affair. The article, a "sociological interpretation" by John H. Lindquist and James Fraser (*Pacific Historical Review*, November 1968), argues that the Bisbee Deportation was a spontaneous, "predictable response" by a group of citizens who were simply protecting their homes against threats from seditious radicals.

The general labor history source which deals best with this period is Philip Taft's *Organized Labor in American History* (1964), while Vernon Jensen's study presents the most detailed account of early labor history in western mining districts. Two works, Melvyn Dubofsky's books, *We Shall Be All*, and *The I.W.W.: A Study of American Syndicalism* (1920) by Paul F. Brissenden, constitute the best studies of the IWW. *Aliens and Dissenters* (1963) by William Preston, Jr., merits examination by those interested in the problem of political repression.

Several good studies of Western hard-rock mining between 1860 and 1920 have appeared in recent years. John Rowe's *The Hard Rock Men* (1974), Stephen M. Voynik's *The Making of a Hardrock Miner* (1978), and Ronald C. Brown, *Hard Rock Miners: The Intermountain West* (1979) are all competent additions to their field. *The Hardrock Miners* (1974) by Richard E. Lingenfelter is a study of the history of the mining labor movement in the American West from 1863 to 1893, while *Hard Rock Epic* (1979) by Mark Wyman emphasizes the impact of the American Industrial Revolution upon the mine workers. Lingenfelter's description of the day-to-day life of underground miners is outstanding. In 1972 George G. Suggs, Jr., published *Colorado's War on Militant Unionism*, a study of the Western Federation of Miners' battle with big industry and Colorado Governor James H. Peabody.

BIBLIOGRAPHY

Libraries

Arizona Law Library and Archives. Capitol. Phoenix, Arizona.
Arizona Historical Society. Tucson, Arizona.
Arizona State University. Tempe, Arizona.
Northern Arizona University. Flagstaff, Arizona.
Phoenix Public Library. Phoenix, Arizona.
University of Arizona. Tucson, Arizona.
———. Law Library. Tucson, Arizona.
———. Science Library. Tucson, Arizona.
University of California at Los Angeles. Los Angeles, California.
University of California at Riverside. Riverside, California.

Records, Private Papers and Manuscript Collections

Arizona Copper Company files. Special Collections, University of Arizona Library. Tucson, Arizona.
Arizona Territorial Court Records. National Archives and Records Service. Laguna Niguel, California.
"Clifton-Morenci Strike, 1915–16" file. Special Collections, University of Arizona Library. Tucson, Arizona.

Department of Labor files. National Archives. Washington, D.C.

Department of Justice files. National Archives. Washington, D.C.

Douglas, Lewis. Papers. Special Collections, University of Arizona Library. Tucson, Arizona.

Greenway, John. Papers. Arizona Historical Society. Tucson, Arizona.

Hunt, G. W. P. Papers. Arizona Law Library and Archives. Phoenix, Arizona.

——. Papers. Special Collections, Arizona State University Library. Tempe, Arizona.

——. "Scrapbooks." Special Collections, University of Arizona Library. Tucson, Arizona.

Ives, Eugene. Letterbooks. Specials Collections, University of Arizona Library. Tucson, Arizona.

Martin, Douglas. Papers. Special Collections, University of Arizona Library. Tucson, Arizona.

McClintock, James H. Clip files. Phoenix Public Library. Phoenix, Arizona.

McCluskey, H. S. Files. Special Collections, Arizona State University Library. Tempe, Arizona.

Records of Clerk of the Superior Court. Yavapai County Court House. Prescott, Arizona.

Simmons v. El Paso and Southwestern Railroad. Exhibits. Special Collections. University of Arizona Library. Tucson, Arizona.

Staunton, William Field. Papers. Special Collections, University of Arizona Library. Tucson, Arizona.

United Verde Copper Company Files. Jerome, Arizona.

——. Special Collections, Northern Arizona University. Flagstaff, Arizona.

United States District Court (Arizona) Records. National Archives and Records Service. Laguna Niguel, California.

Young, Herbert V. Files. Clarkdale, Arizona.

Government Documents and Publications

Arizona. *Abstract of Record*. Appeal to the Supreme Court of the State of Arizona from Superior Court of Maricopa County. George W. P. Hunt, Appellant v. Thomas E. Campbell, Appellee. August 6, 1917.

——. *Abstract of Record*. Appeal to the Supreme Court of the State of Arizona from Superior Court of Cochise County. Wm. Truax, *et al*. v. Bisbee Local Cooks' and Waiters' Union, *et al*. October 13, 1916.

——. Acts, *Resolutions and Memorials of the Regular Session, First Legislature*. March 18, 1912–May 18, 1912.

———. *Biennial Report of the State Tax Commission of Arizona*, 1913–1918.

———. *Constitution*. 1961.

———. Department of Mineral Resources. Frank J. Tuck. *History of Mining in Arizona*. 1955.

———. *First Report of the State Tax Commission*. For the period between May 18, 1912, and December 31, 1912.

———. *Journal of House of Representatives, Third Legislature of the State of Arizona, First Special Session*. May–June, 1918.

———. *Laws of a Local or Special Nature, Resolutions and Memorials Passed by the Third Special Session, First Legislature of the State of Arizona*. April 14, 1913–May 17, 1913.

———. *Report of the Conference of the Tax Commission, Board of Supervisors and County Assessors of the State of Arizona*, 1913–1918.

———. *Senate Journal, Second Special Session*. June 1, 1915–June 28, 1915.

———. *Session Laws of the Twenty-fifth Legislative Assembly of the Territory of Arizona*. Phoenix. 1909.

———. *Session Laws of the Twenty-fourth Legislative Assembly of the Territory of Arizona*. Phoenix. 1907.

———. *Special Reports of the State Tax Commission of Arizona on Mining Taxation*, Special Report to the Governor, March 17, 1913.

———. Territory. *Proceedings of the Territorial Board of Equalization*, 1905–1913 inclusive

U.S. Bureau of Census. *Historical Statistics of the United States, 1789–1945*. Washington, D.C.: Government Printing Office, 1949.

U.S. Committee on Public Information. "Report and Recommendations of President's Mediators on the Underlying Causes and Remedy for Labor Unrest," *Official Bulletin*, Vol. II, No. 231 (February 11, 1918), pp. 9–14.

———. "Report of President Wilson's Mediation Commission on the Bisbee, Ariz., Deportations, Including its Recommendations as Made on Findings of Facts," *Official Bulletin*, Vol. I, No. 170 (November 27, 1917), pp. 6–7.

U.S. Congress. *Congressional Record*. Vols. LIV, LV and LVI.

U.S. Congress. House of Representatives. "Capital and Labor Employed in Mining Industry." Industrial Commission Report. House Document No. 179. 57th Congress, First Session.

———. "Deportation of Certain Aliens." Report No. 7252. Document 127. 65th Congress, 1st Session, August 4, 1917.

U.S. Congress. House of Representatives. "Exclusion and Expulsion of Aliens of Anarchistic and Similar Classes." Report No. 7652. Document 504. 66th Congress, 2nd Session, December 16, 1919.

———. "Select Committee on Expenditures in the War Department." Report No. 1400. 66th Congress, 3rd Session, Vol. 2, March 2, 1921.

U.S. Congress. Senate. "The Colorado Coal Miners' Strike." Commission on Industrial Relations. Senate Document 415, 64th Congress, 1st Session, Vol. 25, April 28, 1916.

————. "A Report on Labor Disturbances in the State of Colorado, from 1880 to 1904, Inclusive." Senate Document No. 122, 58th Congress, 3rd Session, 1904.

U.S. Secretary of Labor and Bureaus. *Sixth Annual Report of the Secretary of Labor, 1918*. Washington, D.C.: Government Printing Office, 1918.

————. *Seventh Annual Report of the Secretary of Labor, 1919*. Washington, D.C.: Government Printing office, 1920.

Cases Cited

Barron v. Branson (No. 7054). Yavapai County, Arizona. May 14, 1918.

Cochise County v. Wheeler. 254 Fed. 612 (Arizona).

Crim. No. 2685. Cochise County, Arizona. September 13, 1919.

George W. P. Hunt v. Campbell. 19 Birdsall 304 (Arizona).

Raich v. Truax, et al. 219 Fed. 272 (Arizona).

Truax, et al. v. Bisbee Local No. 380 Cooks' and Waiters' Union (No. 1544). 171 Pac. 121 (Arizona).

Truax, et al. v. Corrigan, et al. (No. 1580). 20 Ariz. 7.

————. 176 Pac. 570 (Arizona).

————. 257 U.S. 312 (1921).

U.S. v. Phelps-Dodge Mercantile Co., et al. 209 Fed. 910 (Arizona).

United States v. Wheeler. 254 U.S. 381, 65 L.F. 270.

Books

Adamic, Louis. *Dynamite: The Story of Class Violence in America*. New York: The Viking Press, 1935.

Agee, James. *Let Us Now Praise Famous Men*. New York: Ballantine Books, 1939.

Anderson, Nels. *The Hobo*. Chicago: University of Chicago Press, 1923.

Arizona State Business Directory: 1916–1917. Denver: The Gazetteer Publishing & Printing Co., 1916.

Baruch, Bernard M. *American Industry in the War*. New York: Prentice-Hall Inc., 1941.

Baker, Ray Stannard. *Woodrow Wilson: Life and Letters* (8 Vols.) Garden City: Doubleday, Doran & Company, 1931.

Barnes, Will C. *Arizona Place Names*. Tucson: University of Arizona Press, 1935.

Beard, Mary Ritter. *The American Labor Movement*. New York: The MacMillan Co., 1928.

Berman, Edward. *Labor and the Sherman Act*. New York: Harper and Brothers Publishers, 1930.

Bernstein, Irving. *The Lean Years: A History of the American Worker 1920–1933*. Boston: Houghton Mifflin Company, 1960.

Bimba, Anthony. *The History of the American Working Class*. New York: Greenwood Press, Publishers, 1968.

————. *The Molly Maguires*. New York: International Publishers, 1932.

Bing, Alexander M. *War-time Strikes and Their Adjustment*. New York: E. P. Dutton and Co., 1921.

Boyer, Richard D., and Morais, Herbert M. *Labor's Untold Story*. New York: Cameron Associates, 1955.

Branch, E. Douglas. *Westward: The Romances of the American Frontier*. New York: D. Appleton and Company, 1930.

Brissenden, Paul Frederick. *The I.W.W.: A Study of American Syndicalism*. New York: Columbia University Press, 1920.

Brooks, John Graham. *American Syndicalism: The I.W.W.* New York: The MacMillan Company, 1913.

————. *Labor's Challenge to the Social Order*. New York: The MacMillan Company, 1920.

Brooks, Thomas R. *Toil and Trouble*. New York: Dell Publishing Co., 1964.

Brophy, Frank Cullen. *Though Far Away*. Glendale: The Arthur H. Clark Co., 1940.

Browne, J. Ross. *A Tour Through Arizona: 1864*. Tucson: Arizona Silhouettes, repub. 1951.

Budish, J. M., and Soule, George. *The New Unionism*. New York: Russell & Russell, 1920.

Chaplin, Ralph. *Wobbly*. Chicago: University of Chicago Press, 1948.

Clarkson, Grosvenor B. *Industrial America in the World War*. New York: Houghton Mifflin Co., 1923.

Cleland, Robert G. *A History of Phelps Dodge*. New York: Alfred A. Knopf, 1952.

Cross, Jack L. *et al.* (ed.) *Arizona: Its People and Resources*. Tucson: University of Arizona Press, 1960.

David, Henry. *The History of the Haymarket Affair*. New York: Collier Books, 1936.

Dewees, Francis P. *The Molly Maguires*. New York: Burt Franklin, 1877.

Douglas, Paul H. *Real Wages in the United States: 1890–1926*. Boston: Houghton Mifflin Company, 1930.

Dubofsky, Melvyn. *We Shall Be All*. Chicago: Quadrangle Books, 1969.

Dulles, Foster Rhea. *Labor in America*. New York: Thomas Y. Crowell, 1949.

Dunn, Robert W. *Company Unions*. New York: Vanguard Press, 1927.

Faulk, Odie B. *Land of Many Frontiers*. New York: Oxford University Press, 1968.

————. *Too Far North...Too Far South*. Los Angeles: Western Lore Press, 1967.

Faulkner, Harold U. *The Decline of Laissez Faire: 1897–1917*. New York: Rinehart & Company, Inc., 1952.

Fine, Nathan. *Labor and Farmer Parties in the United States: 1828–1928*. New York: Russell & Russell, 1961.

Frankfurter, Felix and Greene, Nathan. *The Labor Injunction*. New York: The MacMillan Company, 1930.

Gambs, John S. *The Decline of the I.W.W.* New York: Columbia University Press, 1932.

Garber, Paul Neff. *The Gadsden Treaty*. Philadelphia: Press of the University of Pennsylvania, 1923.

Gard, Wayne. *Frontier Justice*. Norman: University of Oklahoma Press, 1949.

Garrett, Paul Willard. *Government Control Over Prices*. Washington, D.C.: Government Printing Office, 1920.

Ginger, Ray. *The Burning Cross*. New Brunswick: Rutgers University Press, 1949.

Goff, John. *George W. P. Hunt and His Arizona*. Pasadena: Socio-Technical Publications, 1973.

Goldberg, Harvey (ed.) *American Radicals: Some Problems and Personalities*. New York: Monthly Review Press, 1957.

Greenstone, J. David. *Labor in American Politics*. New York: Alfred A. Knopf, 1969.

Groat, George C. *An Introduction to the Study of Organized Labor in America*. New York: The MacMillan Company, 1917.

Grubbs, Frank L., Jr. *The Struggle for Labor Loyalty*. Durham: Duke University Press, 1968.

"GT-99." *Labor Spy*. New York: The Bobbs-Merrill Company, 1937.

Hamilton, Alice. *Exploring the Dangerous Trades*. Boston: Little, Brown and Company, 1943.

Hamilton, Patrick. *The Resources of Arizona*. Tucson: Pinon Press, 1881.

Hansen, Ole. *Americanism vs. Bolshevism*. New York: Doubleday, 1920.

Harvey, Rowland Hill. *Samuel Gompers, Champion of the Toiling Masses*. Stanford, California: Stanford University Press, 1935.

Hawley, Lowell S. and Potts, Ralph Bushnell. *Counsel for the Damned*. Philadelphia: Lippincott, 1953.

Hays, Samuel P. *Conservation and the Gospel of Efficiency: The Progressive Conservation Movement*. Cambridge: Harvard University Press, 1959.

Haywood, William D. *Bill Haywood's Book*. New York: International Publishers, 1929.

Holbrook, Stewart H. *The Age of the Moguls*. Garden City, New York: Doubleday, 1953.

Hollon, W. Eugene. *The Southwest: Old and New*. Lincoln: University of Nebraska Press, 1961.

Hopkins, Ernest J. *Financing the Frontier*. Phoenix: The Arizona Printers, 1950.

Howard, Sidney. *The Labor Spy*. New York: Republic Publishing Company, 1924.

Huberman, Leo. *The Labor Spy Racket*. New York: Monthly Review Press, 1937.

Hugins, Walter. *Jacksonian Democracy and the Working Class*. Stanford, California: Stanford University Press, 1960.

Hunter, Robert. *Violence and the Labor Movement*. New York: The MacMillan Company, 1914.

James, George Wharton. *Arizona, The Wonderland*. Boston: The Page Company, 1917.

Jensen, Vernon H. *Heritage of Conflict*. Ithaca: Cornell University Press, 1950.

Jones, Mary Harris. *Autobiography of Mother Jones*. Chicago: Charles H. Kerr & Company, 1925.

Karson, Marc. *American Labor Unions and Politics: 1900–1918*. Carbondale: Southern Illinois University Press, 1958.

Kelly, George H. (ed.) *Legislative History: Arizona 1864–1912*. Phoenix: Manufacturing Stationers, 1926.

King, W. L. Mackenzie. *Industry and Humanity*. Boston: Houghton Mifflin Company, 1918.

Kluger, James R. *The Clifton-Morenci Strike*. Tucson: The University of Arizona Press, 1970.

Kolko, Gabriel. *Triumph of Conservatism*. Chicago: Quadrangle Books, 1963.

Kornbluh, Joyce L. *Rebel Voices: An I.W.W. Anthology*. Ann Arbor: The University of Michigan Press, 1964.

Lamar, Howard Roberts. *The Far Southwest 1846–1912: A Territorial History*. New Haven: Yale University Press, 1966.

Langton, H. H. *James Douglas: A Memoir*. Toronto: University of Toronto Press, 1940.

Laslett, John H. *Labor and the Left*. New York: Basic Books, Inc., 1970.

Lens, Sidney. *Left, Right & Center*. Hinsdale, Illinois: Henry Regnery Company, 1949.

Lester, Richard A. *As Unions Mature*. Princeton: Princeton University Press, 1958.

Levinson, Edward. *I Break Strikes! The Technique of Pearl L. Bergoff*. New York: Robert McBride and Company, 1935.

Lieberman, Elias. *Unions Before the Bar*. New York: Harper and Brothers Publishers, 1950.

Lingenfelter, Richard E. *The Hardrock Miners*. Berkeley: University of California Press, 1974.

Link, Arthur. *Wilson: Confusions and Crises 1915–1916*. Princeton: Princeton University Press, 1964.

Lockwood, Frank C. *Pioneer Days in Arizona*. New York: MacMillan Company, 1932.

Lundberg, Ferdinand. *America's Sixty Families*. New York: The Vanguard Press, 1937.

Mangam, William D. *The Clarks: An American Phenomenon*. New York: Silver Bow Press, 1941.

Marot, Helen. *American Labor Unions*. New York: Henry Holt and Company, 1914.

Martin, Douglas D. *An Arizona Chronology*. Tucson: The University of Arizona Press, 1963.

Mereto, Joseph J. *The Red Conspiracy*. New York: The National Historical Society, 1920.

Miller, Joseph. *Arizona: The Last Frontier*. New York: Hastings House, 1956.

Monaghan, Jay (ed.) *The Book of the American West*. New York: Julian Messner, Inc., 1963.

Montgomery, David. *Beyond Equality: Labor and the Radical Republicans 1862–1872*. New York: Alfred A. Knopf, 1967.

Murdock, Angus. *Boom Copper*. New York: The MacMillan Company, 1943.

Murdock, John. *Constitutional Development of Arizona*. Tempe, Arizona: Arizona State Teachers' College, 1930.

Myers, Gustavus. *History of the Great American Fortunes*. New York: Random House, Inc., 1909.

Orth, Samuel P. *The Armies of Labor*. New Haven: Yale University Press, 1919.

Panunzio, Constantine Maria. *The Deportation Cases of 1919–1920*. New York: Federal Council of the Churches of Christ in America, 1921.

Paré, Madeline Ferrin. *Arizona Pageant*. Phoenix: Arizona Historical Foundation, 1965.

Paul, Rodman. *Mining Frontiers of the Far West: 1848–1880*. New York: Holt, Rinehart & Winston, 1963.

Pelling, Henry. *American Labor*. Chicago: University of Chicago Press, 1960.

Perlman, Mark. *Labor Union Theories in America*. Evanston, Illinois: Row, Peterson & Co., 1958.

Perlman, Selig. *A History of Trade Unionism in the United States*. New York: The MacMillan Company, 1922.

——. *A Theory of the Labor Movement*. New York: Augustus M. Kelley, 1928.

Perlman, Selig, and Taft, Philip. *History of Labor in the United States, 1896–1932*. New York: The MacMillan Company, 1935.

Peterson, H. C. *Propaganda for War*. Norman, Oklahoma: University of Oklahoma Press, 1939.

Phillips, Harlan B. *Felix Frankfurter Reminisces*. New York: Reynal & Company, 1960.

Post, Louis F. *The Deportation Delirium of Nineteen-Twenty*. Chicago: Charles H. Kerr & Company, 1923.

Preston, William, Jr. *Aliens and Dissenters*. New York: Harper & Row, 1963.

Quiett, Glenn Chesney. *They Built the West: An Epic of Rails and Cities*. New York: D. Appleton-Century Company, Inc., 1934.

Ravitz, Abe C., and Primm, James N. (eds.) *The Haywood Case*. San Francisco: Chandler Publishing Co., 1960.

Rayback, Joseph G. *A History of American Labor*. New York: The Macmillan Company, 1959.

Rees, Albert. *Real Wages in Manufacturing: 1890–1914*. Princeton: Princeton University Press, 1961.

Renshaw, Patrick. *The Wobblies*. Garden City, New York: Doubleday & Company, Inc., 1967.

Robinson, Will H. *The Story of Arizona*. Phoenix: The Berryhill Company, 1919.

Rudwick, Elliott M. *Race Riot at East St. Louis, July 2, 1917*. New York: The World Publishing Company, 1964.

Saposs, David J. *Left Wing Unionism*. New York: Russell & Russell, 1926.

Siegfried, Andre. *America Comes of Age*. New York: Harcourt, Brace and Company, 1927.

Taft, Philip. *Organized Labor in American History*. New York: Harper and Row, 1964.

Taylor, Albion G. *Labor Policies of the National Association of Manufacturers*. Urbana: University of Illinois, 1928.

Thompson, Fred. *The I.W.W.: Its First Fifty Years*. Chicago: Industrial Workers of the World, 1955.

Tuchman, Barbara W. *The Zimmerman Telegram*. New York: The Mac-Millan Company, 1958.

Tuck, Frank J. *History of Mining in Arizona*. Phoenix: State of Arizona, 1955.

Tyler, Robert L. *Rebels of the Woods: The I.W.W. in the Pacific Northwest*. Eugene: University of Oregon, 1967.

Van Petten, Donald Robinson. *Constitution and Government of Arizona*. Phoenix: Tyler Printing Company, 1960.

Wade, Richard C. *The Urban Frontier*. Cambridge: Harvard University Press, 1959.

Wagoner, Jay J. *Arizona Territory, 1863–1912*. Tucson: University of Arizona Press, 1970.

Walworth, Arthur. *Woodrow Wilson*. Vol. II. New York: Longmans, Green and Co., 1958.

Watkins, Gordon S. *Labor Problems*. New York: Thomas Y. Crowell Co., 1935.

Writers' Program of the Work Projects Administration. *Arizona: A State Guide*. New York: Hastings House, 1940.

Wyllys, Rufus K. *Arizona: The History of a Frontier State*. Phoenix: Hobson and Herr, 1950.

Yellen, Samuel. *American Labor Struggles*. New York: The Harbor Press, 1956.

Young, Herbert V. *Ghosts of Cleopatra Hill*. Jerome, Arizona: Jerome Historical Society, 1964.

Zinn, Howard. *The Politics of History*. Boston: Beacon Press, 1970.

Articles

Abell, Aaron I. "Labor Legislation in the United States." *Review of Politics*, Vol. X, No. 1 (January 1948), pp. 35–60.

"Adjusting Labor to War Demands." *Literary Digest*, Vol. LV, No. 11 (September 15, 1917), pp. 74–75.

"Adjustment of Labor Difficulties in Arizona Copper Region." *Monthly Review of Labor Statistics*, Vol. V, No. 6 (December 1917), pp. 54–55.

"American Institute of Mining Engineers to Meet in Arizona." *Mining Congress Journal*, Vol. II, No. 9 (September 1916), p. 414.

"American Labor in the World War Period 1914 to April 1917." *Monthly Labor Review*, Vol. 49, No. 4 (October 1939), pp. 785–95.

"American Mining Congress, Nineteen Years Old, Has Had Eventful Career." *Mining Congress Journal*, Vol. II, No. 11 (November 1916), pp. 481–89.

"Annual Reports." *Commercial and Financial Chronicle*, Vol. 104, No. 2700 (March 24, 1917), p. 1139.

"Anti-Injunction Law of Arizona Held Unconstitutional." *Monthly Labor Review*, Vol. XIV, No. 2 (February 1922), pp. 124–128.

Arendt, Hannah. "Thoughts on Politics and Revolution." *New York Review of Books*, Vol. XVI, No. 7 (April 22, 1971), p. 8.

"The Arizona Alien Labor Law." *Outlook*, Vol. 109 (January 20, 1915), pp. 109–10.

"Arizona Chapter, American Mining Congress." *Arizona Mining Journal*, Vol. I, No. 10 (April 1918), p. 4.

"Arizona Chapter of Mining Congress Shows Long List of Achievements." *Mining Congress Journal*, Vol. III, No. 5 (May 1917), pp. 170–73.

"The Arizona Copper Strike." *Outlook*, Vol. 116, No. 13 (July 25, 1917), p. 466.

"Arizona Hitches Its Future to Ideas and Industry." *Business Week*, No. 1399 (June 23, 1956), pp. 114–28.

"Arizona is the Premier Copper State . . . ," *Mining and Scientific Press*, Vol. 113 (August 26, 1916), p. 298.

"Arizona Loyalty Leaguers Indicted." *Survey*, Vol. 40, No. 8 (May 25, 1918), p. 226.

"The Arizona Strike." *Arizona Mining Journal*, Vol. I, No. 2 (August 1917), pp. 4–7.

"Arizona's Anti-Alien Law Unconstitutional." *Survey*, Vol. XXXV, No. 7 (November 13, 1915), p. 155.

Austin, Mary. "Arizona: The Land of the Joyous Adventure." *Nation*, Vol. 116, No. 3013 (April 4, 1923), pp. 385–88.

———. "Hunt of Arizona." *Nation*, Vol. 127, No. 3308 (November 28, 1928), pp. 572–573.

Bernstein, Irving. "The Growth of American Unions." *American Economic Review*, Vol. XLIV, No. 3 (June 1954), pp. 301–18.

"Bills Drafted to Curb the I.W.W." *Survey*, Vol. 38, No. 21 (August 25, 1917), pp. 457–58.

"Bisbee." *Survey*, Vol. XLIII, No. 16 (February 14, 1920), p. 571.

"Bisbee and the Warren District." *Arizona Labor Journal*, Vol. I, No. 17 (August 21, 1913), p. 45.

"The Bisbee Deportations Illegal." *Survey*, Vol. 39, No. 10 (December 8, 1917), pp. 291–92.

"The Bisbee Episode." *Arizona*, Vol. VII, No. 8 (August 1917), p. 1.

"The Bisbee Miners." *Arizona Labor Journal*, Vol. I, No. 17 (August 21, 1913), p. 46.

"Blinders." *New Republic*, Vol. II, No. 15 (February 13, 1915), pp. 33–35.

Bogue, Allan C. "Social Theory and the Pioneer." *Agricultural History*, Vol. XXXIV, No. 1 (January 1960), pp. 21–34.

Boudin, Louis B. "The Sherman Act and Labor Disputes: II." *Columbia Law Review*, Vol. XL, No. 1 (January 1940), pp. 14–51.

Bourne, Randolph. "The Price of Radicalism." *New Republic*, Vol. VI, No. 71 (March 11, 1916), p. 161.

Braeman, John. "Albert J. Beveridge and Statehood for the Southwest, 1912." *Arizona and the West*, Vol. 10, No. 4 (Winter 1968), pp. 313–42.

"Branding a Liar and Issuing a Challenge." *Dunbar's Weekly*, Vol. III, No. 23 (July 10, 1916), p. 2.

Brissenden, Paul. "The Butte Miners and the Rustling Card." *American Economic Review*, Vol. X, No. 4 (December 1920), pp. 755–75.

Bronde, Henry W. "The Significance of Regional Studies for the Elaboration of National Economic History." *Journal of Economic History*, Vol. 20, No. 4 (December 1960), pp. 588–89.

Browne, Lewis Allen. "Bolshevism in America." *Forum*, Vol. LIX (June 1918), pp. 703–17.

Bruere, Robert W. "Copper Camp Patriotism." *Nation*, Vol. CVI, No. 2747 (February 21, 1918), pp. 202–03.

———. "Copper Camp Patriotism: An Interpretation." *Nation*, Vol. CVI, No. 2748 (February 28, 1918), pp. 235–36.

———. "The Industrial Workers of the World." *Harper's Magazine*, Vol. CXXXVII, No. DCCCXVIII (July 1918), pp. 250–57.

Burgess, Opie Rundle. "Bisbee." *Arizona Highways*, Vol. XXVIII, No. 2 (February 1952), pp. 12–13, 32–35.

Callender, Harold. "True Facts About Bisbee." (Report Published by The National Labor Defense Council), *Dunbar's Weekly*, Vol. 14, No. 36 (September 15, 1917), pp. 10–12.

"Campbell Carries Water on Both Shoulders." *Dunbar's Weekly*, Vol. III, No. 39 (October 7, 1916), p. 10.

"The Cause of High Prices." *Literary Digest*, Vol. LIV, No. 11 (March 17, 1917), p. 703.

"Changes in Cost of Living in the United States." *Monthly Labor Review*, Vol. X, No. 6 (June 1920), p. 79.

"Changes in Union Wage Scales and in Retail Prices of Goods, 1907 to 1917." *Monthly Review of the Bureau of Labor Statistics*, Vol. VI, No. 6 (June 1918), pp. 1508–09.

"Changes in Wholesale Prices in the United States." *Monthly Review of the Bureau of Labor Statistics*, Vol. VI, No. 6 (June 1918), p. 91.

Clark, Charles W. "The United Verde and Labor." *Mining and Scientific Press*, Vol. 116 (May 25, 1918), pp. 709–10.

"Cochise County." *Arizona Mining Journal*, Vol. I, No. 12 (December 8, 1909), p. 9.

"Colonel McClintock and the 1917 Copper Strike." *Arizoniana*, Vol. III, No. 1 (Spring 1962), pp. 25–26.

"Conciliation Work of the Department of Labor, March 4, 1913, to June 6, 1916." *Monthly Review of the Bureau of Labor Statistics*, Vol. III, No. 1 (July 1916), pp. 30–31.

Connolly, C. P. "The Fight of the Copper Kings." *McClure's Magazine*, Vol. XXIX, No. 1 (May 1907), pp. 1–16.

———. "The Fight of the Copper Kings." *McClure's Magazine*, Vol. XXIX, No. 2 (June 1907), pp. 214–28.

"The Copper Market." *Arizona Mining Journal*, Vol. I, No. 4 (September 22, 1909), p. 3.

"Copper Quotations." *Mining and Scientific Press*, Vol. 113 (September 30, 1916), pp. 482–83.

"Copper Share Dividends." *Mining and Scientific Press*, Vol. 115 (November 3, 1917), p. 666.

Craige, John H. "The Professional Strike-Breaker." *Collier's*, Vol. XLVI, No. 11 (December 3, 1910), pp. 20, 31–32.

Currie, Barton. "How the West Dealt With One Labor Union." *Harper's Weekly*, Vol. LI, No. 2635 (June 22, 1907), pp. 908–10.

Davies, Richard O. "Arizona's Recent Past: Opportunities for Research." *Arizona and the West*, Vol. 9, No. 3 (Autumn 1967), pp. 243–58.

"Deportation of I.W.W. Members Sustained." *Law and Labor*, Vol. I, No. 5 (May 1919), p. 6.

"Deportations from Bisbee and a Resume of Other Troubles in Arizona." Reprinted in "The Arizona Strike." *Arizona Mining Journal*, Vol. I, No. 2 (August 1917), pp. 4–7.

"Development of Collective Bargaining in Metal Mining," *Monthly Labor Review*, Vol. 47, No. 3 (September 1938), pp. 591–98.

Devine, Edward T. "The Bisbee Deportations." *Survey*, Vol. 38, No. 16 (July 21, 1917), p. 353.

Dewey, John. "In Explanation of Our Lapse." *New Republic*, Vol. XIII, No. 157 (November 3, 1917), pp. 18–19.

DeWolf, William P. "Reopening Old Mines in Arizona." *Mining and Engineering World*, Vol. 45, No. 8 (August 19, 1916), pp. 329–31.

"Doing Things for 'Labor.'" *American Review of Reviews*, Vol. LIV, No. 4 (October 1916), p. 361.

Donner, Frank. "The Theory and Practice of American Political Intelligence." *New York Review of Books*, Vol. XVI, No. 7 (April 22, 1971), pp. 27–39.

"Douglas No. 1." *Arizona Labor Journal*, Vol. V, No. 3 (March 22, 1917), p. 2.

Douglas, James. "Historical Sketch of Copper Queen Mine." *Mining and Engineering World*, Vol. 38, No. 11 (March 15, 1913), pp. 525–27.

Douglas, Walter. "The Arizona Strike." *New Republic*, Vol. VI, No. 72 (March 18, 1916), pp. 185–86.

———. "Increased Wages and Decreased Efficiency in the Clifton-Morenci District." *Mining and Scientific Press*, Vol. 115 (September 8, 1917), pp. 339–40.

———. "The Life of James Douglas." *University of Arizona Bulletin*, General Bulletin No. 5, Vol. XI, No. 3 (July 1, 1940), pp. 69–79.

———. "The Strike in Arizona." *Mining and Scientific Press*, Vol. III (November 20, 1915), pp. 771–772.

Dowell, Eldridge Foster. "A History of Criminal Syndicalism Legislation in the United States." *John Hopkins University Studies in Historical and Political Science*, Vol. LVII, No. 1 (1939).

Dubofsky, Melvyn. "The Origins of Western Working Class Radicalism, 1880–1919." *Labor History*, Vol. VII, No. 2 (Spring 1966), pp. 131–54.

Dumke, Glenn S. "Douglas, Border Town." *Pacific Historical Review*, Vol. 17, No. 3 (August 1948), pp. 283–98.

Editorial Board. "Law of Necessity as Applied in the Bisbee Deportation Case." *Arizona Law Review*, Vol. 3, No. 2 (Winter 1961), pp. 264–79.

"Editorial Comment." *Dunbar's Weekly*, Vol. IV, No. 29 (July 28, 1917), p. 6.

"Editorial Comment." *Dunbar's Weekly*, Vol. IV, No. 36 (September 15, 1917), p. 7.

"Editorial Notes." *New Republic*, Vol. V, No. 53 (November 6, 1915), p. 4.

"Editorials." *Dunbar's Weekly*, Vol. IV, No. 27 (July 14, 1917), p. 1.

"Editorials." *Dunbar's Weekly*, Vol. IV, No. 31 (August 11, 1917), p. 1.

"Editorials." *Dunbar's Weekly*, Vol. IV, No. 37 (September 22, 1917), p. 1.

Elliott, W. Y. "The Political Application of Romanticism." *Political Science Quarterly*, Vol. 39, No. 2 (June 1924), pp. 234–64.

Elsing, Morris Jesup. "The Bisbee Mining District: Past, Present, and Future." *Engineering and Mining Journal-Press*, Vol. 115, No. 4 (January 27, 1928), pp. 177–84.

"Employers' Associations in the United States." *International Labour Review*, Vol. VIII, No. 3 (September 1923), pp. 367–79.

"The Employers' I.W.W." *New Republic*, Vol. XI, No. 134 (May 26, 1917), pp. 98–99.

"Employers' Organisations: A Survey." *International Labour Review,* Vol. VI, No. 6 (December 1922), pp. 935–45.

"Employers' Organization Stiffens Unions." *Survey*, Vol. XXXVII, No. 8 (November 25, 1916), pp. 203–04.

"Enemies Within The Camp." *Independent*, Vol. 91, No. 3582 (July 28, 1917), p. 122.

"Equality Before the Law." *Independent and the Weekly Review*, Vol. 108, No. 3800 (January 14, 1922), pp. 30–31.

"Federal Indictment of Bisbeeites." *Arizona Mining Journal*, Vol. I, No. 12 (May 1918), p. 15.

Fishbein, Meyer H. "The President's Mediation Commission and the Arizona Copper Strike, 1917." *Southwestern Social Science Quarterly*, Vol. XXX, No. 3 (December 1949), pp. 175–82.

Fitch, John A. "Arizona's Embargo on Strike-Breakers." *Survey*, Vol. XXXVI, No. 6 (May 6, 1916), pp. 143–46.

———. "Baiting the I.W.W." *Survey*, Vol. XXXIII, No. 23 (March 6, 1917), pp. 634–35.

———. "The I.W.W., An Outlaw Organization." *Survey*, Vol. XXX, No. 10 (June 7, 1913), pp. 355–62.

———. "A Report of Industrial Unrest." *Survey*, Vol. XXXIX, No. 20 (February 16, 1918), pp. 545–46.

Fly, G. F. "Non-Resident Copper Barons Advance Candidate for Governor." *Dunbar's Weekly*, Vol. 3, No. 7 (February 24, 1916), p. 3.

Ford, Lynn. "The Growing Menace of the I.W.W." *Forum*, Vol. LXI, No. 1 (January 1919), pp. 62–70.

Forster, Charles H. "Despised and Rejected Men: Hoboes of the Pacific Coast." *Survey*, Vol. XXXIII, No. 25 (March 20, 1915), pp. 671–72.

French, Thomas A. "Arizona State Federation of Labor." *Arizona Labor Journal*, Vol. VIII, No. 6 (June 11, 1920), p. 4.

"From Governor Hunt." *New Republic*, Vol. VI, No. 76 (April 15, 1916), p. 293.

Gable, Richard W. "Birth of An Employers' Association." *Business History Review*, Vol. 33, No. 4 (Fall 1959), pp. 535–45.

———. "NAM: Influential Lobby or Kiss of Death." *Journal of Politics*, Vol. 157, No. 2 (May 1953), pp. 254–73.

"General Investment News." *Commercial and Financial Chronicle*, Vol. 104, No. 2712 (June 16, 1917), p. 2456.

"General Investment News." *Commercial and Financial Chronicle*, Vol. 105, No. 2725 (September 15, 1917), p. 1109.

George, Harrison. "What a Political Prisoner Thinks About." *Nation*, Vol. 113, No. 2931 (September 7, 1921), p. 266.

"Globe, Arizona." *Mining and Scientific Press*, Vol. 115 (November 3, 1917), p. 659.

"Go To It." *Dunbar's Weekly*, Vol. IV, No. 30 (August 4, 1917), p. 3.

"Governor Hunt's Reply." *Arizona Mining Journal*, Vol. II, No. 1 (June 1918), p. 14.

Gray, J. H. "Bisbee's Future Greatness." *Arizona*, Vol. IV, No. 9 (July 1914), p. 5.

Grass, Louis. "The Story of A Bisbee Crime." Letter to Editor, *Dunbar's Weekly*, Vol. XIV, No. 31 (August 11, 1917), p. 9.

Hanhila, Matt O. "The Bisbee Tea Party." *Maricopa Open Door*, Vol. I, No. 1 (Fall–Winter 1972), pp. 13–15.

Hastings, John B. "Mine Labor." *Mining and Scientific Press*, Vol. 118 (May 24, 1919), p. 696.

Hays, Samuel P. "The Politics of Reform in Municipal Government in the Progressive Era." *Pacific Northwest Quarterly*, Vol. 55, No. 4 (October 1964), pp. 157–69.

Heckman, A. M. "A New Bonus Plan." *Mining and Scientific Press*, Vol. 117 (August 24, 1918), pp. 249–50.

Heney, Ben. "The Trust Price of Copper." *Mining and Scientific Press*, Vol. 118 (February 22, 1919), pp. 241–42.

Hibschman, Harry. "The I.W.W. Menace Self-Revealed." *New York Times Current History*, Vol. XVI, No. 5 (August 1912), pp. 761–68.

"The High Cost of Deporting." *Survey*, Vol. 42, No. 12 (June 21, 1919), p. 457.

High, James. "William Andrews Clark, Westerner." *Arizona and the West*, Vol. 2, No. 3 (Autumn 1960), pp. 245–64.

Hilton, O. A. "Public Opinion and Civil Liberties in Wartime 1917–1919." *Southwestern Social Science Quarterly*, Vol. XXVIII, No. 3 (December 1947), pp. 201–24.

Hofteling, Catherine. "Sunkist Prisoners." *Nation*, Vol. CXIII, No. 2933 (September 21, 1921), p. 316.

Holbrook, Stewart H. "Wobbly Talk." *American Mercury*, Vol. VII, No. 25 (January 1926), pp. 62–65.

Howard, Sidney. "The Labor Spy: A General View of Industrial Espionage." *New Republic*, Vol. XXV, No. 324 (February 16, 1921), pp. 338–41.

——. "The Labor Spy: A General View of Industrial Espionage." *New Republic*, Vol. XXV, No. 325 (February 23, 1921), pp. 263–363.

Hoxie, Robert F. "The Truth About the I.W.W." *Journal of Political Economy*, Vol. 21, No. 9 (November 1913), pp. 785–97.

Hubbard, Howard A. "The Arizona Enabling Act and President Taft's Veto." *Pacific Historical Review*, Vol. III (1934), p. 318.

——. "Political History." *Arizona and Its Heritage* (Tucson: University of Arizona, 1936), pp. 149–56.

Hughes, H. Stuart. "The Historian and the Social Scientist." *American Historical Review*, Vol. LXVI, No. 1 (October 1960), pp. 20–46.

"Hunt Replies to Carmichael." *Dunbar's Weekly*, Vol. 5, No. 24 (June 15, 1918), p. 7.

Hunter, George S. "The Bull Moose Movement in Arizona." *Arizona and the West*, Vol. 10, No. 4 (Winter 1968), pp. 343–62.

"Importation of Labor." *Arizona Mining Journal*, Vol. I, No. 9 (March 1918), pp. 16–17.

"Index Numbers of Changes in Cost of Living, 1913, to December, 1919." *Monthly Labor Review*, Vol. X, No. 6 (June 1920), p. 79.

"The Industrial Workers of the World." *Outlook*, Vol. 116, No. 13 (July 25, 1917), pp. 466–68.

"Industrial Workers Who Won't Work." *Literary Digest*, Vol. LV, No. 4 (July 28, 1917), pp. 20–21.

"Investigation of Bisbee (Ariz.) Deportations." *Monthly Review of the United States Bureau of Labor Statistics*, Vol. VI, No. 6 (June 1918), p. 57.

"The I.W.W. Develops into a National Menace." *Current Opinion*, Vol. LXIII, No. 3 (September 1917), pp. 153–54.

"The I.W.W. Raids and Others." *New Republic*, Vol. XII, No. 150 (September 15, 1917), pp. 175–77.

"The Jerome Strike." *Arizona Mining Journal*, Vol. I, No. 1 (June 1917), p. 16.

"John McBride Killed by Horse's Kick." *Arizona Mining Journal*, Vol. I, No. 5 (October 1917), p. 21.

Johnson, Michael R. "The I.W.W. and Wilsonian Democracy." *Science and Society*, Vol. XXVIII, No. 3 (Summer 1964), pp. 258–74.

"Judges." *Pacific Reporter*, Vol. 176 (St. Paul: West Publishing Co., 1919), p. v.

"Just a Political Move." *Arizona Labor Journal*, October 25, 1915, p. 3.

Keen, Effie R. "Arizona's Governors." *Arizona Historical Review*, Vol. 3, No. 3 (October 1930), pp. 5–20.

Kitchins, F. Harcourt. "The Troubles and Desires of Labor." *Fortnightly Review*, Vol. CII, No. DCX (October 1, 1917), pp. 581–93.

"Labor Conditions in the Southwest." *Engineering and Mining Journal*, Vol. LXXVII, No. 13 (March 3, 1904), p. 510.

"Labor Demanding War-Profits." *Literary Digest*, Vol. LII, No. 20 (May 13, 1916), p. 1354.

"Labor in Arizona." *Arizona*, Vol. VIII, No. 1 (November–December 1916), p. 16.

"The Labor Troubles at Butte." *Mining and Scientific Press*, Vol. 115 (September 1, 1917), pp. 305–08.

"Labor Unrest in the Southwest." *Survey*, Vol. 38. No. 19 (August 11, 1917), pp. 428–29.

Lamar, Howard R. "The Reluctant Admission: The Struggle to Admit Arizona and New Mexico to the Union." *The American West: An Appraisal*. Santa Fe: Museum of New Mexico Press, 1963, pp. 163–75.

Lanier, Alexander Sidney. "To the President." *New Republic*, Vol. XVIII, No. 233 (April 19, 1919), pp. 383–84.

"The Law Relating to Trades-Unions and Industrial Disputes." *Monthly Review of the Bureau of Labor Statistics*, Vol. I, No. 5 (November 1915), pp. 58–59.

Lescohier, D. D. "With the I.W.W. in the Wheat Lands." *Harper's Magazine*, Vol. CXLVII, No. DCCCLXXIX (August 1923), pp. 371–80.

Levine, Louis. "The Development of Syndicalism in America." *Political Science Quarterly*, Vol. XXVIII, No. 3 (September 1913), pp. 451–79.

Lindquist, John H. "The Jerome Deportation of 1917." *Arizona and the West*, Vol. XI, No. 3 (Autumn 1969), pp. 233–46.

Lindquist, John H., and Fraser, James. "A Sociological Interpretation of the Bisbee Deportation." *Pacific Historical Review*, Vol. XXXVII, No. 4 (November 1968), pp. 401–22.

Lippmann, Walter. "The I.W.W.—Insurrection or Revolution?" *New Review*, Vol. I, No. 19 (August 1913), pp. 701–06.

Lipset, Seymour Martin and Ladd, Everett Carll, Jr. " . . . And What Professors Think." *Psychology Today*, Vol. IV, No. 5 (November 1970), pp. 49–51.

Lloyd, Henry Demerest. "Lords of Industry," *North American Review*, Vol. CXXXVIII, No. 331 (June 1884), p. 552.

"Loyalty Leagues Outlawed." *Arizona Mining Journal*, Vol. VI, No. 4 (April 5, 1918), p. 1.

"Lynch-Law and Reason." *Literary Digest*, Vol. LV, No. 7 (August 18, 1917), pp. 12–13.

Lyon, William H. "The Corporate Frontier in Arizona." *Journal of Arizona History*, Vol. 9, No. 1 (Spring 1968), pp. 1–17.

McMahon, Theresa S. "Centralia and the I.W.W." *Survey*, Vol. XLIII, No. 6 (November 29, 1919), pp. 173–74.

Marcy, Leslie. "The Eleven Hundred Exiled Copper Miners." *International Socialist Review*, Vol. XVII, No. 3 (September 1917), pp. 160–62.

Merz, Charles. "The Issue in Butte." *New Republic*, Vol. XII, No. 151 (September 22, 1917), pp. 215–17.

"Mine Taxation in Arizona is Entirely in Hands of State Tax Commission." *Mining Congress Journal*, Vol. I, No. 9 (September 1915), p. 447.

"Miners Resume Work." *Arizona Labor Journal*, February 3, 1916.

"Minimum Wage Established in Arizona." *Survey*, Vol. XXXVIII, No. 6 (May 12, 1917), p. 149.

"Mining Men Confer With Council of Defense." *Arizona Mining Journal*, Vol. I, No. 10 (April 1918), p. 6.

"The Mining News." *Engineering and Mining Journal*, Vol. 99, No. 6 (February 6, 1915), p. 300.

"The Mining Summary." *Mining and Scientific Press*, Vol. 115 (July 17, 1917), pp. 29–30.

"The Mining Summary." *Mining and Scientific Press*, Vol. 115 (July 14, 1917), p. 63.

"The Mining Summary." *Mining and Scientific Press*, Vol. 115 (July 21, 1917), p. 102.

"The Mining Summary." *Mining and Scientific Press*, Vol. 117 (July 20, 1918), p. 95.

"Mr. Carmichael's Rejoinder." *Arizona Mining Journal*, Vol. II, No. 1 (June 1918), pp. 14, 46–47.

"Mrs. McKay Writes of Bisbee." *Dunbar's Weekly*, Vol. 14, No. 32 (August 18, 1917), p. 9.

Murphy, F. M. "Thanks American Mining Congress for Arizona Work." *Mining Congress Journal*, Vol. I, No. 9 (September 1915), p. 443.

"Never Mind What You Think About the I.W.W." (adv.) *New Republic*, Vol. XV, No. 191 (June 29, 1918), p. 242.

"Nineteenth Annual Convention of Mining Congress Was Great Success." *Mining Congress Journal*, Vol. II, No. 12 (December 1916), pp. 523–24.

"Nineteenth Annual Meeting American Mining Congress." *Mining and Engineering World*, Vol. 45, No. 22 (November 25, 1916), p. 906.

"Norman Carmichael Replies to Governor Hunt." *Arizona Mining Journal*, Vol. II, No. 1 (June 1918), pp. 13–14.

"Note." *New Republic*, Vol. VI, No. 72 (March 18, 1916), pp. 186–87.

Notman, Arthur. "Geology of the Bisbee, Arizona, Ore Deposits." *Mining and Engineering World*, Vol. XXXVIII, No. 12 (March 22, 1913), pp. 567–70.

Nyland, Waino. "Western Mining Town." *Scribner's Magazine*, Vol. XCV, No. 5 (May 1934), pp. 365–69.

"Ol' Rags an' Bottles." *Nation*, Vol. CVIII, No. 2795 (January 25, 1919), pp. 114–16.

Oneal, James. "The Passing of the I.W.W." *Current History*, Vol. XXI, No. 4 (January 1925), pp. 528–34.

——. "The Socialists in the War." *American Mercury*, Vol. X, No. 40 (April 1927), pp. 418–26.

"Organization or Anarchy." *New Republic*, Vol. XI, No. 142 (July 21, 1917), pp. 320–322.

Parker, Carleton H. "The California Casual and His Revolt." *Quarterly Journal of Economics*, Vol. 30 (November 1915), pp. 110–26.

——. "The I.W.W." *Atlantic Monthly*, Vol. CXX (November 1917), pp. 651–62.

"Peaceful Picketing Held to be Lawful and Validity of Anti-Injunction Statute Sustained in Arizona." *Law and Labor*, Vol. I, No. 2 (February 1919), p. 7.

Pearce, T. M. "The 'Other' Frontiers of the American West." *Arizona and the West*, Vol. 4, No. 2 (Summer 1962), pp. 105–12.

"Personal." *Mining and Scientific Press*, Vol. 113 (July 29, 1916), p. 183.

"Personal." *Mining and Scientific Press*, Vol. 115 (September 8, 1917), p. 368.

"Personal." *Mining and Scientific Press*, Vol. 115 (October 27, 1917), p. 628.

"Personal." *Mining and Scientific Press*, Vol. 116 (June 29, 1918), p. 905.

Pierson, George W. "A Restless Temper ... " *American Historical Review*, Vol. LXIX, No. 4 (July 1964), pp. 969–89.

Pomeroy, Earl. "Toward a Reorientation of Western History: Continuity and Environment." *Mississippi Valley Historical Review*, Vol. XLI, No. 4 (March 1955), pp. 579–600.

"The Poor Fool." *Dunbar's Weekly*, Vol. III, No. 9 (March 11, 1916), p. 2.

"The President's Commission at Bisbee." *New Republic*, Vol. XIII, No. 162 (December 8, 1917), pp. 140–41.

"Problems of Labor." *Mining and Scientific Press*, Vol. 110 (January 30, 1915), pp. 170–71.

"A Program for Labor." *New Republic*, Vol. X, No. 127 (April 7, 1917), pp. 312–13.

"Raiding the I.W.W." *Literary Digest*, Vol. LV, No. 12 (September 12, 1917), p. 17.

Raley, A. D. "Deportations Justified." *Arizona Mining Journal*, Vol. I, No. 2 (August 1917), p. 8.

"Rates of Wages Per Day in Certain Branches of Metal Mining Where Gold is a Direct or By-Product, September, 1913 to 1918." *Monthly Labor Review*, Vol. VIII, No. 4 (April 1919), pp. 177–78.

Rau-Roesler, S. E. "Recruiting Labor from the Gold Mines." *Mining and Scientific Press*, Vol. 115 (November 24, 1917), p. 747.

Raymer, Robert G. "Early Copper Mining in Arizona." *Pacific Historical Review*, Vol. IV, No. 2 (1935), pp. 123–30.

"The Red Hysteria." *New Republic*, Vol. XXI, No. 269 (January 28, 1920), pp. 249–52.

"Relative Retail Prices of the Principal Articles of Food in the United States, January, 1913 to June, 1919." *Monthly Labor Review*, Vol. IX, No. 2 (August 1919), pp. 90–91.

"Report of the Commission on Industrial Relations." *Monthly Review of the Bureau of Labor Statistics*, Vol. I, No. 5 (November 1915), pp. 48–76.

"Reports and Documents." Phelps Dodge & Company Annual Report, 1916, *Commercial & Financial Chronicle*, Vol. 104, No. 2700 (March 24, 1917), p. 1160.

"Respecting Troops for Arizona." *Arizona Mining Journal*, Vol. I, No. 9 (March 1918), p. 16.

"Review of Mining." *Mining and Scientific Press*, Vol. 116 (April 13, 1918), p. 523.

"Review of Mining." *Mining and Scientific Press*, Vol. 118 (February 8, 1919), p. 194.

"Review of Mining." *Mining and Scientific Press*, Vol. 118 (June 14, 1919), p. 826.

Richter, F. Ernest. "The Amalgamated Copper Company: A Closed Chapter in Corporation Finance." *Quarterly Journal of Economics*, Vol. 30 (February 1916), pp. 387–407.

——. "The Copper-Mining Industry in the United States." *Quarterly Journal of Economics*, Vol. 41 (February 1927), pp. 236–91.

——. "The Copper-Mining Industry in the United States." *Quarterly Journal of Economics*, Vol. 41 (August 1927), pp. 684–717.

Rickard, T. A. "Editorial." *Mining and Scientific Press*, Vol. 112 (January 8, 1916), p. 32.

——. "Editorial." *Mining and Scientific Press*, Vol. 114 (January 13, 1917), p. 37.

——. "Editorial." *Mining and Scientific Press*, Vol. 115 (September 8, 1917), p. 335.

——. "Labor and Capital." *Mining and Scientific Press*, Vol. 111 (October 30, 1915), p. 655.

——. "The Story of the U.V.X. Bonanza—I." *Mining and Scientific Press*, Vol. 116 (January 5, 1918), pp. 9–17.

Rowntree, B. S. "Labour Unrest." *Contemporary Review*, Vol. CXII (October 1917), pp. 368–79.

"Sheriff Wheeler Answers His Defamers." *Arizona Mining Journal*, Vol. I, No. 5 (October 1917), p. 21.

Shreve, E. O. "Objective: Industrial Peace." *Industrial and Labor Relations Review*, Vol. 1, No. 3 (April 1968), pp. 431–42.

Smith, Russell A. "Significant Developments in Labor Law During the Last Half-Century." *Michigan Law Review*, Vol. 50, No. 8 (June 1952), pp. 1265–90.

Soule, George. "Law and Necessity in Bisbee." *Nation*, Vol. 113, No. 2930 (August 21, 1921), pp. 225–27.

Spargo, John. "Why the I.W.W. Flourishes." *World's Work*, Vol. XXXIX, No. 3 (January 1920), pp. 243–47.

Speek, Peter Alexander. "The Psychology of Floating Workers." *Annals of the American Academy of Political and Social Science*, Vol. LXIX, No. 69 (January 1917), pp. 72–78.

"A State With Two Governors." *Independent*, Vol. 89, No. 3554 (January 15, 1917), p. 96.

Stecker, Margaret Loomis. "The National Founders' Association." *Quarterly Journal of Economics*, Vol. 30 (February 1916), pp. 352–86.

Stern, Leon. "The Drifters." *Survey*, Vol. XXXI, No. 5 (November 1, 1913), pp. 136–38.

"The Story of the Clifton-Morenci District." *Arizona*, Vol. VIII, No. 5 (August 1918), pp. 8–9.

"The Strike at Jerome." *Arizona Mining Journal*, Vol. I, No. 1 (June 1917), pp. 5–6.

"A Strike Without Disorder." *New Republic*, Vol. V, No. 64 (January 22, 1916), pp. 304–06.

"Strikes and Lockouts in the U.W., 1916 to 1927." *Monthly Labor Review*, Vol. XXVII, No. 1 (July 1928), pp. 84–89.

Strong, Anna Louise. "Everett's Bloody Sunday." *Survey*, Vol. XXXVII, No. 17 (January 27, 1917), p. 476.

"The Supreme Court Holds That the Bisbee Deportations do not Offend the Federal Law." *Law and Labor*, Vol. 3, No. 1 (January 1921), pp. 11–13.

Sutter, Fred. "Senator Sutter Makes Reply." *Arizona Mining Journal*, Vol. II, No. 1 (June 1918), p. 48.

"The Tables Turned." *Dunbar's Weekly*, Vol. II, No. 39 (October 9, 1915), p. 6.

Taft, Philip. "The Bisbee Deportation." *Labor History*, Vol. XIII, No. 1 (Winter 1972), pp. 3–40.

――――. "The Federal Trials of the I.W.W." *Labor History*, Vol. III, No. 1 (Winter 1962), pp. 57–91.

Taylor, Graham Romeyn. "The Clash in the Copper Country." *Survey*, Vol. XXXI, No. 5 (November 1, 1913), pp. 127–35, 145–49.

――――. "Moyer's Story of Why He Left the Copper Country." *Survey*, Vol. XXXI, No. 15 (January 10, 1914), pp. 433–35.

"Those Copper Quotations." *Mining and Scientific Press*, Vol. 113 (October 14, 1916), p. 550.

Tyler, Robert L. "The I.W.W. and the West." *American Quarterly*, Vol. XII, No. 2 (Summer 1960), pp. 175–87.

――――. "The Rise and Fall of an American Radicalism: The I.W.W." *Historian*, Vol. XIX, No. 1 (November 1956), pp. 48–65.

"U.S. Supreme Court Upholds Law Making Employers In So-Called Hazardous Occupations Liable in Damages for All Accidents Without Fault." *Law and Labor*, Vol. I, No. 7 (July 1919), p. 19.

Van Valen, Nelson. "The Bolsheviki and the Orange Growers." *Pacific Historical Review*, Vol. 22, No. 1 (February 1953), pp. 39–50.

"Vast Profits for the Mines." *American Review of Reviews*, Vol. LIII, No. 5 (May 1916), p. 535.

Walker, Arthur L. "Recollections of Early Day Mining in Arizona." *Arizona Historical Review*, Vol. VI, No. 2 (April 1935), pp. 14–43.

"The Warren District, Arizona." *Engineering and Mining Journal*, Vol. LXXVIII, No. 14 (October 6, 1904), pp. 545–46.

"The Warren Mining District." *Arizona Labor Journal*, Vol. VIII, No. 6 (June 11, 1920), p. 15.

Watkins, Gordon S. "Labor Problems and Labor Administration in the United States During the World War, Part I." *University of Illinois Studies in the Social Sciences*, Vol. VIII, No. 3 (September 1919), pp. 231–331.

Watkins, Gordon S. "Labor Problems and Labor Administration in the United States During the World War, Part II." *University of Illinois Studies in the Social Sciences*, Vol. VIII, No. 4 (December 1919), pp. 338–461.

Watkins, Robert A. "Respecting the Governor's Message." *Arizona Mining Journal*, Vol. II, No. 1 (June 1918), pp. 9, 11.

Webb, Sidney. "British Labour Under War Pressure." *North American Review*, Vol. CCV, No. 739 (June 1917), pp. 874–85.

"The Week." *Nation*, Vol. 105, No. 2716 (July 19, 1917), p. 57.

"The Week." *Nation*, Vol. 105, No. 2721 (August 23, 1917), p. 191.

"The Week." *Nation*, Vol. 107, No. 2783 (November 2, 1918), p. 501.

"The Week." *Nation*, Vol. 107, No. 2789 (December 14, 1917), p. 717.

Wehle, Louis B. "The Adjustment of Labor Disputes Incident to Production for War in the United States."*Quarterly Journal of Economics*, Vol. XXXII (November 1917), pp. 122–33.

———. "Labor Problems in the United States During the War." *Quarterly Journal of Economics*, Vol. XXXII (February 1918), pp. 333–84.

———. "War Labor Policies and Their Outcome in Peace." *Quarterly Journal of Economics*, Vol. XXXIII (February 1919), pp. 321–43.

Weyl, Walter E. "The Strikers at Lawrence." *Outlook*, Vol. 100 (February 10, 1912), pp. 309–12.

"What Haywood Says of the I.W.W." *Survey*, Vol. 38, No. 19 (August 11, 1917), pp. 429–30.

"Wheeler as Cavalry Leader." *Arizona Mining Journal*, Vol. I, No. 9 (March 1918), p. 17.

"Why I Quit the I.W.W." *Sunset*, Vol. 53, No. 5 (November 1924), pp. 15, 92–96.

Willis, Charles F. "The Institute Meeting." *Mining and Scientific Press*, Vol. 113 (October 7, 1916), p. 535.

———. "Mining in Arizona." *Mining and Scientific Press*, Vol. 112 (January 29, 1916), pp. 171–72.

Willoughby, William Franklin. "Employers' Associations for Dealing With Labor in the United States." *Quarterly Journal of Economics*, Vol. XX (November 1905), pp. 110–50.

Willson, Roscoe C. "Echoes of Deportation Heard for Many Years." *Arizona Days and Ways* (November 15, 1964), pp. 54–55.

———. "Sheriff's Aide Tells of Bisbee Deportation." *Arizona Days and Ways* (November 8, 1964), pp. 42–43.

Woehlke, Walter V. "The Greatest Mining Boom in History." *American Review of Reviews*, Vol. LIV, No. 4 (October 1916), pp. 429–32.

———. "I.W.W." *Outlook*, Vol. 101 (July 6, 1912), pp. 531–36.

———. "The I.W.W. and the Golden Rule." *Sunset*, Vol. 38 (February 1917), pp. 16–18, 62–65.

———. "The Red Rebels Declare War." *Sunset*, Vol. 39 (September 1917), pp. 20–21, 75–77.

Wolf, Robert. "Securing the Initiative of the Workman." *American Economic Review*, Vol. IX, No. 1 (March 1919), pp. 120–31.

Woodbridge, Dwight E. "The Copper Queen Consolidated Mining Company." *Engineering and Mining Journal*, Vol. LXXXI, No. 24 (June 16, 1906), pp. 1134–35.

Yarros, Victor S. "The I.W.W. Trial." *Nation*, Vol. 107, No. 2774 (August 31, 1918), pp. 220–23.

———. "The Story of the I.W.W. Trial." *Survey*, Vol. 40, No. 22 (August 31, 1918), pp. 603–04.

———. "The Story of the I.W.W. Trial." *Survey*, Vol. 40, No. 23 (September 7, 1918), pp. 630–32.

———. "The Story of the I.W.W. Trial." *Survey*, Vol. 40, No. 24 (September 14, 1918), pp. 660–63.

Newspapers

Arizona Daily Star. 1910–1920.
Arizona Gazette. 1910–1921.
Arizona Record. 1915–1917.
Arizona Republic(an). 1900–1965.
Arizona Silver Belt. 1915–1917.
Arizona State Herald. 1916.
Bisbee Daily Review. 1903–1948.
Bowie Enterprise. 1915–1916.
Coconino Sun. 1918.
Copper Era. 1915–1917.
Douglas International. 1915–1918.

Jerome News. 1916–1918.
Jerome Sun. 1916–1918.
Los Angeles Times. 1916–1918.
Messenger. 1915–1917.
New York Call. 1916–1917.
New York Post. 1917–1918.
New York Times. 1916–1921.
Tucson Citizen. 1910–1921.
Verde Copper News. 1917–1918.
Winslow Mail. 1915–1916.
Yuma Morning Sun. 1916–1917

Bulletins, Reports, Pamphlets, Proceedings and Transactions

American Civil Liberties Union. *The Truth About the I.W.W. Prisoners*. New York, 1922.

Arizona State Council of Defense. *A Record of the Activities of the Arizona State Council of Defense from Formation April 18, 1917 to Dissolution, June, 1919*. n.d.

———. "Report of Labor Committee." *Arizona Service Bulletin*. Vol. I, No. 1 (May 1, 1918).

Baker, Horace. *Copper*. Published by Chas. A. Stoneham & Co., 1915.

Bank of Douglas. *Arizona*. 1949.

Bimson, Carl A. *Transformation in the Desert*. Newcomer Society, New York, 1962 (delivered at Phoenix, March 20, 1962).

Bisbee Miners' Local 501, Phelps Dodge Council of the IUMMSW. *This is The Face of Phelps Dodge*, n.d.

Blandy, John F. "The Mining Region Around Prescott, Arizona." *AIME Transactions*, Vol. XI, February, 1883. pp. 286–91.

Bruere, Robert. *Following the Trail of the I.W.W.* Published by the *New York Evening Post*, 1918.

Copper Queen Mining Company. *Description of Property.* New York, 1881.

Curley, Frank E. *The Law of Necessity as Applied in Arizona vs. H. E. Wootton, The Bisbee Deportation Case.* Bureau of Information, Tucson. n.d.

Duff, Harvey. *The Silent Defenders: Courts and Capitalism in California.* Industrial Workers of the World. Chicago, n.d.

Ellinwood, E. E. *Making a Modern Constitution.* Bisbee, 1910.

Hunt, George W. P. *The Coming Citizen: An Address Delivered Before the Arizona Federation of Women's Clubs of Nogales, Arizona.* 1914.

——. *Message to the Special Session of the Third State Legislature.* Phoenix, 1918.

——. *So The People Will Know.* Phoenix, 1915.

Industrial Workers of the World. *Proceedings: Tenth Convention 1916.* Chicago, 1917.

International Union of Mine, Mill and Smelter Workers. *The Years From Virginia City, Nevada.* n.d.

Metal Mine Workers Industrial Union #800. *Bulletin Number One.* Phoenix, Arizona, February 24, 1917.

——. *Bulletin Number Two.* Phoenix, Arizona, April 4, 1917.

Phelps Dodge Corporation. *Annual Reports.* New York, 1914–18.

——. Copper Queen Branch. *Employees' Representation Plan.* 1921.

Unpublished

Beeman, William S. *History of the Bisbee Deportations by an Officer in Charge of the Loyalty League.* Unpublished Manuscript. Arizona Law Library and Archives, Phoenix, 1940.

Brannon, Victor DeWitt. *Employers' Liability and Workmen's Compensation in Arizona.* Unpublished Master's Thesis, University of Arizona, 1932.

Brogden, J. Carl. *The History of Jerome, Arizona.* Unpublished Master's Thesis. University of Arizona, 1952.

Campbell, Thomas E. "The I.W.W. in Arizona." *Typescript Concerning Resconstruction of Labor Troubles in Arizona.* San Fernando, California, 1962. Arizona Historical Society, Tucson.

Cox, Annie M. *History of Bisbee from 1877 to 1937.* Unpublished Master's Thesis. University of Arizona, 1938.

Dickenson, S. C. *A Sociological Survey of the Bisbee-Warren District.* Arizona State Bureau of Mines, December 31, 1917. Typescript in Special Collections, University of Arizona.

George W. P. Hunt and the Constitution of Arizona. No author, no date. Typescript in Special Collections, University of Arizona.

Griffith, Victor S. *State Regulation of Railroad and Electric Rates in Arizona to 1925.* Unpublished Master's Thesis, University of Arizona, 1931.

Harre, T. Everett. *The I.W.W.: An Auxiliary of the German Espionage System.* Typescript in Arizona Historical Society, Tucson, Arizona, n.d.

Harrison, Charles Buxton. *The Development of the Arizona Labor Movement.* Unpublished Master's Thesis. Arizona State University, 1954.

Hunter, George. *John C. Greenway and the Bull Moose Movement in Arizona.* Unpublished Master's Thesis. University of Arizona, 1965.

Jeffrey, Robert S. *The History of Douglas, Arizona.* Unpublished Master's Thesis. University of Arizona, 1951.

Johnson, Alan V. *Governor G. W. P. Hunt and Organized Labor.* Unpublished Master's Thesis, University of Arizona, 1964.

LaCagnina, Yolanda. *The Role of the Recall of Judges Issue in the Struggle for Arizona Statehood.* Unpublished Master's Thesis, University of Arizona, 1964.

Landau, Saul. *The Bisbee Deportations: Class Conflict and Patriotism during World War I.* Unpublished Master's Thesis, University of Wisconsin, 1959.

Lindquist, John H. and Fraser, James. *Community Response to Radical Unionism in the United States: The I.W.W. in Arizona. A Sociological Interpretation of the Bisbee Deportation.* Typescript of presentation made to Arizona Historical Society, 1965.

Martin, Douglas. *The Douglas Dynasty.* Typescript in Special Collections, University of Arizona Library, Tucson, n.d.

Morse, Samuel. *The Truth About Bisbee.* Typescript in Arizona Historical Society, Tucson, Arizona, n.d.

McGinnis, Tru Anthony. *The Influence of Organized Labor on the Making of the Arizona Constitution.* Unpublished Master's Thesis, University of Arizona, 1931.

McLeod, Frederick Farquhar. *Old Man Necessity or Have You Talked With Allie Howe?* Typescript in Special Collections, University of Arizona Library. Tombstone, 1920.

Newkirk, William W. *Historical Geography of Bisbee, Arizona.* Unpublished Master's Thesis, University of Arizona, 1966.

Nichols, Charles A. *Four Generations of the Douglas Family in America.* Typescript in Special Collections, University of Arizona Library, Tucson. Douglas, Arizona, 1965.

O'Neil, D. C. *Forty Years of Mine Taxation in Arizona, 1907–1946.* Typescript in Special Collections, University of Arizona Library, Tucson, n.d.

Riell, Robert. *Copper Mine Strikes in 1917, Globe, Arizona.* Typescript in Harwood P. Hinton files (No. 57). University of Arizona Library, Tucson, n.d.

Tenney, James Brand. *History of Mining in Arizona, Vol. I.* Notes compiled 1927–29. Typescript in Special Collections, University of Arizona Library, Tucson.

Todd, Charles Foster. *The Initiative and Referendum in Arizona*. Unpublished Master's Thesis. University of Arizona, 1931.

Vaughan, Jerome A. *All Women and Children Keep Off Streets Today*. Typescript in Arizona Historical Society, Tucson, n.d.

Watt, Roberta. *History of Morenci, Arizona*. Unpublished Master's Thesis. University of Arizona, 1956.

Weintraub, Hyman. *The I.W.W. in California: 1905–1931*: Unpublished Master's Thesis. University of California at Los Angeles, 1947.

Wilson, Marjorie Haines. *The Gubernatorial Career of George W. P. Hunt*. Unpublished Ph.D. Dissertation, Arizona State University, Tempe, Arizona, 1973.

Young, Herbert V. *The Jerome Deportation of 1917*. Typescript in J. Byrkit files.

Interviews

Adams, Minnie. Bisbee, July 19, 1972.
Bledsoe, Nelson A. Tucson, August 15, 1968.
Burrows, Herb. Tucson, June 27, 1968.
Dickenson, John C. Tucson, April 11, 1966.
Douglas, Walter, Jr. Tucson, April 11, 1966.
Eddy, William. Bisbee, July 19, 1972.
Hanhila, Matt O. Glendale, March 13, 1972.
Jones, William. Bisbee, April 18, 1966.
Keahey, George J. Tucson, August 15, 1968.
Pintek, John. Bisbee, April 8, 1966, July 19, 1972.
Pintek, Katie. Bisbee, April 8, 1966, July 19, 1972.
Rapp, John. Tucson, taped August 16, 1968.
Scarlett, Bishop William. Phoenix, March 13, 1972.
Watson, Fred. Bisbee, July 19, 1972.
Young, H. V. Clarkdale, December 20, 1966.

Harwood P. Hinton Oral History Collection
(University of Arizona)

Adams, Minnie.
Berlindis, J. G.
Chukovich, Glisio.

Erving, Thomas M.
Hanhila, Matt O.
Morris, Si.

INDEX

Absentee ownership, 25, 33, 53, 56, 63, 85, 98
Adams Hotel, 86, 113, 176
Agents provocateurs, 43, 134, 139, 142, 158, 186, 268; in Arizona, 120–22
Agricultural Workers Association, 140
Ajo, Arizona, 9, 13, 146, 157, 180, 181
Akers, Charles H., 34, 45, 49, 82, 88, 110
Aldai, Carlos, 121
Allen, Charles W., 220
Allen, Gayle, 89
Allen, Henry J., 41, 76, 89; in Jerome, Arizona, 33–35
American Federation Of Labor, 23, 24, 36, 102 103, 126, 127, 128, 130, 135, 139, 154
American Institute of Mining Engineers, 65, 105, 319
American Mercury, 6
American Mining and Trading Company, 14

American Mining Congress, 65, 82, 87, 104, 105, 114, 304; Arizona Chapter of, 104, 113, 116, 176
American Review of Reviews, 69
American West and Frontier, 3, 18, 26, 138; image of, 6; mining history in, 22–24
Anderson, George W., 281
Anthracite coal strike of 1902, 28
Anti-Semitism, 7
Arizona, 249
Arizona anti-injunction law, 5, 36, 41, 44, 46, 48, 53, 312, 313
Arizona Business Improvement League, 32
Arizona constitution: constitutional convention, 38, 41–45, 138, 311; Enabling Act, 37, 40, 41; direct sovereignty provisions, 9, 41, 43, 44, 46, 48–50; jointure movement, 38; pro-labor provisions, 46; "radical" nature of, 48; ratification of, 47; recall of judges, 46; Taft's veto of, 49